FLOATING
AND RECREATION ON
MONTANA
RIVERS

By Curt Thompson

Acknowledgements

The Author thanks those who have provided valuable information for the publication of this book.

A special thanks to: The Department of Commerce (Travel Montana)
U.S. Geological Survey
Montana Department of Natural Resources

Published by:

Curt Thompson, Box 392, Lakeside, MT 59922

Library of Congress Catalog Card 93-60249

ISBN: 0-9636856-0-0

Printed in the USA
Thomas Printing, Inc., Kalispell, Montana
First Printing May, 1993
Second Printing September, 1994

COVER PHOTO — SMITH RIVER

TABLE OF CONTENTS

APPENDIX

INTRODUCTION

Montana waterways have played a key role in the early exploration and development of the west. Dugout or birch bark canoes, pirogues and later steamships transported people and goods. Montana has it all! High country falls moderating into prairie rivers, the lifeblood of the plains. We are modern day "Huck Finns" as we explore, fantasize the past or "kick back" while floating a river. Whitewater enthusiasts have an abundance of adventurous water and wonderful family recreational opportunities exist. Portions of our streams teem with trout. We need to protect our sparkling free flowing rivers for future generations to enjoy. With civilization encroaching, our wildlife, riparian zones and fisheries need coddling.

In the beautiful high country of Glacier National Park is a three-way watershed caused by Triple Divide Mountain. Water at this point flows either west, north or east. This is one of only two such watersheds on the North American continent. The other occurs in the Canadian Rockies.

A stream being called a river, creek or brook has nothing to do with flow or size. It is simply the name they have been dubbed, usually by early pioneers. Although rivers are thought of as being the largest streams, some creeks are larger than many small rivers.

Progress has been made to harmonize relations between the recreator and the land owner. Respect must be mutual. The Department of Fish, Wildlife and Parks offers aid to property owners, putting in float-thru gates instead of life threatening barb wire fences. The floater should understand access and trespass law and above all, show respect for the landowner. It is the moral responsibility of all outdoor people to ask permission, and illustrate "class" on private land. Leave a place better than you found it!

Rivers are forever changing. A tree can fall down and blockade a river bank-to-bank in seconds. A huge boulder can fall off a cliff and form a large drop overnight. A new channel or a new log jam can form suddenly. Many man made blunders can occur quickly. A new fence or perhaps a diversion dam bulldozed up quickly, and often illegally.

On a recent photography trip, I drove many miles to take a picture of a certain diversion dam. It was gone! I inquired locally if it would be rebuilt and no one knew for sure. I deleted it from this book and made mention that it may be rebuilt. However, I just learned it was already being rebuilt, so I have since re-added it back in.

Try to get current information by inquiring at local sporting goods stores, Fish, Wildlife and Parks, Forest Service or BLM offices. Local guides and outfitters or ranchers along a river can be helpful. Often, certain stretches of stream could be regulated because of bird nesting. Numerous restrictions on catch and release or no fishing while floating can be in effect. Only the locals may be aware of these conditions.

Water hydraulics are enormously powerful. A steep gradient will cause rapid velocity. A boulder streambed not only offers obstacles to maneuver around, but can cause rapids. Waves can be caused by colliding currents. Curves can cause eddies, ledges can create drops, some with dangerous reversals. This resulting whitewater can be very enjoyable for capable paddlers in proper vessels, or a nightmare for others. Knee-deep water can sweep you off your feet, with enough velocity and poor footing. Low water can sometimes be as dangerous as high water, as it exposes obstacles that may be washed out with high water.

I have used the International Grading Scale I-VI for river difficulty. Bear in mind that high or low water makes things different. The definition for each class and skill level required, can be found in the appendix. Paddling a canoe is more difficult than a raft, as a raft is more forgiving. When speaking of a beginner, I mean a "practiced beginner".

1

Practicing should take place in a still body of water.

There is no such thing as a perfect vessel for all conditions. People should enjoy whatever vessel they have, safely, in an appropriate section of river. I have listed some vessel information for people that might be interested in purchasing, in the appendix.

USE OF THIS BOOK: This book is a no-nonsense guide to the rivers. The book is designed for easy cross reference use by whitewater enthusiasts, family recreationers, fishermen, hunters, photographers, archaeologists, historians, rock hounders, disabled, water researchers or search and rescue. It is for the floater or non-floater, alphabetically or by area of the state.

Recent legislature has given 26 streams the distinction of Class 1 designation. All the other streams are Class 2. Complete definitions and rules can be found in the appendix, and are not to be confused with whitewater ratings.

Quick cross references for whitewater rivers, class 1 or 2 designations, all year rivers, fishing and camping are offered. This information can be found in the watershed list by areas. Complete information can then be found for each river of your choice. Fishing by species can be found in the appendix, for the area you are in. Campgrounds are listed by river as well as access sites. Facilities for each campground can be found in the appendix.

Common wildlife sightings, scenery, and other information appear in the text of each river. Good family recreation can be found in most sections of rivers, including or excluding the whitewater sections.

Special agencies, which may have special regulations, include National Parks, Wilderness Areas, Wildlife Refuges, Indian Reservations and the Wild and Scenic River Corridors. These agencies are defined in the appendix and identified by river.

The United States Geological Survey can give you flow information on most rivers, updated every four hours, during regular office hours. This number is (406) 449-5263. Other telephone numbers are listed if special information is available, on that specific river.

A beautiful day can suddenly turn cold and ugly. Be alert to avoid hypothermia even in mid-summer. Carry dry clothes in a waterproof bag and also carry a pocket size rain suit (two piece), with elastic openings. In the event your extra dry clothes are lost or get wet, getting your wet clothes off and getting into this rainsuit will help contain your body heat. Float leaders should be aware of their abilities and limitations as well as the rest of the group. Basic first aid, safety ideas and river etiquette can be found in the appendix.

All floatable sections have been floated. This does not mean that all portions of severe whitewater are recommended. Some whitewater listed is approaching class VI.

68 of the 81 rivers in Montana have floatable sections, of which 31 contain nearly 300 miles of floatable whitewater. It is the intention of this book to cover the rivers for all possible recreational use, including short sections for children "tubing". Kids are not able to go long distances and must find fun with whatever they have. Two creeks in the state have the designation of class 1 streams, and are included in this river book. Other creeks have been included if they have been called a river by cartographers or historians. Some whitewater creeks have been included under the river of which they are a tributary. Lakes are natural bodies of water and reservoirs are dam created.

Of interest to some may be the longest and greatest volume rivers:

Length (in MT)		Volume (ave.in MT)	
Missouri	734.2 miles	Clark Fork	22,240 cfs
Yellowstone	553.7 miles	Kootenai	13,940 cfs
Milk	537.5 miles	Yellowstone	12,790 cfs
Musselshell	364.3 miles	Flathead	11,740 cfs
Clark Fork	333.1 miles	Missouri	10,570 cfs

The 81 rivers in this book total 7823.2 miles.
Class1 portions of class 1 rivers = 3316.4 miles.
The 68 floatable rivers are 7474.8 total miles (Class 1 - 3976.1 miles) -
    (Class 2 - 3498.7)

3484.9 Class 1	3309.4 Class 1
3362.7 Class 2	2846.9 Class 2
6847.6 River miles	6156.3 River floatable

491.2 Class 1	190.4 Class 1
136.0 Class 2	96.3 Class 2
627.2 Lakes & reservoirs	286.7 Floatable whitewater

Float times when given are calculated on a non-stop basis. A guideline to go by:

Slow water	1/2 mile per hour
Ave. low water	2 miles per hour
Ave. mod. water	3-4 miles per hour
Ave. high water	6 miles per hour
High water	8 miles per hour

3-4 mph is great for family recreation, if stream is not narrow and
    curvy.

Winter floating access sites are usually not plowed open. Ice can form in slow water situations. Ice jams can collect in places, usually in narrow areas with slow deep pools. Spring run-off varies each year, but usually east of the divide run-off is earlier, often in March.

June, July, August and September are the most popular times for family floats. Whitewater enthusiasts begin in April and wear wetsuits. The fall can be a wonderful time to float, if water levels allow. Many eastern Montana fishers, float and fish all year.

Large dams can be hydro-electric or irrigation and flood control. Also many diversion dams exist from large to small. Irrigation jettys are partial obstructions to collect pools of water. Usually these jettys can be floated around or even over. Fences, jettys and the small rock diversion dams quite often get washed out during high water. However, it seems they are soon repaired.

Montana has rivers for everyone. Carefully choose some based on your skill level and vessel of your choice. A safe overnight float-camp trip, is an unforgetable experience.

Wishing you a happy and safe float! CAUTION - Watch for symptoms of "float addiction".

4

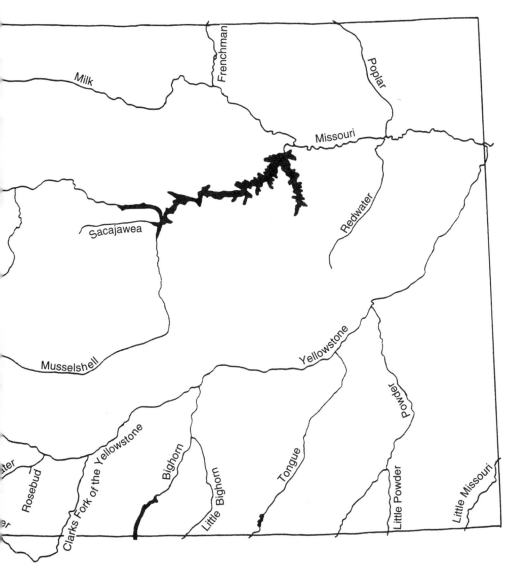

Montana Rivers

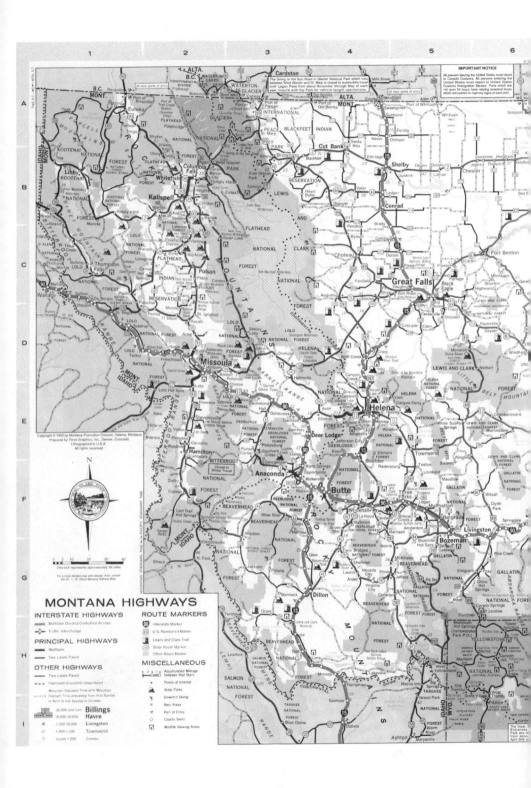

CITIES AND TOWNS (Partial List)

† Hospital • County Seats State Capital: Helena Population: 799,065 (1990 U.S. Census) Land Area: 145,392 sq. miles Total Area (land and water): 147,138 sq. miles

WATERSHEDS

WEST WATERSHED	Class I	All Year	Whitewater	Whitewater (Seasonal)	Unfloatable	Page #
Clark Fork	●	●	●			66
Silverbow				●		230
Little Blackfoot						50
Rock Creek	●		●			206
Blackfoot	●		●			41
North Fork Blackfoot	●		●			46
Clearwater				●		78
Bitterroot	●	●				33
St. Regis				●		222
Flathead	●	●	●			95
Middle Fork Flathead (and Granite Creek)	●	●	●			102
North Fork Flathead	●	●	●			108
South Fork Flathead	●		●			112
White						298
Spotted Bear						239
Stillwater (and Logan Creek)				●		243
Whitefish						302
Swan			●			255
Little Bitterroot				●		37
Jocko						130
Thompson				●		268
Little Thompson						272
Vermilion						290
Bull				●		62

	Class I	All Year	Whitewater	Whitewater (Seasonal)	Unfloatable	Page #
Kootenai	●	●	●			138
Wigwam					●	325
Tobacco						276
Fisher						91
Lake Creek	●					142
Yaak	●		●			310
NORTH WATERSHED						
Belly						16
Mokowanis					●	324
Waterton						294
St. Mary						218
Swiftcurrent				●		259
EAST WATERSHED						
Missouri	●	●	●			164
Jefferson	●	●				126
Red Rock						198
Beaverhead	●					12
Ruby						214
Bighole	●	●	●			20
Wise						306
Boulder				●		54
Little Boulder					●	323
South Boulder					●	323
Madison	●	●	●			146

	Class I	All Year	Whitewater	Whitewater (Seasonal)	Unfloatable	Page #
Elk					●	323
Little Elk					●	324
Gallatin	●		●			122
Dearborn	●			●		87
Smith	●					234
Sun	●		●			251
Roe					●	325
Marias	●					152
Two Medicine			●			284
Cut Bank						83
Teton						263
Arrow					●	323
Judith	●					134
Musselshell						178
Sacajewea					●	325
Milk						157
Red						194
Lost					●	324
Frenchman						118
Redwater						202
Poplar						185
Yellowstone	●	●	●			314
Gardiner					●	324
Shields						226

	Class I	All Year	Whitewater	Whitewater (Seasonal)	Unfloatable	Page #
Boulder				●		58
Stillwater			●			247
Rosebud				●		210
Clarks Fork						74
Broadwater					●	323
Bighorn	●	●				24
Little Bighorn						29
Tongue	●					280
Powder						189
Little Powder					●	324
Little Missouri						174

Triple Divide Mountain in Glacier National Park

BEAVERHEAD

ORIGIN:	Clark Canyon Reservoir Dam (S. of Dillon, MT) El. 5500'
END:	Joins Bighole River to form Jefferson River. (N. of Twin Bridges, MT) El. 4600'
LENGTH:	79.5 river miles (49 air mi.)
FLOATABLE:	79.5 miles (Class I is entire 79.5 miles)
SECTIONS:	Upper (16 mi.) Origin "79.5" to Barrett's Dam "63.5." Middle (23.8 mi.) Barrett's Dam "63.5" to Anderson Lane Bridge. "39.7" Lower (39.7 mi.) Anderson Br. "39.7" to End "0"
DAMS:	Clark Canyon - Forms reservoir and controls flow. Mile "79.5" Barrett's - Portage LEFT - Mile "63.5" Dillon - Float through chute on LEFT bank when dam is raised. Mile "51.7" Twin Bridges - Float through chute on LEFT bank. Mile "1"
WATERFALLS:	None
WHITEWATER:	None
DANGERS:	Dams, fences, low bridges. Sudden dam releases.
DEWATERED:	Severely below Barrett's during irrigation season.
PORTAGES:	1 dam, 4 low irrigation jettys, low bridges, fences, logjams.
SPEC. AGENCIES:	None
REGS - PERMITS:	Ten h.p. motor limit on all streams in Beaverhead and Madison County.
ACCESS-SHUTTLE:	Easy auto access. Roads parallel river. Frequent access points in upper section. Middle and lower sections - infrequent.
SERVICES:	All services in Dillon or Twin Bridges, MT. Commercial fish-float trips available.

CAMPING:	Formal public campgounds few. Some private camp-grounds. Numerous informal campsites.
GAMEFISH:	Rainbow, brown trout. More large trout per mile than any other stream in MT.
VESSEL:	Upper - Raft, canoe, small boat, dory. Middle & Lower - Small raft, canoe, small boat.
SKILL LEVEL:	Upper - Intermediate. Middle - Beginner (many obstructions). Lower - Beginner.
FLOAT TIMES:	Upper - usually good flows. Below Barrett's slow.
FLOW INFO:	(406) 449-5263 USGS - Helena

HYDROGRAPH

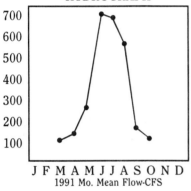

700
600
500
400
300
200
100

J F M A M J J A S O N D
1991 Mo. Mean Flow-CFS

Gage Sta: 1.4 mi. above Barrett's Dam
Drain Area: 2,737 sq. mi. (at gage)
Ave. Flow: (79 years) 441 cfs
Ext. Max: 3720 cfs - 6/20/08 - 6.1'
Ext. Min: 69 cfs - 1/30/39
Gradient: 900' in 79.5 mi. = 11.3' pma
Float Grad: Same
Clarity: Somewhat cloudy to murky
Temp: Jan. 32^0 F.
         Apr. 48^0 F.
         Jul. 71^0 F.
         Oct. 50^0 F.
Total Drain Area: 4200 sq. mi. (approx.)

DRAINAGE:	(East) Jefferson, Missouri, Mississippi, Gulf of Mexico
MAPS:	BLM - #32 "Dillon" (Best map) USFS - Beaverhead NF (Interagency) USGS - "Dillon" CO. - Beaverhead - Madison

BEAVERHEAD

The three forks of the Jefferson River were named after President Jefferson's three cardinal virtues. The Beaverhead being called "Philosophy". Indians felt Beaverhead Rock resembled a swimming beaver. It was here that Sacajewea first recognized her homeland on the Lewis & Clark expedition.

Until 1964, the Beaverhead originated at the confluence of the Red Rock River and Horse Prairie Creek, at the present Clark Canyon Reservoir. Today, the river begins at, and the flow is controlled by, the dam. Dam controlled rivers are unique since flows are regulated and water may be warmer and more clear, as heavy natural runoff is not obvious. The reservoir offers many recreational water opportunities. Historically rich Bannack, our first territorial capitol, is 30 miles southwest of Dillon.

The upper river flows through an arid canyon, paralleled by highways and railroad tracks, which reduce scenic values. For 16 miles to Barrett's Dam the river flows unique from the rest of the river, in that irrigation withdrawals and returns have not yet begun. Access in this upper section is easy, due to proximity of state and federal lands and frontage roads.

Floating and fishing can be competitive as many outfitters also pursue the large rainbow and brown trout inhabiting the undercut and brushy banks. This river produces more large trout per mile than any other steam in the state. Insects alive and artificial abound! Nymph and Girdle Bug patterns work best all year; while dry flies are best in early spring, caddis in summer, and cranefly in the fall. Spinners and spoons work for the spin fisherperson. High water can cause a dangerous clearance situation at low bridges (especially Pipe Organ). At Barrett's Dam a sizeable portage LEFT is necessary if you plan to float on.

Few people float the section from Barrett's to Anderson Lane bridge. The river flows out onto the valley floor and among the cottonwoods are low bridges, irrigation pipe, fences, and log jams that necessitate many portages. From this point the river channels more and an irrigation dewatered and silted situation exists, reducing fishery values. Sometimes, floating is impossible due to reduced flow. The land bordering the remaining river is nearly all private with public access less frequent. In Dillon, a newly designed, float through chute is on left bank of the diversion dam. Floating through Dillon is confusing with numerous small channels.

From Dillon to Anderson bridge the same types of obstacles occur, but with less frequency and severity. Two irrigation jettys will be encountered. Whitetail deer and waterfowl are plentiful, and sandhill cranes are often sighted.

At Anderson bridge obstacles become fewer for the rest of the river. Access is seldom and float times often long as the river is curvy and slow. Two more irrigation jettys occur. The Highway #41 bridge at Point of Rocks access offers easy loading or unloading of small craft.

Between Point of Rocks and Twin Bridges, MT only two places to access are at county road bridges. Put-in or take-out is limited to small vessels. From this point on a small motor could be used if flows are up. In Twin Bridges a fine access occurs by Hwy. 41 bridge on left bank. Beyond Twin Bridges there is no access and your option is to float down the Jefferson R. to access, after floating through chute on LEFT bank of diversion dam 1 mile below Twin Bridges.

Capt. M. Lewis wrote in his journal the evening of 8/22/1805..."in about 2 hours caught 528 good fish, most of them trout"....

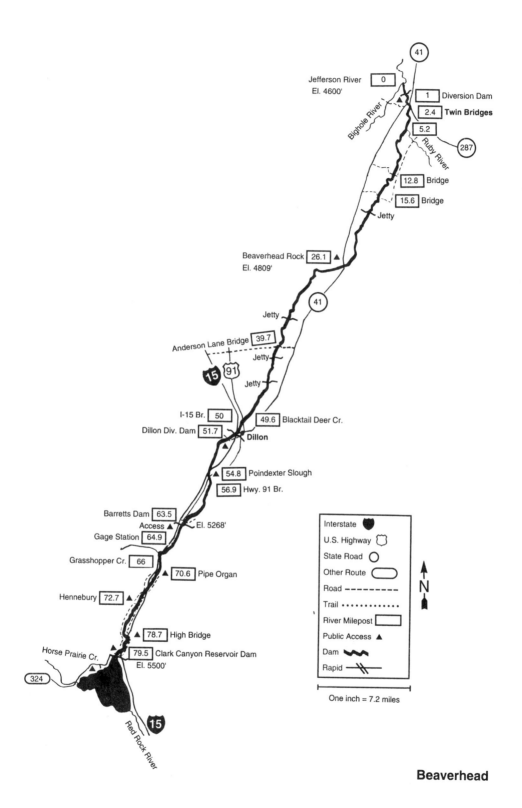

Jefferson River [0]
El. 4600'

[1] Diversion Dam

[2.4] **Twin Bridges**

[5.2]

287

[12.8] Bridge

[15.6] Bridge

Jetty

Beaverhead Rock [26.1] ▲
El. 4809'

41

Jetty

Anderson Lane Bridge [39.7]

Jetty

15 **91**

Jetty

I-15 Br. [50]

[49.6] Blacktail Deer Cr.

Dillon Div. Dam [51.7]
Dillon
▲

▲ [54.8] Poindexter Slough

[56.9] Hwy. 91 Br.

Barretts Dam [63.5]
Access ▲   El. 5268'

Gage Station [64.9]

Grasshopper Cr. [66]

▲ [70.6] Pipe Organ

Hennebury [72.7] ▲

▲ [78.7] High Bridge

Horse Prairie Cr.
▲ [79.5] Clark Canyon Reservoir Dam
El. 5500'

324

15

Red Rock River

Interstate	🛡
U.S. Highway	⬡
State Road	◯
Other Route	⬭
Road	– – – –
Trail	• • • • •
River Milepost	▭
Public Access	▲
Dam	〰
Rapid	⫻

N

One inch = 7.2 miles

Beaverhead

15

BELLY

ORIGIN:	Helen Lake in Glacier National Park. El. 5086'
END:	Enters Canada near Chief Mountain. El. 4400'
LENGTH:	20 total miles in MT (18 river miles plus Elizabeth Lake 2 miles) (12 air miles).
FLOATABLE:	10 miles - Footbridge "12" to last take out (to border) "2"
SECTIONS:	Upper (8 mi.) Origin - Helen Lake "20" to foot bridge "12" Middle (8 mi.) Foot bridge "12" to Three Mile Campsite "4" Lower (4 mi.) Three Mile Campsite "4" to End-Canada border "0"
DAMS:	None.
WATERFALLS:	Dawn Mist "13"
WHITEWATER:	None floatable
DANGERS:	Primitive area (GNP), Dawn Mist Falls
DEWATERED:	Can be too low to float in fall.
PORTAGES:	None
SPEC. AGENCIES:	Glacier National Park
REGS - PERMITS:	Floaters camping overnight need back-country permit (free). You cannot float across the border.
ACCESS-SHUTTLE:	Hiking or horse trail along the river.
SERVICES:	None
CAMPING:	Numerous backcountry campsites (no facilities).
GAMEFISH:	Rainbow, grayling
VESSEL:	Small raft
SKILL LEVEL:	Beginner (if flow is normal).
FLOAT TIMES:	Moderate flows.

FLOW INFO: Call Glacier National Park at Many Glacier and they can radio Belly River Ranger Station for information.

HYDROGRAPH

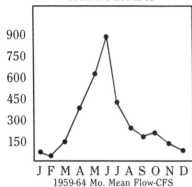

J F M A M J J A S O N D
1959-64 Mo. Mean Flow-CFS

Gage Sta: At Int. Border (Disc. 1964)
Drain Area: 75 sq. mi.
Average Flow: (5 years) 265 cfs
Ext. Max: 8200 cfs 6/08/64
Ext. Min: 30 cfs 2/29/64
Gradient: 686' in 20 miles = 34.3' pma
Float Grad: 200' in 10 miles = 20.0' pma
Clarity: Clear

DRAINAGE: (North) Oldman, S. Sask., Sask., Nelson, Hudson Bay

MAPS:
BLM - #17 "St. Mary"
USGS - "Cut Bank"
Sp.   - "Glacier National Park" USGS
CO.   - Glacier

Belly River

BELLY

The namesake of the river is derived from the Gros Ventre or "Big Belly" Indians who lived downstream. The origin of the river is at Helen Lake in Glacier National Park. The river flows for twenty miles in Montana and enters Alberta near Chief Mountain. The river then flows about 100 miles in Alberta before reaching the Oldman River and eventually on to Hudson Bay.

Access to the river in Montana, is by hiking or horse trails only. Three trails in the Chief Mountain area, or over Ptarmigan Tunnel or Red Gap Pass from the Many Glacier side are possibilities. The trails to the Belly River are through awe inspiring country.

Glacier Park regulations are in effect. You do not need a fishing license, but camping overnight requires a free backcountry permit. Numerous campsites exist and you must choose before you receive your permit. These campsites usually have no facilities, and food preparation areas are distant from tent areas. Some campsites allow horses, others do not. No firearms are allowed and floating across the Canada border is prohibited.

The river meanders slowly for three miles between Helen and Elizabeth lakes. Two miles below Elizabeth Lake and campsite is Dawn Mist Falls. This falls is spectacular. The trail follows the entire river except the lower two miles before the Canada border. In the falls area the river has a steeper gradient and tumbles through a boulder streambed containing much downfall.

One mile below the falls is a foot bridge at river milepost "12". Floating can begin at this point. The unfloatable Mokowanis River "10.5" adds volume to the river. Just below the Mokowanis confluence is the Belly River Ranger Station and campground "10"

The Mokowanis Valley Trail footbridge crosses the Belly River at milepost "9". The very popular Three Mile Campground "4" is the easiest place to exit the river. If alert one could float on two more miles to a point where the trail comes within 100 yards of the river. The trail leaves the river and heads east to the trailhead at Chief Mountain Customs and Immigration. Marking the river at this spot would be wise, as it is difficult to distinguish from the river. This is the last exit possibility in the last two miles to the border.

Wildlife, as well as hikers enjoy the area. Sheep, goats , moose, and elk are all common sights. Grizzlies also inhabit this area. The aspen groves, especially in the fall, with the rugged peaks as a backdrop offer breathtaking beauty. Fishing is quite good. A rainbow or grayling in the evening fry pan is wonderful. This is one of few places that grayling can be found.

A beginner can handle the river in a small or medium raft. Floating is not popular on the river due of course, to packing a raft in. The river can be too low to float in the fall, but if flow permits, this is a trip definitely worth the effort.

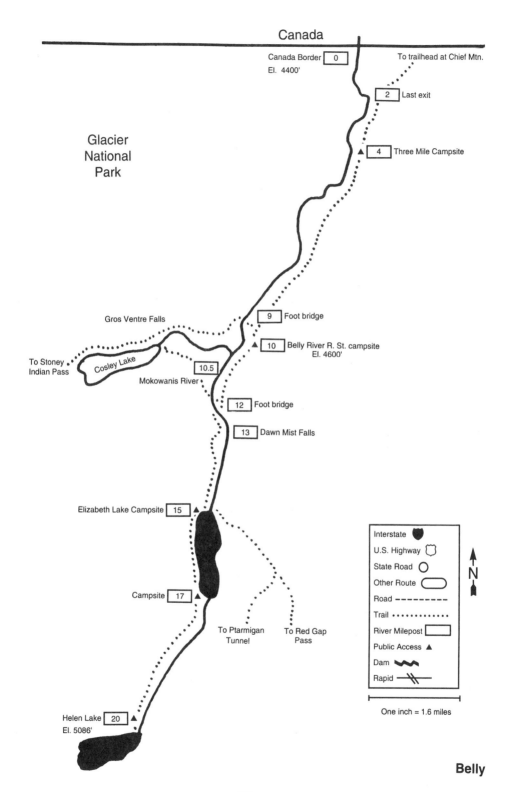

Canada

Canada Border [0]
El. 4400'

To trailhead at Chief Mtn.

[2] Last exit

Glacier
National
Park

▲ [4] Three Mile Campsite

Gros Ventre Falls

[9] Foot bridge

▲ [10] Belly River R. St. campsite
El. 4600'

To Stoney
Indian Pass

Cosley Lake

[10.5]

Mokowanis River

[12] Foot bridge

[13] Dawn Mist Falls

Elizabeth Lake Campsite [15] ▲

Campsite [17] ▲

To Ptarmigan
Tunnel

To Red Gap
Pass

Interstate ⬤
U.S. Highway ⬡
State Road ◯
Other Route ⬭
Road – – – – –
Trail • • • • • • •
River Milepost [   ]
Public Access ▲
Dam 〰
Rapid ⌁

N

One inch = 1.6 miles

Helen Lake [20] ▲
El. 5086'

Belly

19

BIGHOLE

ORIGIN: Skinner Lake (S. of Jackson, MT) El. 7200'

END: Joins Beaverhead R. north of Twin Bridges, MT (Inception of Jefferson River) El. 4600'

LENGTH: 155.6 river miles (65 air miles)

FLOATABLE: 139 miles (Jackson, MT El. 6465' - End) Class 1 portion is 84 miles (Fishtrap Access to End)

SECTIONS: Upper (71.6 mi.) Origin "155.6" to Fishtrap Access "84."
Middle (28.2 mi.) Fishtrap "84" to Dam "55.8"
Lower (55.8 mi.) Dam "55.8" to End "0"

DAMS: Divide Diversion - Dangerous - portage necessary. Pennington Bridge Diversion (right channel)

WATERFALLS: None

WHITEWATER: Moderate (Class II-III, depending on flow) between Jerry Creek Access and Old Divide Bridge (short streches). Also portion between Divide highway access and Salmon Fly Access.

DANGERS: Upper section - fences. Dam between middle and lower sections. A few low rock irrigation jettys. Float through chute on RIGHT "57.5"

DEWATERED: Can be dewatered at times below dam, as millions of gallons are pumped out daily, and some irrigation use.

PORTAGES: Divide Diversion Dam (portage LEFT). Some fences upper, and a few low irrigation jettys (Many of these jettys can be floated over if flows are up). Pennington Div. Dam (portage or use LEFT channel above)

SPEC. AGENCIES: None

REGS - PERMITS: No motors allowed (entire river). Some special fishing regulations.

ACCESS-SHUTTLE: Easy. Roads parallel river with numerous access sites and bridges.

SERVICES:	Limited: Jackson, Wisdom, Wise River, Melrose, Glen, and Twin Bridges, Mt. Commercial fish-float trips available.
CAMPING:	A few formal public campgrounds and numerous access sites.
GAMEFISH:	Brown, rainbow, brook, grayling, mountain whitefish. Blue Ribbon Stream - Divide to Glen.
VESSEL:	Extreme upper - canoe. From Fishtrap Access to end - any vessel. Whitewater section - raft, whitewater canoe, kayak, dory.
SKILL LEVEL:	Upper - Beginner Middle - Intermediate to experienced. Lower - Intermediate.
FLOAT TIMES:	Upper - Slow Middle & Lower - Moderate to fast.
FLOW INFO:	(406) 449-5263 USGS - Helena

HYDROGRAPH

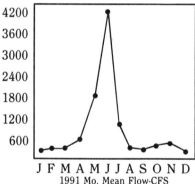

1991 Mo. Mean Flow-CFS

GageSta: 7 miles S. of Melrose
Drain Area: 2,476 sq. mi. (at gage)
Average Flow: (68 years) 1,136 cfs
Ext. Max: 14,300 cfs - 8.04' 6/10/72
Ext. Min: 49 cfs - .70' 8/17/31
Gradient: 2600' in 155.6 mi. = 16.7' pma
Float Grad: 1865' in 139.0 mi. = 13.4' pma
Clarity: Cloudy to Clear
Temp: Jan. 32° F.
        Apr. 43° F.
        Jul. 63° F.
        Oct. 45° F.

DRAINAGE:	(East) Jefferson, Missouri, Mississippi, Gulf.
MAPS:	BLM - #31 "Bighole" (upper) - #32 "Dillon" (lower) USFS - Beaverhead NF (Interagency) USGS - "Dillon" CO. - Beaverhead, Deer Lodge, Silverbow, Madison

BIGHOLE

Captain Lewis of the Lewis & Clark Expedition named the three forks of the Jefferson River for president Jefferson's three cardinal virtues. The Beaverhead was named "Philosophy", Ruby "Philanthropy" and the Bighole "Wisdom". The Shoshoni's called it the "land of the big snows". Local sentiment dictated its present name from early trappers who called valleys "holes".

A trailhead and campground in the Van Houten Lakes area offers the challenge of the backcountry. Unique to most rivers, the upper Bighole meanders through a valley floor with a maze of willows along its banks. Floating can begin at Jackson in a canoe when flow is up if you enjoy a narrow, curvy and brushy experience. The only obstacles would be an occasional fence.

A small campground at the Highway #41 bridge in Wisdom offers an opportunity to rest and a trip west ten miles to Bighole Battlefield National Monument is interesting. Settlers started arriving immediately after the Nez Perce battle. Below Wisdom the river remains similar until reaching the North Fork confluence (14 miles), where it becomes a wider river. Fishtrap Campground begins the Class 1 designation. A beginner can handle the stretch of river to Dickey Bridge in any moderately sized vessel if flows are normal. This access is the last before the Wise River confluence where the river becomes moderately bouncy in places. A few kayakers enjoy the moderate whitewater stretch between Jerry Creek Access and Old Divide Bridge Access (5.7 miles). At Divide a dangerous water supply dam exists that must be portaged (LEFT). The water above Divide Dam holds good fishing but the segment between Divide Access and Glen Access in considered the Blue Ribbon portion. Dry flies work well on these browns when the salmon fly hatch occurs in June. Maidenrock Canyon can be modestly bouncy during high water. You may wish to choose a vessel you can fish from rather than simply HANGING ON. Campgrounds and access sites are frequent.

Rock climbing is popular in the Humbug Spires area and the Bighorn Sheep seem to enjoy it also. Thankfully mining activity is diminishing in the rivers but rockhounding and gold panning can be fun with the mineral content of the Melrose area.

Below Glen, floating pressure dissipates slightly as fish are fewer in numbers but perhaps larger. This portion is an easier float for intermediates with the only problem area being the Pennington Bridge diversion dam. The dam lies just below the bridge in the right channel. Portage or use the left channel just above the bridge, and avoid the dam. An old road which can be muddy with rain parallels the north side of the river. Campground and access sites are adequate.

The Bighole joins the Beaverhead River just below Twin Bridges, MT to form the Jefferson River.

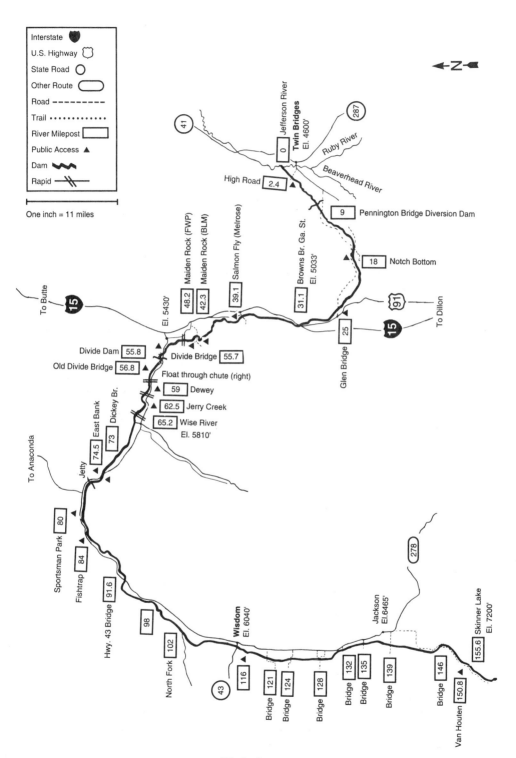

Legend

Interstate
U.S. Highway
State Road
Other Route
Road
Trail
River Milepost
Public Access ▲
Dam
Rapid

One inch = 11 miles

←N→

Jefferson River
Twin Bridges El. 4600'
Ruby River
Beaverhead River

41
287

0

High Road 2.4 ▲

9   Pennington Bridge Diversion Dam

Maiden Rock (FWP)
Maiden Rock (BLM)
Salmon Fly (Melrose)
Browns Br. Ga. St.
El. 5033'

18   Notch Bottom

To Butte
15

48.2
42.3
39.1

El. 5430'

31.1

91

25

15   To Dillon

Glen Bridge

Divide Dam 55.8 ▲
Old Divide Bridge 56.8 ▲
Divide Bridge 55.7

Float through chute (right)

59   Dewey
62.5   Jerry Creek
65.2   Wise River
El. 5810'

East Bank
Dickey Br.

74.5
73

To Anaconda

Jetty ▲

80   Sportsman Park ▲

84   Fishtrap ▲

91.6   Hwy. 43 Bridge

98

102   North Fork

278

Jackson
El.6465'

Skinner Lake
El. 7200'

Wisdom El. 6040'

43

116
121   Bridge
124   Bridge
128   Bridge
132   Bridge
135   Bridge
139   Bridge
146   Bridge
150.8   Van Houten
155.6

Bighole

23

BIGHORN

ORIGIN: Near Thermopolis, WY. Enters MT as Bighorn Reservoir El. 3700'

END: Flows into Yellowstone River near Custer, MT. El. 2670'

LENGTH: 128.4 total miles (84.3 river miles + Bighorn & Afterbay Reservoir 44.1 miles) (90 air mi.)

FLOATABLE: 84.3 river miles 2 reservoirs are floatable.
Class I portion is 86.6 miles (Yellowtail Dam to end) "Navigable river" below Little Bighorn.

SECTIONS: Upper (44.1 mi.) Origin "128.4" to Afterbay Access "84.3"
Middle (44.3 mi.) Afterbay "84.3" to Arapooish Access "40"
Lower (40.0 mi.) Arapooish "40" to End-Yellowstone River "0"

DAMS: Yellowtail (Forms Bighorn Reservoir & controls flow)
Afterbay (Forms Afterbay Reservoir - Access below on North)
Two Leggins Mi. "53.2" - Victory Mi. "13" - Manning Mi. "4"

WATERFALLS: None

WHITEWATER: None

DANGERS: 3 diversion dams, low irrigation jettys, sudden dam release

DEWATERED: No

PORTAGES: 3 diversion dams, (Two Leggins - portage RIGHT), (Victory "13" portage or float over), (Manning "4" portage LEFT)

SPEC. AGENCIES: Bighorn Canyon National Recreation Area (upper) - Crow Indian Reservation (upper & middle sections)

REGS - PERMITS: No motors between Afterbay Access & Bighorn Access. Possible tribal permits if you bank fish or trespass on reservation.

Bighorn River

ACCESS-SHUTTLE:	Roads parallel river. Numerous access sites. A private shuttle business operates out of Fort Smith.
SERVICES:	Fort Smith, St. Xavier, Hardin, MT. Boat rentals and guided fish-float trips.
CAMPING:	Numerous access sites.
GAMEFISH:	Blue Ribbon Stream between Afterbay & Bighorn Access. Brown, rainbow. Also sauger, walleye and catfish in lower section.
VESSEL:	All vessels (Caution - 3 portages). Drift boats (dory) popular between Afterbay & Bighorn Access.
SKILL LEVEL:	Upper - Reservoirs - Beginner Middle & Lower - Beginner (if flows are normal)
FLOAT TIMES:	Upper - Moderately fast. Middle & Lower - Slow.
FLOW INFO:	(406) 449-5263 USGS - Helena

HYDROGRAPH

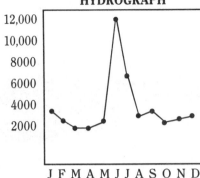

12,000	
10,000	
8000	
6000	
4000	
2000	

J F M A M J J A S O N D
1991 Mo. Mean Flow-CFS

Gage Sta: Below Afterbay Dam
Drain Area: 19,667 sq. mi. (at gage)
Ave. Flow: (57 yrs.) 3,517 cfs
Ext. Max: 37,400 cfs 6/16/35
Ext. Min: 112 cfs 4/02/67
Gradient: 1,030' in 128.4 miles = 8.0' pma
Float Grad: 489' in   84.3 miles = 5.8' pma
Clarity: Cloudy to clear (upper) - M. & L. murky
Temp: Jan. 45⁰ F.
      Apr. 60⁰ F.
      Jul. 75⁰ F.
      Oct. 50⁰ F.
Total Drain Area: 22,885 sq. mi. (WY & MT)

DRAINAGE: (East) Yellowstone, Missouri, Mississippi, Gulf

MAPS: BLM - #81 "Lodge Grass" (upper) - #80 "Hardin" (middle) - #27 "Sumatra" (lower)
USGS - "Billings" (upper) - "Hardin" (middle) - "Forsyth" (lower)
FWP - "Bighorn River Regs" (Afterbay to Arapooish only - not detailed)
CO.   - Bighorn, Treasure

Natures Engineers

26

BIGHORN

The Bighorn river originates at Boysen Reservoir and flows approximately 150 miles in Wyoming before entering Montana as the Bighorn Reservoir. This beautiful setting makes one attempt to imagine how magnificent this sight must have been as a wild river with formidable rapids, prior to the construction of the 525' high Yellowtail Dam which was completed in 1965. The name Bighorn was dubbed from the large population of bighorn sheep found in this area.

Boating on this scenic reservoir can be accessed just above the dam via a backroad from historic Fort Smith. Below Yellowtail is a re-regulating dam which forms Afterbay Reservoir which is also boatable. An airstrip allows "hurry" floats.

River floating may begin at the extremely popular access just below the dam. This 12.3 Blue Ribbon portion to Bighorn Access is preferable to most fisherman. This stretch of river lies in the Bighorn Canyon National Recreation Area, before flowing through the Crow Indian Reservation on its journey to the Yellowstone River. Large brown and rainbow trout are taken using nymphs and streamers. Spinning is difficult due to moss and algae. Fishing is popular in fall and winter as well. Any moderately sized vessel is commonly seen, including dorys, due to ramps at Afterbay and Bighorn Access.

Just below Bighorn Access is St. Xavier, MT, where west is the Chief Plenty Coups State Monument at Pryor. Pryor is the namesake for many landmarks, originating from a young soldier in the Lewis & Clark expedition. From St. Xavier on, the river has a complexion of a slower more turbid stream. You may even encounter jet boats (no motors above)! 8.8 miles below Mallard Campground is the Two Leggins Diversion Dam which must be portaged (RIGHT). From Hwy #313 bridge access the river has no impoundments for nearly 40 miles. Just above Arapooish Access (ramp) the Little Bighorn River adds volume to this now lazy stream. 1 1/2 miles downstream from Arapooish, floaters leave the Crow Reservation and enter mostly private land.

Grant Marsh and General Custer access sites (which may or may not be open sporadically-due to thoughtless individuals garbaging and vandalizing) occur before reaching Victory and Manning Diversion Dams at mileposts "13" and "4". It is possible to float over Victory if the flows are proper, but Manning must be portaged (LEFT).

This lower section is generally accepted as a warm-water fishery. Beginners can handle the entire river in most vessels if flows are normal. Below Manning Dam three miles is the Manual Lisa Access (ramp). Most floaters exit at this point as the last mile to the Yellowstone would require a diversion dam portage and a dozen mile float down the Yellowstone to its first access point.

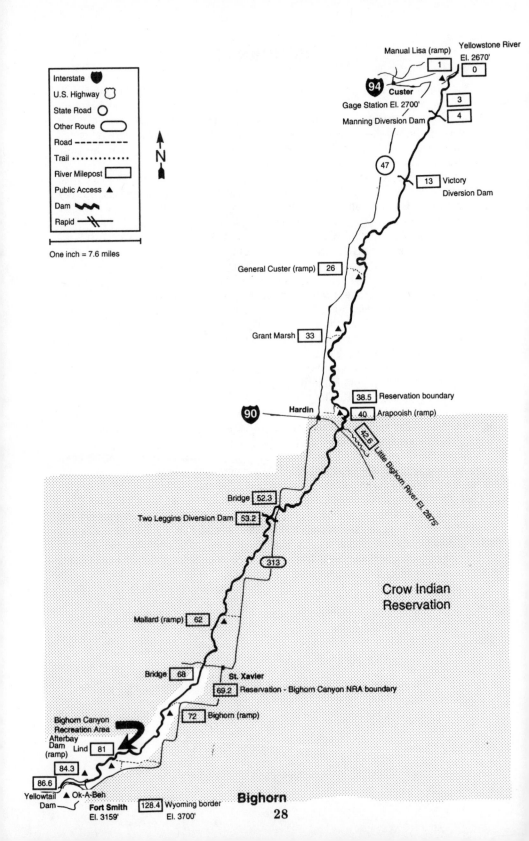

Interstate
U.S. Highway
State Road
Other Route
Road — — — — —
Trail • • • • • • • •
River Milepost
Public Access ▲
Dam
Rapid

One inch = 7.6 miles

N

Manual Lisa (ramp)
Yellowstone River El. 2670'
1
94 Custer
Gage Station El. 2700'
Manning Diversion Dam
3
4
0
47
13 Victory Diversion Dam

General Custer (ramp) 26

Grant Marsh 33

38.5 Reservation boundary
90 Hardin
40 Arapooish (ramp)
42.6
Little Bighorn River El. 2875'

Bridge 52.3
Two Leggins Diversion Dam 53.2
313

Crow Indian Reservation

Mallard (ramp) 62

Bridge 68
St. Xavier
69.2 Reservation - Bighorn Canyon NRA boundary

72 Bighorn (ramp)

Bighorn Canyon Recreation Area
Afterbay Dam (ramp)
Lind 81
84.3
86.6
Yellowtail Dam ▲ Ok-A-Beh
Fort Smith El. 3159'
128.4 Wyoming border El. 3700'

Bighorn
28

LITTLE BIGHORN

ORIGIN:	In the Bighorn Mountains in WY. Enters MT south of Lodge Grass, MT El. 4420'
END:	Flows into Bighorn River at Hardin, MT El. 2875'
LENGTH:	116.1 miles (in MT) 54 air miles
FLOATABLE:	116.1 miles
SECTIONS:	Upper (62.0 mi.) Origin-MT border "116.1" to Hwy 87 Benteen) "54.1" Middle (32.5 mi.) Hwy. 87 "54.1" to Crow Agency "21.6" Lower (21.6 mi.) Crow Agency "21.6" to End-Bighorn River "0"
DAMS:	Sand Creek Diversion Dam (Milepost "55") Crow Agency Diversion Dam (Milepost "21.6")
WATERFALLS:	None
WHITEWATER:	None (under normal conditions)
DANGERS:	Diversion dams, low diversion jettys, fences, logs
DEWATERED:	Often in fall
PORTAGES:	Diversion dams "55" and "21.6"
SPEC. AGENCIES:	Crow Indian Reservation
REGS - PERMITS:	Possible Crow Reservation permits, if you leave the river.
ACCESS-SHUTTLE:	Hwys. and frontage roads parallel river with intersecting bridges. Few formal access sites.
SERVICES:	All - Lodge Grass and Hardin, MT. Limited at Crow Agency, MT
CAMPING:	Few campgrounds. Reservation and private land.
GAMEFISH:	Brown trout, burbot, catfish
VESSEL:	Canoe, small raft, small boat
SKILL LEVEL:	Intermediate (if flows are normal)

FLOAT TIMES: Moderate to slow flow.

FLOW INFO: (406) 449-5263 USGS - Helena

HYDROGRAPH

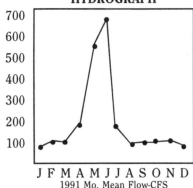

J F M A M J J A S O N D
1991 Mo. Mean Flow-CFS

Gage Sta: 3 1/2 miles North of Wyola, MT
Drain Area: 428 sq. mi. (at gage)
Ave. Flow: (50 yrs.) 208 cfs
Ext. Max: 8,010 cfs - 10.02' ga. ht. 5/19/78
Ext. Min: 12 cfs - .89' ga. ht. 8/08/61
Gradient: 1545' in 116.1 miles = 13.3' pma
Float Grad: Same
Clarity: Cloudy to murky
Temp: Jan. 32° F.
    Apr. 46° F.
    Jul. 73° F.
    Oct. 48° F.

DRAINAGE: (East) Bighorn, Yellowstone, Missouri, Mississippi, Gulf of Mexico.

MAPS: BLM - #81 "Lodge Grass" (upper) - #80 "Hardin" (lower)
USGS - "Hardin"
CO. - Bighorn

Log jams - appear and disappear

LITTLE BIGHORN

The Little Bighorn headwaters in the Bighorn Mountains of Wyoming. The river enters Montana south of Lodge Grass, and flows over 116 miles in Montana before entering the Bighorn River at Hardin.

The entire river is floatable by an intermediate paddler in a canoe, small raft or small boat. This narrow river is often floatable only four months of the year. Two diversion dams, fences, logjams and a few irrigation jettys obstruct the river.

The entire river is within the Crow Indian Reservation. Near Crow Agency (tribal headquarters), is the Custer Battlefield, a national historic monument.

The upper river, flowing between the Bighorn and Rosebud Mountains, can be a little bouncy. The river streambed of gravel and boulders has a steeper gradient. The lower section finds the velocity slowing with sand and gravel streambed. The river becomes more turbid approaching the wide valley floor. As the river is low much of the year, the water warms and fishing is only fair. Brown trout, burbot and catfish inhabit the river. The river is quite pretty, especially in autumn.

Formal campgrounds or access sites are uncommon. Numerous bridges offer access points, with no more than a ten mile float between. Refer to the river milepost for exact locations.

Little Bighorn River

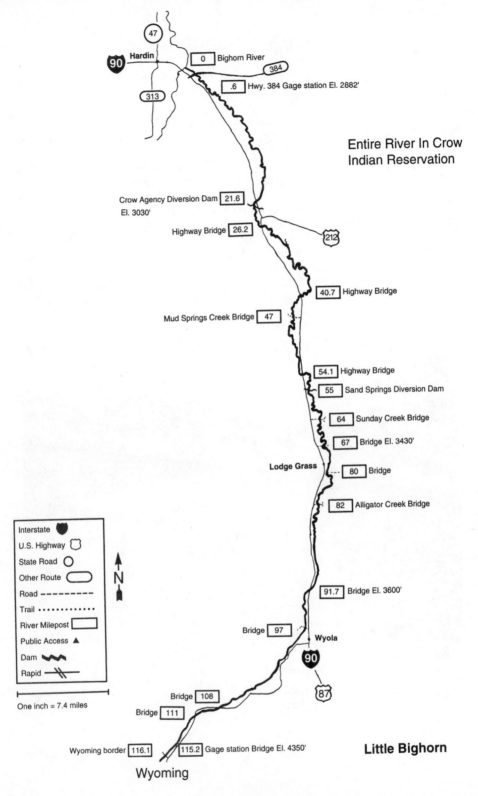

47

90 **Hardin**

0 Bighorn River

384

313

.6 Hwy. 384 Gage station El. 2882'

Entire River In Crow
Indian Reservation

Crow Agency Diversion Dam 21.6
El. 3030'

Highway Bridge 26.2

212

40.7 Highway Bridge

Mud Springs Creek Bridge 47

54.1 Highway Bridge

55 Sand Springs Diversion Dam

64 Sunday Creek Bridge

67 Bridge El. 3430'

Lodge Grass 80 Bridge

82 Alligator Creek Bridge

Interstate
U.S. Highway
State Road
Other Route
Road ----------
Trail ••••••••••
River Milepost
Public Access ▲
Dam
Rapid

One inch = 7.4 miles

91.7 Bridge El. 3600'

Bridge 97

Wyola

90

87

Bridge 108

Bridge 111

Wyoming border 116.1

115.2 Gage station Bridge El. 4350'

Little Bighorn

Wyoming

32

BITTERROOT

ORIGIN:	Confluence of East and West Forks near Conner, MT El. 4,000'
END:	Flows into Clark Fork River at Missoula, MT El. 3090'
LENGTH:	80.2 river miles (67 air miles)
FLOATABLE:	80.2 miles. Class I portion is entire 80.2 miles
SECTIONS:	Upper (26.2 mi.) Origin "80.2" to Hamilton Dam "54" Middle (22 mi.) Hamilton Dam "54" to Stevensville Bridge "32" Lower (32 mi.) Stevensville Bridge "32" to End "0"
DAMS:	2 diversion dams (upper) "64.8" and "60.4" Hamilton Diversion Dam (Rock-Dangerous) portage RIGHT "54" 2 diversion dams between Corvallis and Victor, MT "45.3" and "43.5"
WATERFALLS:	None
WHITEWATER:	None
DANGERS:	5 div. dams, numerous small irrigation jettys, fences
DEWATERED:	Terribly. Between Corvallis and Stevensville, MT. Often not floatable between August 1 until irrigation stops.
PORTAGES:	5 diversion dams (Avoid last 2 by taking left channel)
SPEC.AGENCIES:	Lee Metcalf National Wildlife Refuge (middle section)
REGS - PERMITS:	None
ACCESS-SHUTTLE:	Easy with highways and co. roads paralleling and intersecting. Numerous public access sites. Float down Clark Fork River to exit.
SERVICES:	All. Darby, Hamilton, Victor, Stevensville, Florence, Lolo & Missoula, MT

CAMPING:	A few campgrounds and numerous fish access sites.
GAMEFISH:	Upper - Brook, brown, rainbow and cutthroat trout. Middle & Lower - Brown, mtn. whitefish, largemouth bass and pike.
VESSEL:	Upper & Middle - Small raft, canoe, small boat. Lower -All vessels (Trailer ramps limited). Small motor if flow up.
SKILL LEVEL:	Beginner (if flows are moderate)
FLOAT TIMES:	Upper - moderate flow Middle - slow Lower - moderate
FLOW INFO:	(406) 449-5263 USGS - Helena

HYDROGRAPH

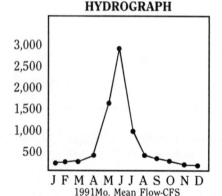

3,000
2,500
2,000
1,500
1,000
500

J F M A M J J A S O N D
1991Mo. Mean Flow-CFS

Gage Sta: 4 mi. S. of Darby, MT
Drain Area: 1,049 sq. mi. (at gage)
Ave. Flow: (54 yrs.) 897 cfs
Ext. Max: 11,500 cfs - 8.2' 5/9/47
Ext. Min: 71 cfs 2/9/39
Gradient: 910' in 80.2 miles = 11.3' pma
Float Grad: Same
Clarity: Cloudy to clear
Temp: Jan. 34⁰ F.
        Apr. 45⁰ F.
        Jul. 66⁰ F.
        Oct. 46⁰ F.
Total Drain Area: 2,814 square miles

DRAINAGE:	(West) Clark Fork, Pend Oreille, Columbia, Pacific
MAPS:	BLM - #14 "Hamilton" (upper) - #13 "Miss. W." (lower) - #15 "Nez Perce" (ext. upper) USFS - Bitterroot NF (Best map-covers entire river) USGS - "Hamilton" - "Elk City" (extreme upper) CO. - Ravalli, Missoula

BITTERROOT

This "handsome" stream as Lewis & Clark called it, begins at the confluence of the East and West Forks and offers a wonderful floating experience; especially in autumn when the foliage comes alive with color.

The river was called Clarks River by the L & C expedition and the Salish Indians called it the Red Willow. It's present name comes from the state flower abundant in the area.

The Bitterroot offers many recreational opportunities including a trailhead up the West Fork, rock climbing, hot springs, cross country skiing and three downhill ski resorts. Rock hounding and recreational gold panning in the lower section, between Victor and Lolo can be fun.

Floating can begin up the West or East Forks or at Hannon Memorial Campground at the Hwy. 93 bridge, south of Darby, MT. Campgrounds and access sites occur before two diversion dams at mileposts "64.8" and "60.4". Also, a dangerous dam exists in Hamilton, mile "54". Fishing in this upper section is quite good year-round, with the Salmon Fly hatch usually beginning mid-June. Salmon Fly, Golden Stone, Drake, Dun and Caddis patterns work best. In the fall, Cahill and Trico are very popular. Fishermen should consult current regulations as certain sections of the river have special fishing regulations as to size and catch-n-release.

Below Hamilton, normal floating continues until reaching Corvallis Road Bridge. Below this bridge for 17 miles floating is lousy or non-existent in August until irrigation stops. Although irrigating is necessary, there needs to be some moderation or correctives in this stretch. The fishery is certainly in jeopardy. Floaters can avoid two diversion dams by taking the left channel below Corvallis Bridge - if that channel hasn't been bulldozed shut.

Below Stevensville Bridge normal floating can again take place. Lee Metcalf National Wildlife Refuge begins one mile downstream, with exceptional opportunity to view waterfowl and other wildlife. Whitetail deer are a common sight, with an occasional moose or elk a possibility. At Stevensville, the historic Fort Owen State Monument would be a worthwhile visit.

Beginners can handle the entire river with caution to the dangers of diversion dams, and curvy, narrow channelization in places. Higher water can, of course, cause the additional problem of increased velocity to make the curves with occasional dead-heads sticking out a threat.

The old adage of "doing as our elders ", certainly does not hold true when it comes to the dumping of everything of no value over the river bank. The thinking must have been that no one will ever see it there and perhaps it will help with flow erosion. What an ugly sight to see car bodies, tires, concrete, and garbage. New law, finally, prohibits dumping of waste. We now, need to get the rivers cleaned up!

Below Florence Crossing, the river broadens and flow slows for the rest of its journey to the Clark Fork River. Maclay Bridge offers the last exit from the river unless your choice is to float down the Clark Fork three miles to the Kona Ranch Road.

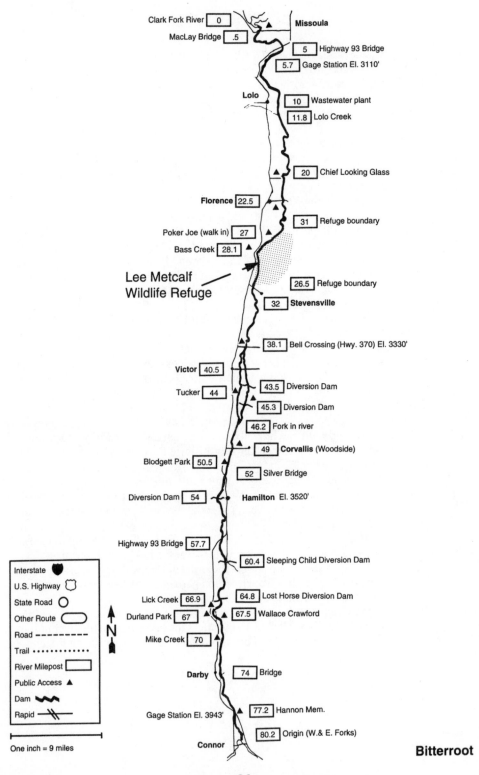

Clark Fork River [0]
△ **Missoula**
MacLay Bridge [.5]
[5] Highway 93 Bridge
[5.7] Gage Station El. 3110'
Lolo
[10] Wastewater plant
[11.8] Lolo Creek
△ [20] Chief Looking Glass
Florence [22.5]
△
[31] Refuge boundary
Poker Joe (walk in) [27] △
Bass Creek [28.1] △
**Lee Metcalf
Wildlife Refuge**
[26.5] Refuge boundary
[32] **Stevensville**
△ [38.1] Bell Crossing (Hwy. 370) El. 3330'
Victor [40.5]
Tucker [44] △ [43.5] Diversion Dam
[45.3] Diversion Dam
[46.2] Fork in river
△ [49] **Corvallis** (Woodside)
Blodgett Park [50.5]
[52] Silver Bridge
Diversion Dam [54] **Hamilton** El. 3520'
Highway 93 Bridge [57.7]
[60.4] Sleeping Child Diversion Dam
Lick Creek [66.9] △ [64.8] Lost Horse Diversion Dam
Durland Park [67] △ △ [67.5] Wallace Crawford
Mike Creek [70]
Darby [74] Bridge
Gage Station El. 3943' △ [77.2] Hannon Mem.
[80.2] Origin (W.& E. Forks)
Connor

Interstate
U.S. Highway
State Road ◯
Other Route ⬭
Road - - - - - -
Trail • • • • • •
River Milepost [   ]
Public Access ▲
Dam 〜〜
Rapid ⫻

N

One inch = 9 miles

Bitterroot

36

LITTLE BITTERROOT

ORIGIN:	Little Bitterroot Lake. El. 3903'
END:	Flows into Flathead River west of Ronan, MT. El. 2550'
LENGTH:	79.6 total miles (76 river miles + Hubbart Reservoir 3.6 miles) (46 air miles)
FLOATABLE:	29 miles (Hot Springs Road Bridge "29" to Flathead River "0" Hubbart Reservoir is also floatable
SECTIONS:	Upper (29.6 mi.) Origin "79.6" to Ranch Road Bridge "50" Middle (21.0 mi.) Bridge "50" to Hot Springs Creek Bridge "29" Lower (29.0 mi.) Bridge "29" to End-Flathead River "0"
DAMS:	Hubbart (Forms reservoir & controls flow)
WATERFALLS:	Falls - Mile "72" (200' high - steep walk around LEFT) 2 Falls - Mile "71" (each 10' high) Falls - Mile "60" (90' high & 8' below. No way to walk around)
WHITEWATER:	2 miles - Mile "2" to Flathead River "0" Class II-III
DANGERS:	Whitewater, fences, rattlesnakes
DEWATERED:	Usually after July
PORTAGES:	Fences, low irrigation jettys, beaver dams
SPEC. AGENCIES:	Flathead Indian Reservation
REGS - PERMITS:	Tribal recreation or fishing permit
ACCESS-SHUTTLE:	Quite round-about. Roads and intersecting road bridges if you study map. No formal access sites.
SERVICES:	All in Hot Springs, MT.
CAMPING:	No formal campgrounds except at Hubbart Reservoir. No access sites. Mostly private land.

GAMEFISH:	Upper - Rainbow, cutthroat, brook, whitefish Middle & Lower - Pike
VESSEL:	Canoe or small boat 2 miles WW section - WW canoe, kayak, small raft
SKILL LEVEL:	Beginner. Experienced in 2 mile WW portion.
FLOAT TIMES:	Slow. Whitewater portion (2 miles) quite fast.
FLOW INFO:	(406) 449-5263 USGS - Helena

HYDROGRAPH

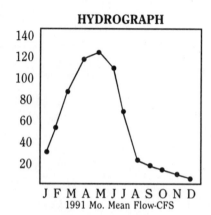

J F M A M J J A S O N D
1991 Mo. Mean Flow-CFS

Gage Sta: Mile "11.1"
Drain Area: 300 sq. mi. (at gage)
Ave. Flow: 65 cfs
Ext. Min: Very little flow often.
Gradient: 1353' in 79.6 miles = 17' pma
Float Grad: 175' in 29.0 miles = 6' pma
Clarity: murky (upper often quite clear)
Temp: Jan. 32^0 F.
          Apr. 60^0 F.
          Jul. 75^0 F.
          Oct. 54^0 F.

DRAINAGE:	(West) Flathead, Clark Fork, Pend Oreille, Columbia, Pacific Ocean
MAPS:	BLM -#10 "Kalispell" (extreme upper)-#11 "Polson" - #12 "Plains" (extreme lower) USFS - Flathead NF (North) upper only - Lolo NF upper only USGS -"Kalispell" (extreme upper)- "Wallace" (lower) CO. - Flathead, Sanders, Lake

LITTLE BITTERROOT

The river begins at the outlet dam, at Little Bitterroot Lake. This river has many faces. Marshy meadows, mountainous gorges, waterfalls, and prairie desert are all scenes.

The upper six miles flow through a marshy bottom with a jungle of willows. Numerous beaver dams create these marshy areas and muddy undercut banks. Finding the river channel is extremely difficult.

Below the Wilderness Boys Ranch "73.5", on the Niarada Road, is a beautiful 200' waterfall "72". The river is now flowing through a narrow mountainous canyon. The stream bed is gravel, boulders, and interlaced with downfall. A steep gradient exists here. A mile below the waterfall is Hidden Lake with two 10' drops below. Below Hidden Lake is an old spur road, off the Hubbart Reservoir Road. This spur road crosses the river and joins the West Side Reservoir Road.

Hubbart Dam "63.4" forms the reservoir. Boating and fishing are popular on the reservoir, even with poor roads leading to it. Rainbow, cutthroat, brookies and whitefish offer good fishing in this upper section. Pike can be found in the middle and lower sections. Numerous campsites on the reservoir are pleasant.

Below Hubbart Dam is a 90' waterfall "60". You can walk the river down to the waterfall, but you cannot go around and continue on. The falls is in a gorge and there is no way around. The best way to view the falls is off the Niarada Road at Little Meadow Creek. It is a 1.3 mile hike upstream across private property to the falls.

Below Little Meadow Creek is the north boundary of the Flathead Indian Reservation. The rest of the river is on tribal or private land.

The river flows out of the mountainous canyon southwest of Niarada. The rest of the river flows through ranchland and has marshy ponds. Rattlesnakes can be found along this lower river. The river flows under the Hwy 28 bridge, north of Hot Springs, MT. Beaver dams, marshes, fences, cottonwood debris and heavy sprinkler irrigating withdrawals, continue to make the river unfloatable.

The Ronan Road bridge "29", east of Hot Springs, marks the beginning of the floatable lower section. Bridges can easily be found for access, with no more than five river miles between. I have seen more turtles in this area, than any other river in Montana.

A beginner in a canoe can handle the river, except the last two miles, which can be whitewater if flow is up. This whitewater should only be approached by an experienced paddler in a whitewater canoe, kayak or small raft. Access to this whitewater can be found above the Sloan Bridge on the Flathead River, and go upstream on an old prairie jeep trail along the east side of the Little Bitterroot River. The lower section is turbid, very curvy, and a few fences and irrigation jettys occur.

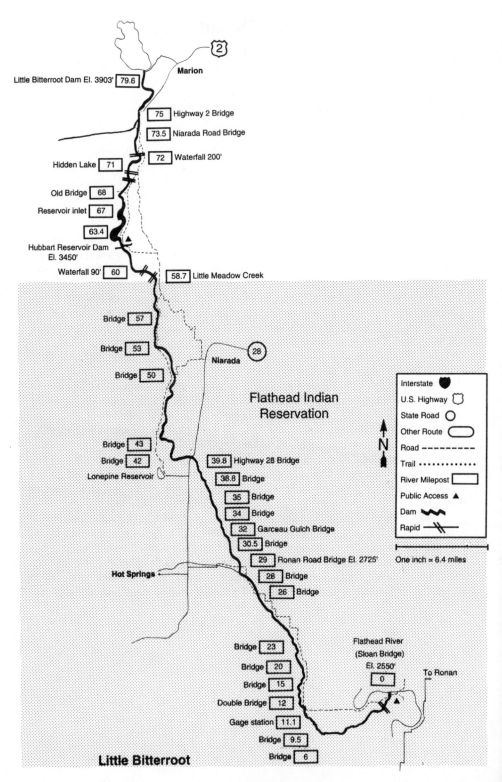

Little Bitterroot Dam El. 3903' | 79.6 |

Marion

| 75 | Highway 2 Bridge

| 73.5 | Niarada Road Bridge

Hidden Lake | 71 | | 72 | Waterfall 200'

Old Bridge | 68 |

Reservoir inlet | 67 |

| 63.4 |

Hubbart Reservoir Dam
El. 3450'

Waterfall 90' | 60 | | 58.7 | Little Meadow Creek

Bridge | 57 |

Bridge | 53 |

Niarada   (28)

Bridge | 50 |

**Flathead Indian
Reservation**

N

Bridge | 43 |

Bridge | 42 | | 39.8 | Highway 28 Bridge

Lonepine Reservoir | 38.8 | Bridge

| 35 | Bridge

| 34 | Bridge

| 32 | Garceau Gulch Bridge

| 30.5 | Bridge

| 29 | Ronan Road Bridge El. 2725'

Hot Springs | 28 | Bridge

| 26 | Bridge

Interstate	🛡
U.S. Highway	⬡
State Road	◯
Other Route	⬭
Road	- - - - - - -
Trail	• • • • • • •
River Milepost	☐
Public Access	▲
Dam	〰〰
Rapid	⫽

One inch ≈ 6.4 miles

Bridge | 23 |

Bridge | 20 | Flathead River
(Sloan Bridge)
El. 2550'

Bridge | 15 | | 0 | To Ronan

Double Bridge | 12 |

Gage station | 11.1 |

Bridge | 9.5 |

Bridge | 6 |

Little Bitterroot

BLACKFOOT

ORIGIN:	At Anaconda Creek near Rogers Pass east of Lincoln. El. 5100'
END:	Flows into Clark Fork River at Bonner, MT El. 3250'
LENGTH:	132.5 river miles (72 air miles)
FLOATABLE:	114.1 miles Landers Fork "116.1" (El. 4875') to dam takeout "2" Class I portion is 66 miles. Cedar Meadows Access to End.
SECTIONS:	Upper (66.5 mi.) Origin "132.5" to Cedar Meadows Access "66" Middle (26 mi.) Cedar Meadows "66" to Sperry Grade Access "40" Lower (40 mi.) Sperry Grade "40" to End "0"
DAMS:	Bonner Dam (take out just above on LEFT)
WATERFALLS:	None
WHITEWATER:	Sperry Grade to Clearwater Bridge (5.3 miles) Moderate whitewater just above and below Roundup Bridge. Whitaker Bridge to Sheep Flats Access (3 miles)
DANGERS:	Bonner Dam.
DEWATERED:	Above Lincoln, MT · could be low in fall.
PORTAGES:	A few log jams mostly between Nevada Creek Bridge for 4 miles downstream.
SPEC. AGENCIES:	Blackfoot River Recreation Corridor (co-op between FWP and landowners) (see appendix) Scotty Brown Bridge to Johnsrud Park (32 miles)
REGS - PERMITS:	This 32 mile corridor has some special restrictions.
ACCESS-SHUTTLE:	Easy, using Hwy 200 and county roads. Numerous fish access sites.
SERVICES:	All. Lincoln, Ovando, Clearwater, and Milltown, MT.
CAMPING:	A few public campgrounds and numerous fish access sites.

| GAMEFISH: | Upper - Cutthroat, brook, bull and whitefish |
| | Middle & Lower - Also brown and rainbow. |

VESSEL:	Upper - Small raft, canoe, small boat
	Middle - Raft, canoe, small boat, small dory.
	Lower - Raft, whitewater canoe, kayak

| SKILL LEVEL: | Upper & Middle - Beginner |
| | Lower - Intermediate to experienced. |

FLOAT TIMES: Moderately fast.

FLOW INFO: (406) 449-5263 USGS - Helena

HYDROGRAPH

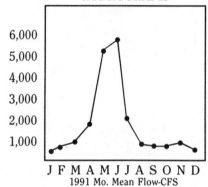

6,000
5,000
4,000
3,000
2,000
1,000

J F M A M J J A S O N D
1991 Mo. Mean Flow-CFS

Gage Sta: 6 miles upstream from Bonner.
Drain Area: 2,290 sq. mi. (at gage)
Ave. Flow: (55 yrs.) 1,606 cfs
Ext. Max: 19,200 cfs - 10.9' 6/10/64
Ext. Min: 156 cfs - 1.2' 2/02/89
Gradient: 1850' in 132.5 miles = 14.0' pma
Float Grad: 1625' in 116.1 miles = 14.0' pma
Clarity: Usually clear
Temp: Jan. 34^0 F.
       Apr. 60^0 F.
       Jul. 71^0 F.
       Oct. 45^0 F.

DRAINAGE: (West) Clark Fork, Pend Oreille, Columbia, Pacific

MAPS:	BLM - #22 "Avon" (upper) - #21 "Granite" (lower) -
	#20 "Seeley Lake" (small middle)
	USFS - L & C NF (Rocky Mountain) upper - Flathead
	NF (South) upper - Lolo NF lower
	USGS - "Butte" - "Choteau"
	FWP - "Blackfoot Guide Map"
	CO. - Lewis & Clark, Powell, Missoula

BLACKFOOT

The Blackfoot is one of my favorite rivers. It has everything! Beautiful scenery, family recreation, fishing, whitewater, and a riparian habitat that supports large populations of big game, eagles, waterfowl and other wildlife.

Indians called the river "Cokalahishkit" meaning river of the road to the buffalo. This valley was guarded by the Blackfoot Indians.

The upper river flows through a cottonwood forest with meandering channels, while the lower river picks up velocity through canyons with numerous whitewater stretches and the coniferous and aspen groves flitting by. Floating can begin as high as Landers Fork Bridge at Hwy. 200, above Lincoln. I once saw a mountain lion stalking a whitetail doe and her fawn as I floated down behind the airport. Hooper Access at Lincoln offers public access to exit or begin a float. Hwy. 200 parallels the river and Willow Creek and Nevada Road bridges are the only ingress or egress possibilities as we go downriver. Mineral Hills Access at the Hwy. 141 bridge, Aunt Molly Access and Cedar Meadows Access lie below. Beginners should have little problem handling the upper section if flows are normal in a small vessel. Numerous log jams occur below Nevada Bridge for four miles which can cause exhausting portages.

Fly and spin fishing can be productive for trout and whitefish. Snowmobiling, rockclimbing, gold panning, and downhill skiing at Great Divide resort and two Missoula resorts, add to the smorgasbord of recreational opportunities this valley has to offer.

Class I designation begins at Cedar Meadows Access "66" for the rest of the river. An old road bridge crosses six miles below and although somewhat difficult to find, a wonderful "River Junction" Campground is at the North Fork confluence. Below River Junction, a short moderate rapids can be handled by intermediates. These rapids are just above Scotty Brown Bridge.

Blackfoot River

43

Fisher

Scotty Brown Bridge (mile "45") begins the "Blackfoot River Recreation Corridor", a co-op between FWP and landowners. This 32 mile corridor to Johnsrud Park has some special courtesy requirements and these landowners are to be commended for their positive approach to recreation. Float-thru gates are provided if fences are necessary. From Scotty Brown Bridge past Russ Gates Campground to Sperry Grade Access the river remains easy to navigate, by beginners in nearly any moderately sized vessel.

Below Sperry Grade (mile "40") begins the whitewater section with numerous sporadic rapids. From mile "40" to the Clearwater River and bridge access (mile "34.7") is a wild ride for a kayak, whitewater canoe, or medium raft. Some good drops and boulders make this perhaps the most challenging run on the river during peak flow. Below Clearwater bridge only a short, moderate rapids occurs, located within sight above the Hwy. 200 bridge at Roundup Access. This rapid is popular with kayakers.

Below Roundup to Whitaker Bridge Access, only intermittent, moderate rapids occur. Intermediates should be able to handle this stretch, especially below Nine Mile. Below Whitaker is the Thibodeau Rapids Campground and rapids. Kayaks, whitewater canoes and rafts are common sights. Just below at Sheep Flats Campground (mile "17") the major whitewater ends. From this point for the rest of the river only occasional, mild rapids occur.

The only wildlife you will probably view in this extremely popular lower portion of the river might be unclad sunbathers lounging on beaches or boulders. A mandatory exit from the river is just above Bonner, MT where the river comes near the highway. A very dangerous dam lies 1/2 mile downstream. The river flows 1 1/2 miles below the dam into the Clark Fork drainage at Milltown Reservoir.

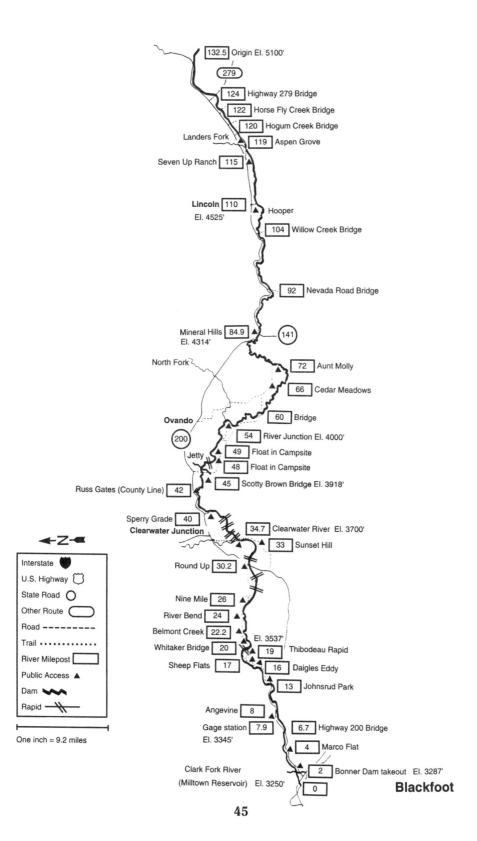

132.5 Origin El. 5100'

279

124 Highway 279 Bridge

122 Horse Fly Creek Bridge

120 Hogum Creek Bridge

Landers Fork
119 Aspen Grove

Seven Up Ranch 115

Lincoln 110
El. 4525'
Hooper

104 Willow Creek Bridge

92 Nevada Road Bridge

Mineral Hills 84.9
El. 4314'
141

North Fork
72 Aunt Molly

66 Cedar Meadows

Ovando
60 Bridge

200
54 River Junction El. 4000'

49 Float in Campsite

48 Float in Campsite

Jetty
45 Scotty Brown Bridge El. 3918'

Russ Gates (County Line) 42

Sperry Grade 40
Clearwater Junction

34.7 Clearwater River El. 3700'

33 Sunset Hill

Round Up 30.2

Nine Mile 26

River Bend 24

Belmont Creek 22.2
El. 3537'

Whitaker Bridge 20
19 Thibodeau Rapid

Sheep Flats 17
16 Daigles Eddy

13 Johnsrud Park

Angevine 8

Gage station 7.9
El. 3345'
6.7 Highway 200 Bridge

4 Marco Flat

2 Bonner Dam takeout El. 3287'

Clark Fork River
(Milltown Reservoir) El. 3250'
0

Blackfoot

←Z←

Interstate
U.S. Highway
State Road
Other Route
Road --------
Trail ....
River Milepost
Public Access ▲
Dam
Rapid

One inch = 9.2 miles

45

BLACKFOOT - NORTH FORK

ORIGIN: At Dabrota Creek near McDonnell Meadow in Scapegoat Wilderness El. 6,000'

END: Flows into Blackfoot River at River Junction Campground (southwest of Ovando) El. 4,000'

LENGTH: 34.6 river miles (20 air miles)

FLOATABLE: 19 miles Big Nelson Trailhead to end.
Class I portion is 6.1 miles (Hwy. 200 Bridge to end)

SECTIONS: Upper (15.6 mi.) Origin "34.6" to Big Nelson Trailhead "19" (unfloatable)
Middle (12.9 mi.) Big Nelson "19" to Hwy. 200 Bridge "6.1"
Lower (6.1 mi.) Hwy. 200 Bridge "6.1" to End "0"

DAMS: None

WATERFALLS: North Fork Falls (1 mile below Dry Fork confluence - unfloatable section)

WHITEWATER: Big Nelson Trailhead "19" to Milepost "10"
Mile 19 to Mile 17 Bridge access Class IV-V (depending on flow)
Mile 17 to Mile 10 Class II-III

DANGERS: Log jams (Mile "7")

DEWATERED: Possibly after August

PORTAGES: 2 log jams (Mile "7")

SPEC. AGENCIES: None

REGS - PERMITS: No motors in Scapegoat Wilderness portion.

ACCESS-SHUTTLE: Big Nelson (200' carry kayak or ww canoe) - Road bridge (mile "17") (carry 50') - Road bridge (mile "8") - Hwy. 200 bridge (mile "6.1") - Harry Morgan access (mile "2") River Junction Campground "0" (19 miles around by road)

SERVICES: Limited in Ovando, MT

CAMPING:	Big Nelson Campground and numerous places along Blackfoot River in addition to River Junction Campground.
GAMEFISH:	Cutthroat, rainbow, brook, bull trout and whitefish.
VESSEL:	Medium raft, whitewater canoe, kayak. (Difficult launch and take out sites)
SKILL LEVEL:	Middle - "19" to "8" Experienced - Highly skilled. Lower - "8" to "0" Beginner.
FLOAT TIMES:	Moderately fast entire river. Upper 2 miles very fast.
FLOW INFO:	Lincoln Ranger District (NFS) 362-4265

HYDROGRAPH

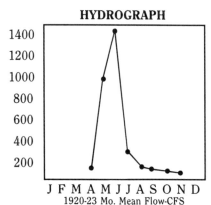

1920-23 Mo. Mean Flow-CFS

Gage Sta: Near Helmville (Disc. in 1923)
Drain Area: 228 sq. mi.
Ext Max: 2820 cfs 06/05/22
Ext Min: 27 cfs 11/16/22
Gradient: 2000' in 34.6 miles = 57.8' pma
Float Grad: 800' in 19.0 miles = 42.1' pma
Clarity: Cloudy to clear

DRAINAGE:	(West) Blackfoot, Clark Fork, Pend Oreille, Columbia, Pacific
MAPS:	BLM - #30 "Dearborn" (upper) - #20 "Seeley Lake" (middle) - #21 "Granite" (lower) USFS - Flathead NF (South) or Lewis & Clark NF (Rocky Mtn. Div.) USGS - "Choteau" - "Butte" CO. - Powell

BLACKFOOT - NORTH FORK

High in the Scapegoat Wilderness is the inception of the North Fork of the Blackfoot River. The unfloatable upper section, accessible only by foot or on horseback, flows over North Fork falls on its journey to the Big Nelson Trailhead and Campground. This is a very popular trailhead leading into much of the wild country protected from civilization.

The stream, although small carries a nice volume of water during the floatable months. A little known stream, it has some versatile floating portions. Beginning at Big Nelson Trailhead (mile "19"), kayakers and whitewater canoe enthusiasts can drag or carry their craft to the river via a poor, steep trail. A wild two mile run (Class IV) down to the county bridge, by highly skilled paddlers is fun.

Below this county bridge (mile "17") experienced persons in kayaks, whitewater canoes or medium rafts can have seven more miles of moderate whitewater in this nine mile run. The lower two miles flatten out. The county bridge at mile "8" is the next modest access point.

Below this county road bridge are two major log jams at mile "7" that must be portaged. The Hwy. 200 Bridge mile "6.1" marks the beginning of the Class I designation. Again, no formal access exists, but by dragging your small vessel through a barb wire fence on the highway right-of-way you can get to the water. This eight mile lower portion can be handled by beginners if flow is normal. Harry Morgan Access at a county road bridge south of Ovando offers a rest stop at mile "2". The river soon joins the Blackfoot at the beautiful but difficult-to-find River Junction Campground on the Blackfoot River.

Access to the upper section and the Big Nelson Trailhead can be found by going two miles east of the Hwy. 200 bridge and turn north on the North Fork Road and following it to road end.

Access to River Junction Campground is by going six miles west of Ovando on Hwy. 200, turn south and go across the Scotty Brown Bridge on the Blackfoot River; and continue 1 1/2 miles further south. Turn left and go back east nearly four miles to an old road that turns off north. By following this old road 2 1/2 miles it will lead you to River Junction Campground. All of this will be worth the trouble of studying a good map and getting lost. Perhaps someday, someone will put up some signs!

North Fork Blackfoot River

48

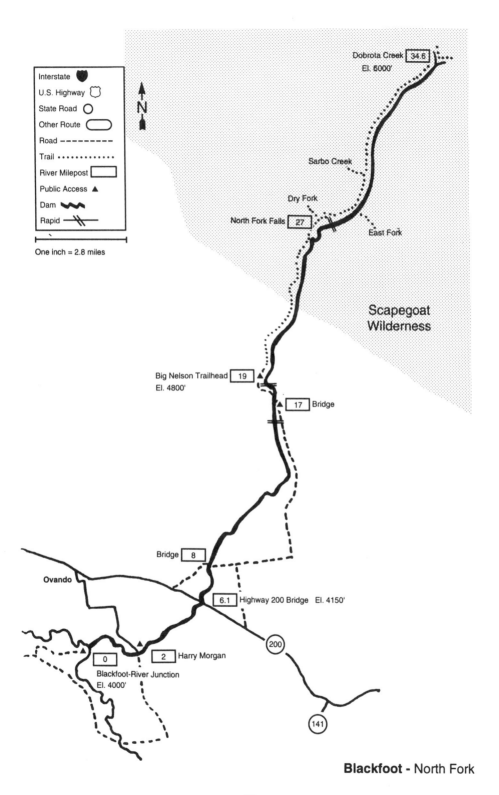

Interstate
U.S. Highway
State Road
Other Route
Road ---------
Trail ....
River Milepost
Public Access ▲
Dam
Rapid

One inch = 2.8 miles

N

Dobrota Creek 34.6
El. 6000'

Sarbo Creek

Dry Fork

North Fork Falls 27

East Fork

Scapegoat
Wilderness

Big Nelson Trailhead 19
El. 4800'

17 Bridge

Bridge 8

Ovando

6.1 Highway 200 Bridge El. 4150'

200

0

2 Harry Morgan

Blackfoot-River Junction
El. 4000'

141

Blackfoot - North Fork

49

LITTLE BLACKFOOT

ORIGIN:	Connors Gulch, near Cliff Mountain south of Elliston. El. 6700'
END:	Flows into Clark Fork River at Garrison, MT El. 4350'
LENGTH:	39.3 miles (20 air miles)
FLOATABLE:	17 miles (Avon "17" to End - Clark Fork "O"
SECTIONS:	Upper (12.3 miles) Origin "39.3" to Hwy. 12 Bridge (Elliston) "27" Middle (10.0 miles) Hwy. 12 Bridge "27" to Avon Road "17" Lower (17.0 miles) Avon Road "17" to End - Clark Fork River "O"
DAMS:	None
WATERFALLS:	None
WHITEWATER:	None
DANGERS:	Fences, low irrigation jettys
DEWATERED:	Often too low to float in fall
PORTAGES:	Jettys, fences
SPEC.AGENCIES:	None
REGS - PERMITS:	None
ACCESS-SHUTTLE:	Easy. Hwy. 12 parallels and crosses river.
SERVICES:	Limited in Avon and Garrison, MT
CAMPING:	Kading Campground in upper section. No formal campgrounds in middle or lower sections, or formal access sites.
GAMEFISH:	Upper - Cutthroat, brook Lower - Brown, whitefish
VESSEL:	Canoe, small raft, small boat
SKILL LEVEL:	Intermediate

Small raft - big fun

FLOAT TIMES:	Moderate flow
FLOW INFO:	(406) 449-5263 USGS - Helena

HYDROGRAPH

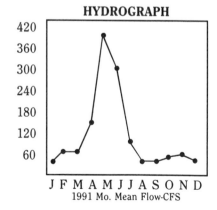

1991 Mo. Mean Flow-CFS

Gage Sta: Mile "5"
Drain Area: 398 sq. mi.
Ave. Flow: (19 yrs.) 162 cfs
Ext. Max: 8,650 cfs - 8.79' ga. ht. 5/21/81
Ext. Min: 6 cfs - 2.94' ga. ht. 8/24/77
Gradient: 2350' in 39.3 mi. = 59.8' pma
Float Grad: 450' in 17.0 mi. = 26.5' pma
Clarity: Cloudy to clear
Temp: Jan. 32° F.
Apr. 40° F.
Jul. 63° F.
Oct. 50° F.

DRAINAGE:	(West) Clark Fork, Pend Oreille, Columbia, Pacific
MAPS:	BLM - #22 "Avon"
	USFS - Helena NF
	USGS - "Butte"
	CO. - Powell

LITTLE BLACKFOOT

The origin of the river is at Connors Gulch, near Cliff Mountain south of Elliston, Montana. The small mountain stream tumbles down through a gravel and boulder streambed, lined with willow and coniferous trees. Much downfall exists. Nearing Elliston and Hwy. 12, the river becomes marshy, caused by less gradient and beaver dams. Kading Campground, Ranger Station and Trailhead are at the headwaters. A forest service road off Hwy. 12, leads upstream to these facilities.

Below Hwy. 12 the river remains unfloatable, due to its narrow stature, fences and irrigation projects. Three bridges offer access as the river meanders through private property.

Fishing can be quite good in the upper section for cutthroat and brookies. The lower section is inhabited by browns and whitefish.

Floating can begin just above Avon. An old road goes through Avon and up along the north side of the river. Putting a small vessel in is no problem. Two Hwy. 12 bridges, at river mileposts "16" and "14.5", occur before the Hwy. 12 Rest Stop at "10".

Below the rest stop, three more bridges offer access at mile posts "8", "7" and "5". The last opportunity to exit on the Little Blackfoot is at the old highway bridge ".5", on the east edge of Garrison, Montana. Floating beyond this point, would require a .7 mile jaunt down the Clark Fork River, to the Garrison bridge located on the west edge of Garrison.

Intermediates in a small raft, canoe or small boat, can handle the entire lower section if flow is normal. This lower section offers beautiful scenery, especially in autumn, if stream volume permits floating.

Little Blackfoot River

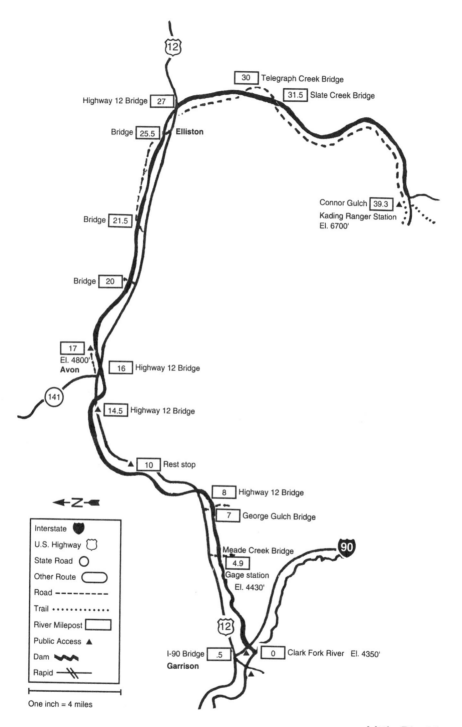

12

30 Telegraph Creek Bridge

31.5 Slate Creek Bridge

Highway 12 Bridge 27

Bridge 25.5 **Elliston**

Connor Gulch 39.3 ▲
Kading Ranger Station
El. 6700'

Bridge 21.5

Bridge 20

17
El. 4800'
Avon

16 Highway 12 Bridge

141

14.5 Highway 12 Bridge

10 Rest stop

←-N-←

8 Highway 12 Bridge

7 George Gulch Bridge

Meade Creek Bridge
4.9
Gage station
El. 4430'

Interstate 🛡
U.S. Highway ⬡
State Road ◯
Other Route ⬭
Road - - - - - -
Trail • • • • • • •
River Milepost ▭
Public Access ▲
Dam 〰
Rapid ⫽

90

12

I-90 Bridge .5
Garrison

0 Clark Fork River   El. 4350'

One inch = 4 miles

Little Blackfoot

53

BOULDER (Jefferson)

ORIGIN: West Fork near Cottonwood Mountain west of Boulder, MT El. 6500'

END: Flows into Jefferson River near Cardwell. El. 4205'

LENGTH: 77.8 miles (38 air miles)

FLOATABLE: 57.5 miles (Basin, MT El. 5560' to End)

SECTIONS: Upper (20.3 mi.) Origin "77.8" to Kleinsmith Gulch Bridge "57.5"
Middle (34.5 mi.) Kleinsmith Bridge "57.5" to county bridge "23"
Lower (23.0 mi.) County bridge "23" to End-Jefferson River "O"

DAMS: Diversion dam (Mile "10") can bypass in other channel
Diversion dam (Mile "5.5") portage

WATERFALLS: None

WHITEWATER: 10.4 miles - Kleinsmith Gulch Bridge (Basin) to Hwy 281 (#69) Bridge 53.8' pma gradient, in whitewater portion. Class IV when flows are up. Bridge dangers.

DANGERS: Low diversion jettys, fences, 2 div. dams, bridges

DEWATERED: Often in fall

PORTAGES: Diversion dam (Mile "5.5")

SPEC. AGENCIES: None

REGS - PERMITS: 10 hp max. on all streams in Jefferson County.

ACCESS-SHUTTLE: Highways parallel river with intersecting road bridges. No formal access sites. Private property.

SERVICES: All in Boulder, MT

CAMPING: No formal campgrounds in floatable portion. Numerous campgrounds in upper section.

GAMEFISH:	Upper (best) - Brook, rainbow, whitefish
	Middle - Rainbow, brook, whitefish
	Lower - Brown trout
VESSEL:	Canoe, medium raft, small boat
	Kayak in whitewater portion.
SKILL LEVEL:	Beginner (if flows are normal)
	Highly skilled (whitewater portion)
FLOAT TIMES:	Moderate flow. Fast in whitewater portion.
FLOW INFO:	(406) 449-5263 USGS - Helena

HYDROGRAPH

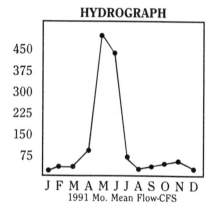

1991 Mo. Mean Flow-CFS

Gage Sta: 2 mi. southeast of Boulder, MT
Drain Area: 381 sq. mi. (at gage)
Ave. Flow: (48 yrs.) 115 cfs
Ext. Max: 3,490 cfs - 10.9' ga. ht. 6/9/64
Ext. Min: No flow at times in 1931
Gradient: 2295' in 77.8 miles = 29.5' pma
Float Grad: 1355' in 57.5 miles = 23.6' pma
Clarity: Clear to murky
Temp: Jan. 34° F.
   Apr. 41° F.
   Jul. 73° F.
   Oct. 43° F.

DRAINAGE:	(East) Jefferson, Missouri, Mississippi, Gulf of Mexico
MAPS:	BLM - #22 "Avon" (upper) - #23 "Townsend" (middle) - #33 "Madison" (lower)
	USFS - Deer Lodge NF (entire river) - Helena NF (upper only)
	USGS - "Butte" (upper) - "White Sulphur" (middle) - "Bozeman" (lower)
	CO. - Jefferson

BOULDER (Jefferson)

The mainstem of the Boulder begins at the West Fork, near Cottonwood Mountain, west of Boulder, MT. Nearly 78 miles later it flows into the Jefferson River near Cardwell.

Below the inception of the river, a bench and numerous beaver dams cause the stream laziness. There are numerous campgrounds in this area, and fishing is best in this upper section. Brookies, rainbow and whitefish are common.

Kleinsmith Gulch Road bridge "57.5", near Basin, marks the beginning of a kayakers run. This seldom used whitewater extends down to the Hwy. 69 bridge at Boulder. This 10.4 mile stretch can be dangerous as bridge pillars and boulders are obstacles in the stream bed that has a steep gradient of 63.5 fpm.

Below Boulder "47.1" the river establishes a normal floating gradient and the boulders disappear. However downfall, numerous channels and irrigation withdrawals make floating difficult in this middle section. The middle and lower sections flow through private land. Campgrounds or access sites are non-existent, so bridge access must suffice. Hwy. 69 parallels the river and intersecting roads with bridges occur at adequate intervals.

The best floating begins at the road bridge "23" near Dunn Creek. Springs upstream add more volume and the river does not channelize as much. Bridges exist at mileposts "14", "11" and "6". Diversion dams occur at mileposts "10" and "5.5". Another road bridge is at milepost "2", and the Hwy. 10 (I-90) bridge ".5" offers the last exit off the river before the Jefferson. Floating beyond this point would require a 1/2 mile float on the lower Boulder, a 1 1/2 mile jaunt through the Jefferson Slough, and 1/2 mile down the mainstream of the Jefferson River to La Hood Access. Brown trout, in addition to the species in the upper section, inhabit the lower river, but in fewer numbers. The warmer water and often dewatered stream take its toll.

A beginner can handle the river except the whitewater section, if flow is normal. A canoe is the best vessel, although a small raft or small boat would work. The whitewater section should only be approached by the highly skilled in a kayak, after careful scouting.

Boulder River

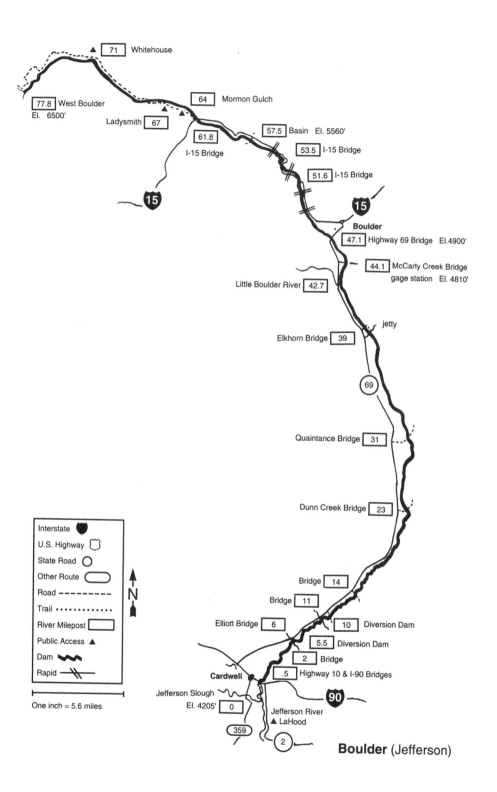

- ▲ 71 Whitehouse
- 77.8 West Boulder El. 6500'
- 64 Mormon Gulch
- Ladysmith 67
- 61.8 I-15 Bridge
- 57.5 Basin El. 5560'
- 53.5 I-15 Bridge
- 51.6 I-15 Bridge
- Boulder
- 47.1 Highway 69 Bridge El. 4900'
- 44.1 McCarty Creek Bridge gage station El. 4810'
- Little Boulder River 42.7
- jetty
- Elkhorn Bridge 39
- Quaintance Bridge 31
- Dunn Creek Bridge 23
- Bridge 14
- Bridge 11
- Elliott Bridge 6
- 10 Diversion Dam
- 5.5 Diversion Dam
- 2 Bridge
- .5 Highway 10 & I-90 Bridges
- Cardwell
- Jefferson Slough
- El. 4205' 0
- Jefferson River
- ▲ LaHood

Legend:
- Interstate
- U.S. Highway
- State Road
- Other Route
- Road - - - - - -
- Trail • • • • • • •
- River Milepost ☐
- Public Access ▲
- Dam
- Rapid

N

One inch = 5.6 miles

Boulder (Jefferson)

BOULDER (Yellowstone)

ORIGIN:	Confluence of South Fork & Basin Creek southwest of Big Timber, MT El. 8800'
END:	Flows into Yellowstone River at Big Timber, MT El. 4000'
LENGTH:	61.8 miles (45 air miles)
FLOATABLE:	34.7 miles - Milepost "51" to Falls Creek "39" (Whitewater - Kayaks only) Milepost "22.7" to End "O"
SECTIONS:	Upper (28.9 mi.) Origin "61.8" to Natural Bridge & Falls "32.9" Middle (10.2 mi.) Natural Bridge "32.9" to East Boulder Bridge "22.7" Lower (22.7 mi.) East Boulder Bridge "22.7" to End Yellowstone River "O"
DAMS:	None
WATERFALLS:	Natural Bridge Falls 105' Milepost "32.9"
WHITEWATER:	12 mi. Put in - Mi. "51" to Falls Creek Takeout "39" Upper 3 miles Class IV to V Next 9 miles Class III
DANGERS:	Natural Bridge Falls. Whitewater above. 22.7 mile lower section can be bouncy also. Occasional diversion jettys, fences, logjams.
DEWATERED:	Can be low in fall.
PORTAGES:	None in the 2 floatable sections.
SPEC. AGENCIES:	None
REGS - PERMITS:	10 hp. max. on all streams in Park Co. (upper portion)
ACCESS-SHUTTLE:	Not difficult. Road parallels river and numerous access points.
SERVICES:	All in Big Timber, MT
CAMPING:	Numerous campgrounds

GAMEFISH:	Above falls - Rainbow, brook trout Below falls - Brown, rainbow
VESSEL:	Upper floatable whitewater section - Kayaks Lower floatable section - Raft, whitewater canoe
SKILL LEVEL:	Upper Whitewater - Highly skilled Lower - Intermediate to Experienced.
FLOAT TIMES:	Moderately fast when flows are normal
FLOW INFO:	(406) 449-5263 USGS - Helena

HYDROGRAPH

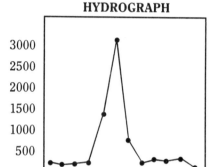

3000
2500
2000
1500
1000
500

J F M A M J J A S O N D
1991 Mo. Mean Flow-CFS

Gage Sta: Big Timber, MT
Drain Area: 523 sq. mi.
Ave. Flow (42 yrs.) 582 cfs
Ext. Max: 9,840 cfs - 7.84' ga. ht. 5/28/56
Ext. Min: 10 cfs 8/27/61
Gradient: 4800' in 61.8 mi. = 77.7' pma
Float Grad: 900' in 22.7 mi. = 40.0' pma
Clarity: Clear to cloudy
Temp: Jan. 32^0 F.
        Apr. 52^0 F.
        Jul. 61^0 F.
        Oct. 54^0 F.

DRAINAGE:	(East) Yellowstone, Missouri, Mississippi, Gulf of Mexico
MAPS:	BLM - #34 "Park" (upper) - #35 "Beartooth" (lower) USFS - Gallatin NF - Custer NF (Beartooth division) (lower portion only) USGS - "Bozeman" (upper) - "Billings" (lower) CO. - Park, Sweetgrass

BOULDER (Yellowstone)

If ever a river was befitting of its name, this would be it. Big boulders! Little boulders! All kinds of boulders! The mainstem begins at the South Fork and Basin Creek confluence, southwest of Big Timber, MT. The headwaters are in the high country of the Absaroka-Beartooth Wilderness.

A road paralleling the river, leads to a trailhead accessing the backcountry. Floating is not extremely popular, possibly due to the short float season; or the geographics of it all. We are blessed with so many wonderful rivers. Above Hells Canyon Campground is a trail leading to the river. Kayakers beginning at this point enjoy up to a twelve mile run down to Falls Creek Campground. The upper three miles through the canyon, down to Church Camp is Class IV-V, depending on flow. From Church Camp to Chippy Park Campground is a four mile Class III stretch. Chippy Park to Falls Creek is five miles of occasional Class III. Falls Creek Campground offers the last public exit before the 105' waterfall at the Natural Bridge State Monument. Below the falls is a ten mile stretch with no public access.

Floating can begin at the East Boulder (East Fork) Road bridge "22.7". Most floaters begin however, at the Boulder Forks Campground and West Boulder (West Fork) confluence "19.4". Kayakers also enjoy a section of the West Boulder.

Even under normal water conditions, the boulders in the river create a bouncy ride. An occasional irrigation jetty and fence will appear. This lower section requires at least intermediate skills in a raft or whitewater canoe.

Fuller Draw bridge "16", Eight Mile Bridge "11" and Big Rock Campground "5" all afford ingress or egress. The Hwy. 10 bridge in Big Timber "1.5" is the last public exit on the Boulder before reaching the Yellowstone River.

Above the falls rainbow and brookies are popular. Below the falls, browns & rainbow are the most common. Fly-fishing is more popular than spinning as "boulder bites" are frequent. In early spring, caddis, mayfly and stonefly imitations work well. Mid-June is the beginning of the salmon fly hatch. In August the trouts fancy turns to grasshoppers. Wade fishing can be difficult on the slippery rocks.

Boulder River

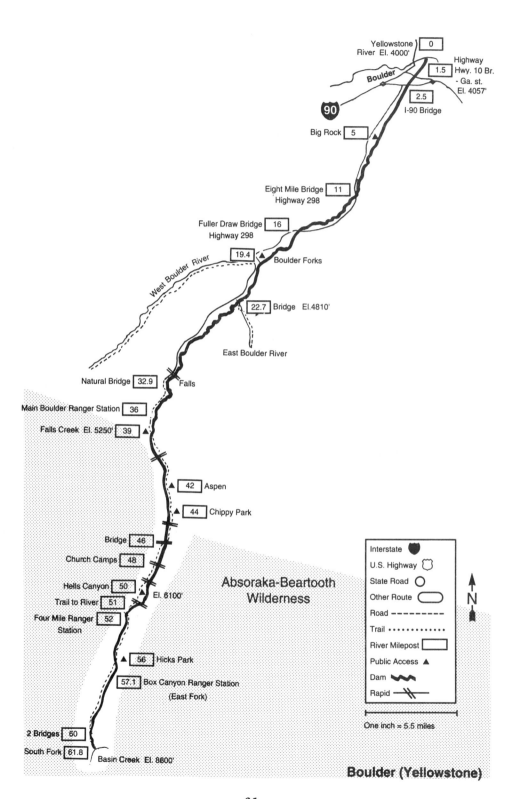

Yellowstone
River El. 4000' [0]

Boulder

Highway
Hwy. 10 Br.
- Ga. st.
El. 4057' [1.5]

[2.5]
I-90 Bridge

90

Big Rock [5]

Eight Mile Bridge [11]
Highway 298

Fuller Draw Bridge [16]
Highway 298

[19.4]
Boulder Forks

West Boulder River

[22.7] Bridge   El.4810'

East Boulder River

Natural Bridge [32.9]
Falls

Main Boulder Ranger Station [36]

Falls Creek El. 5250' [39]

[42] Aspen

[44] Chippy Park

Bridge [46]

Church Camps [48]

Hells Canyon [50]
El. 6100'
Trail to River [51]

Four Mile Ranger [52]
Station

[56] Hicks Park

[57.1] Box Canyon Ranger Station
(East Fork)

2 Bridges [60]

South Fork [61.8]
Basin Creek El. 8600'

Absoraka-Beartooth
Wilderness

Interstate	(symbol)
U.S. Highway	(symbol)
State Road	◯
Other Route	(symbol)
Road	-------
Trail	·········
River Milepost	☐
Public Access	▲
Dam	(symbol)
Rapid	(symbol)

N

One inch = 5.5 miles

Boulder (Yellowstone)

BULL

ORIGIN: Confluence of North & Middle Forks southeast of Bull Lake (not related) El. 2400'

END: Flows into Clark Fork River at Cabinet Gorge Reservoir El. 2175'

LENGTH: 26.3 miles (17 air miles)

FLOATABLE: 22 miles (lower 22 miles)

SECTIONS: Upper (4.3 mi.) Origin "26.3" to Private Rd. "22"
Middle (10.4 mi.) Road "22" to Hwy. # 56 Br. "11.6"
Lower (11.6 mi.) Hwy. 56 Br. "11.6" to End - "O"

DAMS: None

WATERFALLS: None

WHITEWATER: 3 miles (Mile "3" to "O") Class III when water up

DANGERS: Irrigation jettys, fences, whitewater

DEWATERED: Usually not

PORTAGES: Logs, jettys, fences

SPEC. AGENCIES: None

REGS - PERMITS: None

ACCESS-SHUTTLE: Quite easy. Hwy. 56 parallels river. No formal access sites but adequate places.

SERVICES: Limited by Bull Lake (not related to Bull River)

CAMPING: Campground at end on Cabinet Gorge Reservoir

GAMEFISH: Rainbow, cutthroat, brown, brook, bulls, whitefish

VESSEL: Canoe, small boat, medium raft.
3 mile whitewater portion - Whitewater canoe, medium raft, kayak

SKILL LEVEL:	Middle - Beginner
	Lower - Intermediate
	Whitewater - Experienced

FLOAT TIMES: Middle - Extremely slow.
Lower - Moderate to fast. (Flows improve at East Fork confluence)

FLOW INFO: (406) 847-2462 Kootenai NF (Cabinet District at Trout Creek)

HYDROGRAPH

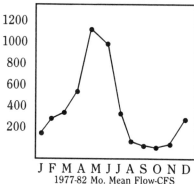

J F M A M J J A S O N D
1977-82 Mo. Mean Flow-CFS

Gage Sta: near Noxon, MT (disc. 1982)
Drain Area: 139 sq. mi.
Ave. Flow: (10 yrs.) 379 cfs
Ext. Max: 3540 cfs 6/17/74
Ext. Min: 43 cfs 1/01/79
Gradient: 225' in 26.3 miles = 8.6' pma
Float Grad: Same
Clarity: Quite clear
Temp: Jan. 38° F.
       Apr. 43° F.
       Jul. 64° F.
       Oct. 45° F.

DRAINAGE: (West) Clark Fork, Pend Oreille, Columbia, Pacific

MAPS: BLM - #5 "Libby"
USFS - Kootenai NF
USGS - "Kalispell"
CO.   - Sanders

BULL

Bull moose horns were found at the mouth of the river in the 1820's and it is ventured to say, this is the namesake of the area. The mainstem of the river is at the confluence of the North and Middle Forks, southeast of Bull Lake. Bull Lake is not related to the Bull River system. Bull Lake forms Lake Creek, which flows to the north. The Bull River flows south and dumps into the Clark Fork at Cabinet Gorge Reservoir.

The short upper section is unfloatable due to downfall and stream channelization. Floating can begin at river milepost "22", at a private road bridge, just off Hwy. 56.

Highway 56 bridge "18.2" crosses the river, and again crosses the river at milepost "11.6". Two miles below this bridge is the East Fork confluence "9.7".

Above the East Fork the river meanders slowly and is quite deep. The river flows through lush hayfields in its sandy streambed. Below the East Fork the river picks up velocity and the coniferous vegetation creates a more mountain stream appearance. A bridge near Basin Creek "5.5" offers ingress or egress. Below this bridge the road comes close to the river above Smoky Creek, at river mile "3".

If flow is high, these last three miles become whitewater. A steeper gradient occurs and the streambed is a boulder garden, through the canyon. A fine campground can be found at the river's mouth to the Cabinet Gorge Reservoir.

The middle section can be handled by a beginner in any moderately sized vessel. A canoe is the best, as the river is very slow. Below the East Fork and down to milepost "3" requires intermediate skills in a canoe or medium raft. The lower three miles of whitewater requires an experienced paddler in a medium raft, whitewater canoe or kayak.

Fishing can be quite good with the presence of rainbow, cutts, browns, brookies, bulls and the omnipresent whitefish. Fly-fishing can be great and in the middle section spinning can be equally productive.

The locals use and enjoy the Bull River. Canoeing is popular. A canoe race on the Cabinet Gorge Reservoir is becoming an annual event.

Bull River

64

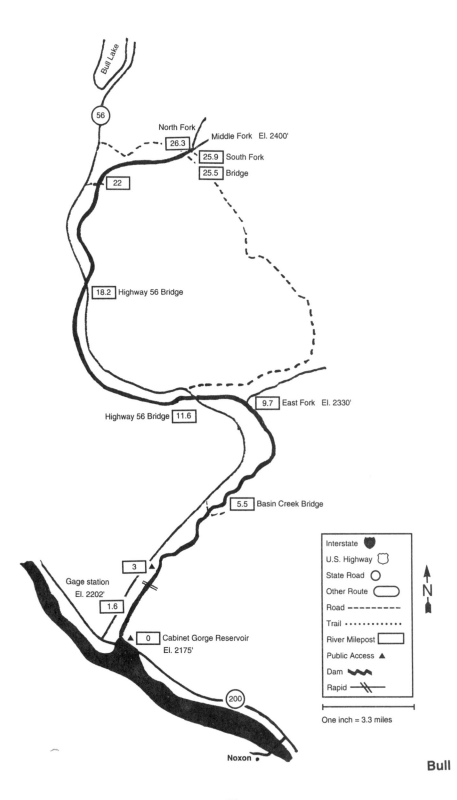

Bull Lake

56

North Fork
Middle Fork   El. 2400'
26.3
25.9   South Fork
25.5   Bridge

22

18.2   Highway 56 Bridge

9.7   East Fork   El. 2330'

Highway 56 Bridge   11.6

5.5   Basin Creek Bridge

3

Gage station
El. 2202'

1.6

0   Cabinet Gorge Reservoir
El. 2175'

200

Noxon

Interstate
U.S. Highway
State Road
Other Route
Road ----------
Trail ············
River Milepost
Public Access ▲
Dam
Rapid

N

One inch = 3.3 miles

Bull

CLARK FORK

ORIGIN:	Confluence of Warm Springs and Silverbow Creek at Warm Springs, MT El. 4800'
END:	Idaho border. (.6 miles above Cabinet Gorge Dam) El. 2175'
LENGTH:	333.1 total miles (282.6 river miles + 4 reservoirs. 50.5 miles) (200 air miles)
FLOATABLE:	282.6 river miles. Class I is entire 333.1 miles Milltown 3.0 miles Thompson Falls 6.6 Noxon 21.6 Cabinet Gorge <u>19.3</u> All floatable 50.5 miles
SECTIONS:	Upper (119.1 mi.) Origin "333.1" to Mill. Dam "214" Middle (128.3 mi.) Milltown Dam "214" to Plains Bridge "85.7" Lower (85.7 mi.) Plains Bridge "85.7" to End "0"
DAMS:	Diversion Dam (Between Bearmouth & Beavertail Mile "240") portage RIGHT Milltown (Mile "214") portage RIGHT Council Grove Diversion Dam (Mile "200.5") portage or use LEFT channel above Thompson Falls (Mile "57.6") MAJOR portage RIGHT Noxon (Mile "19.3") MAJOR portage RIGHT
WATERFALLS:	None
WHITEWATER:	20 miles (Cyr Canyon & Alberton Gorge) Mile "165" to "145" Class IV Also: Cascade Rapids Mi. "102" 300 yards Class III Plains Rapids Mi. "80" 100 yards Class III
DANGERS:	Dams, 2 diversion jettys in Missoula (Mile "208.3" & "207.2"), whitewater sections, sudden dam releases, wind on reservoirs.
DEWATERED:	Possibly above Rock Creek if flow is low.
PORTAGES:	5 dams (listed above)
SPEC. AGENCIES:	None

REGS - PERMITS:	None
ACCESS-SHUTTLE:	A few access sites and bridges.
SERVICES:	All services in many communities. Commercial white-water raft trips through Alberton Gorge. (10.4 miles)
CAMPING:	A few public campgrounds and access sites. Less frequent above Beavertail.
GAMEFISH:	Upper - Poor - recovering brown trout. Below Rock Creek rainbow & cutthroat Middle - Rainbow, brown, whitefish. Below Alberton cutthroat Lower - Rainbow, brown, dollys, largemouth bass, and a few cutts & brookies
VESSEL:	Upper - Canoe, medium raft, small boat Middle - All vessels (Except whitewater - Large raft, kayak) Lower - All vessels (Caution-short whitewater portion & reservoirs
SKILL LEVEL:	Upper - Beginner - if flows are normal Middle - Beginner - (Whitewater portions - Experienced to Highly skilled) Lower - Beginner - (Caution dangers listed above)
FLOAT TIMES:	Upper - Slow to Garrison. Mod. to Turah Br. Middle - Moderate (Whitewater sections fast) Lower - Moderate to Slow. (also many reservoirs)
FLOW INFO:	(406) 449-5263 USGS - Helena

HYDROGRAPH

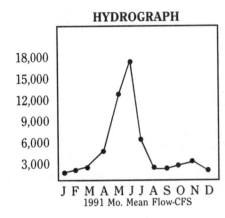

18,000
15,000
12,000
9,000
6,000
3,000

J F M A M J J A S O N D
1991 Mo. Mean Flow-CFS

Gage Sta: 1 mile below Bitterroot River
Drain Area: 9,003 sq. mi. (at this gage)
Ave. Flow: (62 yrs.) 5,407 cfs
Ext. Max: 52,800 cfs - 12.08' rod 5/23/48
Ext. Min: 388 cfs -   .05' rod 1/18/33
Gradient: 1625' in 333.1 miles = 4.8' pma
Float Grad: Same
Clarity: Cloudy to clear
Temp: Jan. 36⁰ F.
      Apr. 50⁰ F.
      Jul. 60⁰ F.
      Oct. 45⁰ F.
Total Drain Area: 22,050 sq. mi. (in MT)

DRAINAGE: (West) Pend Oreille, Columbia, Pacific Ocean

MAPS: BLM - #22 "Avon" - #21 "Granite" - #13 "Miss. W."
- #12 "Plains" - #7 "Wallace" - #11 "Polson" - #6
"Thompson Falls" - #5 "Libby"
USFS - Deer Lodge NF (upper) - Lolo NF (lower) -
Kootenai NF (ext. lower)
USGS - "Butte" - "Hamilton" - "Wallace" - "Kalispell"
CO.   - Deer Lodge, Powell, Granite, Missoula, Min-
eral, Sanders

A tragedy

68

CLARK FORK

The Clark Fork origin is at the confluence of Silverbow and Warm Springs Creeks, and while most rivers headwater in a pristine setting the Clark Fork begins in a mining area. Until recently, fish were non-existent and the river rampant with pollution, from upstream mine effluent. Correctives have been implemented and the upper river is gradually improving its fishery values.

The river above Deer Lodge was called Arrowstone by the Indians as they found a stone in the area from which they made fine arrowheads. A hot springs and Lost Creek State Park near Anaconda and Grant Kohrs National Historic Site in Deer Lodge are worth visits while in the area.

Floating may begin at a county road bridge at the origin, mile "333.1". A canoe is the best vessel to use in this slow moving, curvy and brushy portion. A few bridges offer the only access points to Deer Lodge, MT. 8.7 miles below Deer Lodge and accessible by frontage road, is the only formal access site, located at O'Neil Creek.

Below this access, the river picks up volume and velocity with the addition of the Little Blackfoot River. The river is often dewatered above after mid-summer. Fishing improves in this area, however algae growth often limits it to dry fly attempts come fall. Much of this upper portion flows through private land, so please use the courtesy of the high-water mark.

Below Drummond the river becomes more popular. A diversion dam, which must be portaged exists at Ryan Creek (mile "240") just above Beavertail Hill Access. Below Rock Creek floating pressure increases to Turah Bridge Access, the last access site before Milltown Dam and reservoir.

Milltown Dam "214" has an access site just below, and Sha-Ron Access is three miles below. This Hellgate Canyon was named by the French trappers "Porte de Enfer" for the skulls and bones they found here. In Missoula two jettys occur, one by the University of Montana and the other one mile downstream at Broadway Bridge. As you leave Missoula, the right channel takes you to a diversion dam which must be portaged and Council Hill Access. The left channel allows you to bypass the dam and go to Spurgin Road Access.

The next 31 miles to Alberton have no formal access sites, so bridges need to be used. At St. Johns Access ("165") beginners need to hang up their paddles, as big whitewater lies ahead to Tarkio Access or even Forest Grove. Most whitewater buffs begin this Alberton Gorge float at Cyr Access ("161.4") and exit at Tarkio Access ("151"). Tarkio is a difficult private access across boulder, sand and a steep rutted road.

The early season "Rest Stop" rapid is just below St. Johns Access. This rapid is Class IV at high water and Class II-III at other times of the year. Below Cyr Access are only moderate rapids until the Class III "Cliffside" (Shelf) rapid. Big waves are prevalent in this narrow stretch. Also, some moderate rapids are located just above the triple bridge area.

Below the triple bridges the canyon narrows and contains the biggest whitewater. "Tumbleweed" is a Class IV rapid during high water and mellows to Class III later. A large rock on the right has a large hole below, during normal flow. Scouting this rapid from the left bank is advisable. Below "Tumbleweed" lie the "Boateater" and "Fang" rapids. These last two major rapids are not technically difficult but have high waves. They are rated Class III. Kayakers often exit the river just below "Fang" at the beautiful Fish Creek confluence, however it is a steep climb.

The annual average is 5,000 cfs, however good whitewater can be found anywhere between 2,000 and 10,000 cfs. Up to 20,000 cfs can be difficult and above 20,000 cfs the river can be very dangerous. Peak flows are common to 40,000 cfs and the record is nearly 53,000 cfs.

Plans are on the drawing board for disabled access at each end of this whitewater section. Tarkio to Forest Grove contains only mild whitewater, and can be handled by intermediates. Just below Forest Grove I awoke in my sleeping bag on the beach, surrounded by wild turkeys in their early morning get-a-drink ritual.

The beautiful canyon float from St. Regis to Plains can be handled by beginners, if they would portage the Class III Cascade Rapids at milepost "102". Look for Bighorn Sheep in this area as well as the Thompson Falls area. Below Plains Bridge Access "85.7" lies the Plains Rapids at mile "80". This Class III rapid can be portaged LEFT if desired, and is followed by another Class II just below. Most floaters do not continue past the Thompson River Access "64.2", located under the bridge, as three dams form three nearly continuous reservoirs all the way to the Idaho border. All three of these reservoirs are boatable and offer good fishing.

Clark Fork River

70

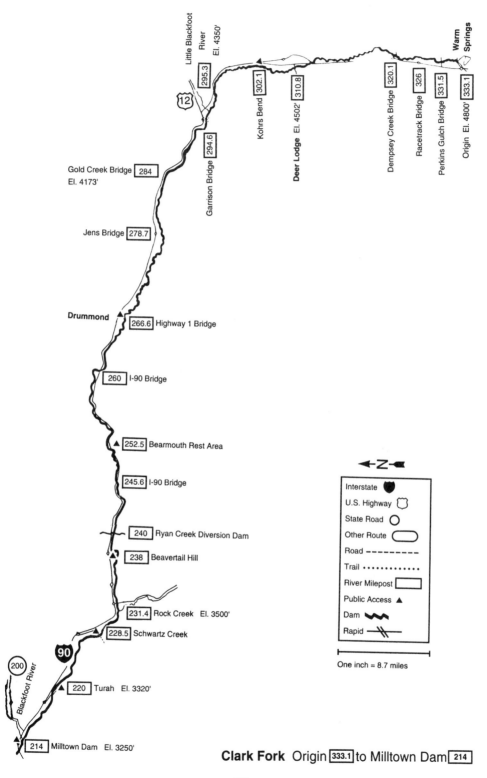

Little Blackfoot
River El. 4350'

[295.3]

(12)

[294.6] Garrison Bridge

Warm
Springs

[302.1] Kohrs Bend

Deer Lodge El. 4502' [310.8]

[320.1] Dempsey Creek Bridge

[326] Racetrack Bridge

[331.5] Perkins Gulch Bridge

[333.1] Origin El. 4800'

Gold Creek Bridge [284]
El. 4173'

Jens Bridge [278.7]

Drummond [266.6] Highway 1 Bridge

[260] I-90 Bridge

[252.5] Bearmouth Rest Area

[245.6] I-90 Bridge

[240] Ryan Creek Diversion Dam

[238] Beavertail Hill

[231.4] Rock Creek El. 3500'

[228.5] Schwartz Creek

<table>
<tr><td>Interstate</td><td></td></tr>
<tr><td>U.S. Highway</td><td></td></tr>
<tr><td>State Road</td><td>○</td></tr>
<tr><td>Other Route</td><td></td></tr>
<tr><td>Road</td><td>- - - - - - - -</td></tr>
<tr><td>Trail</td><td>•••••••••••</td></tr>
<tr><td>River Milepost</td><td>☐</td></tr>
<tr><td>Public Access</td><td>▲</td></tr>
<tr><td>Dam</td><td>〰</td></tr>
<tr><td>Rapid</td><td>≠</td></tr>
</table>

One inch = 8.7 miles

90

(200)

Blackfoot River

[220] Turah El. 3320'

[214] Milltown Dam El. 3250'

Clark Fork Origin [333.1] to Milltown Dam [214]

71

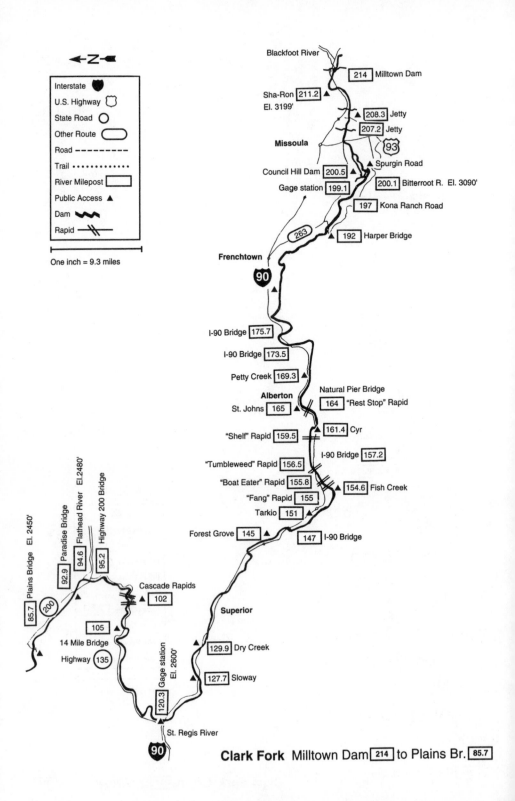

Map Legend

Interstate
U.S. Highway
State Road
Other Route
Road – – – – –
Trail ••••••••
River Milepost
Public Access ▲
Dam
Rapid

One inch = 9.3 miles

Blackfoot River
214 Milltown Dam
Sha-Ron 211.2
El. 3199'
208.3 Jetty
207.2 Jetty
Missoula
93
Spurgin Road
Council Hill Dam 200.5
200.1 Bitterroot R. El. 3090'
Gage station 199.1
197 Kona Ranch Road
263
192 Harper Bridge
Frenchtown
90
I-90 Bridge 175.7
I-90 Bridge 173.5
Petty Creek 169.3
Natural Pier Bridge
Alberton
164 "Rest Stop" Rapid
St. Johns 165
161.4 Cyr
"Shelf" Rapid 159.5
I-90 Bridge 157.2
"Tumbleweed" Rapid 156.5
"Boat Eater" Rapid 155.8
154.6 Fish Creek
"Fang" Rapid 155
Tarkio 151
Forest Grove 145
147 I-90 Bridge
Superior
Plains Bridge El. 2450'
85.7
200
Paradise Bridge
92.9
Flathead River El.2480'
94.6
Highway 200 Bridge
95.2
Cascade Rapids
102
105
14 Mile Bridge
Highway 135
129.9 Dry Creek
Gage station
El. 2600'
127.7 Sloway
120.3
St. Regis River
90

Clark Fork Milltown Dam 214 to Plains Br. 85.7

72

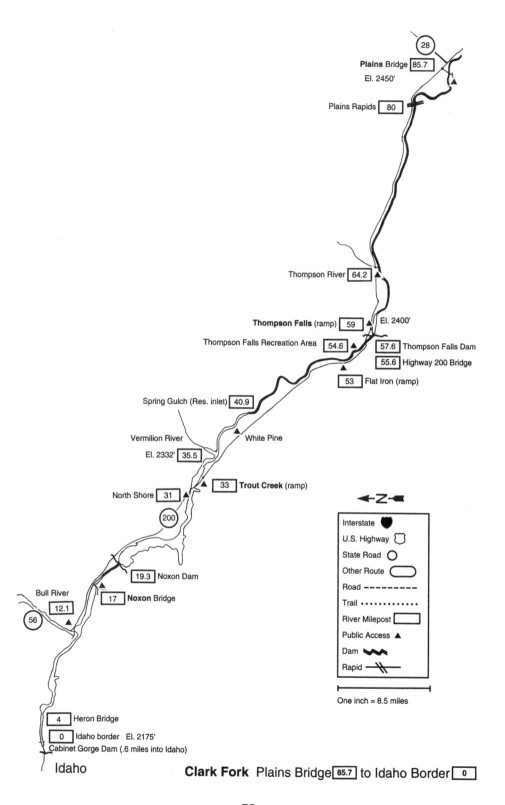

Plains Bridge 85.7
El. 2450'

Plains Rapids 80

Thompson River 64.2

Thompson Falls (ramp) 59   El. 2400'

Thompson Falls Recreation Area 54.6   57.6 Thompson Falls Dam
55.6 Highway 200 Bridge

53 Flat Iron (ramp)

Spring Gulch (Res. inlet) 40.9

Vermilion River   White Pine
El. 2332' 35.5

33 Trout Creek (ramp)

North Shore 31

200

19.3 Noxon Dam

Bull River
12.1   17 Noxon Bridge

56

4 Heron Bridge

0 Idaho border El. 2175'
Cabinet Gorge Dam (.6 miles into Idaho)

Idaho

N

Interstate
U.S. Highway
State Road
Other Route
Road ----------
Trail ....
River Milepost
Public Access ▲
Dam
Rapid

One inch = 8.5 miles

Clark Fork Plains Bridge 85.7 to Idaho Border 0

CLARKS FORK (Yellowstone)

ORIGIN:	At West Fork near Cooke City, MT & Hwy 212 - El. 8300'. Enters Wyoming after 2.5 miles and flows 66.3 miles and re-enters MT south of Belfry. El. 4000'
END:	Flows into Yellowstone R. near Laurel. El. 3200'
LENGTH:	75.1 miles in MT (2.5 miles + 72.6 miles) 70 air miles
FLOATABLE:	72.6 miles (Wyoming border to end)
SECTIONS:	Upper (2.5 mi.) Origin "141.4" to Wyoming border "138.9" Middle (30.2 mi.) Wyoming border "72.6" to Bridger Bridge "42.4" Lower (42.4 mi.) Bridger Bridge "42.4" to End - Yellowstone River "0"
DAMS:	Wills (Wolf Creek) 3' rock "62" Youst (Cem.) 3' rock "61" Mutual 3' rock "59.5" Holland (Belfry) 3' rock "58.5" Golden (Lind) 4' concrete "56" Dry Creek 4' concrete "53.3" Bridger Ditch 3' rock "51" Sand Creek (Cottonwood Creek) 3' rock "47.6" Orchard (Rush. Cr.) 5' concrete Left Channel "44.6" Bartlett (Skunk Creek) 3' rock "37" White Horse 5' concrete "18"
WATERFALLS:	None
WHITEWATER:	None
DANGERS:	Diversion dams, irrigation jettys
DEWATERED:	Can be low in fall
PORTAGES:	Diversion dams, irrigation jettys 3' rock jettys: "72.5" - "67.8" - "44.6" (in right channel) - "32.5" - "29" "26" - "8" - "2.9"
SPEC. AGENCIES:	None

REGS - PERMITS:	10 hp max. on all streams in Park Co.
ACCESS-SHUTTLE:	Easy, with highways and intersecting bridges. Formal access sites are infrequent.
SERVICES:	Belfry, Bridger, Edgar, Laurel, MT
CAMPING:	Formal campgrounds or access sites few.
GAMEFISH:	Extreme upper - Brook trout Middle - Rainbow, cutthroat, whitefish Lower - Brown, rainbow, sauger, burbot (ling), catfish
VESSEL:	Any moderate size craft (if flow is normal)
SKILL LEVEL:	Beginner (if flow is normal)
FLOAT TIMES:	Moderate flow
FLOW INFO:	(406) 449-5263 USGS - Helena

HYDROGRAPH

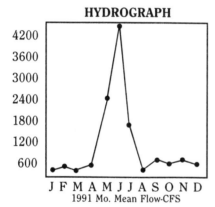

4200
3600
3000
2400
1800
1200
600

J F M A M J J A S O N D
1991 Mo. Mean Flow-CFS

Gage Sta: Edgar, MT
Drain Area: 2,032 sq. mi. (at this gage)
Ave. Flow: (53 yrs.) 1,029 cfs
Ext. Max: 10,900 cfs - 8.62' ga. ht. 6/2/36
Ext. Min: 36 cfs 4/22/61
Gradient: 800' in 72.6 miles = 11' pma
Float Grad: Same
Clarity: Cloudy
Temp: Jan. 34^0 F.
       Apr. 48^0 F.
       Jul. 69^0 F.
       Oct. 48^0 F.

DRAINAGE:	(East) Yellowstone, Missouri, Mississippi, Gulf
MAPS:	BLM - #35 "Beartooth" (upper) - #36 "Pryor" (lower) USFS - Custer NF (Beartooth Division) USGS - "Billings" CO. - Park, Carbon, Yellowstone

CLARKS FORK (Yellowstone)

This river originates in the high country near Yellowstone National Park, in the vicinity of Cooke City, MT. It flows near Hwy. 212 a short distance before entering Wyoming. Returning to Montana, the river descends gradually to a wide valley floor on its journey to the Yellowstone River. The river was named for Captain Clark of the Lewis and Clark Expedition, on the return trip. "A fine place for an establishment" was a comment at the mouth of river near laurel.

Eleven diversion dams completely block the river. These dams vary from 3' rock to 5' concrete structures. In addition, eight rock jettys protrude 2/3 of the way across the channel. Location of these dams and jettys is on the river milepost chart. This river has more diversions, per mile of river length, than any other in Montana. The Orchard Diversion Dam "44.6" occupies the left channel, while its counterpart, a rock jetty, occupies the right channel.

This river can become severely dewatered. This lack of flow is a detriment to the fishery value as well as the scenery and recreation values. Brook trout frequent the extreme upper portion in the high country. The middle section contains rainbow, cutthroat and whitefish. The lower section has browns, rainbow, sauger, burbot (ling), and catfish.

Upon returning to Montana, the river can be floated its entire distance, by portaging the obstructions. The scenery along the river is quite pretty and when the flow is up, it is a good sized stream. Fossils can be found in the Bridger area. A beginner can handle the river in any moderately sized vessel when flow is normal. Highways 310 and 72 parallel and cross the river. Intersecting county road bridges offer adequate access points, as formal campgrounds and access sites are infrequent.

Clarks Fork River

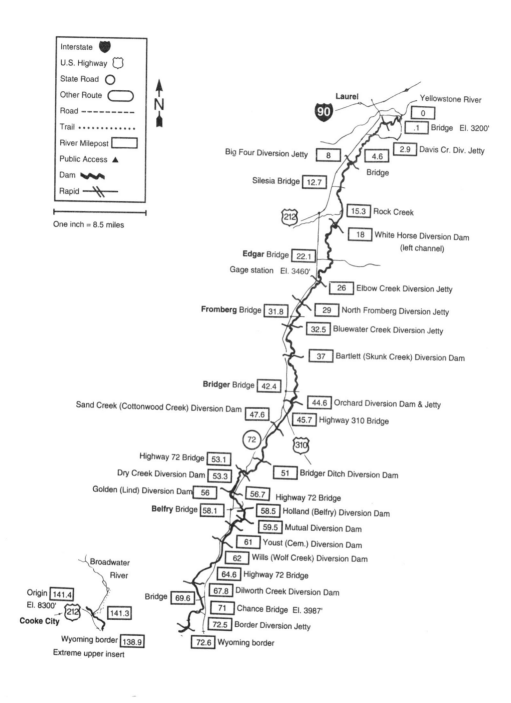

Interstate	(shield)
U.S. Highway	◯
State Road	◯
Other Route	⬭
Road	- - - - - - -
Trail	• • • • • • • •
River Milepost	▢
Public Access	▲
Dam	∿∿
Rapid	⫽

One inch = 8.5 miles

N

Laurel
90

Yellowstone River
0

.1 Bridge El. 3200'

Big Four Diversion Jetty 8

4.6

2.9 Davis Cr. Div. Jetty

Bridge

Silesia Bridge 12.7

212

15.3 Rock Creek

18 White Horse Diversion Dam
(left channel)

Edgar Bridge 22.1

Gage station El. 3460'

26 Elbow Creek Diversion Jetty

Fromberg Bridge 31.8

29 North Fromberg Diversion Jetty

32.5 Bluewater Creek Diversion Jetty

37 Bartlett (Skunk Creek) Diversion Dam

Bridger Bridge 42.4

Sand Creek (Cottonwood Creek) Diversion Dam

47.6

44.6 Orchard Diversion Dam & Jetty

45.7 Highway 310 Bridge

72

310

Highway 72 Bridge 53.1

Dry Creek Diversion Dam 53.3

51 Bridger Ditch Diversion Dam

Golden (Lind) Diversion Dam 56

56.7 Highway 72 Bridge

Belfry Bridge 58.1

58.5 Holland (Belfry) Diversion Dam

59.5 Mutual Diversion Dam

61 Youst (Cem.) Diversion Dam

62 Wills (Wolf Creek) Diversion Dam

64.6 Highway 72 Bridge

67.8 Dilworth Creek Diversion Dam

Bridge 69.6

71 Chance Bridge El. 3987'

72.5 Border Diversion Jetty

72.6 Wyoming border

Broadwater
River

Origin 141.4
El. 8300'
212
141.3
Cooke City

Wyoming border 138.9
Extreme upper insert

Clarks Fork (Yellowstone)

CLEARWATER

ORIGIN: At Clearwater Lake, north of Seeley Lake, MT
El. 4800'

END: Flows into Blackfoot River near Clearwater Junction
El. 3700'

LENGTH: 45.8 total miles (33 river & 7 lakes 12.8 miles)
34 air miles

FLOATABLE: 26 river miles (West Fork Bridge El. 4120' to End)

Rainy	.6 miles
Alva	1.6
Inez	1.8
Seeley	1.8
Salmon	3.9
Elbow	1.5
Blanchard	<u>1.6</u>

All floatable 12.8 miles

SECTIONS: Upper (15.8 mi.) Origin "45.8" to Boy Scout Br. "30"
Middle (19.7 mi.) Boy Scout "30" to Salmon L. "10.3"
Lower (10.3 mi.) Salmon Lake "10.3" to End "0"

DAMS: Rainy Lake Mile "39.9" (8' concrete)
Pond Mile "31.0" (8' concrete)
Blanchard Lake Mile "3.5"

WATERFALLS: None

WHITEWATER: 1.6 miles Salmon Lake outlet "10.3" to Elbow Lake
inlet "8.7" Class III

DANGERS: 3 dams, whitewater

DEWATERED: Usually not

PORTAGES: Pond Dam (RIGHT) - Blanchard Dam (LEFT)

SPEC. AGENCIES: Blackfoot River Corridor - Hwy. 200 "3.5" to
Blackfoot River. (see appendix)

REGS - PERMITS: None

ACCESS-SHUTTLE: Hwy 83 parallels river and roads intersect. Numerous
access sites.

SERVICES:	All services Seeley Lake, MT. Limited Clearwater Junction
CAMPING:	Numerous campgrounds
GAMEFISH:	Rainbow, brook, cutthroat, whitefish, bulls. Also large-mouth bass lower.
VESSEL:	Canoe, small boat, medium raft. Whitewater use kayak, medium raft, or whitewater canoe.
SKILL LEVEL:	Beginner if flows are normal. Whitewater - Experienced
FLOAT TIMES:	Moderate flows. 7 lakes slow.
FLOW INFO:	(406) 449-5263 USGS - Helena

HYDROGRAPH

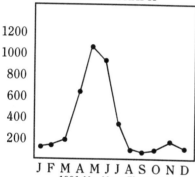

1991 Mo. Mean Flow-CFS

Gage Sta: 1 mile north of Clearwater
Drain Area: 345 sq. mi. (at this gage)
Ave. Flow: (17 yrs.) 287 cfs
Ext. Max: 2,900 cfs - 7.85' ga. ht. 5/17/75
Ext. Min: 16 cfs - 3.56' ga. ht. 9/21/88
Gradient: 1100' in 45.8 mi. = 24' pma
Float Grad: 420' in 38.2 mi. = 11' pma
Clarity: Clear

DRAINAGE:	(West) Blackfoot, Clark Fork, Pend Oreille, Columbia, Pacific Ocean.
MAPS:	BLM - #20 "Seeley Lake" (upper) - #21 "Granite" (extreme lower) USFS - Flathead NF(South) USGS - "Choteau" (upper) - "Butte" (extreme lower) Sp. - "Canoe Trail" (3.5 miles to Seeley L.) USFS CO. - Missoula

CLEARWATER

The namesake is derived from the Salish-Kootenai coming over Jocko Pass and calling the river "Clear Water". This relatively small stream originates at Clearwater Lake "45.8". It flows narrow and congested with downfall, under the Hwy. 83 Bridge, into Rainy Lake, over the Rainy Lake Dam, and into Lake Alva.

Difficult floating can begin below Lake Alva. It takes a patient and physically solid paddler in a canoe to endure the beaver dams and logjams in this multi-channeled portion. This river, connecting a chain of lakes passes through Lake Inez, passes Bear Grass Lane, to a pond dam at milepost "31". This dam backs up water and forms a wildlife marsh. This 8' high dam requires a portage RIGHT. Below this dam is the Boy Scout Road Bridge "30".

Better floating conditions prevail below this Boy Scout Bridge. One mile below is the Canoe Trail Access "29". The canoe trail is three miles long, through a curvy and placid stretch, surrounded by a dense riparian environment of willow and alder. As you enter Seeley Lake, a short paddle across to the National Forest Service Headquarters and a groomed hiking trail back to your vehicle.

Numerous boating activities are common on all these lakes. Camp Paxon and two campgrounds exist at the outlet of Seeley Lake. Fishing can be quite good for rainbow, brook and cutthroat trout. Bulls are also present and whitefish are plentiful. The lower lakes support a largemouth bass fishery.

Below Camp Paxon three bridges cross prior to entering Salmon Lake. Beginners can handle the lakes and the current connecting portions, in a canoe, small boat, or medium raft.

At the Salmon Lake outlet access "10.3" begins a 1.6 mile whitewater run. This run of boulders and steep gradient can be pretty bouncy in high water. Only an experienced paddler in a medium raft, kayak, or whitewater canoe should attempt it.

Clearwater River

Cottontail utilizing natures camouflage

The whitewater ends at Elbow Lake, and there is an access at the lower end of the lake "7.2". Again, a short stretch of current connects to Blanchard Lake and Harpers Campground "5.1". The Blanchard Dam "3.5" at the Hwy. 200 Bridge Access, requires a portage LEFT.

Below Hwy 200 are float-thru fences. These floating gates are pendulum-swinging plastic pipe or 2x4 that keep livestock contained, but allow passage of a vessel or debris. These are wonderful! An access site by the bridge, at the mouth to the Blackfoot River offers exit. Floating on down the Blackfoot would require a more experienced individual, as some rapids occur just above the Roundup Bridge. Roundup Bridge Access is 4.5 miles below the Clearwater River.

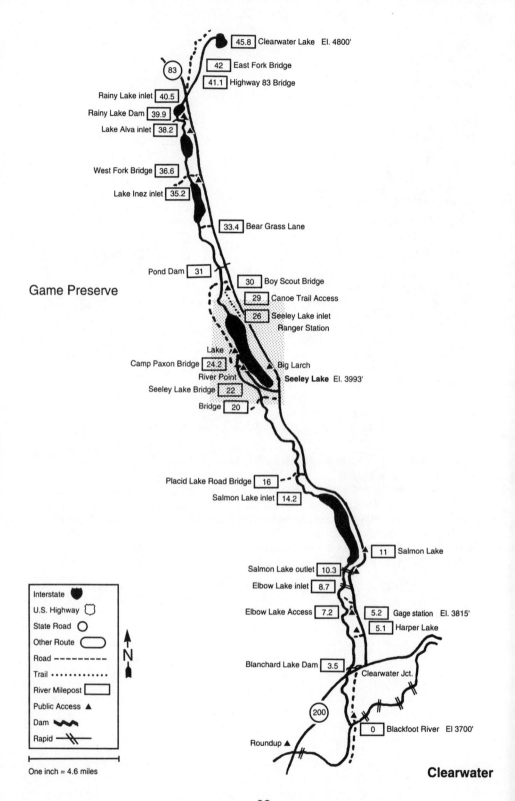

45.8	Clearwater Lake El. 4800'
83	
42	East Fork Bridge
41.1	Highway 83 Bridge
Rainy Lake inlet 40.5	
Rainy Lake Dam 39.9	
Lake Alva inlet 38.2	
West Fork Bridge 36.6	
Lake Inez inlet 35.2	
33.4	Bear Grass Lane
Pond Dam 31	
30	Boy Scout Bridge
29	Canoe Trail Access
26	Seeley Lake inlet
	Ranger Station

Game Preserve

Lake

Camp Paxon Bridge 24.2   Big Larch
River Point
Seeley Lake Bridge 22   **Seeley Lake**   El. 3993'
Bridge 20

Placid Lake Road Bridge 16

Salmon Lake inlet 14.2

11   Salmon Lake

Salmon Lake outlet 10.3
Elbow Lake inlet 8.7

Elbow Lake Access 7.2   5.2   Gage station   El. 3815'
5.1   Harper Lake

Blanchard Lake Dam 3.5   Clearwater Jct.

200

0   Blackfoot River   El 3700'

Roundup ▲

Interstate	🛡
U.S. Highway	⬡
State Road	◯
Other Route	⬭
Road	- - - - - -
Trail	• • • • • •
River Milepost	▭
Public Access	▲
Dam	〰
Rapid	⫻

N

One inch = 4.6 miles

Clearwater

CUT BANK CREEK

ORIGIN:	Confluence of North & South Forks near Starr School, northwest of Browning, MT El. 4600'
END:	Joins Two Medicine River to form the Marias River, south of Cut Bank, MT El. 3300'
LENGTH:	79.8 miles (42 air miles)
FLOATABLE:	79.8 miles
SECTIONS:	Upper (26.1 miles) Origin "79.8" to Del Bonita Hwy. Bridge "53.7" Middle (35.9 miles) Del Bonita Bridge "53.7" to Hwy. 2 Bridge (Cut Bank) "17.8" Lower (17.8 miles) Cut Bank "17.8" to End-Marias River "0"
DAMS:	None
WATERFALLS:	None
WHITEWATER:	None
DANGERS:	Irrigation jettys, remote area, fences, debris.
DEWATERED:	Usually low in fall
PORTAGES:	None
SPEC. AGENCIES:	Glacier National Park (Extreme upper on North & South Forks), Blackfeet Indian Reservation.
REGS - PERMITS:	Glacier National Park rules, Tribal Fishing or Recreation permit.
ACCESS-SHUTTLE:	Difficult and long float distances. Study good map. No formal access sites, Reservation and private land.
SERVICES:	All - in Browning and Cut Bank, MT
CAMPING:	No formal campgrounds or access sites. Reservation and private land.
GAMEFISH:	Upper - Rainbow, brook, cutthroat, burbot Lower - Brown, ling, whitefish
VESSEL:	Canoe, small raft, small boat

SKILL LEVEL:	Intermediate (if flows normal)
FLOAT TIMES:	Moderate flow
FLOW INFO:	(406) 449-5263 USGS - Helena

HYDROGRAPH

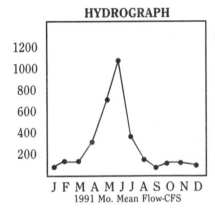

J F M A M J J A S O N D
1991 Mo. Mean Flow-CFS

Gage Sta: Hwy 2 Bridge - Cut Bank, MT
Drain Area: 1065 sq. mi. (at this gage)
Ave. Flow: (48 yrs.) 187 cfs
Ext. Max: 16,600 cfs - 13.93' ga. ht. 6/9/64
Ext. Min: 1 cfs 9/10/88
Gradient: 1300' in 79.8 miles = 16.3' pma
Float Grad: Same
Clarity: Cloudy
Temp: Jan. 32° F.
     Apr. 45° F.
     Jul. 66° F.
     Oct. 40° F.

DRAINAGE:	(East) Marias, Missouri, Mississippi, Gulf of Mexico
MAPS:	BLM - #17 "St. Mary" (extreme upper) - #27 "Cut Bank" - #28 "Valier" (extreme lower) USGS - "Cut Bank" CO. - Glacier

A frequent "site" - thank you

CUT BANK CREEK

The name Cut Bank is named for the steep bank, cut by the stream at Cut Bank, Montana. A few historians and map makers have called this creek a river.

The origin is at the confluence of the North and South Forks at Starr School, northwest of Browning. Nearly eighty miles downstream it joins the Two Medicine River to form the Marias River, south of Cut Bank.

The headwaters of the North and South Forks, are in the beautiful high country of Glacier National Park. After leaving the park the stream flows through the Blackfeet Indian Reservation to a point three miles above Cut Bank.

The creek flows through a cottonwood and willow bottom, with a mostly gravel streambed. Rolling prairie hills surround. Arrowheads and buffalo skulls can be found along the stream and surrounding areas. The float is quite pretty, especially in the fall. No formal campgrounds or access sites exist, so bridges with up to sixteen miles between must suffice for ingress or egress. Floating can continue to the end, where a bridge at the confluence with the Two Medicine River crosses the Marias River.

The upper creek has rainbow, brookies, cutthroat and ling. The lower portion has brown trout, ling and whitefish. An intermediate in a canoe, small raft or small boat can handle the entire stream if flow is normal.

N.F. Cut Bank Creek

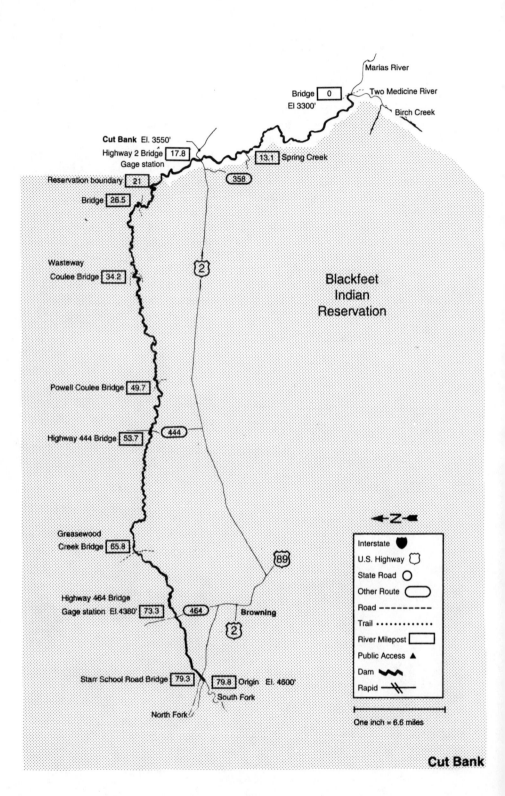

Marias River

Two Medicine River

Bridge 0
El 3300'

Birch Creek

Cut Bank El. 3550'
Highway 2 Bridge 17.8
Gage station

13.1 Spring Creek

358

Reservation boundary 21

Bridge 26.5

2

Wasteway
Coulee Bridge 34.2

Blackfeet
Indian
Reservation

Powell Coulee Bridge 49.7

Highway 444 Bridge 53.7

444

Greasewood
Creek Bridge 65.8

89

Highway 464 Bridge
Gage station El.4380' 73.3

464

Browning

2

Starr School Road Bridge 79.3

79.8 Origin El. 4600'

South Fork

North Fork

N

Interstate ▮
U.S. Highway ⬭
State Road ◯
Other Route ⬯
Road ---------
Trail ....
River Milepost ▭
Public Access ▲
Dam ∿
Rapid ⫻

One inch = 6.6 miles

Cut Bank

DEARBORN

ORIGIN:	Near Scapegoat Mountain in Scapegoat Wilderness El. 6,000'
END:	Flows into Missouri River near Craig, MT El. 3420'
LENGTH:	66.9 river miles (40 air miles)
FLOATABLE:	48 miles (Ranch dam near wilderness boundary (4750') to Missouri River. Class I portion is 41.3 miles (Hwy 434 bridge to Missouri River)
SECTIONS:	Upper (18.9 mi.) Origin "66.9" to Ranch diversion dam "48" Middle (6.7 mi.) Ranch dam "48" to Hwy 434 Bridge access "41.3" Lower (41.3 mi.) Hwy 434 Bridge access "41.3" to End (Missouri River) "0"
DAMS:	None
WATERFALLS:	Dearborn Falls (Milepost "34") 10' falls in 2 steps
WHITEWATER:	Mileposts "41.3" to "34" (Access at mile "29") 3 -4' drops and falls Also - Milepost "26" 3' drop Mileposts "19" to "0" (Actual whitewater is milepost "13" to "0" Class III
DANGERS:	Fences, fallen trees, whitewater and falls Lower 19 miles primitive area.
DEWATERED:	Could be impossible in the fall.
PORTAGES:	Dearborn Falls (Mile "34") Portage LEFT
SPEC. AGENCIES:	Upper - Scapegoat Wilderness
REGS - PERMITS:	Wilderness area - no motors
ACCESS-SHUTTLE:	Intersecting roads upper. Long shuttle from Missouri back up Hwy 287 on lower section.
SERVICES:	Limited in Craig and Wolf Creek, MT
CAMPING:	Public land infrequent. FWP agency asks floaters to try and start early and complete 19 mile lower float in one day, if possible.

GAMEFISH:	Upper - Rainbow, cutthroat Middle - Rainbow, brook Lower - Brown, rainbow
VESSEL:	Upper - Unfloatable Middle - Small raft, canoe, whitewater canoe Lower - Raft, whitewater canoe.
SKILL LEVEL:	Upper - Unfloatable Middle - Intermediate Lower - Intermediate to Experienced
FLOAT TIMES:	Moderate flow
FLOW INFO:	(406) 449-5263 USGS - Helena

HYDROGRAPH

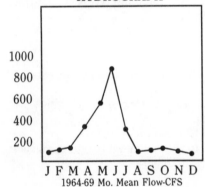

1000
800
600
400
200

J F M A M J J A S O N D
1964-69 Mo. Mean Flow-CFS

Gage Sta: Hwy. 287 Bridge
Drain Area: 325 sq. mi. (at this gage)
Ave. Flow: (5 yrs.) 237 cfs
Ext. Max: 2370 cfs 6/18/65
Ext. Min: 20 cfs 12/9/66
Gradient: 2580' in 66.9 mi. = 38.5' pma
Float Grad: 1330' in 48.0 mi. = 27.7' pma
Clarity: Clear
Temp: 71⁰ F. 8/8/91

DRAINAGE:	(East) Missouri, Mississippi, Gulf of Mexico
MAPS:	BLM - #30 "Dearborn" (upper) - #40 "Great Falls South" (lower) (Best maps) USFS - Lewis & Clark NF (Rocky Mtn. Div.) (Above Hwy 200 Bridge) USGS -"Choteau" (upper)-"Great Falls" (lower) "Bob Marshall, Great Bear, Scapegoat Wilderness" (upper) CO. - Lewis & Clark

DEARBORN

The Dearborn was named "Dearborn's River", in honor of the Secretary of War, in 1805 by Captain Lewis. The river begins in the Scapegoat Wilderness and flows for 22 miles before reaching civilization. The only access is from the popular trailhead used by hikers and horsemen.

This wonderful, transparent but small stream can be floated from below a small irrigation dam located near the dude ranch at the wilderness boundary. This section of 6.7 miles is a beautiful float to the Hwy. 434 Bridge Access. It can be handled by intermediates in a canoe or small raft. It has a relatively steep gradient, but no major obstacles. Low flow after mid-summer might prevent floating.

At Hwy. 434 bridge "41.3" the Class I designation begins. Parking is a problem at this access; it is an old mountainous road and has room for only a couple vehicles. Moderate whitewater begins at this point and only experienced paddlers in canoes or medium rafts should attempt it. Three 4' drops occur at mileposts "37", "36", "35" and a ten foot waterfall (2 steps) occurs at milepost "34" (portage LEFT). The last five miles to the Hwy. 200 Bridge is a gentle float.

The Hwy. 200 Bridge offers only steep access and the Middle Fork confluence just below adds additional volume to the flow. A 3' drop is located three miles below this bridge at mile "26", and is the only obstacle to be encountered in this stretch to the Hwy. #287 Bridge Access (mile "19").

This access begins the most popular floating portion of the Dearborn. The last 19 miles to the Missouri is mostly through private land and camp spots are extremely limited. A sign at this access by the FWP asks people to please get an early start and complete this float the same day. Some intermittent rapids occur below Flat Creek which makes this not only a beautiful, but exciting float trip. This lower portion can be handled by intermediates or experienced paddlers in whitewater canoes or medium rafts.

Fishing in the upper and middle sections is quite good for Rainbow, cutthroat and brookies. The lower portion is predominately brown trout.

A long shuttle from the Missouri River must be expected back to your vehicle at the Hwy. 287 Bridge Access. But it's worth it!

Dearborn River

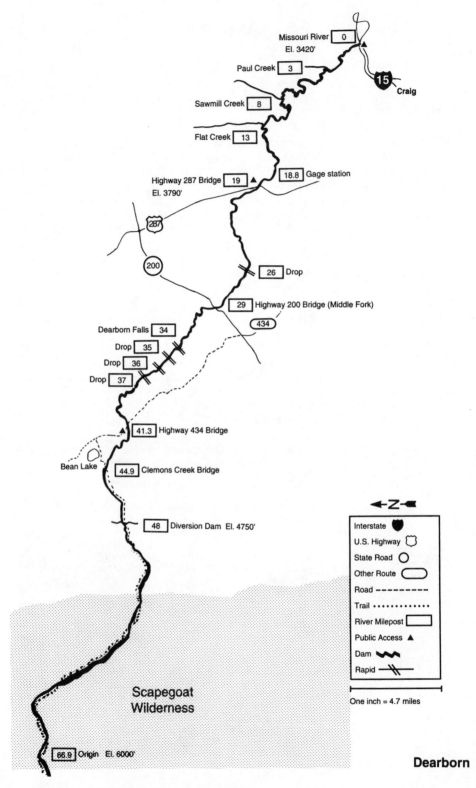

Missouri River 0
El. 3420'

Paul Creek 3

Sawmill Creek 8

Flat Creek 13

18.8 Gage station

Highway 287 Bridge 19
El. 3790'

287

200

26 Drop

29 Highway 200 Bridge (Middle Fork)

434

Dearborn Falls 34

Drop 35

Drop 36

Drop 37

41.3 Highway 434 Bridge

Bean Lake

44.9 Clemons Creek Bridge

48 Diversion Dam El. 4750'

Scapegoat
Wilderness

86.9 Origin El. 6000'

15
Craig

←Z←

Interstate
U.S. Highway
State Road
Other Route
Road ---------
Trail ....
River Milepost
Public Access ▲
Dam
Rapid

One inch = 4.7 miles

Dearborn

FISHER

ORIGIN:	Bear Spring Cr., 5 mi. N. of McGregor Lake. El. 3590'
END:	Flows into Kootenai River near Libby Dam. El. 2200'
LENGTH:	63.9 total mi. (61.9 river mi. + Loon Lakes 2 mi.) (28 air mi.)
FLOATABLE:	30 miles (Silver Butte Fork Bridge "30" to "0")
SECTIONS:	Upper (33.9 mi.) Origin "63.9" to Silver Butte Br. "30" Middle (21.0 mi.) Silver Butte Fork "30" to Fisher River Road Bridge "9" Lower (9.0 mi.) Fisher River Bridge "9" to End-Kootenai River "0"
DAMS:	Low irrigation dams (upper)
WATERFALLS:	None
WHITEWATER:	None. In extremely high water, mileposts "23" to "16.8", can have big waves. Also, erosion jettys exist the last nine miles that form waves in high water.
DANGERS:	Jettys, waves, some remote portions, low bridges.
DEWATERED:	Can be low in fall.
PORTAGES:	None
SPEC. AGENCIES:	None
REGS - PERMITS:	None
ACCESS-SHUTTLE:	Somewhat round-about. Highway 2 and McKillop Road parallel at a distance. Use a good map. No formal access sites, but should be no problem.
SERVICES:	None
CAMPING:	Pleasant Valley Campground at milepost "34.3". Numerous informal places to use as campsites.
GAMEFISH:	Rainbow, whitefish, cutthroat (fishing not very good)
VESSEL:	Canoe, medium raft, small boat
SKILL LEVEL:	Beginner only if flow is normal.

FLOAT TIMES:	Moderately fast flow.
FLOW INFO:	(406) 449-5263 USGS - Helena

HYDROGRAPH

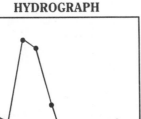

1991 Mo. Mean Flow-CFS

Gage Sta: Mi. "1"
Drain Area: 838 sq. mi.
Ave. Flow: (24 years) 492 cfs
Ext. Max: 8720 cfs - 9.29' ga. ht. 1/16/74
Ext. Min: 29 cfs - 2.37' ga. ht. 1/02/77
Gradient: 1510' in 63.9 mi. = 23.6' pma
Float Grad: 900' in 30.0 mi. = 30.0' pma
Clarity: Cloudy
Temp: Jan. 34^0 F.
         Apr. 43^0 F.
         Jul. 66^0 F.
         Oct. 46^0 F.

DRAINAGE:	(West) Kootenai, Columbia, Pacific Ocean
MAPS:	BLM - #5 "Libby"
	USFS - Kootenai NF
	USGS - "Kalispell"
	CO. - Lincoln

Fisher River

FISHER

The Fisher River is named after John S. Fisher, a miner in the area during the 1860's gold rush era. The river originates at Bear Springs Creek in the Pleasant Valley area, north of McGregor Lake. The river, nearly 69 miles later, flows into the Kootenai, below Libby Dam.

The upper river flows through intermittent timber and hay fields and is surrounded by low mountains. A ranching community in the wide and tranquil valley also supports good numbers of deer and elk. Waterfowl and songbirds are common along the marshland grasses as the stream meanders along a sandy bed with undercut banks. Although not commonly regarded as a good fishing stream, rainbow, cutthroat and whitefish are present.

As the river nears Highway 2 and Loon Lakes, the river picks up velocity in its gravel streambed. Still a small stream, now paralleling Highway 2, it flows through a boulder streambed and is surrounded by the charred remains of a recent forest fire.

Floating can begin as high as the Silver Butte Fork bridge "30". This fork adds the volume of water necessary to make floating possible. The river continues to parallel Highway 2 down to its bridge at milepost "26.2" and the confluence of the West Fork.

McKillop Road, found back upstream, goes north and eventually parallels the river. This road offers access to the river. During high water, big waves are present beginning at river milepost "23". Access can be found at two bridges near McKillop Creek "16.8". A bridge on the McKillop road near Cow Creek "12.8" also offers ingress or egress possibilities. Below Cow Creek is a bridge, near the Wolf Creek confluence "10.9", on the Fisher River Road.

A practiced beginner can handle the river, only if the flow is low. A medium sized raft, canoe or small boat would work nicely. During high water the river commands an experienced paddler in a raft or whitewater canoe. A kayak would also be enjoyable.

Below Wolf Creek, the Fisher River Road parallels the river the rest of its journey. The remaining river has erosion ridges in the streambed to help protect the railroad embankment. These low ridges of rock and gravel cause waves to follow, when the water is high. Also a low bridge occurs that requires a short portage during high water. These railroad tracks certainly detract from the scenic values through this beautiful canyon.

The railroad crosses the river at milepost "3". A short and narrow gorge, with a sharp turn and small drop, exists below this bridge. This railroad bridge is 1/2 mile above Peoples Creek.

One can float into the Kootenai River and go straight across, and work upstream a couple hundred yards to a campground and access site. You could elect to go downstream a short distance along the left bank, and drag your vessel up and over the railroad tracks to an old road. Informal campsites are frequent along the river.

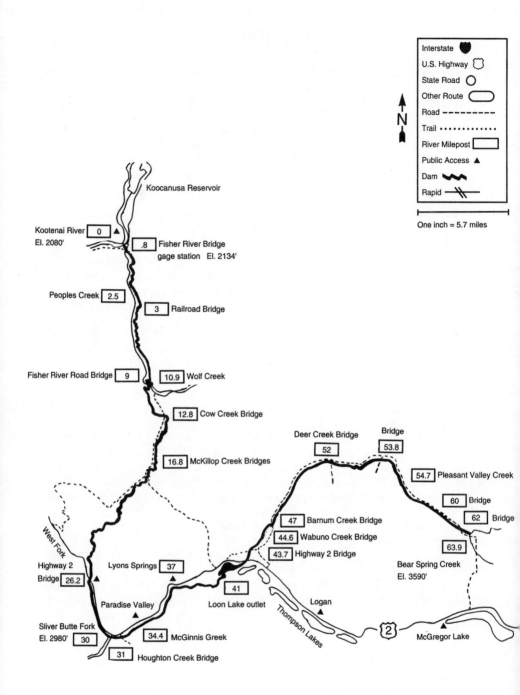

Koocanusa Reservoir

Kootenai River [0] ▲
El. 2080'

[.8] Fisher River Bridge
gage station El. 2134'

Peoples Creek [2.5]

[3] Railroad Bridge

Fisher River Road Bridge [9] [10.9] Wolf Creek

[12.8] Cow Creek Bridge

[16.8] McKillop Creek Bridges

Deer Creek Bridge   Bridge
[52]   [53.8]

[54.7] Pleasant Valley Creek

[60] Bridge

[62] Bridge

[47] Barnum Creek Bridge
[44.6] Wabuno Creek Bridge
[43.7] Highway 2 Bridge   [63.9]

West Fork

Highway 2   Lyons Springs [37]
Bridge [26.2] ▲   Bear Spring Creek
                               El. 3590'

Paradise Valley ▲   [41]
                     Loon Lake outlet   Logan ▲
Sliver Butte Fork   Thompson Lakes
El. 2980' [30]   [2]
          [34.4] McGinnis Greek   McGregor Lake ▲
     [31] Houghton Creek Bridge

Legend:
- Interstate
- U.S. Highway
- State Road ○
- Other Route ⬭
- Road --------
- Trail ••••••••
- River Milepost ▭
- Public Access ▲
- Dam
- Rapid

One inch = 5.7 miles

Fisher

94

FLATHEAD

ORIGIN:	Confluence of Middle & North Forks at Blankenship Bridge El. 3100'
END:	Flows into Clark Fork R. near Paradise, MT El. 2480'
LENGTH:	158.3 total mi. (127.3 river mi. + Flathead Lake 31 mi.) 80 air miles
FLOATABLE:	All 158.3 mi. (Class I designation is entire 158.3 mi.)
SECTIONS:	Upper (36.3 mi.) Origin "158.3" to Foys Bend Access "122" Middle (50 mi.) Foys Bend "122" to Kerr Dam "72" Lower (72 mi.) Kerr Dam Access "72" to End "0"
DAMS:	Kerr Dam (Controls flow below dam)
WATERFALLS:	None
WHITEWATER:	7 miles (Kerr Dam Access "72" to Buffalo Bridge Access "65" 4 major rapids called "Buffalo Rapids". Class IV
DANGERS:	Whitewater, sudden dam releases.
DEWATERED:	No
PORTAGES:	Kerr Dam (MAJOR portage LEFT)
SPEC. AGENCIES:	Upper - Wild, Scenic, Recreation Corridor (Recreational designation) Lower - Flathead Indian Reservation
REGS - PERMITS:	Motors over 10 hp not allowed above South Fork confluence. On Reservation - Motors over 15 hp prohibited. From 3/15 - 6/30 (waterfowl nesting) no motors allowed. No shooting from vessel except hunting waterfowl. Tribal recreation - fish permit.
ACCESS-SHUTTLE:	Easy access and shuttle
SERVICES:	All services - Columbia Falls, Kalispell, Polson

CAMPING:	A few formal public campgrounds and numerous fishing access sites.
GAMEFISH:	Upper - Cutthroat, rainbow, bulls Middle - Also lake trout (Mackinaw), kokanee, whitefish Lower - Largemouth bass, pike, trout
VESSEL:	Upper - Any moderately-sized craft Middle - Any vessel Lower - Any moderately-sized craft (Except Whitewater-Large raft, kayak, whitewater canoe)
SKILL LEVEL:	Upper - Beginner Middle - Beginner Whitewater - Experienced Lower - Beginner
FLOAT TIMES:	14.5 miles Blankenship Bridge to Columbia Falls = 3 1/2 hours nonstop Columbia Falls - Pressentine 6.8 miles = 2 hours Pressentine - Old Steel Bridge 8 miles = 2 1/2 hours Old Steel Bridge - Foys Bend 7 miles = 3 hours Lower - Flow slow
FLOW INFO:	(406) 449-5263 USGS - Helena

Moiese Bison

HYDROGRAPH

30,000
25,000
20,000
15,000
10,000
5,000

J F M A M J J A S O N D
1991 Mo. Mean Flow-CFS

Gage Sta: Columbia Falls, MT
Drain Area: 4,464 sq. mi. (at this gage)
Ave. Flow: (63 yrs.) 9,729 cfs
Ext. Max: 176,000 cfs - 25.58' rod 06/9/64
Ext. Min: 798 cfs -   .08' rod 12/8/29
Gradient: 620' in 158.3 miles = 3.9' pma
Float Grad: Same
Clarity: Upper-clear Slow water-murky
Temp: Jan. 38⁰ F.
      Apr. 41⁰ F.
      Jul. 61⁰ F.
      Oct. 43⁰ F.
Total Drain Area: 8840 square miles

DRAINAGE: (West) Clark Fork, Pend Oreille, Columbia, Pacific

MAPS: BLM - #10 "Kalispell" (upper) - #11 "Polson" (middle)
                    #12 "Plains" (lower)
                    USFS - Flathead NF (North) (upper) - Lolo NF (ex-
                    treme lower)
                    USGS - "Kalispell" (upper) - "Wallace" (lower)
                    CO.   - Flathead, Lake, Sanders

Livestock - groundwater decay?

97

FLATHEAD

The Flathead is perhaps the recreational hub of Montana. Flathead Lake and its proximity to Glacier National Park, wilderness areas, and the National Wild-Scenic-Recreation river designations awarded to certain sections of this river system help preserve this beautiful country in its natural state. The three forks of the Flathead are rivers in their own right, and form the mainstem of the Flathead River.

Named for the Flathead Indians living in the area, by the other tribes, being of the belief that they pressed the heads of their young to flatten them.

The mainstem of the Flathead begins at the confluence of the Middle and North Forks, within sight upstream from Blankenship Bridge Access, near Coram, MT. The entire river has a Class I designation. Some locals call the upper 9.6 miles down to the South Fork the "Big River", and this stretch has "Recreational" desgination, which means motors over 10 hp are prohibited.

The upper section is a moderate velocity and wide river with access points at Columbia Falls, MT, Pressentine Access, and Old Steel Bridge Access at Kalispell. Foys Bend "122" is the beginning of slow water. Many Flathead Lake boaters navigate up to this point.

I suppose anything with the massive attributes that the Flathead has, must have some short-comings. A glaring example is the fishery it should be and isn't! The upper section contains cutthroat, rainbow, and bull trout, and the few remaining kokanee when they migrate upstream in the fall to spawn.

Flathead Lake is the largest freshwater lake west of the Mississippi and holds many recreation opportunities. Boating, skiing, and although the Flathead isn't ordinarily windy, prevailing winds at times offer tremendous sailing and wind-surfing. Big lake trout (Mackinaw) are the most sought after prize today. The state record caught in 1979 is 42 lbs. The FWP has netted Macks in the 70 lbs , and one in the 90 lb. range. Above Flathead Lake, in some of the backwater sloughs are pike of catchable proportions. On the East shore, the best places for Macks are the Woods Bay and Yellow Bay areas. On the West shore, Angel Point and the Table Bay areas are best. Mack Alley is a good spot between Wild Horse Island and Melita Island. The south half of Flathead Lake is on the Flathead Indian Reservation, and tribal fishing permits are necessary on the lower lake and the river remaining as well. These permits can readily be obtained from any sporting goods store. Wild Horse Island, primarily a state owned blessing, supports a small population of Bighorn Sheep, and a watchful eye on a cruise around the island usually picks out a few.

Below Kerr Dam are four major Class III-IV rapids in a seven mile run called Buffalo Rapids. Sudden dam releases can cause great variance in the flow. The best whitewater is between 10,000 and 20,000 cfs. Most rapids wash out over 20,000 cfs and flow can be so low that the rapids become more difficult. Dam releases up to 50,000 cfs are possible and the record at Columbia Falls, Montana is 176,000 cfs in the flood year of 1964. The record below the dam is 110,000 cfs also in 1964.

The "Ledge" rapid is 1.2 miles below the dam. This rapid occurs at the big bend in the river and has a rock ledge caused drop with holes and waves. This rapid washes out over 18,000 cfs. "Pinball" rapid is just below the "Ledge". Rocks exposed during low water make skilled maneuvering critical. As flow increases waves develop and wash out the rapid and form a hole. Immediately below "Pinball" is "Eagle Wave" rapid. At low water this long run is technical and has big waves with higher flow. The "Buffalo" rapid is 1 1/2 miles below. It is perhaps more difficult than the "Ledge". An eddy just above on the left side allows the time to look it over. One can hike up a foot path to a vantage point and scout. This rapid has a big wave that can flip a raft. Most floaters follow the left bank. An experienced skill level is required in a good raft or kayak. Water is usually warmer, after pooling in the lake. A gauge station occurs just below the dam. Ave. Flows are:

April 14,000 cfs - May 25,000 cfs - June 30,000 cfs - July 20,000 cfs - August 7,000 cfs - September 10,000 cfs - October 11,000 cfs. Average annual flow is 12,000 cfs. Buffalo Bridge offers good ingress or egress. Below this bridge the river meanders tranquilly through a semi-arid badlands. Pike fishing can be excellent near the Moiese National Bison Range. The bison range is certainly worth a drive through. Nearly all the big game animals will be sighted, many of them trophy quality.

As the river flows through a popular waterfowl nesting area the tribe has a no motor restriction on the lower river from 3/15 to 6/30. The rest of the year a 15 hp maximum limit is imposed.

From Dixon Access "25", the water flow slows again for the rest of its journey to the Clark Fork River. This stretch is primarily a pike and largemouth bass fishery and most fishermen use motors. The western boundary of the Flathead Indian Reservation is at Knowles Creek "4.4".

Flathead River

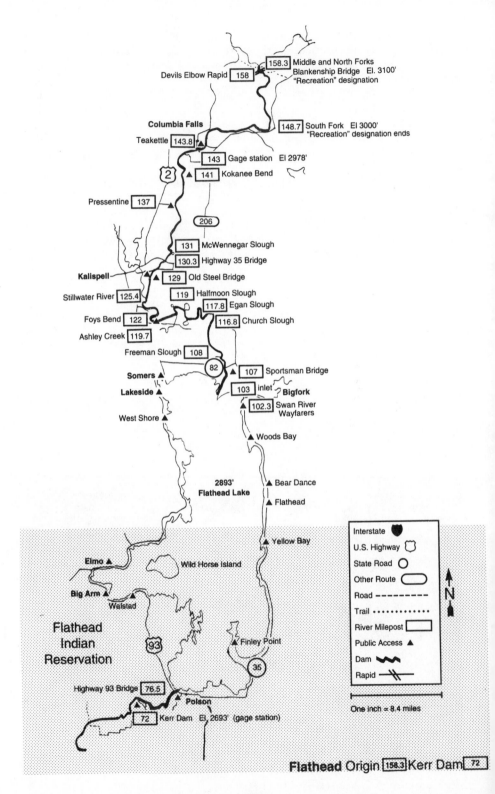

158.3 Middle and North Forks
Blankenship Bridge   El. 3100'
"Recreation" designation

Devils Elbow Rapid 158

Columbia Falls

148.7 South Fork   El 3000'
"Recreation" designation ends

Teakettle 143.8

143 Gage station El 2978'

141 Kokanee Bend

Pressentine 137

206

131 McWennegar Slough

130.3 Highway 35 Bridge

Kalispell

129 Old Steel Bridge

Stillwater River 125.4

119 Halfmoon Slough

117.8 Egan Slough

Foys Bend 122

116.8 Church Slough

Ashley Creek 119.7

Freeman Slough 108

82

107 Sportsman Bridge

Somers

103 inlet Bigfork

Lakeside

102.3 Swan River
Wayfarers

West Shore

Woods Bay

2893'
Flathead Lake

Bear Dance

Flathead

Yellow Bay

Elmo

Wild Horse Island

Big Arm

Walstad

Flathead
Indian
Reservation

93

Finley Point

35

Highway 93 Bridge 76.5

Polson

72 Kerr Dam El. 2693' (gage station)

Interstate	🛡
U.S. Highway	⬡
State Road	◯
Other Route	⬭
Road	- - - - - -
Trail	• • • • • •
River Milepost	▭
Public Access	▲
Dam	〰
Rapid	✕

N

One inch ≈ 8.4 miles

Flathead Origin 158.3 Kerr Dam 72

100

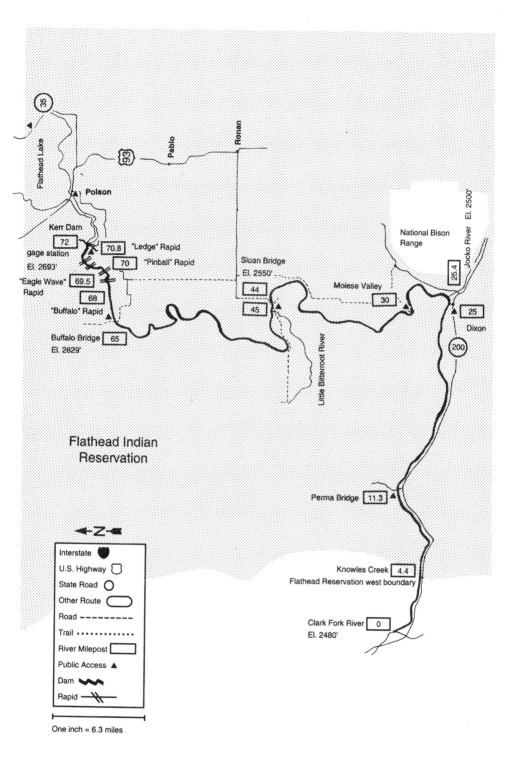

Flathead Lake

35

93

Pablo

Ronan

Polson

Kerr Dam
72
gage station
El. 2693'

70.8 "Ledge" Rapid

70 "Pinball" Rapid

Sloan Bridge
El. 2550'

National Bison
Range

Jocko River El. 2500'

25.4

"Eagle Wave" 69.5
Rapid

68

44

Moiese Valley

30

"Buffalo" Rapid

45

25

Buffalo Bridge 65
El. 2629'

Little Bitterroot River

Dixon

200

Flathead Indian
Reservation

Perma Bridge 11.3

N

Knowles Creek 4.4
Flathead Reservation west boundary

Clark Fork River 0
El. 2480'

Interstate
U.S. Highway
State Road
Other Route
Road – – – – – – – –
Trail • • • • • • • • • •
River Milepost
Public Access ▲
Dam
Rapid

One inch = 6.3 miles

Flathead Kerr Dam 72 to Clark Fork River 0

FLATHEAD - MIDDLE FORK

ORIGIN: Near Gooseberry Park at the confluence of Strawberry and Bowl Creeks, in Bob Marshall Wilderness. El. 5200'

END: Joins North Fork of the Flathead at Blankenship Bridge to form Flathead River. El. 3100'

LENGTH: 92.3 river miles (50 air miles)

FLOATABLE: 73 miles Schaeffer Ranger Station Airstrip El. 4855' to Flathead River. Class I portion is 72.2 miles (Schaeffer Creek to Flathead River).

SECTIONS: Upper (19.3 mi.) Origin "92.3" to Schaeffer Meadow Airstrip "73"
Middle (31.9 mi.) Schaeffer Airstrip "73" to Essex Bridge Access "41.1"
Lower (41.1 mi.) Essex Bridge "41.1" to End (North Fork confluence) "0"

DAMS: None

WATERFALLS: None

WHITEWATER: Middle - Schaeffer Airstrip to Essex Bridge Access. 31.9 miles Class V
Lower - Moccasin Creek Access to West Glacier 8 miles Class IV (John Stevens Canyon)

DANGERS: Upper and most of middle portion is wilderness. Extreme whitewater.

DEWATERED: The middle portion could be low after August some years.

PORTAGES: Possible whitewater portages: 3- Class V rapids
5- Class IV rapids

SPEC. AGENCIES: Wild-Scenic-Recreation Corridor. Bob Marshall & Great Bear Wilderness. Glacier National Park (borders on right from Bear Creek downstream).

REGS - PERMITS: No motors in wilderness or in Wild-Scenic portions. 10 hp motor limit in Recreation portion.

ACCESS-SHUTTLE: Upper and most of middle - Horse, hike, or fly to airstrip
Lower - Highway 2 parallels river.

SERVICES: Upper & Middle - None
Lower - Limited
Whitewater and Wilderness raft trips available

CAMPING: Numerous access sites.

GAMEFISH: Cutthroat, Dolly Varden (bull trout)

VESSEL: Upper - Not floatable.
Middle - Large raft
Lower - Raft, kayak, whitewater canoe, dory

SKILL LEVEL: Middle - Highly skilled - Expert
Lower - Experienced

FLOAT TIMES: Schaeffer to Bear Creek (27.3 miles) 2+ full days
to: Essex   (4.6 miles) 1 1/2 hours. (Non-stop)
    Paola   (8.1 miles) 2 1/2 hours
    Cascadilla   (11. miles) 3 hours
    Moccasin   (8.0 miles) 2 1/2 hours
    West Glacier (8.0 miles) 2 1/2 hours
    Blankenship (6.0 miles) 2 1/2 hours

FLOW INFO: 12 inches ga. ht. best family float.
(406) 888-5700 ga. ht. (mid season)
(406) 449-5263 cfs. flow USGS - Helena

Upper Middle Fork

Pick and choose - tread lightly

HYDROGRAPH

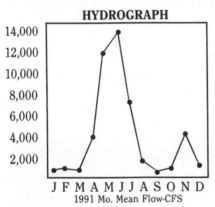

J F M A M J J A S O N D
1991 Mo. Mean Flow-CFS

Gage Sta: 1 mi. west of West Glacier
Drain Area: 1,128 sq. mi.
Ave. Flow: (52 yrs.) 2,922 cfs
Ext. Max: 140,000 cfs - 36.46' ga.ht.6/9/64
Ext. Min: 173 cfs 11/27/52
Gradient: 2100' in 92.3 miles = 22.8' pma
Float Grad: 1755' in 73.0 miles =24.0' pma
Clarity: Clear
Temp: Jan. 36⁰ F.
Apr. 40⁰ F.
Jul. 58⁰ F.
Oct. 45⁰ F.

DRAINAGE: (West) Flathead, Clark Fork, Pend Oreille, Columbia, Pacific Ocean.

MAPS: BLM - #18 "Hungry Horse"
USFS - Flathead NF (South)
USGS - "Cut Bank" (upper) - "Kalispell" (lower)
Sp. - "Bob Marshall" - Great Bear-Scapegoat Wilderness" (USFS Topographic)
"Glacier National Park" (Bear Creek to end)
(USGS Topographic)
"Three Forks-Flathead River" (Glacier Natural Historical Society) Great 2nd map!
CO - Flathead

FLATHEAD - MIDDLE FORK

The Middle Fork begins its rampage in the Bob Marshall Wilderness, and carries with it the distinction of being a "Wild" river, awarded in 1980, by the National Wild & Scenic Rivers Act. The upper section above Schaeffer Meadow Ranger Station and Airstrip, is accessible only by trail, to its headwaters.

A chartered flight or a horse trip through this ruggedly beautiful terrain will get you to the floating start at Schaeffer. Be prepared for the whitewater ride of your life! This river is the biggest whitewater river in the state, and may be unfloatable during peak runoff. This 27.3 mile joyride back to civilization, has nearly continuous Class II whitewater, with eight Class IV & V and lots of Class III thrown in. Having skill, good equipment, and a little courage is essential. Kayakers would have a ball in this section, but since we cannot get a kayak in an airplane or on a horse, we need to settle for a high quality and large raft. Kayakers could enter through Granite Creek downstream. The Class I designation, by legislature, begins at Schaeffer Creek. Wonderful informal camp spots exist wherever you choose, if you have a dry sleeping bag!

The first rapids are called "Three Forks", almost continuous whitewater for 2 miles with 3 Class IV rapids. The most demanding rapids are below Spruce Park Ranger Station, where three Class V rapids occur in succession. These three rapids are difficult to portage as you are in a canyon. Stop and try to get a look ahead and study the drops.

The Great Bear Wilderness boundary lies one mile above Bear Creek Access. Bear Creek marks the legal designation for the "Wild" portion end, and the "Recreational" portion beginning. However, for management purposes the Forest Service has extended the boundary to Essex Bridge Access. Glacier National Park boundary on the right bank is just below Bear Creek, and continues for the rest of the river. The combination of wilderness areas, Glacier National Park and the "Wild" designation of the upper river somewhat assures us that the river's future looks bright.

Those of you arriving at Bear Creek with a couple hours of sunlight left, may wish to continue on to Essex Bridge Access. This 4.6 mile extension takes you through two moderate rapids and past the Goat Lick. Goats can rarely be seen this close and in such a spectacular setting. A short trip east on Highway 2 may give you an opportunity to see a grizzly or black bear, near the corn spill west of Snowslip. Also, the John Stevens Canyon is a popular elk wintering range just east of West Glacier.

Below Essex Bridge moderate Class II rapids occur intermittently. Below Cascadilla Access to Moccasin Creek Access a few logjams may exist. Moccasin Creek begins the very popular whitewater stretch to West Glacier. This is an eight mile float, but only about two miles of it is heavy duty whitewater. Named rapids occur between mile "9.5" and "7.5". "Tunnel" Class II, "Bone-Crusher" II, "Jaws" IV, "Waterfall" II, "Narrows" III, "C.B.T." III, "Pumphouse" II. You can exit at the West Glacier Bridge or continue on a mile to the easier golf course exit.

Below the golf course the five remaining miles to Blankenship Bridge still carries "Recreational" designation and the right bank is still Glacier National Park. Eagles are a common sight in the fall in the McDonald Creek area, as these raptors gather for the kokanee spawning migration. The only rapids is a short and modest Class II at milepost "2". Blankenship Bridge offers adequate access.

GRANITE CREEK: Kayakers can find access to the Middle Fork by going up Highway 2, to 2.5 miles west of the summit at Marias Pass. Take road #569 up to Challenge Ranger Station. A half-mile carry will get you to Granite Creek and you can paddle the creek eight miles with a 75' f.p.m. gradient into the Middle Fork. There are a few downfall portages, but it is done. The confluence of Granite Creek is eleven river miles above the Spruce Park Rapids and five miles beyond Spruce Park is Bear Creek Access. This makes a 24 mile run.

Lower Middle Fork - Flathead River

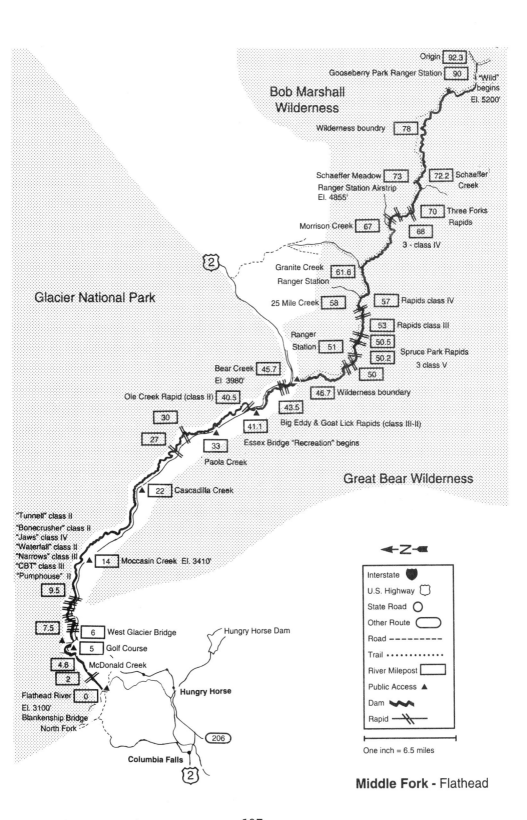

Bob Marshall
Wilderness

Origin 92.3
Gooseberry Park Ranger Station 90 "Wild" begins
El. 5200'

Wilderness boundry 78

Schaeffer Meadow 73 72.2 Schaeffer Creek
Ranger Station Airstrip
El. 4855'
70 Three Forks Rapids
Morrison Creek 67
68
3 - class IV

Granite Creek 61.6
Ranger Station

Glacier National Park

25 Mile Creek 58   57 Rapids class IV

53 Rapids class III
Ranger Station 51 50.5
50.2 Spruce Park Rapids
3 class V
50

Bear Creek 45.7   46.7 Wilderness boundary
El. 3980'

Ole Creek Rapid (class II) 40.5
43.5
30   41.1 Big Eddy & Goat Lick Rapids (class III-II)
27   33   Essex Bridge "Recreation" begins
Paola Creek

Great Bear Wilderness

22 Cascadilla Creek

"Tunnel" class II
"Bonecrusher" class II
"Jaws" class IV
"Waterfall" class II
"Narrows" class III
"CBT" class III
"Pumphouse" II

14 Moccasin Creek El. 3410'

9.5

7.5
6 West Glacier Bridge   Hungry Horse Dam
5 Golf Course
4.8   McDonald Creek
2
Flathead River 0   Hungry Horse
El. 3100'
Blankenship Bridge
North Fork
206
Columbia Falls
2

← Z ←

Interstate	⬟
U.S. Highway	🛡
State Road	◯
Other Route	⬭
Road	- - - - - - -
Trail	• • • • • • •
River Milepost	▭
Public Access	▲
Dam	〰
Rapid	⫽

One inch = 6.5 miles

Middle Fork - Flathead

FLATHEAD - NORTH FORK

ORIGIN:	Near Fernie, British Columbia, north of Polebridge, MT Canada border El. 3900'
END:	Joins Middle Fork at Blankenship Bridge to form Flathead River El. 3100'
LENGTH:	58.3 river miles in Montana (43 air miles)
FLOATABLE:	58.3 miles (Entire 58.3 miles is Class I designation)
SECTIONS:	Upper (25.3 mi.) Origin-Canada border "58.3" to Polebridge Access "33" Middle (17.9 mi.) Polebridge "33" to Big Creek Access "15.1" Lower (15.1 mi.) Big Creek "15.1" to End (Middle Fork confluence) "0"
DAMS:	None
WATERFALLS:	None
WHITEWATER:	Kintla Creek waves (Class II) mile "49" Big Creek Rapids (Class II) mile "14" Great Northern Rapids (Class III) mile "10.5" Fool Hen Rapids (2) (Class III) mile "8" and "7.2"
DANGERS:	An occasional logjam, whitewater.
DEWATERED:	Upper portion from Canada to Ford Access in fall.
PORTAGES:	None, if upper river flows are normal.
SPEC. AGENCIES:	Wild-Scenic-Recreation Corridor. Glacier National Park. Canada customs?
REGS - PERMITS:	No motors above Big Creek ("Scenic" designation). 10 hp limit below Big Creek. ("Recreation" desig.)
ACCESS-SHUTTLE:	Quite good-using North Fork road and a few access sites.
SERVICES:	All services Columbia Falls, MT - limited at Polebridge, MT (gas, food, cabins). Scenic and fishing raft trips available.

CAMPING:	Big Creek Campground and a few access sites.
GAMEFISH:	Upper - Cutthroat, Dolly Varden (bull trout) Middle & Lower - Also kokanee
VESSEL:	Any moderately-sized craft (except extreme upper-if flows are low) small raft, canoe
SKILL LEVEL:	Beginner to Intermediate (CAUTION - Whitewater or portage)

FLOAT TIMES: (Non-stop)

	High	Ave.	Low
Canada border to Ford (14.3 mi.)	2 hr.	4 hr.	6 hr.
Polebridge (11 mi.)	1.5	3	4
Big Creek (17.9 mi.)	2.5	5	6.5
Glacier Rim (11.1 mi.)	1.5	3	4
Blankenship Bridge (4 mi.)	.5	1.5	2

FLOW INFO: (406) 449-5263 USGS - Helena

HYDROGRAPH

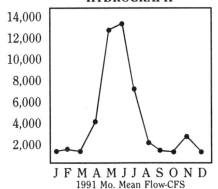

1991 Mo. Mean Flow-CFS

Gage Sta: Milepost "3.7"
Drain Area: 1,548 sq. mi.
Ave. Flow: (60 years) 2,974 cfs
Ext. Max: 69,100 cfs - 18.6' rod 6/9/64
Ext. Min: 198 cfs - .86' rod 1/8/53
Gradient: 800' in 58.3 miles = 13.7' pma
Float Grad: Same
Clarity: Clear
Temp: Jan. 32° F.
      Apr. 40° F.
      Jul. 55° F.
      Oct. 43° F.

DRAINAGE:	(West) Flathead, Clark Fork, Pend Oreille, Columbia,
MAPS:	BLM - #9 "Whitefish" (upper) - #10 "Kalispell" USFS - Flathead NF (North) (Best Map) USGS - "Kalispell" Sp. - "Glacier National Park" (USGS topographic) "Three Forks - Flathead River" (GN Hist. Soc.) CO. - Flathead

FLATHEAD - NORTH FORK

The Kootenai called this stream "Wolf Tail". The North Fork like the rest of the Flathead system is part of the National Wild and Scenic River system. The river begins in British Columbia at McEvoy Creek and flows 47 miles in Canada before reaching the border at milepost "58.3". "Scenic" designation begins here and the entire river has Class I designation. Glacier National Park boundary is along the left bank the entire river. These designations help assure us that this river will continue in its natural state.

Floating can begin right at the border at a fine access site. The first portion down to Ford Access can be low in the fall which might slow your float time and force a few drags across riffles. Some moderate Class II waves at the mouth of Kintla Creek during high flows can be skirted on the right.

Below Ford, floating is possible the entire year. Seeing herds of elk or an occasional bear or moose can be expected. Any moderately sized vessel is adequate in this stretch. Intermediate skills are necessary in this upper section. Polebridge has an access at the Glacier National Park bridge.

Beginners can handle the section between Polebridge and Big Creek, watching carefully for an occasional partial logjam, during normal conditions. Beginners should not attempt it in the spring when the river is really cookin'. The "Scenic" designation ends and the "Recreational" designation begins legally at Camas Bridge. However, for management purposes the Forest Service has extended it to Big Creek Access.

Below Big Creek, four moderate rapids occur intermittently with deep, beautiful green pools and canyon walls. Rafts or canoes are the best vessel for this lower section and at least intermediate skills are necessary. Lots of open canoes end up swamped in "Fool Hen" rapids. Just two miles above Great Northern Flats Access is a short class II rapid and another class III rapid lies 1.5 mile below. Fool Hen rapids are really two class III rapids located at mile "8" and "7.2". Long waves are formed after the rapids. One mile below Canyon Creek is the Glacier Rim Access or you can float on four miles to the Blankenship Bridge Access and the mainstem of the Flathead River.

Fishing in the North Fork is spotty. Cutthroat and bull trout are native to the area with a small kokanee salmon spawning run in the fall. The Flathead system does not have the nutrients of some of the "Blue Ribbon" streams and the fishery is fragile. Fish do not grow fast and catch-and-release is good practice.

North Fork honeymoon

110

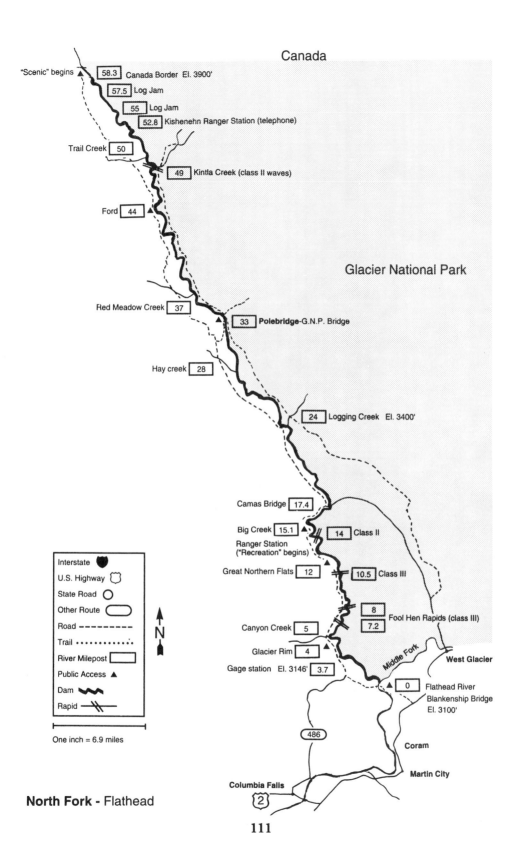

Canada

"Scenic" begins ▲

58.3 Canada Border El. 3900'

57.5 Log Jam

55 Log Jam

52.8 Kishenehn Ranger Station (telephone)

Trail Creek 50

49 Kintla Creek (class II waves)

Ford 44 ▲

Glacier National Park

Red Meadow Creek 37

33 ▲ Polebridge-G.N.P. Bridge

Hay creek 28

24 Logging Creek El. 3400'

Camas Bridge 17.4

Big Creek 15.1 ▲

14 Class II

Ranger Station
("Recreation" begins)

Great Northern Flats 12

10.5 Class III

8

Fool Hen Rapids (class III)

Canyon Creek 5

7.2

Glacier Rim 4 ▲

Gage station El. 3146' 3.7

Middle Fork

West Glacier

▲ 0 Flathead River
Blankenship Bridge
El. 3100'

486

Coram

Martin City

Interstate 🛡
U.S. Highway 🛡
State Road ◯
Other Route ⬭
Road --------
Trail ·········
River Milepost ☐
Public Access ▲
Dam 〰
Rapid ⫽

N

One inch = 6.9 miles

North Fork - Flathead

2

FLATHEAD - SOUTH FORK

ORIGIN: Confluence of Danaher and Youngs Creek above Big Prairie in the Bob Marshall Wilderness. El. 4800'

END: Flows into Flathead River at Hungry Horse, MT El. 3000'

LENGTH: 100 total miles (65.4 river miles and 34.6 miles Hungry Horse Reservoir) (80 air miles)

FLOATABLE: 65.4 river miles and Hungry Horse Reservoir is floatable. (60.1 miles are Class I - Youngs Creek to Hungry Horse Reservoir)

SECTIONS: Upper (38.4 mi.) Origin "100" to Take-Out "61.6"
Middle (21.7 mi.) Take-Out "61.6" to H. H. Res. "39.9"
Lower (39.9 mi.) H. H. Res. "39.9" to End (Flat. R.) "0"

DAMS: Hungry Horse (Forms Hungry Horse Reservoir and regulates flow below)

WATERFALLS: None

WHITEWATER: 7.8 miles - Meadow Creek Gorge (Floating not recommended) 4.5 miles
Below Hungry Horse Dam 3.3 miles Class III - IV depending on dam release.

DANGERS: Wilderness area and primitive setting. Meadow Creek Gorge. Sudden dam releases (below dam)

DEWATERED: Upper portion can get low in fall.

PORTAGES: Meadow Creek Gorge (5 mile hike or horse pack)
Take-Out point "61.6" to Cedar Flats Access (Harrison Creek) "57.1"
Dam - Major portage LEFT and over dam - difficult access below

SPEC. AGENCIES: Wild-Scenic Corridor. Bob Marshall Wilderness

REGS - PERMITS: No motors in wilderness area or in Wild or Scenic sections.

ACCESS-SHUTTLE: Difficult. Horse-pack or back-pack into wilderness. Middle and lower sections are also difficult to shuttle or access. Horse rentals and pack trips available at Spotted Bear.

SERVICES:	Gas, meals, cabins at guest ranches at Spotted Bear. Wilderness scenic and fishing raft trips available.
CAMPING:	Camping in wilderness is no problem. Numerous campgrounds and access sites in middle section.
GAMEFISH:	Cutthroat, bull trout, mountain whitefish.
VESSEL:	Entire river - Medium sized raft.
SKILL LEVEL:	Upper and Middle - Experienced Meadow Creek Gorge - Expert Below dam - Highly skilled
FLOAT TIMES:	Wilderness area - 2 or 3 days nonstop Cedar Flats to Spotted Bear (9.1 miles) 3.5 hours Spotted Bear to Hungry Horse Res. (8.1 mi.) 3.5 hrs.
FLOW INFO:	(406) 449-5263 USGS - Helena Also possible to phone Spotted Bear Ranger Station and they can radio Big Prairie Ranger Station 752-7345

Meadow Creek Gorge - S.F.

HYDROGRAPH

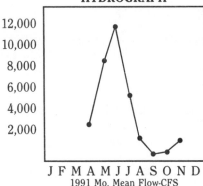

12,000
10,000
8,000
6,000
4,000
2,000

J F M A M J J A S O N D
1991 Mo. Mean Flow-CFS

Gage Sta: 1/2 mile above Twin Creek
Drain Area: 1,160 sq. mi. (at gage)
Ave. Flow: (18 years) 2,310 cfs
Ext. Max: 30,200 cfs - 15.2' ga. ht. 06/16/74
Ext. Min: 127 cfs - 4.13' ga. 11/30/79
Gradient: 1800' in 100 miles = 18' pma
Float Grad: Same
Clarity: Clear
Temp: Jan. 38⁰ F. Taken below H. H. Dam
      Apr. 40⁰ F.
      Jul. 45⁰ F.
      Oct. 41⁰ F.
Total Drain Area: 1663 square miles

DRAINAGE: (West) Flathead, Clark Fork, Pend Oreille, Columbia,

MAPS: BLM - #19 "Swan River" (upper) - #18 "Hungry
Horse Reservoir" (lower)
USFS - Flathead NF (South and North) (best map)
USGS - "Choteau" (upper) - "Cut Bank" (middle) -
"Kalispell" (lower)
Sp.   - "Bob Marshall, Great Bear, Scapegoat Wilder-
ness" (USFS topographic). "Three Forks-Flathead
River" (Glacier Natural Historical Society)
CO.   - Powell - Flathead

Meadow Creek Gorge - S.F.

114

FLATHEAD - SOUTH FORK

The South Fork is Montana's most pristine and inaccessible river. Accessible only by horse or backpacking forty miles up the river from Meadow Creek Trailhead, over the Swan Range from the Holland Lake areas or up the North Fork of the Blackfoot. Only a fortunate few ever experience this fabulous outdoor adventure.

The "Wild" designation awarded to this stream begins at its origin (Mile "100"). Floating from this point past Big Prairie Ranger Station and down to the White River confluence may be a problem if low water conditions exist. Below the White River ("83.1") floating can take place anytime, during the float season. The heat of summer is the most popular, but an autumn float is spectacular. The White River makes its presence known with its milky colored, glacier fed water. Camp anywhere that rings your bell, but treat your intrusion with respect for your hostess "Mother Nature". A raft large enough to carry your gear and an experienced skill level, are the pre-requisites for this trip that will remain in your fantasies for life. The cutthroat fishing is fabulous, but please keep only enough for the evening or breakfast frying pan. Fly or spin fishing is equally productive.

Immediately below the pack bridge at Black Bear Ranger Station is a short Class II rapid on the curve. Below Black Bear Creek are short Class II and III rapids at mile "65". The take out point at mile "61.6" is difficult to see and get stopped. A sign just upstream on the right bank gives you a quick clue, but the flow is fast and getting stopped can be difficult unless you are alert. This take out place is recommended rather than floating through the dangerous Meadow Creek Gorge. It is a three mile portage around the upper half of the gorge by trail, to the Meadow Creek Trailhead and packbridge. You may wish to pre-schedule an outfitter to meet you or pre-plan to carry your gear out. Below the trailhead it is a two mile portage down the road to the Cedar Flats walk in access at Harrison Creek ("57.1"). This is a steep 200 yard access that enables floating on to Spotted Bear ("48"). This is also a wonderful float! The "Wild" designation ends and the "Recreation" status begins at the Spotted Bear Ranger Station. Floating can continue on to Log Landing Access ("39.9") which is the inlet of Hungry Horse Reservoir. Boating and fishing on the reservoir is popular.

MEADOW CREEK GORGE: I have purposely left out details of the gorge because it is a myth or story of its own. May we regress back upstream to the take out at mile "61.6" and discuss the gorge to mile "57.1".

If you will pardon the personal experience, years ago while doing research on the gorge, I collected feedback from about fifty people in official positions or "people-in-the-know". I was told some ghostly stories that it never had been floated successfully nor could it be floated! Even today, some people live with that myth. My mind played games with me until I equipped myself with a modified two man raft and took off. I bounced my old football helmet off the cliffs and was happy I had a wet suit and life jacket on. A week later I did it again. I only desire to accomplish one thing with this story and that is to emphasize the importance of positive factual and precise information be shared between floaters. I have been "tuned-in" to gorge activity and am aware of perhaps twenty people who have floated it, but I cannot be certain that they did not portage the narrow places and drops.

Below the normal take out are two Class II rapids, followed by a Class III. A class IV with rocks forming a chute and dangerous four foot drop is just below. These rapids are followed by beautiful, deep, green pools. A narrow place 3 1/2' wide follows and soon a class III occurs. A class IV and class III follow, just above a very dangerous 5' drop in a 3 1/2' wide place. This drop could be a "keeper". Another class IV drop with a wave is just below. An area only 6' wide follows in a still pool. The water hydraulics are enormous in places. Time has eroded the cliffs, forming caves. Strong eddies could pull you in and under the rock. A possible exit occurs at Bunker Creek, but you have a 1/2 mile steep climb to the trailhead.

A mild class II rapid occurs at Bunker Creek where you enter the steep wall cliff area. A couple of sharp turns follow, directly under the packbridge, just above Meadow Creek, entering as a waterfall. The gorge is only a dozen feet wide through the quiet pool in this eery stretch. The Cedar Flats Access is 1.8 miles below the packbridge. Below the quiet pool the cliffs open up some and below are three class III rapids and two class IV drops. You can stop and scout these on the LEFT.

It really serves no purpose to float the gorge. Floating in a raft the size you would be coming out of the wilderness in would be difficult to portage often and long oars would be unusable. Lining or standing your raft on edge is also difficult. It is not desirable kayaking water and the three mile hike in makes it less appealing. I suggest those wishing to view the gorge do so from the packbridge or scaling along the cliffs.

I floated in late summer, but after a huge rain and the water was really cookin'. A week later it was easier, but more sharp rocks were exposed. I have made a map of the gorge and would be willing to share it with anyone interested.

Those interested in floating below Hungry Horse Dam must slide their vessel down a steep bank for 100 yards. Be cautious of sudden dam releases, but a couple miles of good whitewater can be found. "Devils Elbow" is a bouncy class IV consisting of two drops and a sharp turn. The river soon flattens out before joining the Flathead River at Hungry Horse, Montana. You can exit along the old river road a couple miles up from the Highway 2 bridge or at the bridge itself.

Lower South Fork

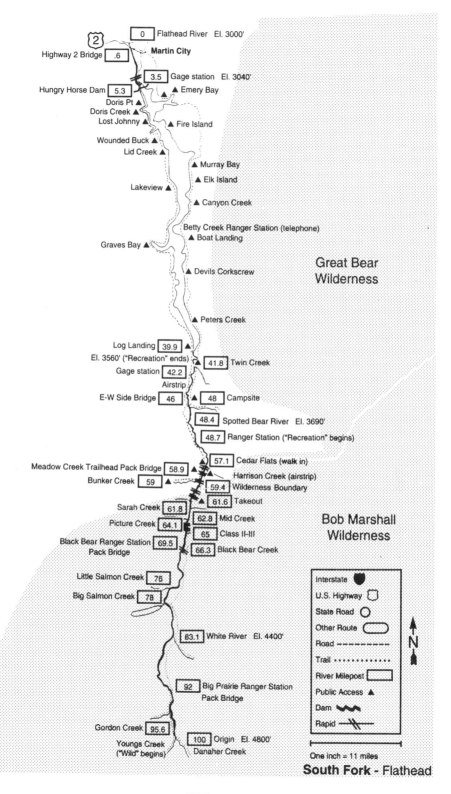

2

| 0 | Flathead River El. 3000' |

Highway 2 Bridge | .6 |
Martin City

| 3.5 | Gage station El. 3040'

Hungry Horse Dam | 5.3 | ▲ ▲ Emery Bay
Doris Pt ▲
Doris Creek ▲
Lost Johnny ▲ ▲ Fire Island

Wounded Buck ▲
Lid Creek ▲

▲ Murray Bay

▲ Elk Island

Lakeview ▲ ▲ Canyon Creek

Betty Creek Ranger Station (telephone)
▲ Boat Landing

Graves Bay ▲

▲ Devils Corkscrew

Great Bear Wilderness

▲ Peters Creek

Log Landing | 39.9 |
El. 3560' ("Recreation" ends) ▲ | 41.8 | Twin Creek
Gage station | 42.2 |
Airstrip
E-W Side Bridge | 46 | ▲ | 48 | Campsite
| 48.4 | Spotted Bear River El. 3690'
| 48.7 | Ranger Station ("Recreation" begins)

| 57.1 | Cedar Flats (walk in)
Meadow Creek Trailhead Pack Bridge | 58.9 | ▲
Harrison Creek (airstrip)
Bunker Creek | 59 | ▲ | 59.4 | Wilderness Boundary
| 61.6 | Takeout
Sarah Creek | 61.8 | ▲
Picture Creek | 64.1 | | 62.8 | Mid Creek
| 65 | Class II-III
Black Bear Ranger Station | 69.5 |
Pack Bridge | 66.3 | Black Bear Creek

Bob Marshall Wilderness

Little Salmon Creek | 76 |

Big Salmon Creek | 78 |

| 83.1 | White River El. 4400'

| 92 | Big Prairie Ranger Station
Pack Bridge

Gordon Creek | 95.6 |
Youngs Creek
("Wild" begins) | 100 | Origin El. 4800'
Danaher Creek

Interstate 🛡
U.S. Highway ⬡
State Road ◯
Other Route ⬭
Road – – – – – –
Trail • • • • • •
River Milepost ▭
Public Access ▲
Dam 〰
Rapid ⫽

N

One inch = 11 miles

South Fork - Flathead

FRENCHMAN

ORIGIN:	At Cypress Lake, near Eastend, Sask. Enters MT north of Saco, MT. El. 2420'
END:	Flows into Milk River northwest of Saco, MT El. 2150'
LENGTH:	76.3 total mi. (74.3 river mi. + Frenchman Res. 2 mi.) (35 air mi.)
FLOATABLE:	46 river mi. (Reservoir is floatable) Mi. "48" to "0"
SECTIONS:	Upper (28.3 mi.) Origin (Border) "76.3" to End of road "48" Middle (17.5 mi.) Road end "48" to Frenchman Dam "30.5" Lower (30.5 mi.) Dam "30.5" to End - Milk River "0"
DAMS:	Frenchman Dam (Forms Res. & controls flow) "30.5" 2 diversion dams Mi. "15" and "10"
WATERFALLS:	None
WHITEWATER:	None
DANGERS:	Frenchman dam, 2 diversion dams, irrigation jettys, remote area, fences, muddy roads.
DEWATERED:	Low most of the time, especially during irrigation season and fall.
PORTAGES:	Frenchman Dam (15' high-concrete spillway) portage RIGHT best. 2 diversion dams
SPEC. AGENCIES:	None
REGS - PERMITS:	None
ACCESS-SHUTTLE:	No formal access sites. Private land. Road goes up west side of river, across dam and eventually goes up east side of the middle section to end of road.
SERVICES:	None
CAMPING:	No campgrounds or access sites. Private land.
GAMEFISH:	Pike, catfish, walleye, sauger

VESSEL:	Canoe, small raft, small boat
SKILL LEVEL:	Intermediate
FLOAT TIMES:	Slow flow.
FLOW INFO:	(406) 449-5263 USGS - Helena

HYDROGRAPH

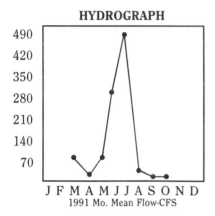

490
420
350
280
210
140
70

J F M A M J J A S O N D
1991 Mo. Mean Flow-CFS

Gage Sta: Intl. border
Drain Area: 2,120 sq. mi. (at this locale)
Ave. Flow: 80 cfs
Ext. Max: 22,700 cfs - 19.9' ga. ht. 4/15/52
Ext. Min: No flow often
Gradient: 270' in 76.3 mi. = 3.5' pma
Float Grad: Same
Clarity: Murky

DRAINAGE:	(East) Milk, Missouri, Mississippi, Gulf of Mexico
MAPS:	BLM - #7 "Bowdoin"
	USGS - "Glasgow"
	CO. - Phillips, Valley

Unfloatables - early spring

FRENCHMAN

The Frenchman River originates at Cypress Lake near Eastend, Saskatchewan. It flows for 281.1 miles in Canada before entering Montana, north of Saco. The river then flows for 76.3 miles before joining the Milk River. The Frenchman is called a river in Canada, but is often called a creek in Montana.

The upper 28 miles are unfloatable as no access exists in this remote and roadless countryside. The valley is quite pretty. Cottonwood and willow bottoms are surrounded by rolling prairie hills and an occasional bluff. The streambed is primarily silt and sand with undercut banks, however some gravel sections occur.

A road north of Saco parallels the river on the west, and crosses the Frenchman Dam and Reservoir. This road then eventually parallels the river again above the reservoir on the east bank. These roads can be extremely muddy when wet.

Floating can begin as high as the end of the road, where an old concrete ford crosses the river at milepost "48". No formal access sites or campgrounds exist, so bridge access must suffice. Bridges in two places are nearly 15 miles apart. Floating is not popular on the river, as the dam, two diversion dams, irrigation jettys and fences obstruct the river. The river is often low, due to lack of spring runoff and irrigation use. Fishing has not been good recently, however pike, catfish, walleye and sauger inhabit the stream.

An intermediate in a canoe, small boat or small raft can handle the river. The last place to exit on the Frenchman is at a county road bridge at milepost "2". Floating could continue on and into the Milk River, and downstream two miles to the Bjornberg Access.

Frenchman River

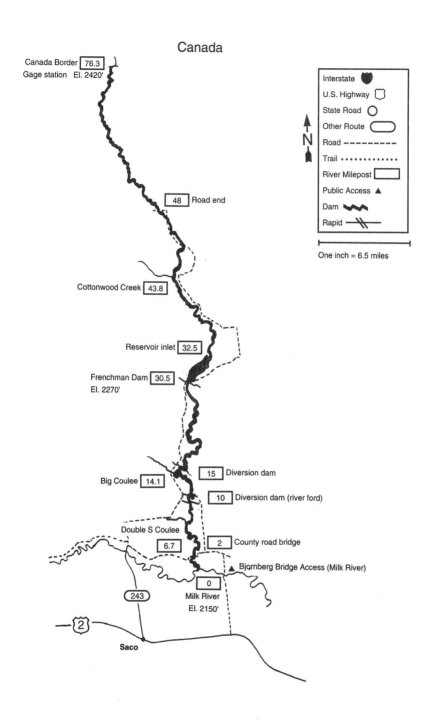

Canada

Canada Border [76.3]
Gage station   El. 2420'

Interstate	
U.S. Highway	
State Road	
Other Route	
Road	- - - - -
Trail	• • • • • • • •
River Milepost	☐
Public Access	▲
Dam	∿∿∿
Rapid	⧺

One inch = 6.5 miles

[48]   Road end

N

Cottonwood Creek [43.8]

Reservoir inlet [32.5]

Frenchman Dam [30.5]
El. 2270'

[15]   Diversion dam

Big Coulee [14.1]

[10]   Diversion dam (river ford)

Double S Coulee

[6.7]

[2]   County road bridge

▲ Bjornberg Bridge Access (Milk River)

[0]

(243)

Milk River
El. 2150'

(2)

Saco

Frenchman

121

GALLATIN & WEST FORK

ORIGIN:	Gallatin Lake in Yellowstone National Park in WY Enters MT near Highway #191 El. 7,000'
END:	Flows into Missouri River at Missouri River Headwaters State Park near Three Forks, MT. El. 4,000'
LENGTH:	100.5 river mi. (72 air mi.)
FLOATABLE:	88.8 mi. (Y.N.P. boundary (El. 6775') to End). (Class I = 85.4 mi. - Taylors Fork to Missouri River)
SECTIONS:	Upper (23.5 mi.) Origin (WY border) "100.5" to Red Cliff Camp "77" Middle (29.3 mi.) Red Cliff "77" to Gage Station Access "47.7" Lower (47.7 mi.) Gage Station "47.7" to End "0"
DAMS:	8 Diversion dams (See map)
WATERFALLS:	None
WHITEWATER:	13 mi. Deer Creek Access "66" to Squaw Creek Bridge Access "53" (Class IV) 15.4 mi. Taylor Creek Access "85.4" to West Fork Access "70" (Class II-III high water only)
DANGERS:	Diversion dams, fences, logjams, whitewater.
DEWATERED:	Below Gallatin Gateway bridges in the fall and above Red Cliff
PORTAGES:	Upper - None Middle - None Lower - 8 div. dams, numerous logjams and fences
SPEC. AGENCIES:	Upper - Yellowstone National Park
REGS - PERMITS:	Floating not allowed in Yellowstone National Park. No fishing from vessel above Gallatin Forks. 10 hp limit on all streams in Gallatin County.
ACCESS-SHUTTLE:	Easy. Highways and roads parallel and intersect frequently. Numerous access sites.
SERVICES:	All in Bozeman, MT. Upper river adequate. Commercial whitewater raft trips available.

CAMPING:	Upper & Middle - Numerous campgrounds and access sites. Lower - Adequate access sites and a few campgrounds.
GAMEFISH:	Upper - Rainbow, cutthroat, whitefish Middle - Rainbow, brown, brook, whitefish Lower - Brown, whitefish, rainbow
VESSEL:	Upper - Medium size raft, canoe (whitewater canoe or kayak when high) Middle - Large raft, kayak Lower - Small raft, canoe, (small boat below Gallatin Forks)
SKILL LEVEL:	Upper - Inter.to Experienced (depending on flow) Middle - Experienced to Highly skilled Lower - Intermediate
FLOAT TIMES:	Upper - High water-fast. Low water - much slower Middle - Good float speed. Lower - Slow (Slow water, many obstacles to portage)
FLOW INFO:	(406) 449-5263 USGS - Helena

HYDROGRAPH

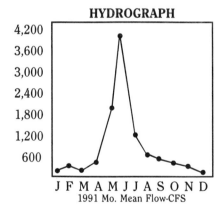

4,200
3,600
3,000
2,400
1,800
1,200
600

J F M A M J J A S O N D
1991 Mo. Mean Flow-CFS

Gage Sta: Milepost "47.4"
Drain Area: 825 sq. mi. (at this location)
Ave. Flow: (61 years) 806 cfs
Ext. Max: 9,100 cfs - 7.38' ga. ht. 6/17/74
Ext. Min: 117 cfs - .68' ga. ht. 1/19/35
Gradient: 3,000' in 100.5 mi. = 30.0' pma
Float Grad: 2775' in 88.8 mi. = 31.3' pma
Clarity: Clear to murky (lower)
Temp: Jan. 32^0 F.
       Apr. 46^0 F.
       Jul. 71^0 F.
       Oct. 46^0 F.
Total Drain Area: 1,830 sq. mi.

DRAINAGE:	(East) Missouri, Mississippi, Gulf of Mexico
MAPS:	BLM - #33 "Madison" (best map) USFS - Gallatin NF (Origin to Four Corners only) USGS - "Bozeman" CO. - Gallatin

123

GALLATIN & WEST FORK

Although the true main stem is only 12.4 miles long, it is generally accepted that the west stem is a continuation of the Gallatin River and the east stem is a fork flowing into it. Lewis & Clark named the river after the Secretary of Treasury Albert Gallatin. The origin is at Gallatin Lake within Yellowstone National Park in Wyoming and flows 15 miles before reaching the Montana border, still within Yellowstone National Park, at milepost "100.5". Since floating streams is not allowed in Yellowstone National Park, floating can begin at the park boundary "88.8" in a beautiful alpine meadow.

Taylor Creek Access "85.4" is where the class I designation begins. If flow is low, Red Cliff Campground "77" or West Fork "70" is a better place to begin and avoid the boulder gardens above. When water is high these boulder gardens create moderate whitewater.

Deer Creek Access "66" marks the beginning of the 13 mile Gallatin whitewater. One mile below, a Class III rapid exists and one mile below that, is the Portal Creek rapid (class IV). Below Greek Creek "59" the more frequent rapids occur. "Hilarity Hole" a class IV at mile "57.5", "Straightaway" (class IV) at "56.5" and "House Rock", another Class IV, just below Cascade Creek Bridge Access, create most of the excitement. Below House Rock is the one mile, continuous Class II-III boulder garden known as the "Mad Mile". Squaw Creek Access is the end of the whitewater.

A dangerous diversion dam, which requires portage LEFT, is at mile "46". Use the left channel at Gallatin Gateway Bridges "39" to avoid the dangerous diversion dam 1 mile downstream in the right channel!

Axtell Bridge Access "36", is the beginning of the most miserable portion of the river. Four diversion dams, fences, logjams and many channels can make this stretch frustrating. Below Sheds Bridge "32.7" on Highway 84 these same obstacles appear but are less frequent. Diversion Dams at mile "30" and "20" both require portages RIGHT. Central Park Access, under the I-90 Bridge offers easier floating for the last 19.2 miles of river.

At present, fishing is spotty on the river, and fishing from a vessel is not permitted above Gallatin Forks "12.4". The Gallatin offers diverse scenery, from the alpine meadows to the canyons, and the cottonwood groves on the valley floor. The Gallatin joins the Madison and Jefferson at Missouri Headwaters State Park, near Three Forks to form the Missouri River.

House Rock Rapids

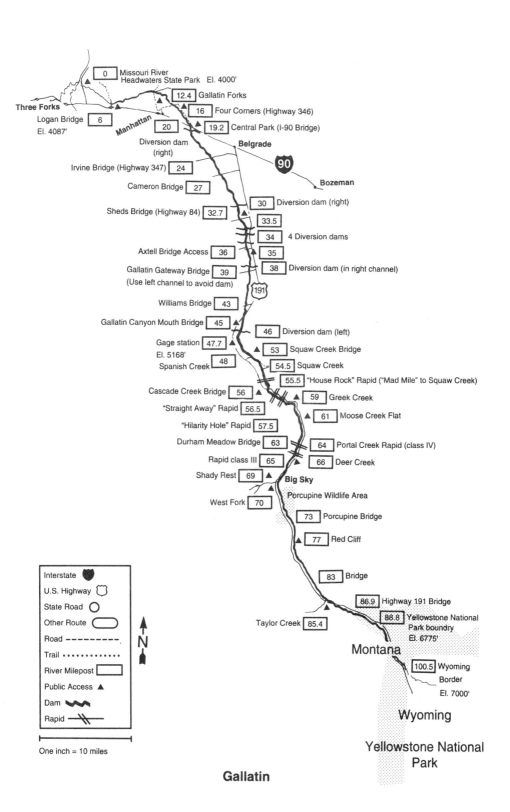

0	Missouri River Headwaters State Park El. 4000'
12.4	Gallatin Forks
16	Four Corners (Highway 346)
19.2	Central Park (I-90 Bridge)

Three Forks

Logan Bridge **6**
El. 4087'

Manhattan **20**

Diversion dam (right)

Belgrade

Irvine Bridge (Highway 347) **24**

Cameron Bridge **27**

Bozeman

Sheds Bridge (Highway 84) **32.7**

30	Diversion dam (right)
33.5	
34	4 Diversion dams
35	

Axtell Bridge Access **36**

Gallatin Gateway Bridge **39**
(Use left channel to avoid dam)

| **38** | Diversion dam (in right channel) |

191

Williams Bridge **43**

Gallatin Canyon Mouth Bridge **45**

| **46** | Diversion dam (left) |
| **53** | Squaw Creek Bridge |

Gage station **47.7**
El. 5168'

Spanish Creek **48**

| **54.5** | Squaw Creek |
| **55.5** | "House Rock" Rapid ("Mad Mile" to Squaw Creek) |

Cascade Creek Bridge **56**

| **59** | Greek Creek |

"Straight Away" Rapid **56.5**

"Hilarity Hole" Rapid **57.5**

| **61** | Moose Creek Flat |

Durham Meadow Bridge **63**

| **64** | Portal Creek Rapid (class IV) |

Rapid class III **65**

| **66** | Deer Creek |

Shady Rest **69**

Big Sky

Porcupine Wildlife Area

West Fork **70**

73	Porcupine Bridge
77	Red Cliff
83	Bridge
86.9	Highway 191 Bridge
88.8	Yellowstone National Park boundry El. 6775'

Taylor Creek **85.4**

Montana

| **100.5** | Wyoming Border El. 7000' |

Wyoming

Yellowstone National Park

Gallatin

Interstate	
U.S. Highway	
State Road	
Other Route	
Road	- - - - - - -
Trail	• • • • • • •
River Milepost	
Public Access	▲
Dam	〰
Rapid	—

N

One inch = 10 miles

JEFFERSON

ORIGIN:	Confluence of Beaverhead and Bighole rivers, north of Twin Bridges, MT. El. 4600'
END:	Joins Madison and Gallatin rivers to form Missouri River at Headwaters State Park north of Three Forks, MT. El. 4,000'
LENGTH:	83.5 river mi. (48 air mi.)
FLOATABLE:	83.5 mi. (Entire 83.5 mi. is Class I)
SECTIONS:	Upper (44.5 mi.) Origin "83.5" to Cardwell Br. "39" Middle (30.5 mi.) Cardwell "39" to Hwy #10 "8.5" Lower (8.5 mi.) Drouillard Campground "8.5" to "0"
DAMS:	Parsons Bridge diversion dam Parrot Castle Access diversion dam
WATERFALLS:	None
WHITEWATER:	None
DANGERS:	2 diversion dams
DEWATERED:	No
PORTAGES:	2 - Portage each diversion dam LEFT
SPEC. AGENCIES:	None
REGS - PERMITS:	10 hp motor limit on all streams in Madison, Jefferson, and Gallatin County (Entire river)
ACCESS-SHUTTLE:	Numerous access sites with road access not overly difficult.
SERVICES:	All services - Twin Bridges, Whitehall, Three Forks.
CAMPING:	A few campgrounds and numerous access sites.
GAMEFISH:	Brown, rainbow
VESSEL:	Any moderate-size craft (CAUTION - portages)
SKILL LEVEL:	Beginner

FLOAT TIMES: Upper & Middle - Moderate flow
                    Lower - Very slow.

FLOW INFO: (406) 449-5263 USGS - Helena

HYDROGRAPH

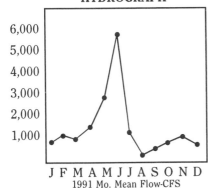

J F M A M J J A S O N D
1991 Mo. Mean Flow-CFS

6,000
5,000
4,000
3,000
2,000
1,000

Gage Sta: Highway 10 Bridge by Three Forks.
Drain Area: 9,532 sq. mi.
Ave. Flow: (13 years) 2,061 cfs
Ext. Max: 15,900 cfs - 8.06' ga. ht. 5/24/81
Ext. Min: 43 cfs - 1.31' ga. ht. 9/07/88
Gradient: 600' in 83.5 mi. = 7.2' pma
Float Grad: Same
Clarity: Cloudy
Temp: Jan. 32^0 F.
        Apr. 52^0 F.
        Jul. 78^0 F.
        Oct. 48^0 F.

DRAINAGE: (East) Missouri, Mississippi, Gulf of Mexico

MAPS: BLM - #32 "Dillon" (upper) - #33 "Madison" (lower)
             USFS - Deer Lodge NF (Origin to L & C Caverns) -
             Beaverhead NF (upper)
             USGS - "Dillon" (upper) - "Bozeman" (lower)
             CO.   - Madison, Jefferson, Gallatin, Broadwater

Parsons Diversion Dam (Jefferson)

127

JEFFERSON

Named in honor of their expedition promoter and president, Thomas Jefferson in 1805, by Lewis & Clark. The river begins at the confluence of the Beaverhead and Bighole Rivers, near Twin Bridges, MT at milepost "83.5".

The river meanders through brushy, cottonwood bottoms, surrounded by numerous backwater sloughs; vital to the waterfowl, upland birds and other wildlife in the area. Irrigation withdrawals and returns are evident in the often cloudy water. Excessive nutrients in the river cause rapid growth of algae late in the summer, which makes spin fishing difficult. Most fishermen fish wet flies or streamers.

Below LaHood, near the Lewis & Clark Caverns State Park the river enters a semi-arid canyon before sprawling out again on a wide valley floor.

Some effects of the mineralization in the valley are apparent. Gold, silver, lead, zinc and copper exist, and hopefully their presence will not cause the valley to further deteriorate.

Beginners can handle the entire river in any moderately sized vessel, if flows are normal. A 10 hp motor limitation is in effect for the entire river. A diversion dam at Parsons Bridge Access "63" usually needs to be portaged LEFT. High water often washes out some boulders and forms a chute that skilled paddlers can navigate. Scouting this dangerous dam is important. The diversion dam at Parrot Castle Access "55" also requires portage. Below these diversion dams numerous access sites occur at bridges making short floats possible.

Jefferson River

128

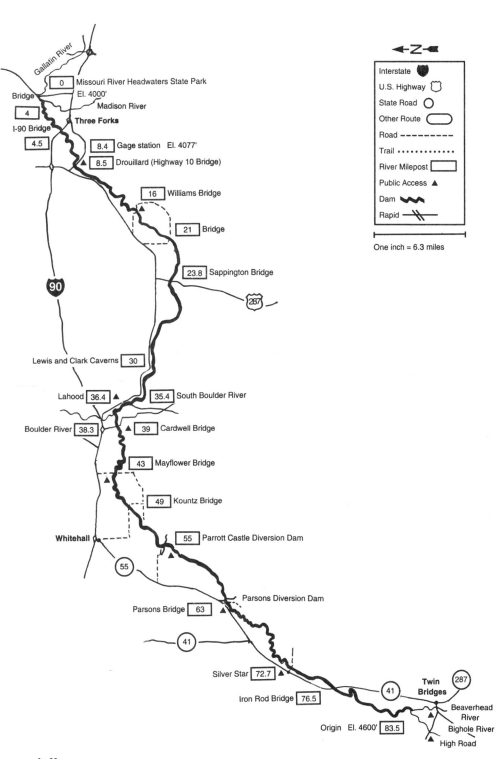

One inch = 6.3 miles

Jefferson

JOCKO

ORIGIN:	Jocko Lakes east of Arlee, MT. El. 4750'
END:	Flows into Flathead River at Dixon, MT. El. 2500'
LENGTH:	39.5 miles (25 air miles)
FLOATABLE:	25 miles (Bridge at - Mi. "25" to Flathead River "0")
SECTIONS:	Upper (14.5 mi.) Origin "39.5" to Big Knife Br. "25" Middle (7.3 mi.) Bridge "25" to Hwy 93 Br. "17.7" Lower (17.7 mi.) Highway 93 Br. "17.7" to End - "0"
DAMS:	Ravalli Diversion Dam Mi. "7.5"
WATERFALLS:	None
WHITEWATER:	None
DANGERS:	Fences, logs, irrigation jettys, Ravalli Diversion Dam
DEWATERED:	Can be low in fall.
PORTAGES:	Ravalli Diversion Dam (.2 mi. below Highway 200 Bridge) portage RIGHT. Also fences and logjams
SPEC. AGENCIES:	Flathead Indian Reservation (entire river)
REGS - PERMITS:	Recreation or fishing permit (Tribal)
ACCESS-SHUTTLE:	Highway 93 or 200 parallel the river. Only formal access site at Mi. "5". Private property.
SERVICES:	Limited in Arlee, Ravalli, Dixon, MT
CAMPING:	No formal campgrounds, and only 1 access site. Private property.
GAMEFISH:	Rainbow, cutthroat, brown, brook, bulls, whitefish
VESSEL:	Canoe, small raft, small boat
SKILL LEVEL:	Intermediate
FLOAT TIMES:	Moderate flow.
FLOW INFO:	(406) 449-5263 USGS - Helena

HYDROGRAPH

600	
500	
400	
300	
200	
100	

J F M A M J J A S O N D
1991 Mo. Mean Flow-CFS

Gage Sta: Dixon, MT
Drain Area: 380 sq. mi.
Ave. Flow: (2 years) 227 cfs
Ext. Max: 1130 cfs - 3.35' ga. ht. 5/19/91
Ext. Min: 95 cfs 12/30/90
Gradient: 2250' in 39.5 mi. = 57.0' pma
Float Grad: 950' in 25.0 mi. = 38.0' pma
Clarity: Clear

DRAINAGE: (West) Flathead, Clark Fork, Pend Oreille, Columbia,

MAPS: BLM - #20 "Seeley Lake" (extreme upper) - #12 "Plains" (lower)
USFS - Flathead NF (South) upper - Lolo NF upper
USGS - "Choteau" (upper) - "Wallace" (lower)
CO. - Lake, Sanders

Bull Trout - Once upon a time - common

131

JOCKO

The Jocko River is named after Jocko Finley, a member of the Northwest Fur Company. The origin of the river is at the outlet of Lower Jocko Lake.

The upper river is small and tumbles down from the mountain basin through much downfall. The river gains volume after the South and Middle Forks enter.

Floating can begin as high as the county road bridge "25", near Big Knife Creek. This bridge is east of Arlee, at the base of the mountains. The six mile float down to the fish hatchery and its walk-in access, at Arlee, has a few barb wire fences and logjams.

Below the fish hatchery "19", floating gets better as there are fewer man-made obstacles. The Highway 93 bridge at river milepost "17.7", offers ingress or egress.

Fishing gets easier below the Highway 93 bridge as bank vegetation is not as thick. Rainbow, cutts, browns, brookies, bulls and whitefish inhabit the stream. The entire river flows through the Flathead Indian Reservation or private land. Stay within the high water marks, or preferably, seek landowner permission. If you bank fish or camp, a tribal fishing or recreational use permit is required.

An intermediate can handle the river if flow is normal. A small raft, canoe or small boat will work, however the river can be low in the fall. A curvy stream, fences, logjams, a few irrigation jettys and the very dangerous Ravalli Diversion Dam command caution.

Below the Highway 93 bridge, bridges can be found at river mileposts "14" and "10.8". The Highway 200 bridge "7.7" at Ravalli, offers steep access. Just below this bridge is a large diversion dam "7.5", that must be portaged RIGHT. A fishing access and campsite is found at milepost "5". This access is along the south boundary of the Moiese Bison Range. Bighorn sheep and other wildlife can often be spotted.

Below this fishing access is the Highway 212 bridge ".8". This bridge is the last opportunity to exit the Jocko. Floating the balance of the river would require a 1/2 mile float down to the Flathead River to the Dixon Access, located on the left bank.

Jocko River

132

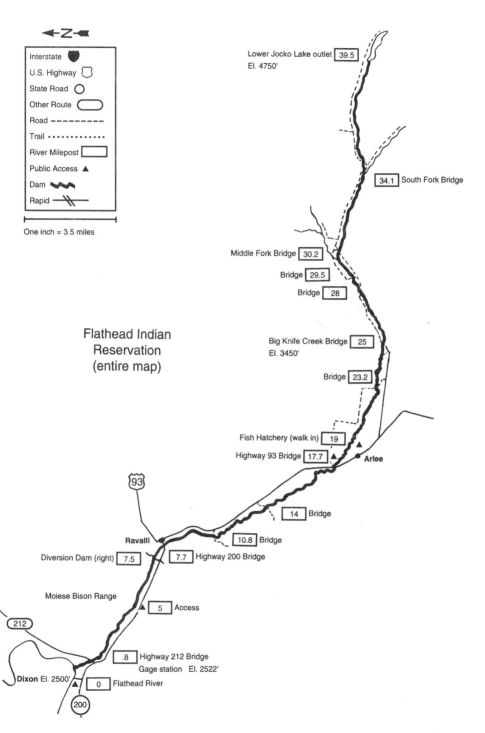

Interstate

U.S. Highway

State Road

Other Route

Road ----------

Trail ....

River Milepost

Public Access ▲

Dam

Rapid

One inch = 3.5 miles

Lower Jocko Lake outlet 39.5
El. 4750'

34.1 South Fork Bridge

Middle Fork Bridge 30.2

Bridge 29.5

Bridge 28

Flathead Indian
Reservation
(entire map)

Big Knife Creek Bridge 25
El. 3450'

Bridge 23.2

Fish Hatchery (walk in) 19

Highway 93 Bridge 17.7 ▲

Arlee

93

14 Bridge

Ravalli

10.8 Bridge

Diversion Dam (right) 7.5

7.7 Highway 200 Bridge

Moiese Bison Range

▲ 5 Access

212

.8 Highway 212 Bridge
Gage station El. 2522'

Dixon El. 2500'

▲ 0 Flathead River

200

Jocko

133

JUDITH

ORIGIN: Confluence of Middle & South Forks above Sapphire Village, southwest of Utica, MT El. 5,000'

END: Flows into Missouri near Judith Landing Br. Access, Hwy 236 north of Winnifred, MT. El. 2440'

LENGTH: 129.8 river miles
(80 air miles)

FLOATABLE: 103 mi. (Hobson, MT. (El. 4,000') to Missouri River)
Class I des. is 72.3 mi. - Big Springs Cr. to Missouri

SECTIONS: Upper (26.8 mi.) Origin "129.8" to Hobson "103"
Middle (30.7 mi.) Hobson "103" to Big Sp. Cr. "72.3"
Lower (72.3 mi.) Big Sp. Cr. "72.3" to Missouri "0"

DAMS: None

WATERFALLS: None

WHITEWATER: None, except short boulder garden at milepost "62"

DANGERS: Remote country, fences, irrigation jettys

DEWATERED: Could be dewatered in fall.

PORTAGES: None, except some fences or irrigation jettys

SPEC. AGENCIES: None

REGS - PERMITS: None

ACCESS-SHUTTLE: Access and shuttle is not easy and round-about.

SERVICES: Limited at Utica and Hobson, MT.

CAMPING: Difficult. Private land basically. Seek permission

GAMEFISH: Upper - Rainbow, brown, brook, cutthroat
Middle - Above plus sauger
Lower - Brown, sauger, burbot, catfish, shovelnose sturgeon

VESSEL: Canoe, medium raft, small boat

SKILL LEVEL: Beginner

FLOAT TIMES: Moderate to slow current.

FLOW INFO: (406) 449-5263 USGS - Helena
Lewis & Clark NF (Jefferson division - Judith Dist. at
Stanford) 566-2292

HYDROGRAPH

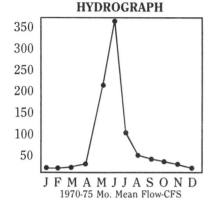

1970-75 Mo. Mean Flow-CFS

Gage Sta: Utica, MT (Discontinued)
Drain Area: 328 sq. mi. (at this location)
Ave. Flow: (16 years) 60 cfs
Ext. Max: 1020 cfs 6/09/64
Ext. Min: .5 cfs 3/17/62
Gradient: 2560' in 129.8 mi. = 19.7' pma
Float Grad: 1560' in 103.0 mi. = 15.1' pma
Clarity: Cloudy to murky
Temp: Aug. 66⁰ F.

DRAINAGE: (East) Missouri, Mississippi, Gulf of Mexico

MAPS: BLM - #24 "Castles" #25 "Snowy" (upper) - #15
"Judith" (lower)
USFS - Lewis & Clark NF (Jefferson Div.) (upper)
USGS - "White Sulphur" & "Roundup" (upper) -
"Lewistown" (lower)
CO.   - Judith Basin, Fergus

Muskrat Castle

JUDITH

The Judith River headwaters in the Little Belt Mountains and the main stem begins at the confluence of the Middle and South Forks, above Sapphire Village. Captain Clark on 5/29/1805 named the stream Judieths River, for Julia (Judy) Hancock of Virginia, whom he later married.

. The upper section down to Hobson, is infested with beaver dams and fences and for the most part, unfloatable. Rock hounding in the Yogo Gulch area is a popular pastime. "Montana Diamonds", gold, silver and copper are traceable in the Moccasin and Judith Mountains and evidence of the old mining activity still exists.

Below Hobson "103", floating is possible if flow is normal, with county bridges being the only possibilities of access. Ross Fork "87.7" adds a little volume to the stream. Big Spring Creek "72.3", a wonderful fishing stream, enters on private property. The class I designation begins here and the current owners are very congenial. A detailed map can guide you to this secluded spot on the west bank. Most floaters however, put in just below at a county road bridge at milepost "66". A 1/2 mile long boulder garden occurs at mile "62" and can be slightly bouncy. This section of the river meanders through a brushy, but otherwise open valley. Fishing is "so-so" above this point for numerous trout species and sauger.

At Highway #81 Bridge "60", the remote portion of the float begins. The first 1/2 dozen miles the river flows through rolling prairie country and at Warm Springs Creek "53.4", the scenery improves with cottonwood groves and some sparse coniferous and juniper growth. The White Cliffs area "44" is very pretty. A private game ranch exists about mile "29", perhaps enabling you to focus on some elk on the surrounding hillsides. Brown trout along with a warmer water fishery would offer a stubborn fisherperson a mixed creel.

Anderson Bridge "21.9", west of Winnifred, MT is the only access along this extended river trip. 79 Coulee at milepost "12.6" offers floaters a landmark as some of the ranchers ford the river in their 4x4 during normal flow. The current slows below this point, for the remaining dozen mile journey to the Missouri. Paddling through a huge cottonwood bottom you finally reach "Old Misery", and an .8 mile jaunt downstream takes you to Judith Landing Campground and ramp access.

Practiced beginners in a canoe, medium raft or even a small boat can handle the entire Judith; with caution for the inherent dangers of fences, boulder garden, and a few irrigation jettys. Bear in mind the remoteness of the area!

Judith River

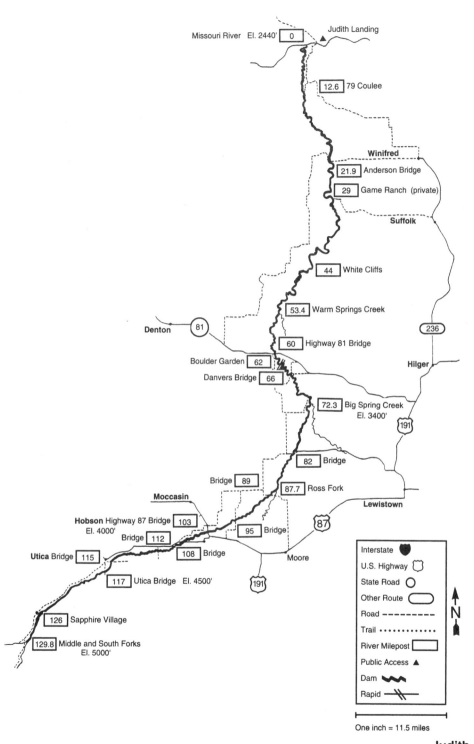

Missouri River El. 2440' [0] ▲ Judith Landing

[12.6] 79 Coulee

Winifred

[21.9] Anderson Bridge

[29] Game Ranch (private)

Suffolk

[44] White Cliffs

[53.4] Warm Springs Creek

(81)
Denton

[60] Highway 81 Bridge

(236)

Boulder Garden [62]

Hilger

Danvers Bridge [66]

[72.3] Big Spring Creek
El. 3400'

(191)

[82] Bridge

Bridge [89]

Moccasin

[87.7] Ross Fork

Lewistown

Hobson Highway 87 Bridge [103]
El. 4000'

Bridge [112]

[95] Bridge

(87)

Utica Bridge [115]

[108] Bridge

Moore

[117] Utica Bridge El. 4500'

(191)

[126] Sapphire Village

[129.8] Middle and South Forks
El. 5000'

Interstate	⬢
U.S. Highway	⬭
State Road	◯
Other Route	⬭
Road	- - - - - -
Trail	• • • • • • •
River Milepost	▭
Public Access	▲
Dam	〰
Rapid	╫

N

One inch = 11.5 miles

Judith

137

KOOTENAI

ORIGIN:	Near Radium Hot Springs, BC. Enters MT near Eureka. El. 2400'
END:	Flows into Idaho El. 1800' (back into Canada and the Columbia River)
LENGTH:	99.6 total mi. (50.3 river mi. + Koocanusa Res. 49.3 mi.) (48 air mi.)
FLOATABLE:	50.3 river mi. (Libby Dam to Idaho border) - Koocanusa Reservoir is floatable. Class I is entire 50.3 river mi.
SECTIONS:	Upper (49.3 mi.) Origin (Canada border) "99.6" to Libby Dam "50.3" Middle (28.6 mi.) Libby Dam "50.3" to Kootenai Falls "21.7" Lower (21.7 mi.) Kootenai Falls "21.7" to End - Idaho border "0"
DAMS:	Libby Dam (Forms Koocanusa Res. and reg. flow)
WATERFALLS:	Kootenai Falls
WHITEWATER:	3.5 mi. China Rapids-portage Kootenai Falls - Kootenai Falls gorge (Class IV) Also Jennings Rapid and Yaak River waves Class III
DANGERS:	Waterfall, whitewater, sudden dam releases
DEWATERED:	No
PORTAGES:	Kootenai Falls (portage LEFT) Jennings (LEFT) - China Rapids (LEFT) Gorge Rapids (LEFT along Railroad) Yaak River waves (RIGHT thru Yaak River)
SPEC. AGENCIES:	None
REGS - PERMITS:	None
ACCESS-SHUTTLE:	Fair with roads, bridges, access sites and close to highways.
SERVICES:	All in Libby or Troy, MT Commercial float fishing trips available.
CAMPING:	A few campgrounds and access sites.

GAMEFISH:	Upper (Reservoir) - Kokanee, cutthroat, rainbow Middle - Rainbow, cutthroat, big hybrids. Lower - Also white sturgeon (below Kootenai Falls) (Illegal to fish white sturgeon)
VESSEL:	Upper (Reservoir) - All craft Middle - Any moderate-sized vessel to Libby Bridge. Medium raft, whitewater canoe, kayak below Lower - Medium raft, whitewater canoe, kayak through gorge. Any moderate-sized vessel below
SKILL LEVEL:	Upper (Reservoir) - Beginner Middle - Intermediate to Libby. Experienced below to Kootenai Falls. Lower - Highly skilled in gorge below Kootenai Falls. Beginner below (caution Yaak River waves)
FLOAT TIMES:	3,000 cfs (normal), 4500 - 8000 (good floating), 12,000 (Great Whitewater), 20,000-25,000 (not rec- ommended). Dam dictates flow.
FLOW INFO:	(406) 293-3421 (Recorded dam flow-release info.) 449-5263 USGS - Helena

HYDROGRAPH

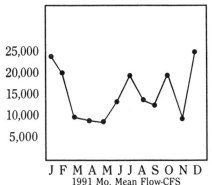

25,000
20,000
15,000
10,000
5,000

J F M A M J J A S O N D
1991 Mo. Mean Flow-CFS

Gage Sta: Just below Libby Dam
Drain Area: 8,985 sq. mi. (at this location)
Ave. Flow: (20 years) 11,210 cfs
Ext. Max: 47,200 cfs - 27.5' ga. ht. 8/5/74
Ext. Min: 1,900 cfs 1/29/72
Gradient: 600' in 99.6 mi. = 6.0' pma
Float Grad: 300' in 50.3 mi. = 6.0' pma
Clarity: Clear
Temp: Jan. 38° F.
        Apr. 39° F.
        Jul. 53° F.
        Oct. 51° F.
Total Drain Area: 11,740 sq. mi. (border)

DRAINAGE:	(West) Columbia, Pacific Ocean
MAPS:	BLM - #4 "Yaak" (upper) - #5 "Libby" (lower) USFS - Kootenai NF (Best map) USGS - "Kalispell" CO. - Lincoln

KOOTENAI

The free-flowing course of the Kootenai was shortened considerably in 1973, upon completion of the 400' high Libby Dam. The resulting Koocanusa Reservoir, is backed up a considerable distance into Canada. Another hydro-electric project just below, is now pending before the Federal Energy Regulatory Commission.

The Indians called the river "Flatbow", and it was named later for these Kutenai Indians (People of the waters). The Kootenai originates in Kootenay National Park in British Columbia.

Boating on the ever-fluctuating reservoir is moderately popular. Kokanee, along with rainbow and cutthroat are the most popular species. Some evening fishermen, catch the odd looking creatures called ling (Burbot). Below the reservoir bridge, one might spot rock climbers, as this is an international pastime in the area.

River floating can begin immediately below Libby Dam "50.3". A campground at the bridge, near the Fisher River confluence, offers easy access also. A class III Jennings Rapid occurs at milepost "46". This rapid causes little concern to most floaters, but it can be portaged easily. The Libby Bridge "33.2" (on the left) offer good access; however below this, access on the Highway 2 side is difficult. Using the highway and carrying across the railroad tracks is about it. The west side of the river does have a river road going downstream for a short distance.

The China Rapids, a long Class III at milepost "24", may have a story to tell. It is rumored that Chinese miners were floating a raft of gold down river to avoid the land route and a hold-up. The raft disintegrated and only one survived to tell the story. The Kootenai flow is dictated by dam releases. 8,000 cfs is a pleasant float (3,000 normal), however, releases to 25,000 cfs are common. These heavy discharges are dangerous. Updated flow information is available through a telephone recording. Below the China Rapids are the spectacular 30' Kootenai Falls and gorge "21.7". A portage LEFT is necessary. Below the falls is a dangerous one mile gorge. This gorge has five Class IV and two Class III rapids with nearly no recovery time between. Once you have committed to floating the gorge, stopping or portaging is not possible because of the sheer walls. I have an adventuresome story to tell sometime, if someone would like to listen. Most people would carry their raft or canoe along the railroad tracks a short mile to less hostile water or up to Highway 2.

Below this gorge may be the only place in Montana where the White Sturgeon (called Wyal by the Kootenais) may still exist. Fishing is no longer allowed in Montana for this species. Also, this is the only place in Montana where the rare Harlequin duck congregates, other than McDonald Creek in Glacier National Park. On a recent outing, I watched a pair of river otters playing on the river bank just above the falls. Fishing on this river is excellent. Rainbow, cutthroat and some big hybrids are commonly the reward.

Any moderate sized vessel is fine from the dam to above China Rapids; and from below the gorge whitewater, on and into Idaho. The gorge requires a kayak, good raft, or a highly skilled individual in a whitewater canoe.

Throops Lake Access, on private land, is two miles below the end of the gorge whitewater. The slower flow for the rest of the river begins here. A fine access at the Troy Bridge and at the Yaak River Campground, offers ingress or egress. Class II waves occur at the mouth of the Yaak River "6.1". As you approach the Idaho border you are at the lowest elevation in the state, and only a difficult access point exists without floating on into Idaho.

140

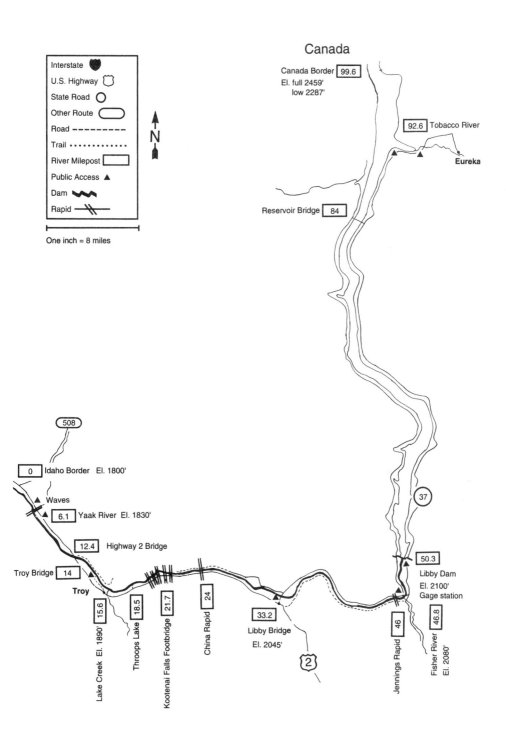

Canada

Canada Border [99.6]
El. full 2459'
   low 2287'

[92.6] Tobacco River

Eureka

Reservoir Bridge [84]

Interstate
U.S. Highway
State Road
Other Route
Road ---------
Trail ....
River Milepost [   ]
Public Access ▲
Dam 〰〰
Rapid —//—

N

One inch = 8 miles

(508)

[0] Idaho Border El. 1800'

▲ Waves
▲ [6.1] Yaak River El. 1830'

[12.4] Highway 2 Bridge

Troy Bridge [14]
▲
Troy

[15.6] Lake Creek El. 1890'

[18.5] Throops Lake

[21.7] Kootenai Falls Footbridge

[24] China Rapid

[33.2]
Libby Bridge
El. 2045'

(2)

(37)

[50.3]
Libby Dam
El. 2100'
Gage station

[46] Jennings Rapid

[46.8] Fisher River El. 2080'

Kootenai

141

LAKE CREEK

ORIGIN:	Bull Lake - south of Troy, MT El. 2300'
END:	Flows into Kootenai River at Troy, MT El. 1890'
LENGTH:	13.9 total mi. (13.5 river mi. and Troy Reservoir .4 mi.) (12 air mi.)
FLOATABLE:	11.1 river mi. (Mine Br. (El. 2270') to Kootenai R.) Class I is 6 mi. (Chase Road Bridge to Kootenai River)
SECTIONS:	Upper (2.4 mi.) Bull Lake "13.9" to Mine Br. "11.5" Middle (10.4 mi.) Mine Br. "11.5" to Troy Dam "1.1" Lower (1.1 mi.) Troy Dam "1.1" to Kootenai R. "0"
DAMS:	Troy Dam (Forms reservoir and controls flow)
WATERFALLS:	None
WHITEWATER:	None
DANGERS:	Upper - Swamps below Bull Lake Middle - Logjams, fences (above Chase Road Bridge) Lower - Sudden dam releases
DEWATERED:	Can be low in fall.
PORTAGES:	Troy Dam (MAJOR portage RIGHT) Many logjams Mi. "11.5" to "6"
SPEC. AGENCIES:	None
REGS - PERMITS:	None
ACCESS-SHUTTLE:	Few access points and quite round-about shuttling. Class I portion is easy.
SERVICES:	All in Troy, MT
CAMPING:	The only campground is on Bull Lake. Troy Reservoir has an access site.
GAMEFISH:	Rainbow, cutthroat, brook, bulls, whitefish.
VESSEL:	Upper - On lake any vessel. Not floatable Bull Lake to Mine Road Bridge. Middle - Small raft, small canoe (above Chase Road) Medium raft, canoe below Lower - Medium raft, canoe, kayak

SKILL LEVEL:	Beginner if flows are normal. (Many logjams between Mine Bridge and Chase Bridge)
FLOAT TIMES:	Middle - Slow (logjams) to Chase Road. Below normal. Lower - Short and fast.
FLOW INFO:	(406) 449-5263 USGS - Helena

HYDROGRAPH

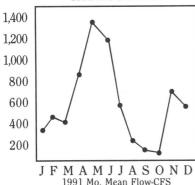

1,400
1,200
1,000
800
600
400
200

J F M A M J J A S O N D
1991 Mo. Mean Flow-CFS

Gage Sta: Just below Troy Dam
Drain Area: 210 sq. mi.
Ave. Flow: (21 years) 459 cfs
Ext. Max: 3,820 cfs - 5.64' ga. ht. 11/25/90
Ext. Min: 2 cfs 9/15/48
Gradient: 410' in 13.9 mi. = 29.5' pma
Float Grad: 380' in 11.5 mi. = 33.0' pma
Clarity: Clear
Temp: Jan. 34° F.
        Apr. 45° F.
        Jul. 54° F.
        Oct. 41° F.

DRAINAGE:	(West) Kootenai, Columbia, Pacific Ocean
MAPS:	BLM - #5 "Libby"
	USFS - Kootenai NF (Best map)
	USGS - "Kalispell"
	CO. - Lincoln

Kootenai Falls

143

LAKE CREEK

Lake Creek gets its name from the 1890's when Troy was called Lake City. The creek flows right along the edge of Troy and into the Kootenai River. Lake Creek, is one of only two creeks in Montana to have the distinction of being included by legislation, as a Class I stream.

The origin of Lake Creek is at the Bull Lake outlet "13.9". It meanders through a marshy beaver dam and logjam area, where moose are present, to the Mine Road Bridge "11.5". Floating can begin at this bridge for those who are patient and well equipped physically, in a canoe or small raft. At the time of this writing, 14 logjams are present in the next 5.5 mile stretch. Four of these logjams require stumbling and crawling with your vessel, through a thick brush portage.

The Chase Road Bridge "6" marks the beginning of the Class I portion. Easy floating, except for a couple fences can be enjoyed the rest of the way to the Troy Reservoir. An informal campsite may be used at the reservoir.

Floating is not popular on Lake Creek and pretty fair fishing for trout and whitefish can be found. Beginners can handle Lake Creek if flow is normal. Portaging Troy Dam, for those who wish to continue on, can best be handled by putting your vessel on your vehicle, driving around and up the lower dam road. 1.1 mile of stream is left before entering the Kootenai River. A short distance down the Kootenai will be the Troy Bridge Access.

Lake Creek

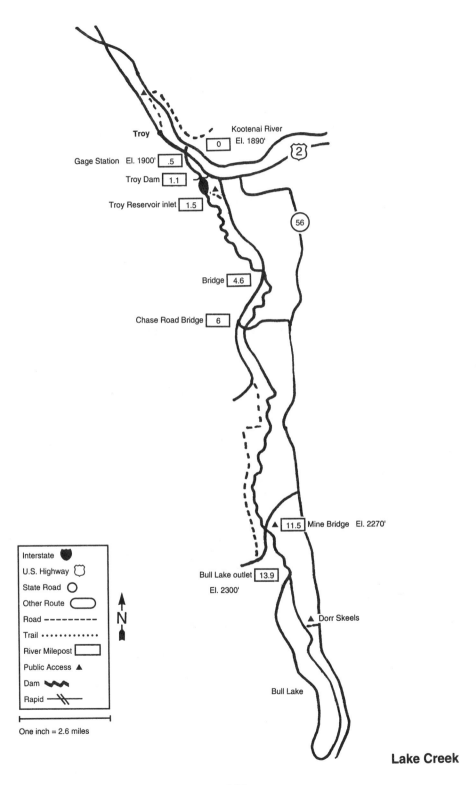

Troy

Kootenai River
El. 1890'

[2]

Gage Station El. 1900' [.5]

Troy Dam [1.1]

Troy Reservoir inlet [1.5]

[56]

Bridge [4.6]

Chase Road Bridge [6]

Mine Bridge El. 2270' [11.5] ▲

Bull Lake outlet [13.9]

El. 2300'

▲ Dorr Skeels

Bull Lake

Lake Creek

Interstate 🛡️
U.S. Highway ⬭
State Road ◯
Other Route ⬯
Road --------
Trail ••••••••••
River Milepost ☐
Public Access ▲
Dam 〰️
Rapid ⫽

N

One inch = 2.6 miles

MADISON

ORIGIN: Confluence of Firehole & Gibbon Rivers in Yellowstone National Park, WY. Enters MT near West Yellowstone. El. 6660'

END: Joins Jefferson River to form Missouri River at Headwaters State Park, near Three Forks, MT El. 4,000'

LENGTH: 133.4 mi. (110.2 river mi. + 23.2 reservoir miles)
Hebgen	14.9
Quake Lake	3.6
Ennis	<u>4.7</u>
(90 air mi.)	23.2 miles - all floatable

FLOATABLE: 103 river mi. (YNP to Missouri R.) + 3 res.
Class I portion is 101.4 mi. (Quake Lake to end)

SECTIONS: Upper (35.4 mi.) Origin-Wyoming border "133.4" to Hwy 87 Access "98"
Middle (57.7 mi.) Hwy 87 "98" to Madison Dam "40.3"
Lower - (40.3 mi.) Madison Dam "40.3" to End "0"

DAMS: Hebgen (Forms res. - controls flow in middle portion)
Quake Lake (A natural rock dam caused by landslide)
Madison (Forms Ennis Res. and controls flow below)
Diversion dam (below Varney Bridge)

WATERFALLS: None

WHITEWATER: 19.7 mi.   Quake Lake slide dam to Madison Campground = 10.4 mi.   Class V-VI (upper)
Madison Dam to Hwy. 84 access = 9.3 mi. Class IV

DANGERS: Sudden releases 2 dams. Quake Lake slide dam and dangerous rapids below. Whitewater, rattlesnakes and remoteness of Bear Trap Canyon. Diversion dam.

DEWATERED: Can be low in fall, but floatable.

PORTAGES: Hebgen Dam, Quake Lake slide dam and rapids, Madison Dam (all 3 portage RIGHT). Caution 4 rapids in Bear Trap Canyon (see map). Diversion Dam

SPEC. AGENCIES: Yellowstone National Park, Lee Metcalf Wilderness.

REGS - PERMITS:	Floating streams not allowed in Yellowstone National Park. No motors in wilderness. 10 hp motor limit on Gallatin & Madison County streams. No fishing while floating in a few sections. No camping allowed in Bear Trap Canyon.
ACCESS-SHUTTLE:	Highways and roads parallel and intersect river often. Access to and around Bear Trap Canyon lengthy on rough road. Numerous access points, especially in middle portion.
SERVICES:	All services in West Yellowstone and Ennis, MT. Whitewater and fishing float trips available.
CAMPING:	Numerous campgrounds and access sites.
GAMEFISH:	Upper - Brown, rainbow, whitefish, cutthroat Middle - To Varney Bridge - Rainbow, brown Varney to res. - Brown, rainbow, grayling Lower - Brown, rainbow, whitefish, grayling
VESSEL:	Upper (Quake L. to Hwy 87 Br.) Kayak, large raft. Middle - upper 7 mi. bouncy - Raft, whitewater canoe, kayak - any moderate size craft below Bear Trap Canyon - Large raft, kayak, whitewater canoe. Highway 84 Access to end - any moderate size vessel
SKILL LEVEL:	Milepost 126.2 to 101.4 - Beginner Milepost 101.4 to 101 - Expert (not recommended) Milepost 101 to 91 - Experienced Milepost 91 to 40.3 - Beginner to Intermediate Milepost 40.3 to 31 - Highly skilled Milepost 31 to 0 - Beginner to Intermediate
FLOAT TIMES:	Upper - Extreme upper-moderate. Below Quake Lake extremely fast. Middle - Moderate flow. Lower - Moderate flow. (best whitewater flows 1700-2200 cfs.)
FLOW INFO:	(406) 449-5263 USGS - Helena

HYDROGRAPH

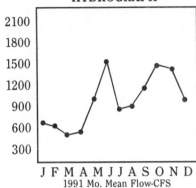

2100
1800
1500
1200
900
600
300

J F M A M J J A S O N D
1991 Mo. Mean Flow-CFS

Gage Sta: Below Hebgen Dam
Drain Area: 905 sq. mi. (at this location)
Ave. Flow: (82 years) 1,004 cfs
Ext. Max: 5,980 cfs - 3.69' ga. ht. 6/3/43
Ext. Min: 5 cfs 5/12/60
Gradient: 2660' in 133.4 mi. = 19.9' pma
Float Grad: 2600' in 101.4 mi. = 25.6' pma
Clarity: Clear to cloudy
Temp: Jan. 36° F.
Apr. 38° F.
Jul. 58° F.
Oct. 48° F.

DRAINAGE: (East) Missouri, Mississippi, Gulf of Mexico

MAPS: BLM - #45 "Hebgen Lake" & #42 "Centennial" (upper) - #33 "Madison" (lower)
USFS - Gallatin NF (Wyoming border to Grey Cliff)
USGS - "Ashton" (upper) - "Bozeman" (lower)
Sp. - "Bear Trap Canyon Float Guide" (USDI)
CO. - Gallatin, Madison

A tasty Brown

MADISON

Yellowstone National Park in Wyoming marks the inception, at the confluence of the Firehole and Gibbon Rivers. It flows 16 miles in Wyoming before entering Montana at milepost "133.4". Still within Yellowstone National Park, the river reaches the park boundary "126.2" just above the Highway 191 Bridge, near West Yellowstone, MT. Floating streams is not allowed in Yellowstone National Park.

Floating in this upper section is not popular because of the two reservoirs interrupting the flow. The short stretch above Hebgen Reservoir and between Hebgen Dam and Quake Lake can be floated by beginners. The two reservoirs are also boatable. Quake Lake slide dam was naturally caused by the 1959 earthquake. A mountain rockslide completely blocked the river channel and also created severe whitewater below. "No trespassing" signs have been erected immediately below "Quake Dam". Floating on this 3.4 mile stretch to the Highway 87 Bridge Access, is not advised. Huge sharp boulders, big drops, and a torrent of water caused by steep gradient create big-time whitewater. I have floated the lower three miles of this 3.4 mile stretch in a small raft, enabling me to maneuver. The upper .4 mile however, either the no trespassing signs, not having my kayak on that trip, or FEAR deterred my float.

Below Highway 87 Bridge Access "98" are seven bouncy miles of Class II turbulence, not conducive to good float fishing. Madison Campground "91" begins the popular float fishing portion to Ennis, MT. All kinds of vessels are visible, handled by all skill levels. Many of the serious fishermen and most of the outfitters prefer a dory (banana river-boat). The river flows swiftly and the rather shallow bottom creates a continuous riffle. Numerous campgrounds and access points exist along the entire river. Fishermen are more commonly awarded catches of brown and rainbow trout in this "blue ribbon stream". Check locally for current regulations, as some stretches may be closed to float fishing and others catch and release only. This river, named by Lewis & Clark, for then Secretary of State and successor to the presidency, James Madison; has international fame as a fishing and floating stream.

Even man has an equal

Lower Madison River

Below Varney Bridge Access "59.7" to the reservoir, is probably home to the largest trout of the river. Take the right channel below Varney to avoid the diversion dam nearly four miles below. Ennis Campground at the Highway 287 Bridge "50.6", is a popular exit. The slower water below to Ennis Reservoir and a long paddle across this often windy reservoir is the reason.

Below Madison Dam "40.3" is the very popular Bear Trap Canyon whitewater run. This 9.3 mile float through the Lee Metcalf Wilderness Area, is remote and beautiful. Access to the dam is difficult. Follow the road north of Ennis along the east side of the reservoir. Near the dam the road becomes rocky and very narrow, making trailering a raft and parking a problem.

Warm water discharges from 900-10,000 cfs occur. The best whitewater flow is between 1700-2200 cfs. Floaters should study the updated flow sign just upstream from the power plant and weigh the consequences. A good raft, kayak or whitewater canoe, driven by the experienced, is imperative, through this Class IV portion. Portaging, if desired, is easy and I've included the side to portage. "Double Drop" (RIGHT), is a rapids between the dam and the power plant. "Whitehorse" (LEFT), the difficult "Kitchen Sink" (RIGHT), and "Greenwave" or "Youthful Folly" (LEFT) all follow with ample time to recover between. Although I have not seen any, rattlesnakes and a few poisonous plants live in this area. A popular exit at Highway 84 Access, and a short jaunt up the highway to Norris Hot Springs is a super way to end the day.

Beginners can handle the rest of the river below Highway 84 Access for its remaining 31 miles in any moderate sized vessel. A few access sites and campgrounds are available, and you float by, at some distance to, the Buffalo Jump State Monument. Flows slow as you near the Missouri Headwaters State Park.

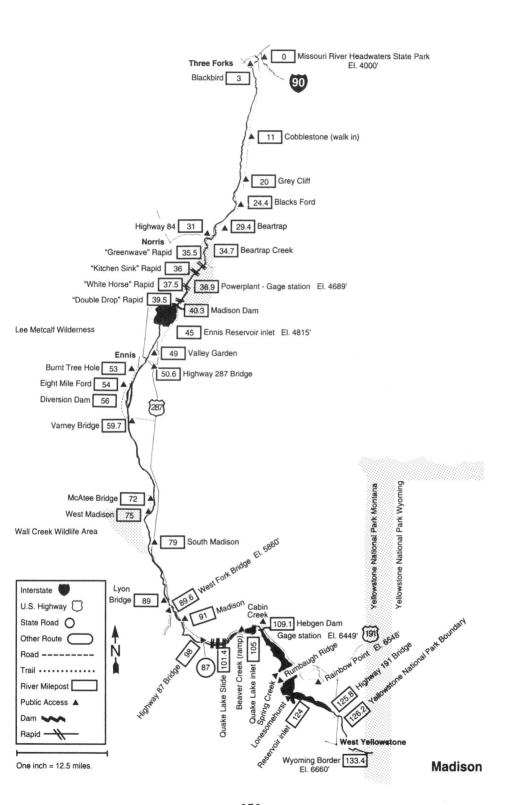

Three Forks
Blackbird [3]

[0] Missouri River Headwaters State Park El. 4000'

[11] Cobblestone (walk in)

[20] Grey Cliff

[24.4] Blacks Ford

Highway 84 [31]
[29.4] Beartrap
Norris
"Greenwave" Rapid [35.5]   [34.7] Beartrap Creek
"Kitchen Sink" Rapid [36]
"White Horse" Rapid [37.5]   [36.9] Powerplant - Gage station   El. 4689'
"Double Drop" Rapid [39.5]
[40.3] Madison Dam

Lee Metcalf Wilderness
[45] Ennis Reservoir inlet   El. 4815'

Ennis
[49] Valley Garden
Burnt Tree Hole [53]
Eight Mile Ford [54]   [50.6] Highway 287 Bridge
Diversion Dam [56]
287
Varney Bridge [59.7]

McAtee Bridge [72]
West Madison [75]
Wall Creek Wildlife Area
[79] South Madison

West Fork Bridge El. 5860'

Lyon Bridge [89]
[89.6]
[91] Madison   Cabin Creek
[109.1] Hebgen Dam
Gage station   El. 6449'
191
Rumbaugh Ridge
Rainbow Point   El. 6548'
Highway 87 Bridge [98]
87
[101.4]
Quake Lake Slide
Beaver Creek (ramp)
Quake Lake inlet [105]
Spring Creek
Lonesomehurst
[124] Reservoir inlet
Highway 191 Bridge
[125.8]
[126.2]
Yellowstone National Park Boundary
Yellowstone National Park Montana
Yellowstone National Park Wyoming
West Yellowstone

Wyoming Border [133.4]
El. 6660'

Madison

Interstate
U.S. Highway
State Road
Other Route
Road
Trail
River Milepost
Public Access ▲
Dam
Rapid

N

One inch = 12.5 miles.

MARIAS

ORIGIN:	Confluence of Two Medicine River and Cut Bank Creek, south of Cut Bank, MT. El. 3300'
END:	Flows into Missouri River at Loma, MT. El. 2550'
LENGTH:	170.5 total mi. (143.8 river mi. + Tiber Res. 26.7 mi.) (90 air mi.)
FLOATABLE:	143.8 river mi. and Tiber Reservoir is floatable Class I portion is 80.3 river mi. (Tiber Dam to Missouri)
SECTIONS:	Upper (53.7 mi.) Origin "170.5" to F Bridge "116.8" Middle (36.5 mi.) F Br. "116.8" to Tiber Dam "80.3" Lower (80.3 mi.) Tiber Dam "80.3" to Missouri "0"
DAMS:	Tiber (Forms reservoir and controls flow below)
WATERFALLS:	None
WHITEWATER:	None
DANGERS:	Remote area
DEWATERED:	Occasionally in the fall
PORTAGES:	Tiber Dam (major portage RIGHT)
SPEC. AGENCIES:	None
REGS - PERMITS:	None
ACCESS-SHUTTLE:	Difficult. Very round-about. Few access sites
SERVICES:	All services in Cut Bank, Shelby and Fort Benton. Limited in Loma, MT
CAMPING:	Formal campground below Tiber Dam only. Very few access sites. Mostly private land.
GAMEFISH:	Above dam- Rainbow, brown, whitefish, catfish, pike, walleye, burbot Below dam- Also, sauger, shovelnose sturgeon.
VESSEL:	Any moderate size vessel, unless flows are low. When flows are up a small motor could be used.

SKILL LEVEL:	Beginner (CAUTION - remote area and winds)
FLOAT TIMES:	Flows are slow to moderate.
FLOW INFO:	(406) 449-5263 USGS - Helena

HYDROGRAPH

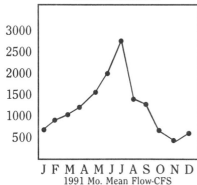

3000
2500
2000
1500
1000
500

J F M A M J J A S O N D
1991 Mo. Mean Flow-CFS

Gage Sta: Below Tiber Dam
Drain Area: 4,927 sq. mi. (at this location)
Ave. Flow: (38 years) 856 cfs
Ext. Max: 10,400 cfs - 10.63' ga. ht. 6/16/64
Ext. Min: .2 cfs 11/10/55
Gradient: 750' in 170.5 mi. = 4.4' pma
Float Grad: Same
Clarity: Cloudy to murky
Temp: Jan. 38⁰ F.
         Apr. 50⁰ F.
         Jul. 71⁰ F.
         Oct. 52⁰ F.

DRAINAGE:	(East) Missouri, Mississippi, Gulf of Mexico
MAPS:	BLM - #28 "Valier" & #38 "Tiber Reservoir" (upper) #4 "Fresno" & #14 "Highwood" (lower) USGS - "Cut Bank" (extreme upper) - "Shelby" - "Great Falls" (extreme lower) CO. - Ponderosa, Toole, Liberty, Blaine, Chouteau.

Pike - A prolific gamefish

MARIAS

The Indians called it "the river that scolds at all others". Captain Lewis named it "Maria's River" in honor of his cousin Maria Wood, while camped at the mouth, near Loma, MT on 6/8/1805.

The river begins with the joining of the Two Medicine River and Cut Bank Creek, south of Cut Bank, MT. A bridge at this juncture offers good access. The next access is at the Shelby Golf Course, two miles above I-15 bridge, a distance of 28 miles. The river meanders along a cottonwood bottom, with rolling prairie hills in the background. This float can be completed in 1 day if flow is normal.

The annual Marias float race begins at the Shelby Golf Course "142.7" and ends at the F - Bridge "116.8". This early summer event is more of a "funfest" than a race, considering one "racer" used a bathtub. Current slows below the F - Bridge as Tiber Reservoir is only ten miles away, and the dam 27 miles beyond.

Rainbow and brown trout, whitefish, big catfish, pike, walleye and burbot (ling) are found above the dam. Below the dam, sauger and shovelnose sturgeon are also found. A beginner in any moderate sized vessel, can handle the entire river and I have seen small motors used when water is high. Caution for the remoteness of the area and the possibility of high winds is in order.

The Class I portion of the Marias begins at Tiber Dam "80.3". A campground just below is a wonderful place to begin a float. Four miles below is the Paisley (Pugsley) Bridge, and six miles beyond is the Moffatt Bridge. It is then a ten mile float to the Highway 223 (Circle) Bridge "59".

Below Highway 223 you enter a very remote area with nearly no access. The only access being down the Rudyard road to river milepost "39", before reaching Loma "2.4". A little rain can cause the roads to turn to impassable grease. A cottonwood bottom surrounded by sandstone formations creates a beautiful badland environment. Wildlife of all kinds enjoy the inaccessibility and seclusion.

The Teton River enters at the Highway 87 Bridge Access in Loma. Floating the last 2.4 miles into the Missouri River would result in a 17 mile float downstream to its first access at Virgelle.

Marias River

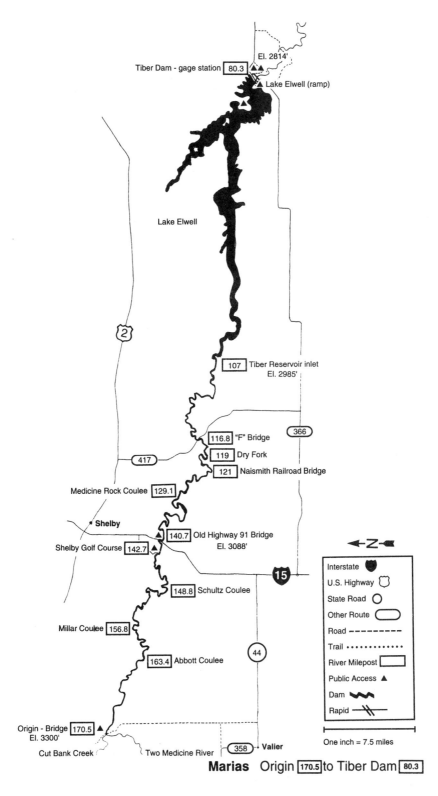

El. 2814'

Tiber Dam - gage station 80.3

Lake Elwell (ramp)

Lake Elwell

2

107 Tiber Reservoir inlet
El. 2985'

366

116.8 "F" Bridge

119 Dry Fork

121 Naismith Railroad Bridge

Medicine Rock Coulee 129.1

417

Shelby

140.7 Old Highway 91 Bridge
El. 3088'

Shelby Golf Course 142.7

15

148.8 Schultz Coulee

Millar Coulee 156.8

44

163.4 Abbott Coulee

Origin - Bridge 170.5
El. 3300'

Cut Bank Creek

Two Medicine River

358 Valier

Interstate

U.S. Highway

State Road

Other Route

Road ----------

Trail ••••••••••

River Milepost

Public Access ▲

Dam

Rapid

One inch = 7.5 miles

Marias Origin 170.5 to Tiber Dam 80.3

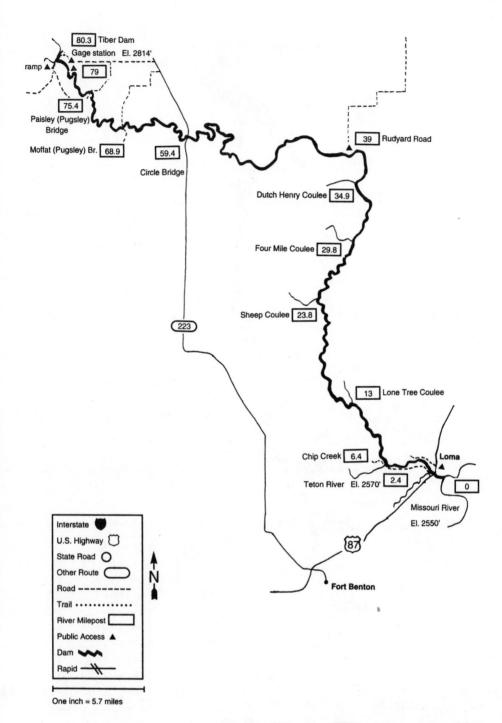

80.3 Tiber Dam
Gage station El. 2814'
ramp
79
75.4
Paisley (Pugsley)
Bridge
Moffat (Pugsley) Br. 68.9   59.4
Circle Bridge

39 Rudyard Road

Dutch Henry Coulee 34.9

Four Mile Coulee 29.8

Sheep Coulee 23.8

223

13 Lone Tree Coulee

Chip Creek 6.4
Teton River El. 2570'   2.4
Loma
0
Missouri River
El. 2550'

87

Fort Benton

Interstate
U.S. Highway
State Road
Other Route
Road -----------
Trail ....
River Milepost
Public Access ▲
Dam
Rapid

N

One inch = 5.7 miles

Marias   Tiber Dam 80.3 to Missouri River 0

156

MILK

ORIGIN:	Confluence of Middle & South Forks, north of Browning, MT. El. 4400' After 47.3 mi. enters Canada. After 167.4 mi. in Canada, re-enters US northwest of Havre, MT. El. 2660'
END:	Flows into Missouri River below Fort Peck Dam. El. 2020'
LENGTH:	537.5 total MT mi. (516.8 river mi. + Fresno Reservoir 20.7 mi.) (317 air mi.)
FLOATABLE:	516.8 river mi. + Fresno Reservoir is floatable.
SECTIONS:	Upper (100.2 mi.) Origin "704.9" minus 167.4 Mi. in Canada to Fresno Dam "437.3" Middle (163.0 mi.) Fresno Dam "437.3" to Dodson Dam "274.3" Lower (274.3 mi.) Dodson Dam "274.3" to End - Missouri River "0"
DAMS:	Fresno (Forms reservoir & controls river flow) (major portage) Mi. "437.3" Havre Mi. "419.7" portage (10' high concrete) East Havre Mi. "414.5" portage LEFT (6' high rock) Lohman Mi. "393.5" portage Chinook weir Mi. "379.2" portage (Built 1993) Paradise (Chinook) Mi. "374.5" portage RIGHT best (15' concrete) (Built 1966) Ft. Belknap (double dam) Mi. "333.2" portage LEFT (4' rock - 15' concrete) 100 yards apart Dodson Mi. "274.3" portage RIGHT best (20' concrete) (Built 1910) Vandalia Mi. "117.3" portage LEFT best (20' concrete) (Built 1917)
WATERFALLS:	None
WHITEWATER:	None
DANGERS:	9 dams, some irrigation jettys, upper river remote. Winds on Fresno Reservoir. Irrigation returns.
DEWATERED:	Sometimes during irrigation or in fall.
PORTAGES:	9 dams (see above)

SPEC. AGENCIES:	Glacier National Park - Blackfeet Reservation - Fort Belknap Reservation - Fort Peck Indian Reservation
REGS - PERMITS:	Tribal fish license on Blackfeet Reservation - Fort Belknap Reservation - Fort Peck Indian Reservation
ACCESS-SHUTTLE:	Upper - ext. difficult (few roads, poor access, remote) Middle & Lower - Not too difficult
SERVICES:	All services in many towns along entire river.
CAMPING:	Upper - No campgrounds or formal access sites. Middle & Lower - Few campgrounds or access sites.
GAMEFISH:	Walleye, sauger, catfish, pike
VESSEL:	Canoe, small boat, medium raft, entire river
SKILL LEVEL:	Beginner (Caution: remote, dams, wind)
FLOAT TIMES:	Flows are normally slow.
FLOW INFO:	(406) 449-5263 USGS - Helena

HYDROGRAPH

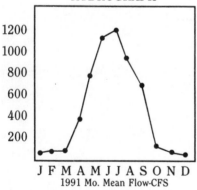

1200
1000
800
600
400
200

J F M A M J J A S O N D
1991 Mo. Mean Flow-CFS

Gage Sta: Havre, MT
Drain Area: 5,785 sq. mi. (at this location)
Ave. Flow: (43 years) 418 cfs
Ext. Max: 20,000 cfs - 19.3' ga. ht. 4/12/1899
Ext. Min: No flow at times
Gradient: 2380' in 704.9 mi. = 3.4' pma
Float Grad: Same
Clarity: Cloudy to turbid
Temp: Jan. 32⁰ F.
      Apr. 50⁰ F.
      Jul. 75⁰ F.
      Oct. 46⁰ F.

DRAINAGE:	(East) Missouri, Mississippi, Gulf of Mexico
MAPS:	BLM - #17 "St. Mary" - #27 "Cut Bank" - #4 "Fresno" - #5 "Havre" - #6 "Belknap" - #7 "Bowdoin" - #8 "Glasgow" USGS - "Cut Bank" - "Shelby" - "Havre" - "Glasgow" CO. - Glacier, Hill, Blaine, Phillips, Valley

MILK

Named in 1805 by Captain M. Lewis, "The water of this river possesses a peculiar whiteness, being about the colour of a cup of tea with the admixture of a tablespoonful of milk". The mainstem of the Milk begins at the confluence of the Middle and South Forks north of Browning. After 47.3 miles the river enters Canada, and flows 167.4 miles before re-entering Montana northwest of Havre.

Floating could begin at its origin, 1/4 mile upstream from a bridge north of Browning, on the Blackfeet Indian Reservation. The only point of access would be at the Highway 213 bridge, 21 miles downstream. Below the 213 bridge there is no access before the river enters Canada 26 miles distant. The river re-enters Montana at milepost "490.2". A possible point of entry is where a road comes close to the river ten miles below. Floating through the borders is not allowed. Fresno Reservoir begins at milepost "458", with Fresno Dam at "437.3". Boating activities and fishing are popular on Fresno, but pay respect to the possibility of wind.

The most popular floating section of the Milk begins just below the dam on the south side of the river. Plans are on the drawing board for a disabled access at the dam, and again below at Upper Rookery Access "429.6". Three Cheers! The Lower Rookery Access "423.8", also on the north side of the river, offers egress before the Havre City Dam. Another dam, a 6' rock diversion, is at the east edge of Havre.

The Milk begins as a clear mountain stream, but after its journey into Canada, returns turbid due to natural siltation. It meanders through beautiful prairie country, lined with dense vegetation that abounds with wildlife. Swatting mosquitoes will break the monotony of total solitude! Some trout are present below Fresno, however it is primarily known as a warm water fishery, consisting of walleye, sauger, catfish and pike. A canoe or small boat is your best choice of vessel, as a raft is difficult in windy or slow moving water conditions. A beginner can handle the entire river with caution for diversion dams, irrigation jettys, and remoteness of certain portions.

Milk River

Above the Highway 2 bridge west of Chinook, is the Lohman Diversion Dam. Just south of Chinook, construction of a new irrigation weir has already begun. This weir is just above the Highway 240 bridge. Just below this bridge is the Paradise Dam "374.5". As water is precious on the dry prairie, I suppose we must forgive the presence of these dams. It would be our hope however, that only enough water be withdrawn to meet actual needs. Dewatered streams not only create ugly aesthetic scenes, but they reduce recreational values, and jeopardize fisheries and wildlife habitat.

As floating is not extremely popular on the Milk, formal campgrounds or access sites are infrequent. Bridges may have to suffice for access. Landowners are usually congenial, and should the situation arise, would probably grant permission.

The Belknap Dam "333.2", located on the Fort Belknap Indian Reservation south of Harlem, is just above the Highway 2 bridge. The Belknap Dam, a large concrete structure, is preceded upstream by a rock diversion. A 100 yard portage LEFT will get you around both dams. Dodson Dam "274.3" requires portage and the right side is best. Camping at Belknap or Dodson Dams is a possibility. The reservation lies along the south bank of the river in this area. Check current tribal regulations to see if a special fishing or recreational use permit is necessary.

Below Malta "230" are the Cole Ponds and campground "172". To use these facilities would require a 1/2 mile hike north of the river. Bjornberg Bridge Access "152.3" would be a good spot. 7 miles below the Highway 2 bridge is the Vandalia Dam "117.3". This dam requires a portage LEFT and a campsite here is a possibility.

Below Glasgow "67" is the Nashua Bridge "23", before reaching the Missouri River below Fort Peck Dam. Campgrounds in this area are numerous.

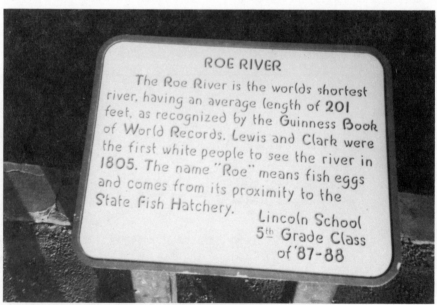

World's shortest river

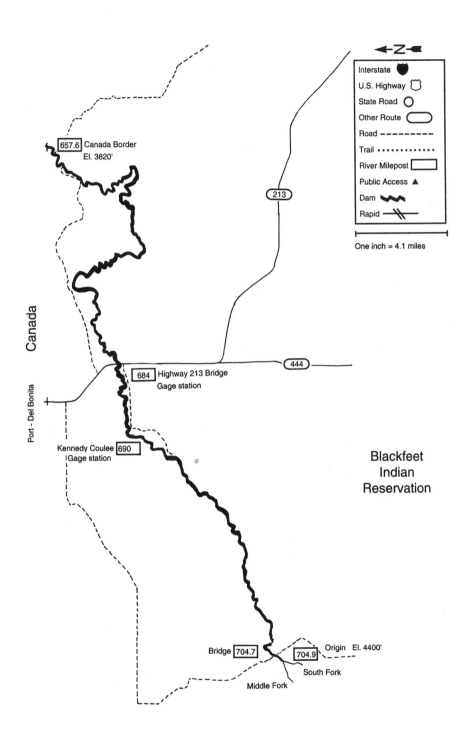

Milk Origin 704.9 to Canada Border 657.6

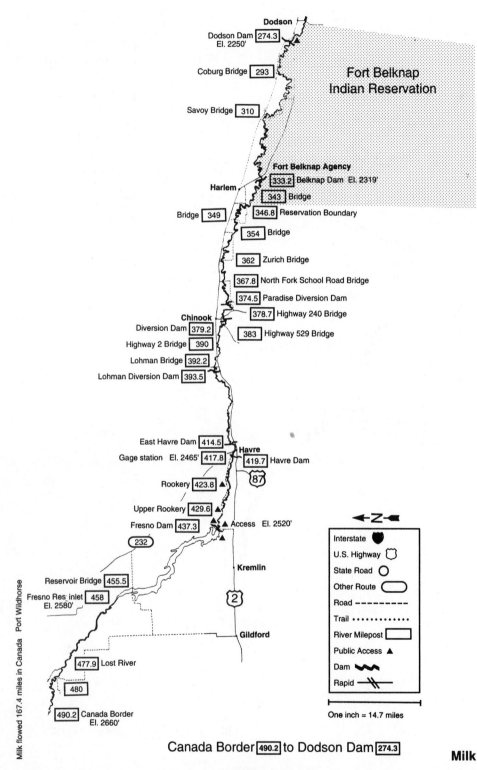

Dodson

Dodson Dam 274.3
El. 2250'

Coburg Bridge 293

Savoy Bridge 310

Fort Belknap
Indian Reservation

Fort Belknap Agency
333.2 Belknap Dam El. 2319'
Harlem
343 Bridge
Bridge 349
346.8 Reservation Boundary
354 Bridge
362 Zurich Bridge
367.8 North Fork School Road Bridge
374.5 Paradise Diversion Dam
378.7 Highway 240 Bridge
Chinook
383 Highway 529 Bridge
Diversion Dam 379.2
Highway 2 Bridge 390
Lohman Bridge 392.2
Lohman Diversion Dam 393.5

East Havre Dam 414.5
Havre
Gage station El. 2465' 417.8
419.7 Havre Dam
87
Rookery 423.8 ▲

Upper Rookery 429.6 ▲
Fresno Dam 437.3 ▲
▲ Access El. 2520'
232
▲
Kremlin
Reservoir Bridge 455.5
Fresno Res. inlet 458
El. 2580'
2
Gildford

477.9 Lost River

480

490.2 Canada Border
El. 2660'

Milk flowed 167.4 miles in Canada   Port Wildhorse

N

Interstate
U.S. Highway
State Road
Other Route
Road ----------
Trail ••••••••••••
River Milepost
Public Access ▲
Dam
Rapid

One inch = 14.7 miles

Canada Border 490.2 to Dodson Dam 274.3

Milk

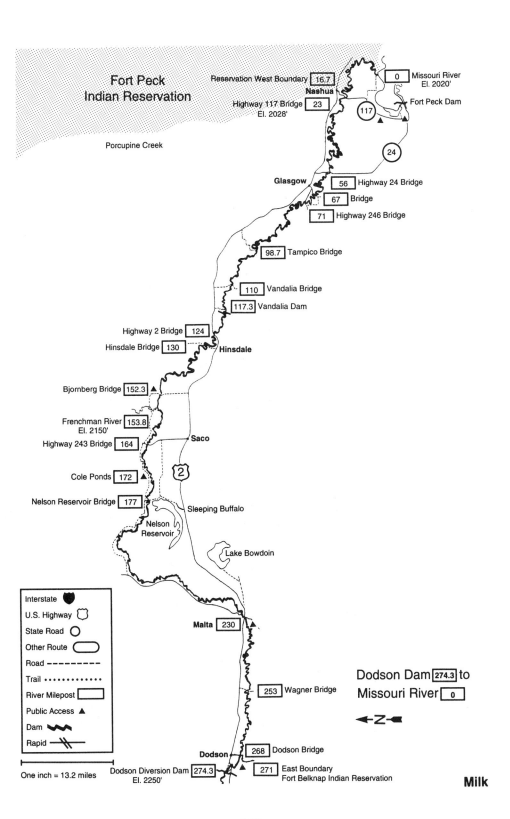

Fort Peck
Indian Reservation

Porcupine Creek

Reservation West Boundary 16.7
Nashua

Missouri River
El. 2020'

Highway 117 Bridge 23
El. 2028'

117

Fort Peck Dam

0

24

Glasgow

56 Highway 24 Bridge

67 Bridge

71 Highway 246 Bridge

98.7 Tampico Bridge

110 Vandalia Bridge

117.3 Vandalia Dam

Highway 2 Bridge 124

Hinsdale Bridge 130

Hinsdale

Bjornberg Bridge 152.3

Frenchman River 153.8
El. 2150'

Highway 243 Bridge 164

Saco

Cole Ponds 172

2

Nelson Reservoir Bridge 177

Sleeping Buffalo

Nelson
Reservoir

Lake Bowdoin

Interstate
U.S. Highway
State Road
Other Route
Road
Trail
River Milepost
Public Access ▲
Dam
Rapid

Malta 230

253 Wagner Bridge

Dodson Dam 274.3 to
Missouri River 0

◄-N-◄

Dodson

268 Dodson Bridge

One inch = 13.2 miles

Dodson Diversion Dam 274.3
El. 2250'

271 East Boundary
Fort Belknap Indian Reservation

Milk

163

MISSOURI

ORIGIN: Confluence of Jefferson, Madison and Gallatin rivers at Missouri River Headwaters State Park, near Three Forks, MT. El. 4,000'

END: Flows into N. D., north of Fairview, MT. El. 1,800'

LENGTH: 734.2 total mi. (510.7 river mi. & 10 res. 223.5 mi.) (382 air mi.)

Toston	6.0 mi.
Canyon Ferry	25.7
Hauser	15.5
Holter	26.3
Black Eagle	3.9
Rainbow*	3.1
Cochrane*	3.2
Ryan*	1.9
Morony*	3.9
Fort Peck	134.0
	223.5

* not floatable

FLOATABLE: 510.7 river mi. & 211.4 reservoir miles
Class I portion is entire 734.2 mi.
"Navigable river" below Fort Benton

SECTIONS: Upper (215.2 mi.) Origin "734.2" to Morony Dam Access "519"
Middle (334 mi.) Morony Access "519" to Fort Peck Dam "185"
Lower (185 mi.) Fort Peck Dam "185" to End - North Dakota border "0"

DAMS: 10 All 10 listed in Reservoirs above (in river sequence).

WATERFALLS: Waterfalls exist below Great Falls dams (unfloatable)

WHITEWATER: Below Morony Dam for four miles Class III (depends on flow). Next exit is Carter Ferry 16.4 mi.

DANGERS: Whitewater below Morony Dam including shelf by Belt Creek (right). Remote areas.

DEWATERED: No

PORTAGES: All dams are MAJOR portages.

SPEC. AGENCIES:	Montana Power Co., Wild & Scenic Act, C.M. Russell Wildlife Refuge, Fort Peck Indian Reservation
REGS - PERMITS:	Permits required between the weekend before Memorial Day and the weekend after Labor Day from Fort Benton to James Kipp State Park (Wild-Scenic-Recreational sections). Available free from BLM river rangers at each major launch point. Information 538-7461. No extended upstream traffic (prime season). No wake speed in these wild or scenic portions (prime season). No motors in Great Falls.
ACCESS-SHUTTLE:	Quite easy with highways and roads paralleling and intersecting river. Also numerus access points in upper section. Middle and Lower sections access points are much less frequent.
SERVICES:	All services available at many locations along river. Canoe rentals (Virgelle)
CAMPING:	Upper - numerous campgrounds and access sites. Middle - occassional camping and access sites. Many river floaters' campsites along remote portion. Lower - Access sites are far-between.
GAMEFISH:	Upper - Brown, rainbow Below Holter Dam - Brown, rainbow, whitefish, walleye Below Great Falls dams - All Montana's warmer water species.
VESSEL:	Any moderate-sized craft.
SKILL LEVEL:	Beginner, except Morony whitewater - Experienced. (CAUTION - remote areas).
FLOAT TIMES:	Upper - Ave. 4 mph flow. Below Smith River slow, and approaching each reservoir. Middle & Lower - Ave. 3 1/2 mph flow.
FLOW INFO:	(406) 449-5263 USGS - Helena 538-7461 Permits - "Wild & Scenic" portion

HYDROGRAPH

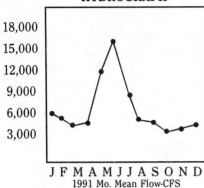

18,000
15,000
12,000
9,000
6,000
3,000

J F M A M J J A S O N D
1991 Mo. Mean Flow-CFS

Gage Sta: Fort Benton, MT
Drain Area: 24,749 sq. mi. (at this location)
Ave. Flow: (101 years) 7,722 cfs
Ext. Max: 140,000 cfs - 18.5' ga. ht. 6/6/08
Ext. Min: 627 cfs 7/5/36
Gradient: 2200' in 734.2 mi. = 3' pma
Float Grad: Same
Clarity: Cloudy to murky
Temp: Jan. 40⁰ F.
         Apr. 46⁰ F.
         Jul. 71⁰ F.
         Oct. 53⁰ F.
Total Drain Area: Approx. 95,000 sq. mi.
(North Dakota border)

DRAINAGE: (East) Mississippi, Gulf of Mexico

MAPS: BLM - #33 "Madison" - #23 "Townsend" - #40 "Great Falls South" - #39 "Great Falls North" - #14 "Highwood" - #4 "Fresno" - #15 "Judith" - #67 "Zortman" - #76 "Fort Peck West" - #77 "Sand Springs" - #18 "Haxby" - #8 "Glasgow" - #9 "Poplar" #10 "Muddy".
USFS - Helena NF (Toston Dam to Holter Reservoir)
USGS - "Bozeman" - "White Sulphur" - "Great Falls" "Shelby" - "Lewistown" - "Jordan" - "Wolf Point"
Sp.   - "Missouri River Guide" (Holter to Great Falls)
DFWP - "Upper Missouri National Wild & Scenic River" (Fort Benton to James Kipp) BLM 2 maps
CO.   - Gallatin, Broadwater, Lewis & Clark, Cascade, Chouteau, Blaine, Fergus, Phillips, Petroleum, Garfield, Valley, McCone, Roosevelt, Richland.

MISSOURI

Indians called the Missouri the "Long River", and long it is; 2,615.4 miles long, (when the Jefferson, Beaverhead and Red Rock Rivers are included). These rivers are merely extensions of the Missouri. The name Missouri originated downstream in St. Louis (town of large canoes!). Locally, it is nicknamed "Big Muddy", "Big Mo" or "Old Misery".

Floating can begin at Missouri Headwaters State Park "734.2", near Three Forks, MT; at the confluence of the Gallatin, Madison and Jefferson Rivers. Fairweather Access "723" offers the only access before Toston Dam creates the rivers first reservoir. Floating can continue on, below the dam to Townsend, MT before flow is again interrupted by the Canyon Ferry Reservoir. Canyon Ferry Dam is followed closely by Hauser and Holter Dams, creating a nearly continuous reservoir system. These 3 reservoirs do offer a variety of recreational boating activities.

Below Holter Dam "624.5" to Cascade "589" is the "Blue Ribbon" fishing portion. Big brown and rainbows offer excellent fishing and commercial outfitters frequent the area. Even late fall is an excellent time to fish. The scenery is gorgeous through this canyon area and numerous access sites and campgrounds are available. Below the Prewett Creek Recreation Area are the short and moderate "Half Breed" rapids. These rapids would only cause some concern for the beginner.

The Highway 330 bridges at Cascade and Ulm offer access. Below Ulm "565", the river slows due to the water backed up by the five dams in the Great Falls area. Motors are commonly used in this area, but are not allowed within Great Falls. Broadwater Bay Access, across from the Sun River confluence in Great Falls offers a place to exit. Floating is not possible between the five dams, due to no access, shortness of float, and sudden dam discharges.

Below Morony Dam Access "519" is four miles of whitewater in the 16.4 mile float to Carter Ferry Access "502.6". Immediately below Morony are numerous shelfs, causing waves. A dangerous shelf and waves at Belt Creek (east bank) should be avoided. The magnitude of the whitewater is dependent on Morony Dam discharge. The greater the discharge, the bigger the waves. Belt Creek also offers some whitewater thrills.

Below Carter Access begins the National Wild, Scenic and Recreation designation at milepost "487.8". In 1976, this 153.2 mile section was inducted into the river "Hall of Fame". This designation remains downstream to the James Kipp State Park, at the Highway 191 Fred Robinson Bridge "334.6". International floating popularity has caused a free permit being required between the weekend before Memorial Day and the weekend after Labor Day. These permits are available from BLM river rangers at each major launch point. No extended upstream traffic and a "no wake" speed in the "wild" and "scenic" portions exist during prime season.

History and scenery is in abundance in this area. Off the river, southwest of Great Falls is the Ulm Pishkun State Park. The C.M. Russell Museum in Great Falls and the Sluice Boxes State Monument southeast of Great Falls are worth seeing. The Fort Benton area, Pilot Rock, White Cliffs, LaBarge Rock, Citadel Rock, and the Hole-in-the-wall areas offer historical hikes. Original Lewis & Clark campsites and other historical locations are too numerous to mention here, so may I refer you to the river milepost maps. These maps also break down the divisions between Wild, Scenic or Recreation designations. The BLM waterproof two map edition "Upper Missouri National Wild & Scenic River" are great to buy and take along. They cover this entire corridor. The historical rapids that these maps show should not cause any concern to the floater today.

The ramp at the Judith Landing Bridge and campground offers easy ingress or egress. Below the Judith Landing Bridge "396.9" is the McClelland Ferry Access "383.1" and the Charles M. Russell Wildlife boundary "346". Mile "334.6" at the Highway 191 bridge marks the end of this special corridor.

Below the Fred Robinson Bridge (James Kipp) is the Siparyann Campground "326" and the Rock Creek boat ramp "319". This is a popular paddlefish snagging area in late May. These huge prehistoric fish (record 142 lbs. 8 oz.), do not take bait or lures, but ingest plankton as their diet. Home to these fish is the Fort Peck Reservoir and they migrate upstream to spawn on these gravel bars.

Fort Peck Dam "185" creates the very large, often dangerously windy, reservoir. Boating on this reservoir is quite popular and offers a wonderful opportunity to view wildlife in this extremely remote area.

Below Fort Peck Dam, at the confluence of the Milk River "174.9", is the western boundary of the Fort Peck Indian Reservation. The reservation follows along the river on the north bank. Access sites are very infrequent. A ramp exists at Wolf Point and the Highway 13 bridge campground "114.8". Poplar bridge and campground "77" and Brockton ramp access "64", offer exit or entry. The east boundary of the Fort Peck Indian Reservation occurs at Big Muddy Creek "43.8". Culbertson bridge "34.2" offers only difficult access for small vessels. After reaching the North Dakota border and Fort Union, a 3 mile float to Fort Buford, North Dakota offers a ramp and campground.

Missouri River

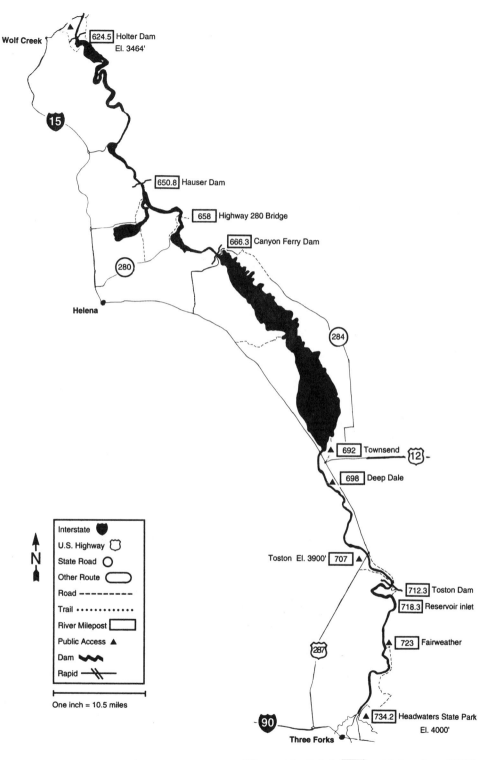

Wolf Creek

15

624.5 Holter Dam
El. 3464'

650.8 Hauser Dam

658 Highway 280 Bridge

280

666.3 Canyon Ferry Dam

Helena

284

692 Townsend 12

698 Deep Dale

Toston El. 3900' 707

712.3 Toston Dam

718.3 Reservoir inlet

287

723 Fairweather

734.2 Headwaters State Park
El. 4000'

90

Three Forks

Interstate	⬟
U.S. Highway	⬡
State Road	◯
Other Route	⬭
Road	- - - - - -
Trail	•••••••••••
River Milepost	▭
Public Access	▲
Dam	〰
Rapid	⫽

↑
N
▲

One inch = 10.5 miles

Missouri Origin 734.2 to Holter Dam 624.5

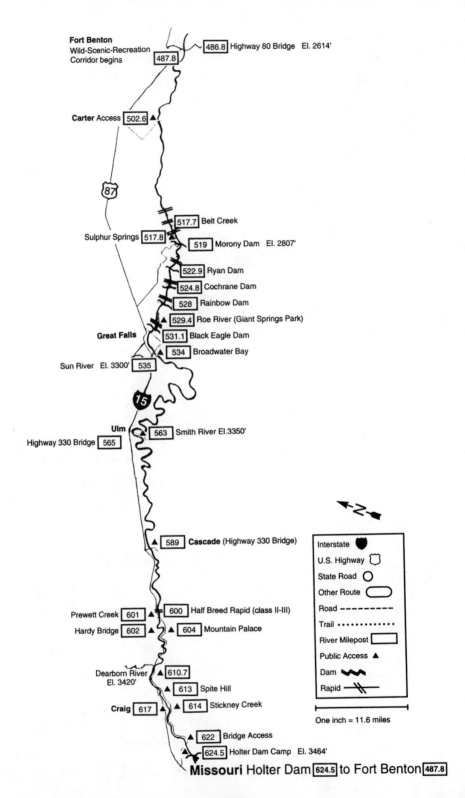

Fort Benton
Wild-Scenic-Recreation
Corridor begins [487.8]

[486.8] Highway 80 Bridge   El. 2614'

Carter Access [502.6] ▲

(87)

[517.7] Belt Creek

Sulphur Springs [517.8]

[519] Morony Dam   El. 2807'

[522.9] Ryan Dam

[524.8] Cochrane Dam

[528] Rainbow Dam

[529.4] Roe River (Giant Springs Park)

Great Falls

[531.1] Black Eagle Dam

[534] Broadwater Bay

Sun River   El. 3300' [535]

(15)

Ulm

[563] Smith River El.3350'

Highway 330 Bridge [565]

[589] **Cascade** (Highway 330 Bridge)

Prewett Creek [601] ▲ [600] Half Breed Rapid (class II-III)

Hardy Bridge [602] ▲ ▲ [604] Mountain Palace

Dearborn River ▲ [610.7]
El. 3420'

▲ [613] Spite Hill

Craig [617] ▲ ▲ [614] Stickney Creek

▲ [622] Bridge Access

▲ [624.5] Holter Dam Camp   El. 3464'

Interstate
U.S. Highway
State Road ◯
Other Route ⬭
Road — — — — —
Trail • • • • • • • •
River Milepost ☐
Public Access ▲
Dam 〰
Rapid ⊬

One inch = 11.6 miles

Missouri Holter Dam [624.5] to Fort Benton [487.8]

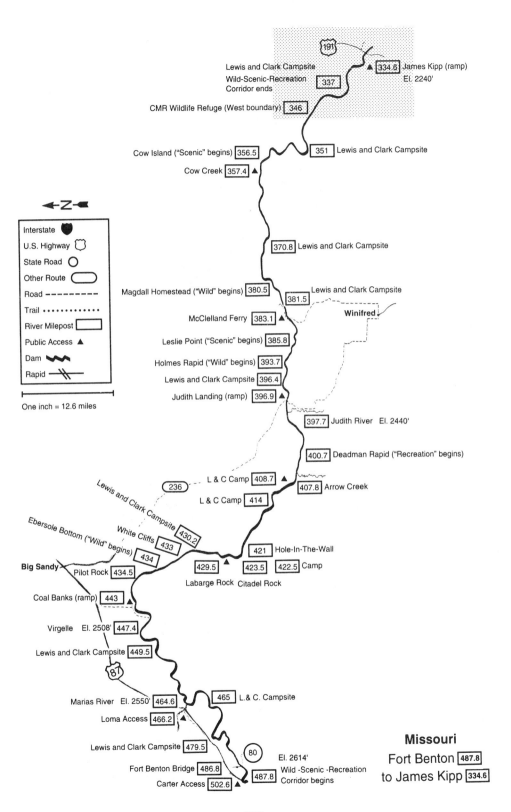

Lewis and Clark Campsite
Wild-Scenic-Recreation Corridor ends | 337
CMR Wildlife Refuge (West boundary) | 346

▲ 334.6 | James Kipp (ramp)
El. 2240'

Cow Island ("Scenic" begins) | 356.5
Cow Creek | 357.4 ▲

351 | Lewis and Clark Campsite

370.8 | Lewis and Clark Campsite

Magdall Homestead ("Wild" begins) | 380.5
381.5 | Lewis and Clark Campsite
Winifred
McClelland Ferry | 383.1 ▲
Leslie Point ("Scenic" begins) | 385.8
Holmes Rapid ("Wild" begins) | 393.7
Lewis and Clark Campsite | 396.4
Judith Landing (ramp) | 396.9 ▲
397.7 | Judith River   El. 2440'
400.7 | Deadman Rapid ("Recreation" begins)
L & C Camp | 408.7 ▲
236
L & C Camp | 414
407.8 | Arrow Creek

Lewis and Clark Campsite
Ebersole Bottom ("Wild" begins)
White Cliffs | 430.2
433
434
Big Sandy
Pilot Rock | 434.5
421 | Hole-In-The-Wall
429.5 ▲
423.5 | 422.5 | Camp
Labarge Rock   Citadel Rock

Coal Banks (ramp) | 443 ▲

Virgelle   El. 2508' | 447.4

Lewis and Clark Campsite | 449.5

87

Marias River   El. 2550' | 464.6
Loma Access | 466.2 ▲
465 | L. & C. Campsite

Lewis and Clark Campsite | 479.5
80   El. 2614'
Fort Benton Bridge | 486.8
487.8 | Wild -Scenic -Recreation Corridor begins
Carter Access | 502.6 ▲

Missouri
Fort Benton 487.8
to James Kipp 334.6

Legend:
Interstate
U.S. Highway
State Road
Other Route
Road - - - - - - - -
Trail ••••••••••••
River Milepost
Public Access ▲
Dam
Rapid

One inch = 12.6 miles

171

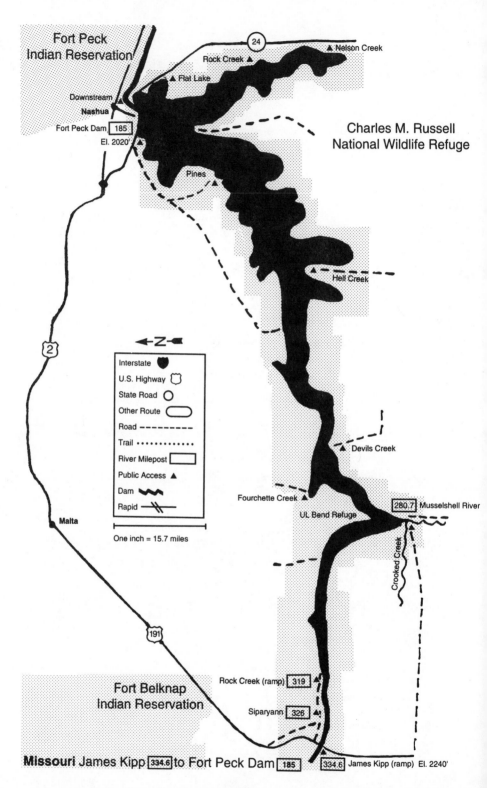

Fort Peck
Indian Reservation

24

▲ Nelson Creek
Rock Creek ▲

▲ Flat Lake

Downstream
Nashua

Fort Peck Dam 185

El. 2020'

Charles M. Russell
National Wildlife Refuge

Pines

Hell Creek ▲

2

←Z←

Interstate 🛡
U.S. Highway ⬡
State Road ◯
Other Route ⬭
Road -------
Trail ••••••••
River Milepost ▭
Public Access ▲
Dam 〰〰
Rapid ⫻

One inch = 15.7 miles

Devils Creek ▲

Fourchette Creek ▲

280.7 Musselshell River

UL Bend Refuge

Malta

Crooked Creek

191

Rock Creek (ramp) 319 ▲

Fort Belknap
Indian Reservation

Siparyann 326 ▲

Missouri James Kipp 334.6 to Fort Peck Dam 185   334.6 James Kipp (ramp) El. 2240'

172

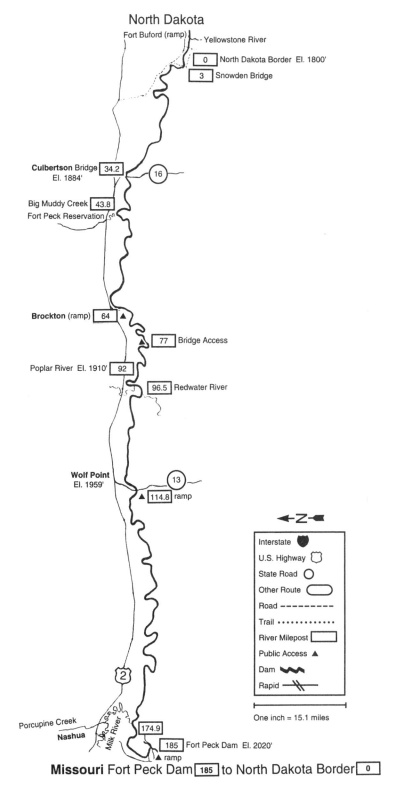

North Dakota

Fort Buford (ramp)
-- Yellowstone River

| 0 | North Dakota Border El. 1800' |
| 3 | Snowden Bridge |

Culbertson Bridge | 34.2 |
El. 1884'
(16)

Big Muddy Creek | 43.8 |
Fort Peck Reservation

Brockton (ramp) | 64 | ▲

▲ | 77 | Bridge Access

Poplar River El. 1910' | 92 |

| 96.5 | Redwater River

Wolf Point
El. 1959'
(13)
▲ | 114.8 | ramp

Interstate
U.S. Highway
State Road
Other Route
Road -------
Trail ••••••••••
River Milepost [ ]
Public Access ▲
Dam
Rapid

One inch = 15.1 miles

Porcupine Creek
Nashua

| 174.9 |
| 185 | Fort Peck Dam El. 2020'
▲ ramp

Missouri Fort Peck Dam | 185 | to North Dakota Border | 0 |

LITTLE MISSOURI

ORIGIN:	Near New Haven, WY. Enters MT south of Alzada, MT El. 3450'
END:	Flows into South Dakota northeast of Alzada, MT El. 3100'
LENGTH:	80 miles (in MT) (39 air miles)
FLOATABLE:	80 miles (during high water only)
SECTIONS:	Upper (33 mi.) Origin "80" to Albion Bridge "47" Middle (13 mi.) Albion Br. "47" to road br. "34" Lower (34 mi.) Camp Crook Road Bridge "34" to End-South Dakota border "0"
DAMS:	None
WATERFALLS:	None
WHITEWATER:	None
DANGERS:	Irrigation diversions, fences, remote areas, logjams, curvy, brushy
DEWATERED:	Usually in fall and until spring runoff
PORTAGES:	Irrigation diversions, fences
SPEC. AGENCIES:	None
REGS - PERMITS:	None
ACCESS-SHUTTLE:	Not easy. Long distances between access points. Road parallels river, but mostly private land. Muddy roads
SERVICES:	Limited in Alzada, MT
CAMPING:	No formal campgrounds or access sites. Private land.
GAMEFISH:	Catfish, sauger, pike, also sunfish and pumpkinseed
VESSEL:	Canoe, small boat
SKILL LEVEL:	Beginner
FLOAT TIMES:	Slow flow.

174

HYDROGRAPH

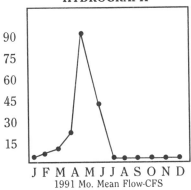

1991 Mo. Mean Flow-CFS

Gage Sta: Highway 20 Bridge at Camp Crook
Drain Area: 1,970 sq. mi. (at this locale)
Ave. Flow: (38 years) 123 cfs
Ext. Max: 9,420 cfs - 16.9' ga. ht. 3/24/78
Ext. Min: No flow at times
Gradient: 350' in 80 mi. = 4.4' pma
Float Grad: Same
Clarity: Murky

DRAINAGE: (East) Missouri (in North Dakota), Mississippi, Gulf

MAPS: BLM - #40 "Box Elder"
USFS - Custer NF (Sioux Division) lower only
USGS - "Ekalaka"
CO.   - Carter

Endangered prairie chicken

LITTLE MISSOURI

The Little Missouri is a big river! Big in length. The river headwaters near New Haven, Wyoming and flows for approximately 90 miles in Wyoming, 80 miles in Montana, 90 miles in South Dakota and 500 miles in North Dakota. The river empties into the Sakakawea Reservoir, on the Missouri system, at Charging Eagle Bay.

The river enters Montana south of Alzada and snakes its way across the extreme southeast corner of Montana. This is not a popular floating stream, but it does have enough water four months of the year.

This turbid river meanders through an arid rolling prairie ranch land. The muddy streambed is lined with sagebrush, willow thickets and marsh grasses, with steep eroded banks. A few irrigation diversions and debris collecting fences obstruct the river.

As the river flows through private land, formal campgrounds or access sites are non-existant. Numerous bridges must suffice for access. The Custer National Forest is on the north and does break up the prairie profile.

The low gradient causes slow flow, so a canoe or small boat is the answer. Some locals use a small motor when flow is up. A beginner can handle the entire river, but be cautious of rattlesnakes and bring a "fly swatter". Catfish, sauger, pike and the sporting sunfish and pumpkinseed inhabit the river.

Little Missouri River

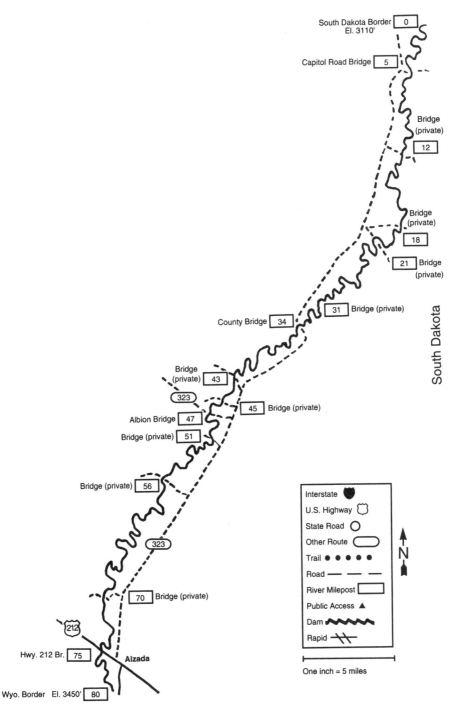

South Dakota Border
El. 3110'   0

Capitol Road Bridge   5

Bridge
(private)

12

Bridge
(private)

18

21   Bridge
(private)

31   Bridge (private)

County Bridge   34

Bridge
(private)   43

323

45   Bridge (private)

Albion Bridge   47

Bridge (private)   51

Bridge (private)   56

323

70   Bridge (private)

212

Hwy. 212 Br.   75   Alzada

Wyo. Border   El. 3450'   80

South Dakota

Interstate
U.S. Highway
State Road
Other Route
Trail ● ● ● ● ●
Road — — —
River Milepost
Public Access ▲
Dam
Rapid

N

One inch = 5 miles

Wyoming

Little Missouri

MUSSELSHELL

ORIGIN: Confluence of North & South Forks east of White Sulphur Springs, MT along Highway #12. El. 4700'

END: Flows into Fort Peck Reservoir on Missouri, north of Mosby, MT. El. 2234'

LENGTH: 364.3 miles
(132 air mi.)

FLOATABLE: 364.3 miles

SECTIONS: Upper (113.4 mi.) Origin "364.3" to Lavina Highway 3 Bridge "250.9"
Middle (120.5 mi.) Highway 3 Bridge "250.9" to Highway 12 Bridge "130.4"
Lower (130.4 mi.) Highway 12 Br. "130.4" to End "0"

DAMS: 34 diversion dams:

3' unnamed rock	357.3
Two Dot Concrete 10'	354.5
Unnamed	348.5
Unnamed	337
Unnamed	336.5
Unnamed	334.5
Milton Creek	333.1
Harlowton 3' rock	328.5
Harlowton 3' rock	322
Amer. Fork rock 5'	318.2
Winnecook 6' concrete	309.7
Deadmans 6' concrete	308.9
Webster 3' rock	308.3
Jensen 3' rock	307
Brady 3' rock	304.5
Vonica 3' rock	302.6
OK 3' rock	302
Taber 3' rock	300.8
Tierney 3' rock	297.5
Simms 3' rock	280.3
Dale 3' rock	268.5
Slayton 6' concrete	260.7
Lavina 6' concrete	257.3
Egge 6' concrete	240.5
Parrot 6' concrete	233
Naderman 6' concrete	223.2
Rodeghiero 12' concrete	217
Brown 5' concrete (narrow)	199.5
Goffena-Sudan 3' concrete	190

Kruger-Spendrift 3' rock	182
Delphia 3' concrete	178.9
Davis-Cooley-Goffena 6' concrete	170.3
Melstone 5' concrete	163
Musselshell 5' steel	160.5

WATERFALLS: None

WHITEWATER: None

DANGERS: Diversion dams, fences, remote area and poor roads near F.P. Reservoir. Irrigation returns.

DEWATERED: Often. Usually too low to float in fall.

PORTAGES: Diversion dams, fences.

SPEC. AGENCIES: None

REGS - PERMITS: None

ACCESS-SHUTTLE: Upper & Middle sections quite easy. Few access sites but adequate bridges. Lower section extremely difficult.

SERVICES: Lots of towns along river with most services.

CAMPING: Few formal campgrounds and access sites.

GAMEFISH: Upper - Brown, rainbow, whitefish
Middle - Also smallmouth bass (not good fishing)
Lower - Sauger, walleye, catfish, crappie, ling, pike

VESSEL: Canoe, medium raft, small boat

SKILL LEVEL: Beginner (Caution - dangers listed) if flows are normal.

FLOAT TIMES: Moderate to slow flow.

FLOW INFO: (406) 449-5263 USGS - Helena

HYDROGRAPH

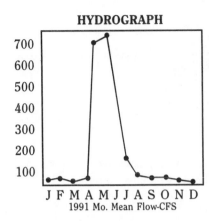

JFMAMJJASOND
1991 Mo. Mean Flow-CFS

Gage Sta: Harlowton, MT
Drain Area: 1,125 sq. mi. (at this locale)
Ave. Flow: (81 years) 159 cfs
Ext. Max: 7,270 cfs - 10.01' ga. ht. 6/20/75
Ext. Min: No flow at times
Gradient: 2466' in 364.3 mi. = 6.8' pma
Float Grad: Same
Clarity: Cloudy to murky
Temp: Jan. 32⁰ F.
      Apr. 43⁰ F.
      Jul. 69⁰ F.
      Oct. 50⁰ F.

DRAINAGE: (East) Missouri, Mississippi, Gulf of Mexico

MAPS: BLM - #24 "Castles" - #25 "Snowy" - #26 "Roundup"
#27 "Sumatra" - #17 "UL Bend"
USFS - Lewis & Clark NF (Jefferson Div.) (upper)
USGS - "White Sulphur" - "Roundup" - "Forsyth" - "Jordan"
CO. - Meagher, Wheatland, Golden Valley, Musselshell, Rosebud, Petroleum, Garfield

Dangerous current reversals

MUSSELSHELL

The mainstem of the Musselshell begins at the confluence of the North and South Forks, east of White Sulphur Springs, MT. The headwaters assist in the drainage of the Little Belt and Castle Mountains. The river meanders for nearly 365 miles before entering the remote Fort Peck Reservoir on the Missouri.

The rivers entire distance is floatable for those patient enough to deal with the 34 diversion dams found along its course. These diversion dams vary between 3' rock and 12' concrete structures. The river milepost maps, elsewhere in this writing, will give their locations.

As floating is not extremely popular on this river, few campgrounds or access sites occur. Bridges must suffice. A beginner can handle the entire river, when flow is normal. Incoming water returns deserve caution and the roads get slippery after rain, especially below Melstone. The river is often dewatered after spring runoff and heavy irrigation withdrawals are taking place. A canoe would be the best choice of craft, as slow moving water is prevalent.

Lewis & Clark on 5/30/1805 said the Menatares named it because of the quantities of "mussell shells" along the banks.

The upper and middle sections are very pretty, especially in the fall. The river meanders through private land, with ranching and some farming being the bases of the economy. From rolling prairie hills to surrounding high bluffs, followed by a panorama of the Bull Mountains and the pristine environment of the lower section, is an offering of many ecosystems.

Below Melstone, irrigation is not common and access to the river is difficult. This lower 130.4 mile section requires a good map and some shuttle exploring will be necessary. Attempting to explain the remote points here would be futile. It certainly is worth the effort if floating a remote and extended day portion of a river is your "bag". Fossils appear in the area and this is "where the deer and the antelope play".

Because of its proximity to Harlowton, locals commonly float between the two bridges (2.9 mi.). Fishing in the Musselshell is spotty at best. Above Harlowton, before the water has warmed and the heaviest irrigation withdrawals occur, brown trout are often caught. Below Harlowton is a struggling smallmouth bass fishery. The lower section has walleye, sauger, catfish, ling and pike.

Musselshell River

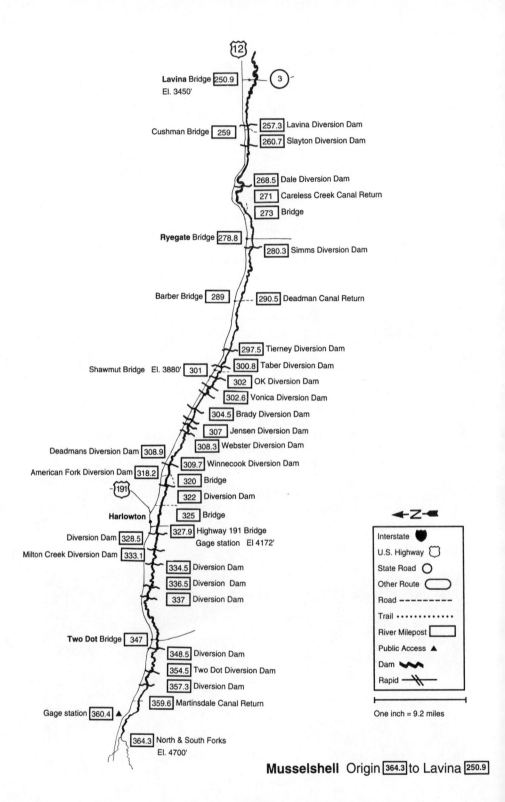

🛡12

Lavina Bridge 250.9 ◯3
El. 3450'

Cushman Bridge 259
257.3 Lavina Diversion Dam
260.7 Slayton Diversion Dam

268.5 Dale Diversion Dam
271 Careless Creek Canal Return
273 Bridge

Ryegate Bridge 278.8
280.3 Simms Diversion Dam

Barber Bridge 289
290.5 Deadman Canal Return

297.5 Tierney Diversion Dam
Shawmut Bridge   El. 3880' 301
300.8 Taber Diversion Dam
302 OK Diversion Dam
302.6 Vonica Diversion Dam
304.5 Brady Diversion Dam
307 Jensen Diversion Dam
308.3 Webster Diversion Dam
Deadmans Diversion Dam 308.9
309.7 Winnecook Diversion Dam
American Fork Diversion Dam 318.2
320 Bridge
🛡191
322 Diversion Dam
Harlowton
325 Bridge
327.9 Highway 191 Bridge
Gage station El 4172'
Diversion Dam 328.5
Milton Creek Diversion Dam 333.1
334.5 Diversion Dam
336.5 Diversion Dam
337 Diversion Dam

Two Dot Bridge 347
348.5 Diversion Dam
354.5 Two Dot Diversion Dam
357.3 Diversion Dam
359.6 Martinsdale Canal Return
Gage station 360.4 ▲
364.3 North & South Forks
El. 4700'

◀—Z—◀

Interstate	🛡
U.S. Highway	◯
State Road	◯
Other Route	⬭
Road	- - - - - - - -
Trail	• • • • • • • • •
River Milepost	▭
Public Access	▲
Dam	〰
Rapid	⤫

One inch = 9.2 miles

Musselshell Origin 364.3 to Lavina 250.9

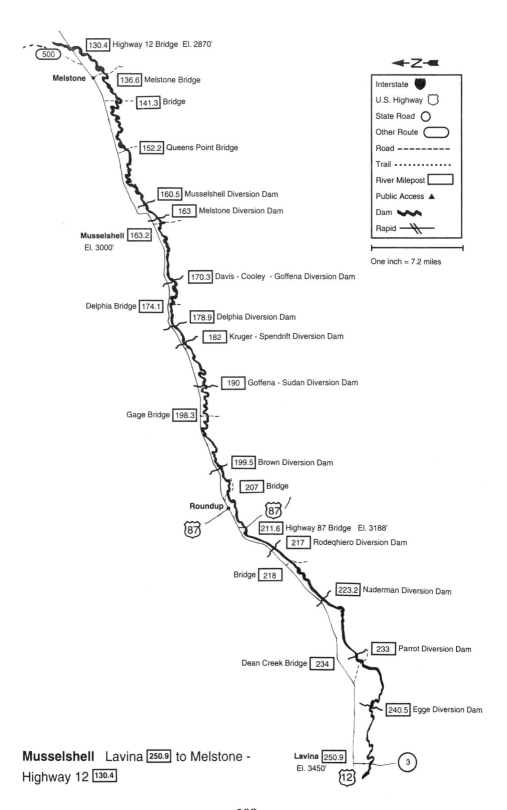

130.4 Highway 12 Bridge El. 2870'

500

Melstone

136.6 Melstone Bridge

141.3 Bridge

152.2 Queens Point Bridge

160.5 Musselshell Diversion Dam

163 Melstone Diversion Dam

Musselshell 163.2
El. 3000'

170.3 Davis - Cooley - Goffena Diversion Dam

Delphia Bridge 174.1

178.9 Delphia Diversion Dam

182 Kruger - Spendrift Diversion Dam

190 Goffena - Sudan Diversion Dam

Gage Bridge 198.3

199.5 Brown Diversion Dam

207 Bridge

Roundup

87

211.6 Highway 87 Bridge   El. 3188'

217 Rodeqhiero Diversion Dam

Bridge 218

223.2 Naderman Diversion Dam

233 Parrot Diversion Dam

Dean Creek Bridge 234

240.5 Egge Diversion Dam

Lavina 250.9
El. 3450'

3

12

Map Legend:

Interstate	(shield)
U.S. Highway	(shield)
State Road	◯
Other Route	⬭
Road	---------
Trail	•••••••••••
River Milepost	☐
Public Access	▲
Dam	〰
Rapid	/ /

←—N—→

One inch = 7.2 miles

Musselshell   Lavina 250.9 to Melstone -
Highway 12 130.4

183

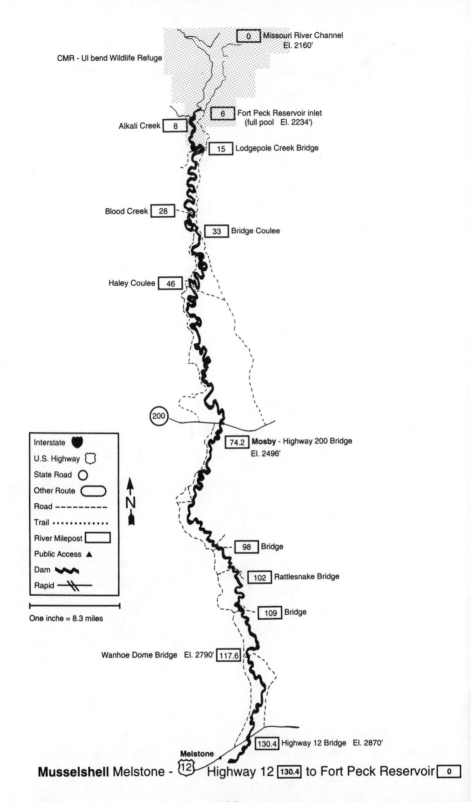

CMR - Ul bend Wildlife Refuge

| 0 | Missouri River Channel
El. 2160'

| 6 | Fort Peck Reservoir inlet
(full pool El. 2234')

Alkali Creek | 8 |

| 15 | Lodgepole Creek Bridge

Blood Creek | 28 |

| 33 | Bridge Coulee

Haley Coulee | 46 |

(200)

| 74.2 | **Mosby** - Highway 200 Bridge
El. 2496'

Interstate
U.S. Highway
State Road
Other Route
Road -------
Trail ....
River Milepost [   ]
Public Access ▲
Dam
Rapid

N

One inch = 8.3 miles

| 98 | Bridge

| 102 | Rattlesnake Bridge

| 109 | Bridge

Wanhoe Dome Bridge   El. 2790' | 117.6 |

| 130.4 | Highway 12 Bridge   El. 2870'

Melstone

Musselshell Melstone - (12) Highway 12 | 130.4 | to Fort Peck Reservoir | 0 |

POPLAR

ORIGIN:	Near Rockglen, Sask. Enters MT northwest of Scobey. El. 2460'
END:	Flows into Missouri River south of Poplar, MT. El. 1910'
LENGTH:	141.4 mi. (in MT) (70 air mi.)
FLOATABLE:	107.9 mi. (East Fork confluence to end)
SECTIONS:	Upper (33.5 mi.) Origin-Canada border "141.4" to East Fork Bridge "107.9" Middle (61.1 mi.) East Fork Br. "107.9" to Br. "46.8" Lower (46.8 mi.) Bridge "46.8" to Missouri River "0"
DAMS:	None
WATERFALLS:	None
WHITEWATER:	None
DANGERS:	Fences, remote area, irrigation jettys
DEWATERED:	Often in fall
PORTAGES:	None
SPEC. AGENCIES:	Fort Peck Indian Reservation
REGS - PERMITS:	Possible reservation recreation or fishing permits.
ACCESS-SHUTTLE:	Not easy. Long distances between access points, and roads can be poor.
SERVICES:	All services in Scobey and Poplar, MT
CAMPING:	No formal campgrounds and few access sites.
GAMEFISH:	Upper & Middle - Pike, walleye Lower - Walleye, ling, pike, sauger, catfish, smallmouth bass
VESSEL:	Any small vessel
SKILL LEVEL:	Beginner (if flows are normal)

FLOAT TIMES: Moderate to slow.

FLOW INFO: (406) 449-5263 USGS - Helena

HYDROGRAPH

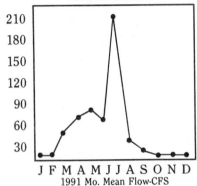

1991 Mo. Mean Flow-CFS

Gage Sta: 4 mi. North of Poplar, MT
Drain Area: 3,174 sq. mi. (at this locale)
Ave. Flow: (52 years) 124 cfs
Ext. Max: 37,400 cfs - 17.86' ga. ht. 4/6/54
Ext. Min: No flow at times
Gradient: 550' in 141.4 mi. = 3.9' pma
Float Grad: Same
Clarity: Cloudy to turbid
Temp: Jan. 32° F.
      Apr. 55° F.
      Jul. 71° F.
      Oct. 40° F.

DRAINAGE: (East) Missouri, Mississippi, Gulf of Mexico

MAPS: BLM - #9 "Poplar"
      USGS - "Wolf Point"
      CO.   - Daniels, Roosevelt

Mallards

186

POPLAR

Early settlers called the river "Porcupine", because of the quilly little nuisances that were common. Its present name comes from the poplar trees that grow in abundance. The river begins near Rockglen, Saskatchewan and flows for approximately twenty five miles in Canada before entering Montana, northwest of Scobey. The river flows for nearly 142 miles to the Missouri River south of Poplar, Montana.

The upper section flows through a remote area with access difficulty. The Middle and East Forks add volume to the river and a bridge crosses just below this confluence. Floating can begin at this bridge "107.9". Bridges in the Scobey area offer access points at no more than nine river miles between.

The Highway 13 bridge "90.9" near Scobey, is the beginning of a 22 mile section with no access, down to a bridge at milepost "69". The Fort Peck Indian Reservation begins midway between these two bridges, and continues for the rest of the river.

The West Fork, six miles below this bridge, adds more volume to the river. A dam impounds a small reservoir at milepost "50.5", however it is possible to float right around this dam.

The best place to begin floating is at the gage station bridge "46.8", due to the added water from the West Fork. Below the gage station bridge are the remains of two old diversion dams at mileposts "43.3" and "40.6". One can float right through these. Another bridge occurs at mile "28" and numerous bridges below this point offer ingress or egress with no more than seven river mile intervals. Four miles below Poplar, Montana the river enters the Missouri.

The fall is a beautiful time to float if flow permits. The autumn foliage is exquisite. A beginner can handle the river in any small vessel. A canoe is the best as some "dead" water occurs and winds are common.

The upper and middle sections are inhabited by pike and walleye. The lower section also has ling, sauger, catfish and smallmouth bass.

Snow and Blue phase geese

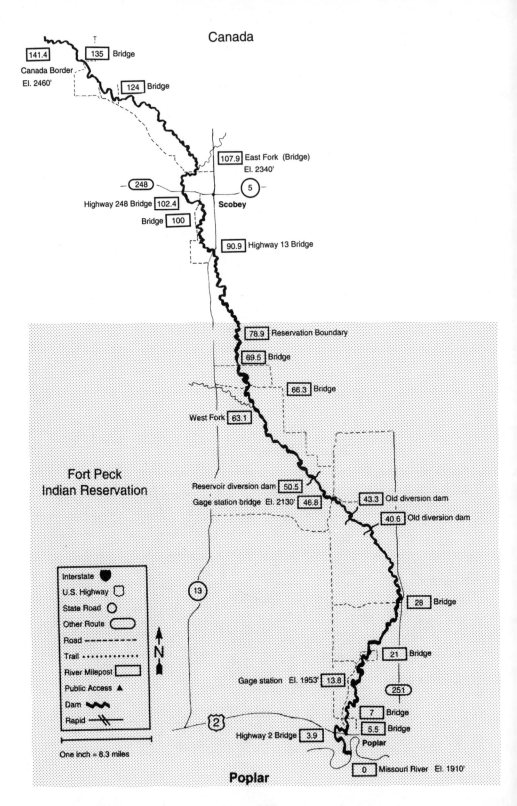

Canada

141.4
Canada Border
El. 2460'

135 Bridge

124 Bridge

107.9 East Fork (Bridge)
El. 2340'

248

5

Highway 248 Bridge 102.4

Bridge 100

Scobey

90.9 Highway 13 Bridge

78.9 Reservation Boundary

69.5 Bridge

66.3 Bridge

West Fork 63.1

Fort Peck
Indian Reservation

Reservoir diversion dam 50.5

Gage station bridge El. 2130' 46.8

43.3 Old diversion dam

40.6 Old diversion dam

Interstate	⬛
U.S. Highway	⬭
State Road	◯
Other Route	⬭
Road	- - - -
Trail	· · · ·
River Milepost	▭
Public Access	▲
Dam	〜
Rapid	⧸

N

One inch = 8.3 miles

13

28 Bridge

21 Bridge

251

Gage station El. 1953' 13.8

7 Bridge

5.5 Bridge

2

Highway 2 Bridge 3.9

Poplar

0 Missouri River El. 1910'

Poplar

188

POWDER

ORIGIN:	Near Kaycee, WY. Enters MT southwest of Broadus. El. 3350'
END:	Flows into Yellowstone River near Terry, MT. El. 2250'
LENGTH:	217.5 mi. (in MT) (125 air mi.)
FLOATABLE:	217.5 mi.
SECTIONS:	Upper (62.5 mi.) Origin - WY border "217.5" to Little Powder River "155" Middle (108.2 mi.) L. Powder "155" to Mizpah Creek Bridge "46.8" Lower (46.8 mi.) Mizpah Bridge "46.8" to End - Yellowstone River "0"
DAMS:	None
WATERFALLS:	None
WHITEWATER:	None
DANGERS:	Shallow, mud & quicksand, fences, irrigation projects, remote area, muddy roads.
DEWATERED:	Usually in fall.
PORTAGES:	None
SPEC. AGENCIES:	None
REGS - PERMITS:	None
ACCESS-SHUTTLE:	Difficult. Roads parallel river - but distant. Few access sites. Mostly private land. Muddy roads.
SERVICES:	All in Broadus, MT only.
CAMPING:	No formal campgrounds, and very few access sites. Private land.
GAMEFISH:	Catfish, shovelnose sturgeon, sauger
VESSEL:	Any small craft.

SKILL LEVEL:	Beginner, with caution to dangers, if flows are normal.
FLOAT TIMES:	Moderate to slow flows.
FLOW INFO:	(406) 449-5263 USGS - Helena

HYDROGRAPH

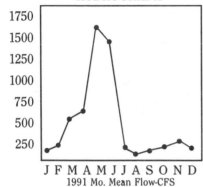

1750
1500
1250
1000
750
500
250

J F M A M J J A S O N D
1991 Mo. Mean Flow-CFS

Gage Sta: Highway 12 Bridge at Locate, MT
Drain Area: 13,194 sq. mi. (at this locale)
Ave. Flow: (53 years) 580 cfs
Ext. Max: 31,000 cfs - 12.2' ga. ht. 2/19/43
Ext. Min: No flow at times
Gradient: 1100' in 217.5 mi. = 5.1' pma
Float Grad: Same
Clarity: Turbid
Temp: Jan. 32⁰ F.
      Apr. 45⁰ F.
      Jul. 73⁰ F.
      Oct. 43⁰ F.

DRAINAGE:	(East) Yellowstone, Missouri, Mississippi, Gulf
MAPS:	BLM - #39 "Powder" - #40 "Box Elder" - #29 "Custer" USGS - "Ekalaka" (upper) - "Miles City" (lower) CO. - Powder River, Custer, Prairie

Our prairie neighbors

190

POWDER

The etymology of this river begins with the Lewis and Clark Expedition calling it "Redstone" for the red rocks nearby. A Frenchman, Roubidoux, during an Indian attack shouted, "cacher le poudre" (hide the powder!). It has also been jokingly described as "an inch deep and a mile wide".

The Powder River begins near Kaycee, Wyoming and flows for approximately 185 miles before entering Montana. This turbid river then sluggishly flows for nearly 218 more miles, before adding more silt to the Yellowstone near Terry, Montana.

Floating is often impossible in late summer and the fall, but when flow permits, its entire distance in Montana is floatable. The upper section offers rugged "badlands" beauty. This environment supports large populations of mule deer, many of the bucks being magnificent. Access points are rare, as private land, and the areas remoteness, require few bridges. Since the river is not popular for floating, formal campgrounds are nearly non-existent. Roads do parallel the river at a distance, with a very few intersecting points. An extended day outing is enjoyable.

A beginner can handle the river in any moderately sized vessel, when flow permits. The stream bed is muddy and shallow. These shallow place are often not distinguishable due to the waters turbidity, and getting out to drag your craft can be dangerous. Quicksand also occurs in a few areas. Although there are no major portages, fences and a few irrigation projects along the bank deserve caution. Since this a remote area and roads can become impassable with a little rain, careful trip planning is imperative.

The middle and lower sections support large cottonwood bottoms and are surrounded by rolling prairie hills. Not commonly thought of as a fishing stream, a few catfish, sauger and shovelnose sturgeon are present. An informal campsite is offered at the mouth of the river, to the Yellowstone.

Powder River

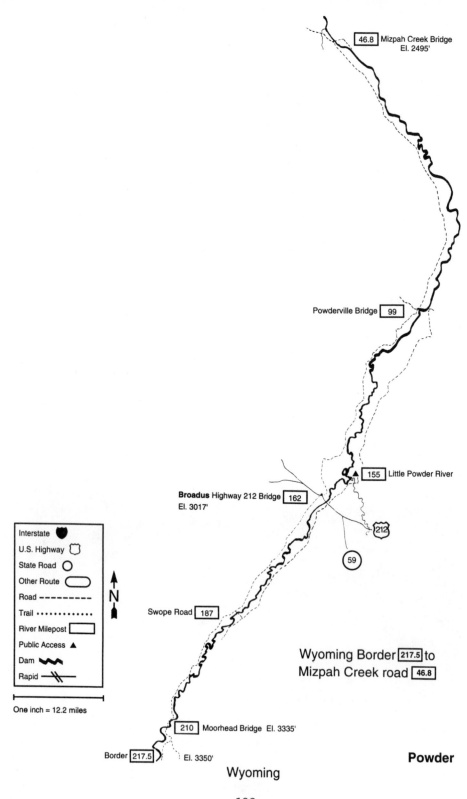

46.8 Mizpah Creek Bridge
El. 2495'

Powderville Bridge 99

155 Little Powder River

Broadus Highway 212 Bridge 162
El. 3017'

212

59

Swope Road 187

Wyoming Border 217.5 to
Mizpah Creek road 46.8

210 Moorhead Bridge El. 3335'

Border 217.5   El. 3350'

Powder

Wyoming

Interstate
U.S. Highway
State Road
Other Route
Road ----------
Trail ....
River Milepost
Public Access ▲
Dam
Rapid

N

One inch = 12.2 miles

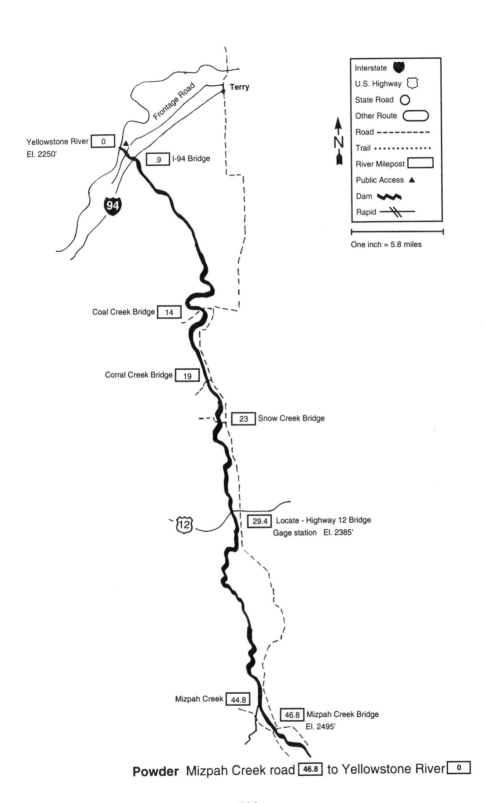

Terry

Frontage Road

Yellowstone River [0]
El. 2250'

[.9] I-94 Bridge

94

Interstate
U.S. Highway
State Road
Other Route
Road --------
Trail ....
River Milepost [   ]
Public Access ▲
Dam 〰〰
Rapid ⫽

↑
N
↑

One inch = 5.8 miles

Coal Creek Bridge [14]

Corral Creek Bridge [19]

[23] Snow Creek Bridge

(12)   [29.4] Locate - Highway 12 Bridge
Gage station   El. 2385'

Mizpah Creek [44.8]

[46.8] Mizpah Creek Bridge
El. 2495'

Powder Mizpah Creek road [46.8] to Yellowstone River [0]

193

RED

ORIGIN:	Fitzpatrick Creek northeast of Cut Bank, MT. El. 4000'
END:	Flows into Canada (Milk River), near Milk River, Alberta after re-entering MT for 1 mi. El. 3600'
LENGTH:	13.7 total mi. in MT. (12.7 river mi. + Buckley Reservoir 1 mi.) (7 air mi.)
FLOATABLE:	0 river mi. (However, Buckley Reservoir is floatable) Mi. "1" to "0"
DAMS:	Buckley Reservoir Dam (actually a low spillway impoundment)
WATERFALLS:	None
WHITEWATER:	None
DANGERS:	Remote area, wind, muddy roads, fences and culverts in unfloatable river.
DEWATERED:	No water except during runoff or a heavy rain. Buckley Reservoir usually has some water.

A camping friend

194

SPEC. AGENCIES:	None
REGS - PERMITS:	Canada border (no Immigration)
ACCESS-SHUTTLE:	County road and through gravel pit on Buckley private property, to reservoir. Need good map.
SERVICES:	None
CAMPING:	No campgrounds. Private property.
GAMEFISH:	Catfish (in reservoir)
VESSEL:	Canoe on reservoir and backwater
SKILL LEVEL:	Beginner (if no wind)
GRADIENT:	400' in 15.7 mi. = 25.5' pma
WATER:	Murky, warm, no flow usually.
DRAINAGE:	(East) Milk, Missouri, Mississippi, Gulf of Mexico
MAPS:	BLM - #27 "Cut Bank" USGS - "Cut Bank" CO. - Glacier, Toole

Shuttle option

RED

    The origin of the river is at Fitzpatrick Creek, northeast of Cut Bank, Montana. The river then flows into Canada for two miles, re-enters Montana for 1.9 miles, before re-entering Canada and flowing for 11.2 miles into the Milk River near Milk River, Alberta.

    The river only flows during spring runoff or after heavy rains. This prairie river flows through culverts under roads and numerous fences are obstacles. The one-mile long Buckley Reservoir is floatable. A beginner can canoe or use a small boat on the often windy reservoir. Occasionally, one can canoe beyond the reservoir upstream for another mile of backwater.

    The locals use a picnic site at the reservoir. Catfish are present and catchable. Access to this reservoir can be north and east from Cut Bank or west of Sweetgrass. Roads can be muddy after moisture. Canoeing across the International Border is not allowed.

Red River

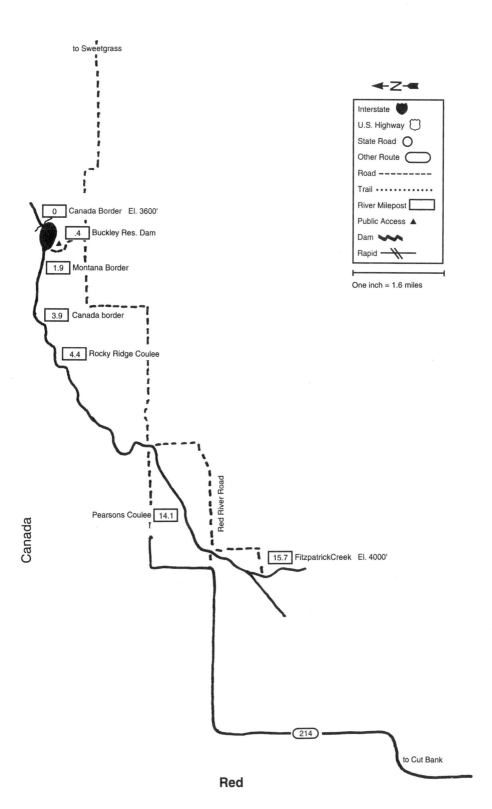

to Sweetgrass

←-N-←

Interstate
U.S. Highway
State Road
Other Route
Road ----------
Trail ••••••••••••
River Milepost
Public Access ▲
Dam
Rapid

One inch = 1.6 miles

0 Canada Border   El. 3600'

.4 Buckley Res. Dam

1.9 Montana Border

3.9 Canada border

4.4 Rocky Ridge Coulee

Red River Road

Canada

Pearsons Coulee 14.1

15.7 FitzpatrickCreek El. 4000'

214

to Cut Bank

Red

197

RED ROCK

ORIGIN:	Lillian Lake near Red Rock Mtn. El. 9,000'
END:	Flows into Clark Canyon Reservoir south of Dillon. El. 5542'
LENGTH:	131.5 total mi. (103.8 river mi. + 2 lakes & 2 reservoirs 27.7 mi.)

Upper & Lower Red Rock Lake 10.8 mi.
Lima Reservoir   12.7
Clark Canyon Reservoir   <u>4.2</u>
                     All floatable   27.7 mi.
(70 air mi.)

FLOATABLE:	91.3 river mi. (Mi. "119" El. 6750' to end)
SECTIONS:	Upper (37.5 mi.) Origin "131.5" to Brundage "94" Middle (35.7 mi.) Brundage Bridge "94" to Lima Dam "58.3" Lower (58.3 mi.) Lima Dam "58.3" to CC Dam "0"
DAMS:	Lower Red Rock Lake dam Mi. "101.9" portage Lima Mi. "58.3" portage Clark Canyon Mi. "0" Forms reservoir & controls flow of Beaverhead River
WATERFALLS:	None
WHITEWATER:	None
DANGERS:	Dams, irrig. jettys, fences, remote area, levee Mi. "83"
DEWATERED:	Can be dewatered in fall.
PORTAGES:	2 dams (see above).
SPEC. AGENCIES:	Deptartment of Interior (Red Rock Lakes Refuge)
REGS - PERMITS:	No motors on refuge, except during waterfowl season in hunting area (10 hp max.). No air thrust boats. Numerous fish regulations. No bait or lead sinkers. 10 hp max. on all streams in Beaverhead County.
ACCESS-SHUTTLE:	Somewhat difficult around lakes and upper area. Lower area easier, but mostly private land.
SERVICES:	Very limited at Red Rock Lakes and Lima, MT.

CAMPING:	Campgrounds at Red Rock Lakes and Clark Canyon Reservoir. Little opportunity to camp at informal sites.
GAMEFISH:	Lakes area - Brook, grayling, cutthroat, ling Below Lima Dam - Cutthroat, rainbow, brown trout.
VESSEL:	Canoe, small boat, medium raft (lots of dead water). Float tubes not allowed on Red Rock Lakes.
SKILL LEVEL:	Beginner (Caution - dangers above and wind)
FLOAT TIMES:	Upper - SLOW and very curvy through Middle section. Lower - Moderate flow.
FLOW INFO:	(406) 449-5263 USGS - Helena

HYDROGRAPH

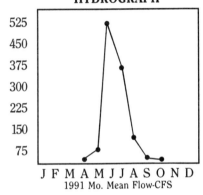

J F M A M J J A S O N D
1991 Mo. Mean Flow-CFS

Gage Sta: Below Dam near Lima, MT
Drain Area: 570 sq. mi. (at this location)
Ave. Flow: (48 years) 143 cfs
Ext. Max: 2500 cfs - 6.4' ga. ht. 5/15/33
Ext. Min: No flow at times.
Gradient: 3458' in 131.5 mi. = 26.4' pma
Float Grad: 1208' in 119.0 mi. = 10.2' pma
Clarity: Cloudy to clear

DRAINAGE:	(East) Beaverhead, Jefferson, Missouri, Mississippi
MAPS:	BLM - #42 "Centennial" (upper) - #41 "Red Rock" USFS - Beaverhead NF (Interagency) entire river USGS - "Ashton" (upper) - "Dubois" (lower). Sp. - "Red Rock Lakes Recreation Guide" (upper only) US Fish & Wildlife CO. - Beaverhead

RED ROCK

Lillian Lake, near Red Rock Mountain in the Centennial Range, is the inception of the river. Red Rock Lakes National Wildlife Refuge covers 40,000 acres of this high country prairie. Ornithologists and bird watchers enjoy over 200 species on this natural aviary. Moose also inhabit the area. The headwaters of the Red Rock mark the beginning of the longest river system on the North American continent. Upper and Lower Red Rock Lakes are connected by marsh, with channels difficult to distinguish. Current regulations on recreational use are available at refuge headquarters. Regulations are researched with wildlife habitat uppermost in mind, and still allow recreational use. This refuge may be one of the reasons the Trumpeter Swan has avoided extinction.

Floating can begin above the Upper Red Rock Lake, and you can canoe through the lakes. A dam at the outlet of Lower Red Rock Lake "101.9" exists, before the stream starts snaking its way along the valley floor. Fishing in the lakes area, can be quite good for brookies, cutthroat and ling. This is also one of the few places grayling are found. A beginner can handle the entire river in a canoe or small boat. Rafts do not work well without current or in windy areas. A small raft will work nicely below Lima Dam.

Brundage Bridge "94" offers access to the river below the lakes. Watch for a levee at milepost "83", and the Lyons Bridge "72.7", on the inlet side of Lima Reservoir offers access. Some people use motors here.

Below Lima Dam "58.3" is the most popular floating section. Beginners should be alert for irrigation jettys and fences, as the river velocity increases with abrupt curves. The river can be dewatered in autumn. The banks again are lined with trees that have been void above.

There are campgrounds at the Red Rock Lakes and also at Clark Canyon Reservoir. There are no formal access points between, so bridges will have to suffice. Most of the land is private in this lower segment so try to stay within the high water marks. Cutthroat, rainbow and brown trout inhabit this lower section. The Clark Canyon Reservoir offers fishing and numerous boating activities.

The commonly used name "Red Rock", dates back to the early settlers and the red rock formations along the river.

Red Rock River

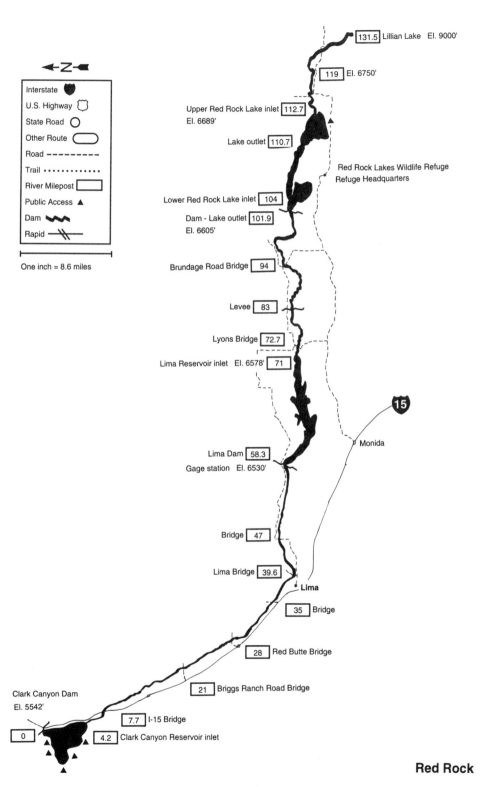

Map Legend

Interstate	🛡
U.S. Highway	⬡
State Road	○
Other Route	⬭
Road	- - - - - -
Trail	· · · · · · · ·
River Milepost	☐
Public Access	▲
Dam	〰
Rapid	≠

One inch = 8.6 miles

131.5 Lillian Lake   El. 9000'

119   El. 6750'

Upper Red Rock Lake inlet 112.7
El. 6689'

Lake outlet 110.7

Red Rock Lakes Wildlife Refuge
Refuge Headquarters

Lower Red Rock Lake inlet 104

Dam - Lake outlet 101.9
El. 6605'

Brundage Road Bridge 94

Levee 83

Lyons Bridge 72.7

Lima Reservoir inlet   El. 6578' 71

15

Lima Dam 58.3
Gage station   El. 6530'

Monida

Bridge 47

Lima Bridge 39.6

Lima

35 Bridge

28 Red Butte Bridge

21 Briggs Ranch Road Bridge

Clark Canyon Dam
El. 5542'

7.7 I-15 Bridge

0

4.2 Clark Canyon Reservoir inlet

Red Rock

REDWATER

ORIGIN: Confluence of Trail and Lisk Creeks southwest of Brockway, MT El. 2600'

END: Flows into Missouri River near Poplar, MT El. 1920'

LENGTH: 149.1 miles
(65 air mi.)

FLOATABLE: 132.2 miles (Brockway Bridge "132.2" to end) High water only!

SECTIONS: Upper (16.9 mi.) Origin "149.1" to Brockway Bridge "132.2"
Middle (101.5 mi.) Brockway Bridge "132.2" to East Fork Bridge "30.7"
Lower (30.7 mi.) East Fork Bridge "30.7" to End - Missouri River "0"

DAMS: None

WATERFALLS: None

WHITEWATER: None

DANGERS: Irrigation, fences, remote areas

DEWATERED: Floatable only during high water. May - July

PORTAGES: Fences

SPEC. AGENCIES: None

REGS - PERMITS: None

ACCESS-SHUTTLE: Extremely difficult. Few paralleling roads and bridges. No formal access sites.

SERVICES: Limited in Brockway, MT. All services in Circle, MT

CAMPING: No formal campgrounds or access sites. Private land.

GAMEFISH: Upper - Pike
Middle & Lower - Sauger, walleye, pike, ling, catfish

VESSEL: Canoe, small boat

SKILL LEVEL: Beginner

FLOAT TIMES: Extremely slow. Usually little or no current.

FLOW INFO: (406) 449-5263 USGS - Helena

HYDROGRAPH

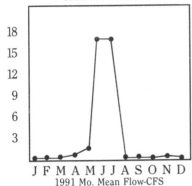

1991 Mo. Mean Flow-CFS

Gage Sta: Circle, MT
Drain Area: 547 sq. mi. (at this locale)
Ave. Flow: (53 years) 12 cfs
Ext. Max: 6,960 cfs - 12.85' ga. ht. 6/29/86
Ext. Min: No flow at times (most years!)
Gradient: 680' in 149.1 mi. = 4.6' pma
Float Grad: Same
Clarity: Murky
Temp: Jul. 76° F.
　　　 Oct. 43° F.

DRAINAGE: (East) Missouri, Mississippi, Gulf of Mexico

MAPS: BLM - #19 "Circle" - #9 "Poplar" (extreme lower)
USGS - "Glendive" - "Wolf Point" (extreme lower)
CO. - McCone, Dawson

Sandhill Crane

203

REDWATER

The river is named for the red shale lining the banks and coloring the water in places. The origin of the Redwater is above Brockway, Montana at the confluence of Trail and Lisk Creeks. The river then flows into the Missouri, nearly 150 miles distant, at Poplar, Montana.

The crooked meandering stream flows through private ranchland and the middle section is remote and quite inaccessible. The streambed varies from silt to sand and has marsh grasses growing along its undercut banks.

The prairie runoff allows floating for only three spring or summer months. Some locals feel the river flows underground in places. However I am of the opinion that the stream becomes dewatered, due to lack of runoff and sprinkler irrigation withdrawals. Below the dewatered portion, perhaps irrigation returns, springs or feeder creeks, create the appearance of more water.

A beginner can handle the river in a canoe or small boat. A canoe is the best vessel, as "dead" water is common and windy conditions may occur. The only dangers are a few fences and some low irrigation jettys and pipe.

Pike can be found in the upper section and the middle and lower sections also have sauger, walleye, ling and catfish.

No formal campgrounds or access sites exist, so infrequent bridges must suffice. In the middle section, one float must be 27 miles between bridges. Another portion is 24 miles between bridges. Refer to the river milepost for exact locations of these bridges. Use of a good and detailed map, showing all access backroads, is also recommended.

Older and wiser - Great Horned Owl

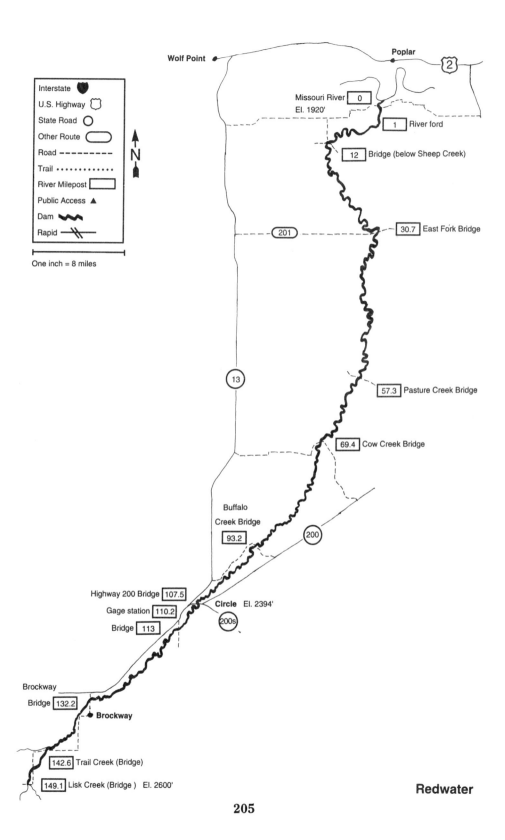

Legend (One inch = 8 miles)

- Interstate
- U.S. Highway
- State Road
- Other Route
- Road ---------
- Trail ....
- River Milepost ☐
- Public Access ▲
- Dam 〰〰
- Rapid

N

Wolf Point

Poplar

2

Missouri River 0
El. 1920'

1   River ford

12   Bridge (below Sheep Creek)

201

30.7   East Fork Bridge

13

57.3   Pasture Creek Bridge

69.4   Cow Creek Bridge

Buffalo
Creek Bridge
93.2

200

Highway 200 Bridge 107.5

Gage station 110.2

Circle   El. 2394'

Bridge 113

200s

Brockway

Bridge 132.2

Brockway

142.6   Trail Creek (Bridge)

149.1   Lisk Creek (Bridge)   El. 2600'

Redwater

ROCK CREEK

ORIGIN:	Confluence of West and Middle Forks. El. 5200'
END:	Flows into Clark Fork R. near Clinton. El. 3500'
LENGTH:	51.4 mi. (35 air mi.)
FLOATABLE:	51.4 mi. (Class I portion is entire 51.4 mi.)
SECTIONS:	Upper (15.4 mi.) Origin "51.4" to Bridge "36" Middle (23.0 mi.) Bridge "36" to Fish access site "13" Lower (13.0 mi.) Access site "13" to End "0"
DAMS:	None
WATERFALLS:	None
WHITEWATER:	4.5 mi. Harrys Flat Campground "17.5" to Fish Access "13". Class III-IV depending on flow.
DANGERS:	Dalles Whitewater portion.
DEWATERED:	Can be low in fall.
PORTAGES:	Possibly the whitewater section 4.5 mi.
SPEC. AGENCIES:	Welcome Creek Wilderness
REGS - PERMITS:	Wilderness area (left bank). No fishing while floating 7/1 to 11/30 (entire river).
ACCESS-SHUTTLE:	Easy. Road parallels river.
SERVICES:	Gas, food, lodging at Guest Ranches along river.
CAMPING:	Numerous campgrounds and access sites.
GAMEFISH:	Upper - Rainbow, cutthroat Lower - Rainbow, brown, brook, cutthroat, bulls, whitefish
VESSEL:	Medium raft, canoe, small boat all except whitewater section: Good raft, kayak, whitewater canoe.
SKILL LEVEL:	Beginner, except whitewater - Experienced.

FLOAT TIMES: Moderately fast.

FLOW INFO: (406) 449-5263 USGS - Helena

HYDROGRAPH

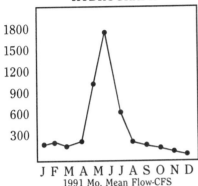

1800
1500
1200
900
600
300

J F M A M J J A S O N D
1991 Mo. Mean Flow-CFS

Gage Sta: .2 mi. upstream from mouth
Drain Area: 885 sq. mi.
Ave. Flow: (19 years) 538 cfs
Ext. Max: 5,520 cfs - 7.49' ga. ht. 6/20/75
Ext. Min: 41 cfs 2/20/89
Gradient: 1700' in 51.4 mi. = 33' pma
Float Grad: Same
Clarity: Clear
Temp: Jan. 34⁰ F.
          Apr. 43⁰ F.
          Jul. 58⁰ F.
          Oct. 43⁰ F.

DRAINAGE: (West) Clark Fork, Pend Oreille, Columbia, Pacific

MAPS: BLM - #21 "Granite"
          USFS - Deer Lodge NF (Best map) - Lolo NF
          USGS - "Butte"
          CO.   - Granite, Missoula

Marmot

207

ROCK CREEK

Rock Creek is one of only two creeks in Montana to receive the distinction of being a Class I stream. Rock Creek begins at the confluence of the West and Middle Forks "51.4" and is a wonderful trout stream throughout. Rainbow, browns, cutts, brookies, bulls and whitefish all exist in this well-managed stream. Fishing while floating is not allowed from 7/1 to 11/30. Floating can begin as high as its origin, and frequent campgrounds and access sites are made possible by a road that parallels the entire creek. Floaters should be courteous to the many bank or wading fisherpersons they will probably encounter.

The Welcome Creek Wilderness Area begins at Cinnamon Bear Creek "18.6" and follows along the left bank for 12 1/2 miles. Rock Creek has 4 1/2 miles of whitewater known as the Dalles Rapids. This whitewater begins at Harrys Flat Campground "17.5" and continues past the Dalles Campground to the access site below at milepost "13". A steep gradient and big boulders to maneuver around make this quite challenging. While beginners can handle the entire creek normally, this whitewater portion should only be run by an experienced paddler in a medium raft, kayak, or whitewater canoe.

Valley of the Moon Access "3" or the private campground "1" are your last opportunities to exit. You may continue however, on into the Clark Fork and exit at Schwartz Creek Access above Clinton, 3 miles downstream.

Rock Creek

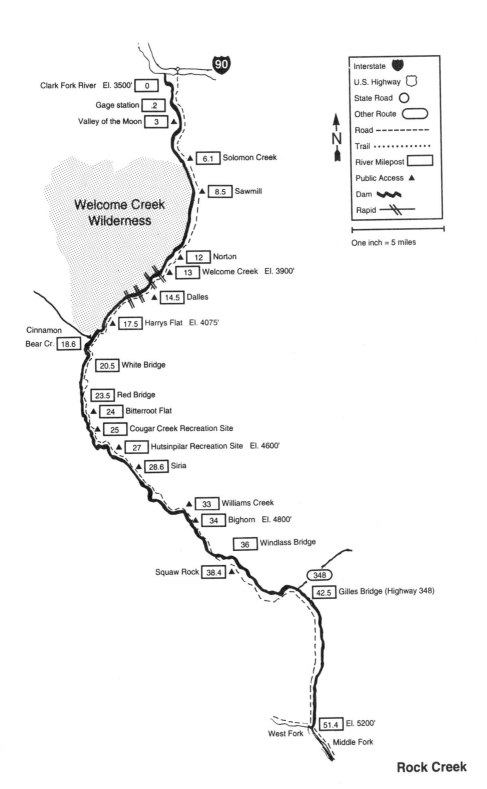

Clark Fork River El. 3500' `0`

Gage station `.2`

Valley of the Moon `3` ▲

▲ `6.1` Solomon Creek

▲ `8.5` Sawmill

Welcome Creek Wilderness

▲ `12` Norton

`13` Welcome Creek El. 3900'

▲ `14.5` Dalles

▲ `17.5` Harrys Flat El. 4075'

Cinnamon
Bear Cr. `18.6`

`20.5` White Bridge

`23.5` Red Bridge

▲ `24` Bitterroot Flat

▲ `25` Cougar Creek Recreation Site

▲ `27` Hutsinpilar Recreation Site El. 4600'

▲ `28.6` Siria

`33` Williams Creek

▲ `34` Bighorn El. 4800'

`36` Windlass Bridge

Squaw Rock `38.4` ▲

(348)

`42.5` Gilles Bridge (Highway 348)

`51.4` El. 5200'
West Fork
Middle Fork

Legend:

Interstate 🛡
U.S. Highway ⬡
State Road ◯
Other Route ⬭
Road -- -- --
Trail • • • • •
River Milepost ▭
Public Access ▲
Dam 〰〰
Rapid ⫽

One inch = 5 miles

N

Rock Creek

ROSEBUD (Stillwater)

ORIGIN:	Confluence of East & West Forks south of Absarokee. El. 4200'
END:	Flows into Stillwater River just north of Absarokee. El. 3990'
LENGTH:	4 miles (3 air mi.)
FLOATABLE:	4 miles
SECTIONS:	None
DAMS:	3 low diversion jettys
WATERFALLS:	None
WHITEWATER:	4 mi. when water high (entire river!)
DANGERS:	3 diversion jettys, whitewater, narrow, curvy, logs
DEWATERED:	Can be too low in fall
PORTAGES:	None
SPEC. AGENCIES:	None
REGS - PERMITS:	None
ACCESS-SHUTTLE:	Easy, but round-about. Secondary road along upper river with easy access. Takeout on Stillwater River
SERVICES:	All in Absarokee or Columbus, MT
CAMPING:	Campgrounds available on Stillwater River.
GAMEFISH:	Brown, rainbow
VESSEL:	Whitewater canoe, small raft, canoe, kayak
SKILL LEVEL:	Experienced
FLOAT TIMES:	Fast
FLOW INFO:	446-2103 Custer NF (Beartooth Division)

HYDROGRAPH

1400
1200
1000
800
600
400
200

J F M A M J J A S O N D
1964-69 Mo. Mean Flow-CFS

Gage Sta: Absarokee, MT
Drain Area: 401 sq. mi.
Ave. Flow: (5 years) 438 cfs
Ext. Max: 4880 cfs 6/15/67
Ext. Min: 82 cfs 2/8/67
Gradient: 210' in 4 mi. = 52.5' pma
Float Grad: Same
Clarity: Clear

DRAINAGE: (East) Stillwater, Yellowstone, Missouri, Mississippi, Gulf of Mexico

MAPS: BLM - #35 "Beartooth"
USFS - Custer NF (Beartooth Division)
USGS - "Billings"
CO.   - Stillwater

Pheasant

211

ROSEBUD (Stillwater)

The name Rosebud is inspired by the profusely growing wild roses, found in the area. The origin is at the confluence of the East and West Forks, just south of Absarokee, Montana. The mainstem is only four miles long. The feeder forks, sometimes called the East and West Rosebud, are 37 and 29 miles long respectfully. Some floating can be done on these two forks.

An old road going south from Absarokee along the river, offers access at the East and West Fork confluence. This entire four miles is whitewater when flow is high, and is often unfloatable in the fall.

This narrow and steep gradient stream has sharp curves, boulders and some partial downfall. Avoiding these obstacles is a challenge. The river requires an experienced pilot in a whitewater canoe, kayak or small raft. Three diversion jettys, which can be floated over, add to the excitement.

Midway between the starting point and the Highway 420 bridge ".9" in Absarokee, the old road comes close to the river at one jetty. The bridge in Absarokee, is the last place to exit on the Rosebud. However, floating can continue on into the Stillwater River and down to a bridge access, one mile below.

Browns and rainbow offer good fishing. Campgrounds can be found downstream on the Stillwater River.

Rosebud River

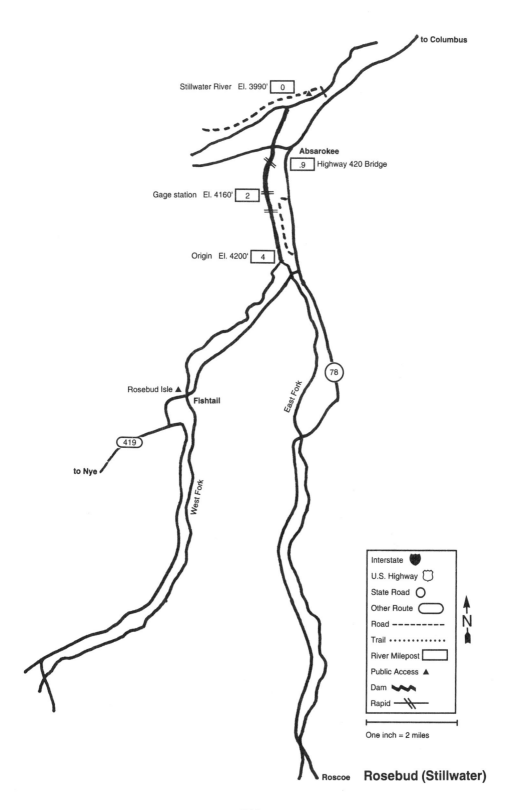

to Columbus

Stillwater River   El. 3990'   0

Absarokee

.9   Highway 420 Bridge

Gage station   El. 4160'   2

Origin   El. 4200'   4

East Fork

78

Rosebud Isle ▲   **Fishtail**

419

to Nye

West Fork

Interstate
U.S. Highway
State Road
Other Route
Road - - - - - - -
Trail · · · · · · · · · · ·
River Milepost
Public Access ▲
Dam
Rapid

N

One inch = 2 miles

Roscoe   **Rosebud (Stillwater)**

RUBY

ORIGIN:	At Divide Creek, south of Alder, MT. El. 7000'
END:	Flows into Beaverhead R. south of Twin Bridges, MT. El. 4650'
LENGTH:	102.9 total mi. (99.8 river mi. + Ruby Res. 3.1 mi.) (55 air mi.)
FLOATABLE:	88.9 river mi. (Cow Camp "92" El. 6600' to end "0") Reservoir is floatable.
SECTIONS:	Upper (10.9 mi.) Origin "102.9" to Cow Camp "92" Middle (44.1 mi.) Cow Camp "92" to Ruby Dam "47.9" Lower (47.9 mi.) Ruby Dam "47.9" to End "0"
DAMS:	Ruby (Forms res. & controls flow below) Mi. "47.9" Clovis & Powder Gulch Diversion Dam "75" Sweetwater Creek Diversion Dam "58" Canyon Canal Diversion Dam Headgate "47"
WATERFALLS:	None
WHITEWATER:	None (Extreme upper when flows are up)
DANGERS:	Upper portion of Middle section, Ruby Dam, diversion dams, fences, remote area.
DEWATERED:	Can be low in fall.
PORTAGES:	Ruby Dam (RIGHT), 3 diversion dams, fences and 5 low irrigation diversions between Mi. "39" and Mi. "7"
SPEC. AGENCIES:	None
REGS - PERMITS:	10 hp motor limit on all streams in Madison County
ACCESS-SHUTTLE:	Quite a few intersecting bridges.
SERVICES:	Limited in Alder. All services in Sheridan and Twin Bridges, MT.
CAMPING:	Few formal campgrounds and access sites.
GAMEFISH:	Above reservoir - Cutthroat, rainbow, brown trout. Below reservoir - Brown trout.

VESSEL:	Canoe, small boat, medium raft.
SKILL LEVEL:	Beginner - if flows are normal (Very curvy and brushy)
FLOAT TIMES:	Moderate to slow flows.
FLOW INFO:	(406) 449-5263 USGS - Helena

HYDROGRAPH

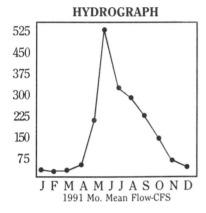

1991 Mo. Mean Flow-CFS

Gage Sta: Below Ruby Dam
Drain Area: 596 sq. mi. (at this locale)
Ave. Flow: (28 years) 213 cfs
Ext. Max: 3,010 cfs - 8.52' ga. ht. 5/16/84
Ext. Min: 19 cfs 1/9/89
Gradient: 2350' in 102.9 mi. = 22.8 pma
Float Grad: 1950' in 92.0 mi. = 21.2 pma
Clarity: Cloudy to Clear
Temp: Jan. 36^0 F.
         Apr. 48^0 F.
         Jul. 66^0 F.
         Oct. 46^0 F.

| DRAINAGE: | (East) Beaverhead, Jefferson, Missouri, Mississippi. |
| MAPS: | BLM - #32 "Dillon" (lower) - #33 "Madison" & #42 "Centennial" (extreme upper)
USFS - Beaverhead NF (Interagency) entire river
USGS - "Dillon" - "Bozeman" - "Ashton" & "Dubois" (extreme upper).
CO. - Madison |

UGLY - Dangerous - Not necessary

RUBY

The etymology of the Ruby seems to flow through time. Named "Philanthropy" by Lewis and Clark, for one of President Jefferson's three cardinal virtues. The three feeder streams to the Jefferson River were named "Philosophy" (Beaverhead) and "Wisdom" (Bighole). Early pioneers gave it the temporary connotation of "Stinkingwater", due to rotten buffalo carcasses found along the river. Its present name "Ruby" is reflected upon the garnets found in the stream bed. Some locals refer to the river as the Beaverheads' "little sister".

Gold, silver, lead, zinc and copper are all traceable in the area. Virginia City, Nevada City, Alder Gulch and Robbers Roost are all historical landmarks. Evidence still remains from "the good ol' days". Today, garnets and insect fossils are found below the dam.

The origin of the Ruby is at Divide Creek, in the high country. Floating can begin as high as Cow Camp, at the confluence of the West and East Forks "92". Cottonwood Camp six miles below and two bridges near the Vigilante Ranger Station offer ingress or egress. The Clovis-Powder Gulch Diversion Dam is five miles below. Ledford Creek Bridge "69" and Sweetwater Creek bridge and diversion dam "58" occur before the inlet of the Ruby Reservoir "51".

A beginner can handle the entire river, if flows are normal. This stream is narrow, curvy and brushy and has many man-made obstacles. A canoe would be the best choice, or a small raft or boat could be possibilities. Above Ruby Dam cutthroat, rainbow and brown trout are found. Below the dam, browns are the most common.

Below Ruby Dam "47.9", six diversion dams exist and many fences. Some of these diversions get washed out in the spring and some large landowners, it is rumored, install new ones any old place they want to; often without official approval. Water is precious in dry country, but ones conscience must prevail. Dewatered rivers ruin fisheries and wildlife habitat and aesthetically are just plain ugly. There needs to be a compromise. Float-thru gates are easy and inexpensive to install, especially with state aid, and seem preferable to solid barb wire. Debris, normally collecting on fences and causing them to topple, floats right through.

Highway 287 parallels the river on the north and a county road parallels on the south. These roads are connected frequently with bridges offering access. The Ruby flows into the Beaverhead 2.8 miles south of Twin Bridges, MT. A fine access at the Highway 41 bridge (on the left) in Twin Bridges offer exit.

Ruby River

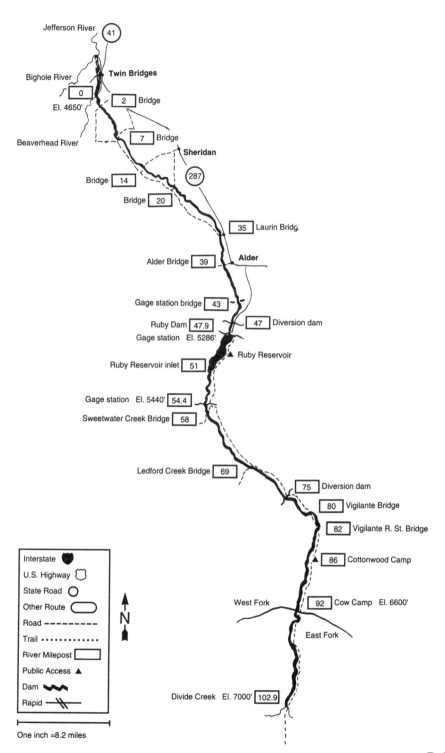

Jefferson River 41

Bighole River

Twin Bridges

0

El. 4650'

2 Bridge

Beaverhead River

7 Bridge

Sheridan

287

Bridge 14

Bridge 20

35 Laurin Bridg.

Alder Bridge 39 **Alder**

Gage station bridge 43

Ruby Dam 47.9 47 Diversion dam

Gage station El. 5286'

▲ Ruby Reservoir

Ruby Reservoir inlet 51

Gage station El. 5440' 54.4

Sweetwater Creek Bridge 58

Ledford Creek Bridge 69

75 Diversion dam

80 Vigilante Bridge

82 Vigilante R. St. Bridge

▲ 86 Cottonwood Camp

West Fork 92 Cow Camp El. 6600'

East Fork

Divide Creek El. 7000' 102.9

Interstate 🛡️
U.S. Highway ⬡
State Road ◯
Other Route ⬭
Road - - - - - -
Trail ....
River Milepost ☐
Public Access ▲
Dam 〰️
Rapid ╫

N

One inch =8.2 miles

Ruby

ST. MARY

ORIGIN: At Gunsight Lake in Glacier National Park. El. 5200'

END: Enters Canada north of Babb, MT. El. 4120'

LENGTH: 41 total mi. in MT (25 river mi. + 2 lakes 16 mi.)
St. Mary Lake   10 mi.
Lower St. Mary Lake   6
Floatable   16 mi.
(31 air mi.)

FLOATABLE: 15 miles
(1.5 mi. between lakes)
(13.5 mi. below lake Mi. "15.5" to "2")

SECTIONS: Upper (18.2 mi.) Origin "41" to Glacier National Park Bridge "22.8"
Middle (9.8 mi.) Bridge "22.8" to Babb access "13"
Lower (13.0 mi.) Babb "13" to Canada border "0"

DAMS: Babb Diversion Dam (Mi. "15") (Built 1915)

WATERFALLS: St. Mary Falls (Mi. "34")

WHITEWATER: None floatable

DANGERS: Diversion dam, primitive park

DEWATERED: Usually not

PORTAGES: Diversion dam (Mi. "15") portage RIGHT

SPEC. AGENCIES: Glacier National Park (upper) - Blackfeet Indian Reservation (lower)

REGS - PERMITS: If camping in Glacier National Park, a back-country camping permit is required. No firearms in Glacier National Park. On reservation a recreation or fishing permit may be necessary if leaving the river. No floating across border.

ACCESS-SHUTTLE: Upper - Hiking or boat on St. Mary Lake
Middle - Highway parallels Lower St. Mary Lake
Lower - Highway parallels river at a distance. Use poor roads to exit river.

SERVICES: All in St. Mary, MT. Limited in Babb, MT.

CAMPING:	Campgrounds in Glacier National Park. No public campgrounds on reservation.
GAMEFISH:	Cutthroat, rainbow, whitefish, bulls
VESSEL:	Canoe, medium raft, small boat
SKILL LEVEL:	Beginner - if flow is normal
FLOAT TIMES:	Moderate flow.
FLOW INFO:	(406) 449-5263 USGS - Helena

HYDROGRAPH

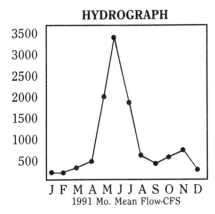

1991 Mo. Mean Flow-CFS

Gage Sta: at International border
Drain Area: 465 sq. mi.
Ave. Flow: (75 years) 683 cfs
Ext. Max: 40,000 cfs - 12.75' ga. 6/5/08
Ext. Min: 16 cfs - 11/29/36
Gradient: 1080' in 41 mi. = 26.3' pma
Float Grad: 364' in 23 mi. = 15.8' pma
Clarity: Cloudy
Temp: Jan. 32⁰ F.
         Apr. 36⁰ F.
         Jul. 69⁰ F.
         Oct. 41⁰ F.

DRAINAGE:	(North) Oldman, S. Sask., Sask., Nelson, Hudson Bay
MAPS:	BLM - #17 "St. Mary"
	USGS - "Cut Bank"
	Sp. - "Glacier National Park" USGS
	CO. - Glacier

219

ST. MARY

The Indians called the river "Blue Banks", and later Father Lacombe named the area St. Mary. The origin of the river is at Gunsight Lake, in the beautiful high country of Glacier National Park.

It would be worthy to note here, that Triple Divide Mountain causes a three-way watershed. The Blackfeet term is "Niuoxkai-itahtai" meaning "three streams". Waters from this mountain, drain either to the Pacific Ocean, Gulf of Mexico or Hudson Bay. This is one of only two triple watersheds on the North American Continent. The other occurs in the Canadian Rockies.

The upper river cascades down the valley and over St. Mary Falls. This falls is one mile above St. Mary Lake. A hiking trail along the river, will take you to Gunsight Lake and beyond. St. Mary Lake offers boating activities and is a photographer's paradise. A tour boat on the lake affords spectacular views of towering peaks.

Floating can begin at the Going to the Sun Road bridge at the park entrance. This entrance also marks the beginning of the Blackfeet Indian Reservation. A short canoe jaunt leads to Lower St. Mary Lake.

Floating on the river again continues at the Highway 89 bridge "15.5" near Babb. This is a beautiful float, especially in autumn. The coniferous and deciduous trees blend along the banks in the valley, where the prairie meets the mountains.

Fishing can be quite good on the river. Cutthroat, rainbow, bulls and whitefish inhabit the undercut banks and gravel streambed. A fishing license is not necessary in Glacier Park, however a tribal permit is required, if you go above the high water marks. A beginner can handle the river if flow is normal. A medium sized raft, canoe or small boat would work fine.

Just below the Highway 89 bridge is a dangerous diversion dam which requires a portage RIGHT. Two miles below the dam is an informal access site north of Babb.

Below the Babb access one can float to the Siphon Road bridge "6". Permission can be gained from the Paisley Ranch (downstream on the east bank), to float to milepost "2". This is the last possible exit before the Canadian border. Floating through the border is not allowed. The river then enters Alberta and flows for a hundred miles before joining the Oldman River. The South Saskatchewan, Saskatchewan and Nelson rivers lead to Hudson Bay.

St. Mary River

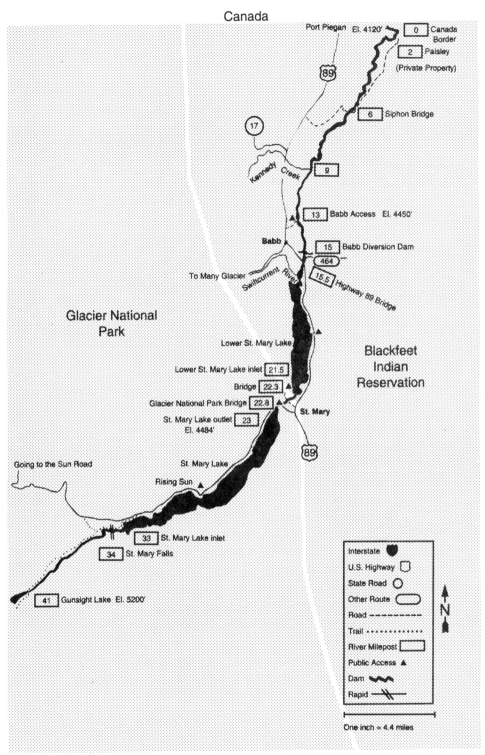

Canada

Port Piegan   El. 4120'
0 Canada Border
2 Paisley
(Private Property)

89

6 Siphon Bridge

17

Kennedy   Creek

9

13 Babb Access El. 4450'

Babb

15 Babb Diversion Dam

464

To Many Glacier   Swiftcurrent   River

15.5 Highway 89 Bridge

Glacier National Park

Lower St. Mary Lake

Blackfeet Indian Reservation

Lower St. Mary Lake inlet 21.5

Bridge 22.3

Glacier National Park Bridge 22.8

St. Mary Lake outlet 23
El. 4484'

St. Mary

89

Going to the Sun Road   St. Mary Lake

Rising Sun

33 St. Mary Lake inlet

34 St. Mary Falls

41 Gunsight Lake El. 5200'

Interstate
U.S. Highway
State Road
Other Route
Road --------
Trail ....
River Milepost
Public Access ▲
Dam
Rapid

N

One inch = 4.4 miles

St. Mary

221

ST. REGIS

ORIGIN:	Cooper Gulch near Lookout Pass, west of St. Regis, MT El. 4600'
END:	Flows into Clark Fork River at St. Regis, MT El. 2600'
LENGTH:	36.3 miles (29 air miles)
FLOATABLE:	32 miles (Rest Area Mile "32" to Clark Fork River "0")
SECTIONS:	Upper (4.3 mi.) Origin "36.3" to Rest Area "32" Middle (15.0 mi.) Rest Area "32" to DeBorgia Br. "17" Lower (17.0 mi.) DeBorgia Bridge "17" to End - "0"
DAMS:	None
WATERFALLS:	None
WHITEWATER:	5.5 miles Mile "31" to "27" Class III when water up. Mile "9.5" to "8.0" Class II-III when water up.
DANGERS:	Logjams, whitewater portions
DEWATERED:	Can be low in fall
PORTAGES:	None, except possible logjams
SPEC. AGENCIES:	None
REGS - PERMITS:	None
ACCESS-SHUTTLE:	Easy. I-90 and especially the frontage road offer good access with bridges. Only a few formal access sites, but should be no problem.
SERVICES:	Limited in Saltese, DeBorgia and St. Regis, MT.
CAMPING:	A few formal campgrounds near the river, but numerous informal places.
GAMEFISH:	Cutthroat, brook trout
VESSEL:	Canoe, medium raft, small boat. Kayakers would enjoy these short whitewater runs when water is high.
SKILL LEVEL:	Intermediate. Whitewater portion - Experienced

FLOAT TIMES: Moderately fast flow.

FLOW INFO: (406) 449-5263 USGS - Helena

HYDROGRAPH

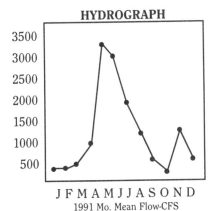

J F M A M J J A S O N D
1991 Mo. Mean Flow-CFS

Gage Sta: Milepost "1.7"
Drain Area: 303 sq. mi.
Ave. Flow: 1234 cfs
Gradient: 2000' in 36.3 mi. = 55.0' pma
Float Grad: 1300' in 32.0 mi. = 40.6' pma
Clarity: Cloudy
Temp: Jan. 35^0 F.
            Apr. 41^0 F.
            Jul. 66^0 F.
            Oct. 46^0 F.

DRAINAGE: (West) Clark Fork, Pend Oreille, Columbia, Pacific

MAPS: BLM - #7 "Wallace"
USFS - Lolo NF (West) entire river (best map)
USGS - "Wallace"
CO.   - Mineral

What a weekend

ST. REGIS

Etymologists seem to agree on the namesake of St. Regis. Belonging to the same Jesuit Order, Father DeSmet in 1842, named the area in honor of St. Regis DeBorgia.

The origin of the river is at Cooper Gulch near Lookout Pass, and flows into the Clark Fork at the community of St. Regis. This small but pretty stream, has survived the bumps and bruises of the I-90 construction.

Floating can begin as high as the Rest Area "32" on I-90. By using the old frontage road one can follow the river quite easily. The upper six miles is moderate whitewater, and should be approached by an experienced paddler in a whitewater canoe, small raft or kayak. The river is narrow, has a steep gradient and contains some boulders. Saltese is the end of this run.

Below Saltese "26" the river quits buckin' and an intermediate can handle the river down to Drexel Exit "9.5", in a small raft, canoe or small boat.

Below Drexel, is 1 1/2 miles of bouncy water. This whitewater is caused by a steeper gradient and trout holding boulders, placed in the river in an attempt to mitigate the highway construction. Both of these whitewater portions should be considered Class II-III depending on flow.

Just below Ward Creek Bridge "8.2" gentle water can be enjoyed for the rest of the river. Two Mile Creek Bridge "4.5" and Little Joe Creek Bridge "1.6" offer ingress or egress. The old frontage road bridge (by I-90 bridge) ".4" offers difficult exit, or one may elect to float into the Clark Fork. Just downstream on the left is the St. Regis Gage Station.

Fishing is quite popular on the river, with respectable numbers of cutthroat, brookies and a few rainbow. Let's not forget the whitefish! Fly fishing can be good as well as the "old standby" Mepps.

St. Regis River

224

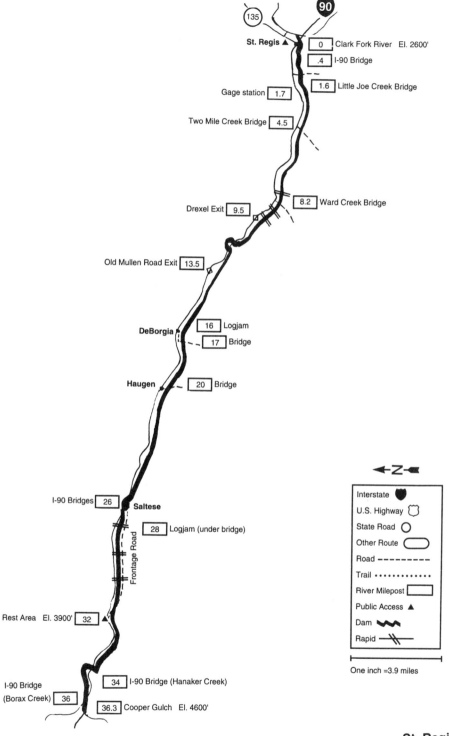

St. Regis

SHIELDS

ORIGIN:	Fawn Creek in Crazy Mountains northeast of Wilsall. El. 6700'
END:	Flows into Yellowstone River east of Livingston, MT El. 4390'
LENGTH:	62 miles (32 air miles)
FLOATABLE:	22.9 miles
SECTIONS:	Upper (9.5 mi.) Origin "62" to S. F. Br. "52.5" Middle (29.6 mi.) S. F. Br. "52.5" to Hwy 89 Br. "22.9" Lower (22.9 mi.) Hwy 89 Br. "22.9" to End - "0"
DAMS:	None
WATERFALLS:	None
WHITEWATER:	None
DANGERS:	Irrigation jettys, fences, logjams
DEWATERED:	Can be low in fall
PORTAGES:	None
SPEC. AGENCIES:	None
REGS - PERMITS:	10 hp. maximum on all streams in Park County
ACCESS-SHUTTLE:	Quite easy. Highway 89 parallels river with intersecting bridges. No formal access sites.
SERVICES:	Limited in Wilsall or Clyde Park, MT
CAMPING:	No formal campgrounds or access sites
GAMEFISH:	Upper - Cutthroat, brook Lower - Brown, rainbow
VESSEL:	Canoe, medium raft, small boat
SKILL LEVEL:	Beginner if flows are normal. River is curvy.

FLOAT TIMES: Moderate flow

FLOW INFO: (406) 449-5263 USGS - Helena

HYDROGRAPH

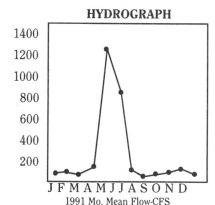

1991 Mo. Mean Flow-CFS

Gage Sta: 2 miles upstream from mouth
Drain Area: 852 sq. mi.
Ave. Flow: (13 years) 282 cfs
Ext. Max: 5,600 cfs - 6.80' ga. ht. 6/20/79
Ext. Min: 17 cfs - 1.44' ga. ht. 8/20/88
Gradient: 2310' in 62.0 miles = 37.3' pma
Float Grad: 435' in 22.9 miles = 19.0' pma
Clarity: Clear to cloudy
Temp: June 61^0 F.

DRAINAGE: (East) Yellowstone, Missouri, Mississippi, Gulf of Mexico

MAPS: BLM - #24 "Castles" (upper) - #34 "Park" (lower)
USFS - Gallatin NF (East) entire river - Lewis & Clark
NF (Jefferson) upper only
USGS - "White Sulphur" (upper) - "Bozeman" (lower)
CO. - Park

Forest friend

SHIELDS

The Shields River was named for John Shields, a member of the Lewis and Clark expedition. Fawn Creek, in the Crazy Mountains northeast of Wilsall, Montana is the beginning of the Shields. The river flows for 62 miles before reaching the Yellowstone River east of Livingston.

The upper river beginning in a mountainous setting, soon enters the ranching community in the valley. The Shields River Campground at Crandall Creek "57.7" is the only formal campground on the river.

Although the upper and middle sections are unfloatable, bridges do offer access to the bank fisherperson, pursuing cutts and brookies. The entire river flows through private land, so stay between the high water marks, or better, seek permission. The river above Clyde Park has a lot of downfall and some irrigation diversions.

Floating can begin just north of Clyde Park, at the Highway 89 bridge "22.9". A county road bridge at milepost "20" is also a possibility. Below Clyde Park, the highway again crosses the river at milepost "13.7". Side road bridges at Bangtail Creek "10.5" and Crazyhead Creek "4.2" would offer difficult ingress or egress. The last place to exit on the Shields is at the county road bridge ".5" that leads to Sheep Mountain Campground four miles downstream on the Yellowstone River.

The Shields is a narrow and curvy stream, with a few irrigation jettys and some downfall. The river can be too low to float after summer. A beginner can handle the river when flow is normal, in a small raft or canoe.

Browns and rainbow are found in this lower section. Bank erosion and siltation is obvious, and the river environment does not support great insect hatches, which is so important to a good trout fishery. The river does however, offer an alternative to the "Big Yellowstone".

Shields River

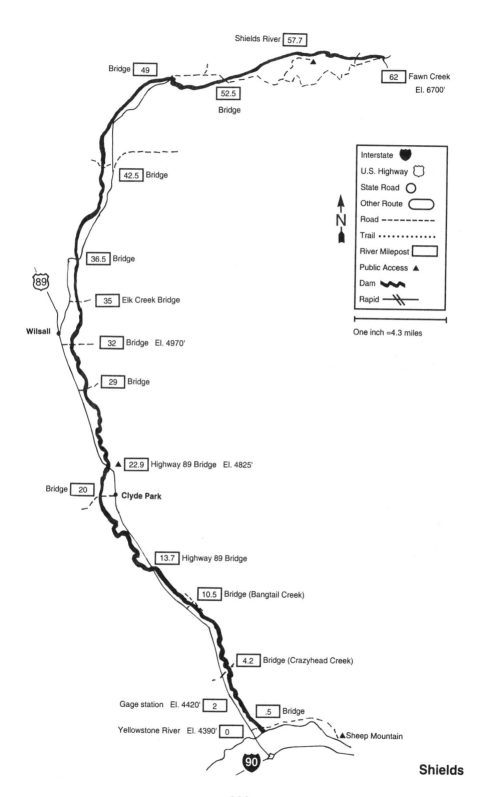

Shields River [57.7]

Bridge [49]

[52.5]
Bridge

[62] Fawn Creek
El. 6700'

[42.5] Bridge

N

[36.5] Bridge

89

[35] Elk Creek Bridge

Wilsall

[32] Bridge   El. 4970'

[29] Bridge

▲ [22.9] Highway 89 Bridge   El. 4825'

Bridge [20]

Clyde Park

[13.7] Highway 89 Bridge

[10.5] Bridge (Bangtail Creek)

[4.2] Bridge (Crazyhead Creek)

Gage station   El. 4420' [2]

[.5] Bridge

Yellowstone River   El. 4390' [0]

▲Sheep Mountain

90

Interstate
U.S. Highway
State Road
Other Route
Road - - - - - - -
Trail • • • • • • • •
River Milepost
Public Access ▲
Dam
Rapid

One inch = 4.3 miles

Shields

SILVERBOW CREEK

ORIGIN:	Yankee Doodle Gulch, above Butte, MT El. 6350'
END:	Joins Warm Springs Creek to form Clark Fork River near Warm Springs, MT El. 4800'
LENGTH:	33.2 total mi. (29.7 river miles + Settling ponds 3.5 mi.) 18 air miles
FLOATABLE:	11.2 miles (Miles Crossing Bridge "16.7" to I-90 frontage road "5.5")
SECTIONS:	Upper (6.2 mi.) Origin "33.2" to I-90 Br. (Butte) "27" Middle (10.3 mi.) Butte "27" to Miles Crossing "16.7" Lower (16.7 mi.) Miles Crossing "16.7" to End "0"
DAMS:	Fairmont Hot Springs Diversion Dam (Mile "11.5") (.1 mi. below bridge)
WATERFALLS:	None
WHITEWATER:	4 miles Mile "16" to Mile "12" (5.1 mile float) Class III - water high
DANGERS:	Diversion dam, whitewater, fences, debris, quicksand, water contamination, 4' drop Mile "13.5"
DEWATERED:	Often low in fall.
PORTAGES:	Fences and possible debris 4' drop portage RIGHT Diversion dam (Mile "11.5") portage RIGHT
SPEC. AGENCIES:	None
REGS - PERMITS:	10 hp maximum on all streams in Silverbow County
ACCESS-SHUTTLE:	Using old Finlen Road paralleling creek between Miles Crossing and Fairmont Hot Springs. I-90 and frontage road for rest of river. No formal access sites.
SERVICES:	All-in Butte. Also limited in Opportunity and Fairmont Hot Springs.
CAMPING:	No formal campgrounds, or access sites.
GAMEFISH:	Rainbow, brook, brown trout (poor - but improving!)

VESSEL:	Canoe, small raft (Whitewater - whitewater canoe, kayak or small raft if water high.)
SKILL LEVEL:	Intermediate (if normal flow)
FLOAT TIMES:	Moderate flow
FLOW INFO:	(406) 449-5263 USGS - Helena

HYDROGRAPH

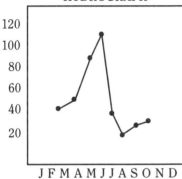

120
100
80
60
40
20

J F M A M J J A S O N D
1991 Mo. Mean Flow-CFS

Gage Sta: 1/2 mile east of Opportunity, MT
Drain Area: 284 sq. mi. (at this gage)
Ave. Flow: 40 cfs
Ext. Max: 654 cfs - 5.61' ga. ht. 3/9/89
Ext. Min: 13 cfs 8/7/90
Gradient: 1550' in 33.2 mi. = 46.7' pma
Float Grad: 450' in 16.7 mi. = 27.0' pma
Clarity: Cloudy to murky
Temp: Oct. 41⁰ F.
Water Quality: Poor - but improving!

DRAINAGE:	(West) Clark Fork, Pend Oreille, Columbia, Pacific
MAPS:	BLM - #22 "Avon"
	USFS - Deer Lodge NF (entire river - best map)
	USGS - "Butte"
	CO. - Silverbow, Deer Lodge

Wapiti

SILVERBOW CREEK

It seems the name Silverbow came from "Screw-up Pete", a prospector, who named it for the curves and sun reflecting off the stream, looking like "silver bows". The stream begins at Yankee Doodle Gulch, above Butte.

This stream has been called the Silverbow portion or extension of the Clark Fork River. A few historians and cartographers have termed it a river.

After flowing through Butte, Rocker and Ramsay, the Miles Crossing Bridge "16.7", west of Ramsay, marks the beginning of float potential. If flow is up, there can be whitewater (moderate) between river mileposts "16" and "12". A four foot drop exists at the footbridge at North Creek and German Gulch "13.5". An intermediate can handle this whitewater in a small raft, whitewater canoe or kayak. Access to this portion can be found by using the old Finlen Road, paralleling the stream and railroad tracks between Miles Crossing and Fairmont Hot Springs. Access to the lower portion is by using the old paved frontage road.

Below the Gregson-Fairmont Hot Springs Road bridge "11.6", is a concrete diversion dam "11.5" with spillway. This dam requires a portage RIGHT. The stream flows under the Highway 441 bridge "10", Highway 1 bridge "7.9" and the Opportunity bridge "6.9". Floating must end at the I-90 or frontage road bridge "5.5". Below these bridges the settling ponds begin.

The canyon from Ramsay to the hot springs is beautiful. Mining has certainly battered this stream. Effluent was dumped directly into the water and fish could not survive. The effects of this carelessness has been felt a long way downstream in the Clark Fork River. Today, thanks to overdue controls, rainbow, brookies and brown trout are on the rebound. A beginner in a canoe or small raft can handle the stream below the hot springs road.

Silverbow River

232

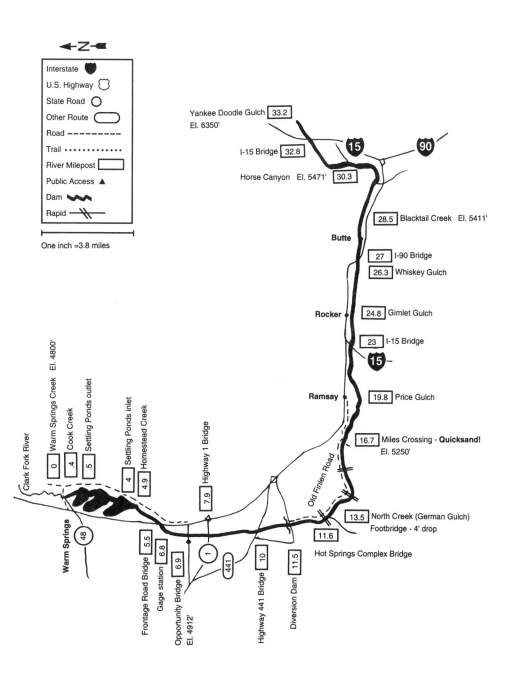

Legend

- Interstate
- U.S. Highway
- State Road
- Other Route
- Road
- Trail
- River Milepost
- Public Access ▲
- Dam
- Rapid

One inch = 3.8 miles

Yankee Doodle Gulch [33.2] El. 6350'

I-15 Bridge [32.8]

Horse Canyon El. 5471' [30.3]

[28.5] Blacktail Creek El. 5411'

Butte

[27] I-90 Bridge

[26.3] Whiskey Gulch

Rocker [24.8] Gimlet Gulch

[23] I-15 Bridge

15

Ramsay [19.8] Price Gulch

[16.7] Miles Crossing - **Quicksand!** El. 5250'

Old Finlen Road

[13.5] North Creek (German Gulch) Footbridge - 4' drop

[11.6]

Hot Springs Complex Bridge

Clark Fork River

Warm Springs Creek El. 4800' [0]

Cook Creek [.4]

Settling Ponds outlet [.5]

Settling Ponds inlet [4]

Homestead Creek [4.9]

Highway 1 Bridge [7.9]

Warm Springs (48)

Frontage Road Bridge [5.5]

Gage station [6.8]

Opportunity Bridge [6.9] El. 4912'

(1)

(441)

Highway 441 Bridge [10]

Diversion Dam [11.5]

Silverbow

SMITH

ORIGIN: Confluence of South and North Forks - west of White Sulphur Springs, MT El. 4900'

END: Flows into Missouri River east of Ulm, MT El. 3350'

LENGTH: 124.8 miles (66 air miles)

FLOATABLE: 98.4 miles (Fort Logan Hwy 360 Br. (El. 4620') to End) Class I portion is 83.7 miles (Camp Baker Access to Missouri River)

SECTIONS: Upper (41.1 mi.) Origin "124.8" to Camp Baker Access "83.7"
Middle (61.1 mi.) Camp Baker Access "83.7" to Eden Bridge Access "22.6"
Lower (22.6 mi.) Eden Bridge "22.6" to End "0"

DAMS: Diversion dam - Milepost 89.4
A few low-float over irrigation jettys

WATERFALLS: None

WHITEWATER: No whitewater sections. There are 2 moderate Class II rapids milepost "34.7"

DANGERS: Diversion dam, irrigation jettys, fences. Long section in remote area, often crowded.

DEWATERED: Can be severely dewatered by summer. Fall float trips are often wonderful.

PORTAGES: Diversion dam, occasional fences, irrigation jettys

SPEC. AGENCIES: Dept. Fish, Wildlife and Parks

REGS - PERMITS: $15.00 float fee and reservation required. Campsites designated. Camp Baker to Eden Bridge 61.1 miles
No motors - entire river.

ACCESS-SHUTTLE: Upper & Middle - Access and shuttle round-about.
Lower- Easier as road parallels river.
Commercial shuttle service available in White Sulphur Springs, MT

SERVICES:	All services in White Sulphur Springs, MT and limited in Ulm, MT. Commercial raft trips available.
CAMPING:	Upper - Good spot at milepost "92" Middle - Numerous campsites in remote section. Lower - No campgrounds and 2 access sites.
GAMEFISH:	Upper - Rainbow, brown, whitefish, brook, cutthroat Lower - Rainbow, brown, whitefish.
VESSEL:	Any moderate sized vessel.
SKILL LEVEL:	Beginner (CAUTION - dangers)
FLOAT TIMES:	Flows moderate to slow. Allow 3 days + for remote 61.1 mile float Lower 9 miles slow.
FLOW INFO:	(406) 453-2081 Flow info. (3.0' is ideal - 2.7' min.) 454-3441 River Reservations 449-5263 USGS - Helena - Flow information

HYDROGRAPH

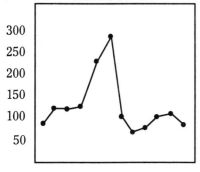

300
250
200
150
100
50

J F M A M J J A S O N D
1991 Mo. Mean Flow-CFS

Gage Sta: Camp Baker
Drain Area: 846 sq. mi. (at this location)
Ave. Flow: (14 years) 149 cfs
Ext. Max: 4,600 cfs - 7.80' ga. ht. 05/22/81
Ext. Min: 16 cfs - 2.12' ga. ht. 11/11/78
Gradient: 1550' in 124.8 mi. = 12.4' pma
Float Grad: 1270' in 98.4 mi. = 12.9' pma
Clarity: Clear to cloudy - lower murky.
Temp: 70° F. 8/8/91
         60° F. 9/9/91
Total Drain Area: Approx. 2100 sq. mi.

DRAINAGE:	(East) Missouri, Mississippi, Gulf of Mexico

MAPS: BLM - #24 "Castles" (extreme upper) - #23 "Townsend" (upper) - #40 "Great Falls South" (lower)
USFS - Lewis & Clark NF (Jefferson) or Helena NF (These cover upper only)
USGS - "White Sulphur" (upper) - "Great Falls" (lower)
Sp. - "Smith River Guide" (Fort Logan Br. to Eden Br.) DFWP
CO. - Meagher, Cascade.

Smith River

SMITH

Lewis and Clark named the river in honor of their Secretary of the Navy, Robert Smith on 7/15/1805. The mainstem of the river begins at the confluence of the South & West Forks, near White Sulphur Springs, MT.

Floating may begin as high as the Fort Logan Bridge on Highway 360 "98.4".A few hardy spring floaters could begin at the Forks Bridge "124.8". A diversion dam mandates a portage at milepost "89.4". Camp Baker Bridge Access "83.7", is the beginning of the Class I portion and the most popular float section. This float has become so popular that the DFWP has had to implement a reservation system and charge a floating fee. They have also limited the outfitters and the number of times they can embark. Designated campsites are also part of the permit. June and July of course, are the most popular months, however, April and late September or early October are great times. I made this trip the middle of October one year, and luckily, had beautiful suntanning weather and the autumn foliage was magnificent. On this trip I saw no other floaters and only 1/2 dozen bank fishermen near the dude ranch.

Irrigation withdrawals are a major problem and floating is usually not possible from the end of July to well into September when irrigation subsides. These draw-downs not only limit the float season, but also force the fish into the deeper pools. Even with the congestion and the irrigation dewatering, I still recommend this float as one of the finer family oriented trips in the state. A three day trip is necessary to make this remote 61.1 mile trip to Eden Bridge Campground "22.6". If you stop to fish a fourth day is needed. Wildlife abounds in the form of elk, trophy mulies, and black bear, with an un-ending list of birds. The face of the river is one of riffles and deep green pools, usually surrounded by canyon walls and a couple small waterfalls. The only whitewater in the entire river are two Class II rapids at mile "34.7". Rafts and canoes are the most popular vessels, with the raft lending itself to easier fishing and more cargo. The canoe however is fun, faster and less resistant to the occasional winds blowing up the valley. A beginner could handle the Smith, but because of its remoteness and a few sharp curves, an intermediate skill level is recommended. Fishing is wonderful, with rainbow, browns and whitefish numerous. Some cutts and brookies are also present. Even a beginner should have no problem putting a fish in the evening fry pan. Stonefly nymphs, salmon flies, caddis imitations and dry flies work well, depending on the time of the year and weather and water conditions. Hammered brass lures and small Mepps spinners are good, or find a grasshopper to put on the hook. The river slows as it leaves the canyon and approaches Eden Bridge. Shuttling is very round-about and long. An old gravel road, always distant to the river, goes south to eventually meet Highway 360. Going east past Fort Logan to the Camp Baker road going north, and following this Camp Baker road north for ten miles will finally get you to your vehicle. Hitch hiking is nearly impossible on this seldom used road. A shuttle service in White Sulphur Springs, MT may be the answer or use two vehicles. I often carry a small Honda 90 trail bike for situations like this.

Below Eden Bridge moderate flow remains and the scenery is still beautiful. Below Truly Bridge "9.3" the river slows considerably and a canoe is your best choice. The river banks are extremely brushy and the water turbid for the rest of its journey to the Missouri. Below Truly Bridge I have seen more Great Horned Owls than any other trip in the state. Highway 330 Bridge "3.6" offers the last exit off the Smith. Floating into the Missouri and downstream to access is a long distance, and since motors are not allowed on the entire Smith, going upstream on the Missouri to Ulm, MT is difficult.

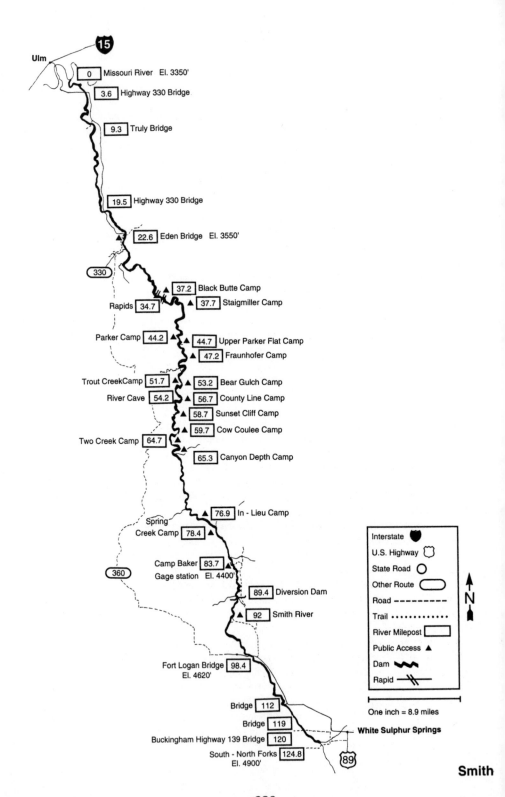

15

Ulm

0 Missouri River El. 3350'

3.6 Highway 330 Bridge

9.3 Truly Bridge

19.5 Highway 330 Bridge

22.6 Eden Bridge El. 3550'

330

37.2 Black Butte Camp

37.7 Staigmiller Camp

Rapids 34.7

Parker Camp 44.2

44.7 Upper Parker Flat Camp

47.2 Fraunhofer Camp

Trout Creek Camp 51.7

53.2 Bear Gulch Camp

River Cave 54.2

56.7 County Line Camp

58.7 Sunset Cliff Camp

59.7 Cow Coulee Camp

Two Creek Camp 64.7

65.3 Canyon Depth Camp

76.9 In - Lieu Camp

Spring
Creek Camp 78.4

360

Camp Baker 83.7
Gage station El. 4400'

89.4 Diversion Dam

92 Smith River

Fort Logan Bridge 98.4
El. 4620'

Bridge 112

Bridge 119

Buckingham Highway 139 Bridge 120

South - North Forks 124.8
El. 4900'

White Sulphur Springs

89

Interstate
U.S. Highway
State Road
Other Route
Road - - - - - - -
Trail ·············
River Milepost
Public Access ▲
Dam 〰〰
Rapid ⫤

One inch = 8.9 miles

N

Smith

238

SPOTTED BEAR

ORIGIN:	Hoop Creek near Spotted Bear Pass in Bob Marshall Wilderness El. 6000'
END:	Flows into South Fork - Flathead River near Spotted Bear Ranger Station El. 3690'
LENGTH:	33.3 miles (20 air miles)
FLOATABLE:	14.7 mi. (Silvertip Cr. Ranger Sta. "14.7" to S. F. "0")
SECTIONS:	Upper (11.9 mi.) Hoop Cr. "33.3" to Dean Falls "21.4" Middle (11.6 mi.) Dean Falls "21.4" to Beaver Cr. "9.8" Lower (9.8 mi.) Beaver Cr. "9.8" to End-S. F. "0"
DAMS:	None
WATERFALLS:	Dean Falls (20' high) Mile "21.4" Spotted Bear Falls (actually a large drop) Mile "8.5"
WHITEWATER:	None (except Spotted Bear Falls)
DANGERS:	Wilderness area, Spotted Bear Falls
DEWATERED:	Can be low in fall
PORTAGES:	Spotted Bear Falls Mile "8.5" (portage RIGHT best)
SPEC. AGENCIES:	Bob Marshall & Great Bear Wilderness.
REGS - PERMITS:	No motors in wilderness.
ACCESS-SHUTTLE:	Upper & Middle - Hiking or horse trail only. Lower - Road parallels river.
SERVICES:	Gas, meals, cabins at guest ranches at Spotted Bear. Also, guided raft trips and horse concession.
CAMPING:	Beaver Creek Campground, Spotted Bear campground and Spotted Bear Access on South Fork River.
GAMEFISH:	Below Dean Falls - Cutthroat, whitefish, bulls
VESSEL:	Upper - unfloatable Middle - small raft Lower - medium raft, canoe, small boat

SKILL LEVEL:	Intermediate (Caution - dangers above) - (if flows are normal)
FLOAT TIMES:	Moderately fast flow.
FLOW INFO:	752-7345 Flathead NF - Spotted Bear District. They can radio Spotted Bear Ranger Station

HYDROGRAPH

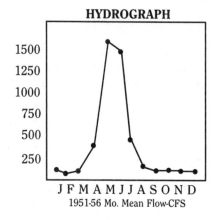

1500
1250
1000
750
500
250

J F M A M J J A S O N D
1951-56 Mo. Mean Flow-CFS

Gage Sta: Spotted Bear, MT (Disc. 1956)
Drain Area: 184 sq. mi.
Ave. Flow: (5 years) 378 cfs
Ext. Max: 4780 cfs 5/20/54
Ext. Min: 22 cfs 11/26/52
Gradient: 2310' in 33.3 miles = 69.4' pma
Float Grad: 610' in 14.7 miles = 41.5' pma
Clarity: Clear to cloudy
Temp: Jan. 32^0 F.
      Apr. 40^0 F.
      Jul. 63^0 F.
      Oct. 43^0 F.

DRAINAGE:	(West) South Fork Flathead, Flathead, Clark Fork, Pend Oreille, Columbia, Pacific Ocean
MAPS:	BLM - #19 "Swan River"
	USFS - Flathead NF (South) entire river - Lewis & Clark NF (RMD) upper only
	USGS - "Choteau"
	Sp. - "Bob Marshall - Great Bear - Scapegoat Wilderness" entire river USFS
	Spotted Bear Ranger District map
	CO. - Flathead

SPOTTED BEAR

Etymologists seem to agree on the namesake of the area. Baptiste, while guiding two miners through the area in the 1861 era, saw a spotted black bear near the mouth of the river.

Hoop Creek, near Spotted Bear Pass within the Bob Marshall Wilderness, marks the origin of the river. The river then flows 33.3 miles into the South Fork of the Flathead at the Spotted Bear Ranger Station.

The Spotted Bear area is accessible by forest service roads, up each side of the reservoir created by Hungry Horse Dam. A bridge over the South Fork River connects the two roads. An airstrip, four miles below Spotted Bear also offers light plane access. There are no year-round residents at the ranger station or the guest ranches, as the roads are not plowed. Snowmobile or a ski-rigged plane would be winter access possibilities. Gas, meals and cabins are offered at the guest ranches, as well as guided float fishing, horse concession, and pack trips. Trailheads in all directions, offer access to the Bob Marshall and Great Bear Wilderness areas.

A road above Spotted Bear, follows the river up to Beaver Creek Campground. Above Beaver Creek the river is accessible only by a hiking and horse trail, leading up to Spotted Bear Pass and beyond. In its upper reaches the small stream is congested with downfall and boulders as it tumbles down by Pentagon Ranger Station and over 20' Dean Falls. Floating is impossible above Dean Creek.

A friend packed me into Dean Creek "19.1" and I floated out through a number of logjams. Thick brush makes portaging even a small raft difficult. Better floating begins at Silvertip Creek Ranger Station "14.7". The added volume of water provided by Silvertip Creek and the absence of logjams below, make this pleasant. The river and its surrounding mountains creating a narrow canyon, offer spectacular scenery.

Beaver Creek Campground "9.8" marks the beginning of the more popular floating, as you can drive to this point. Spotted Bear Falls (actually a large drop), occurs at Big Bill Creek "8.5". Some floaters float through the falls, when flow is high; however an easy portage RIGHT is recommended. An unmarked trail affords a 200 yard steep access to the falls.

Below the falls, the river gradually gets larger, due to numerous feeder streams. The river channels more in its gravel streambed and can be too low to float in the fall. No major obstructions impede floating and soon you reach a short gorge just above the ranger station and the South Fork confluence. Floating must continue down the South Fork 1/2 mile, to a fine access site on the right bank. Numerous formal campgrounds and informal sites exist in the area. Below Beaver Creek, a medium sized raft, canoe or small boat would work well. An intermediate skill level can handle the river.

Fishing in this beautiful and remote river is excellent. Cutthroat, bulls and ubiquitous whitefish offer the fly fisherperson a paradise. Spinning in the deeper pools is also productive.

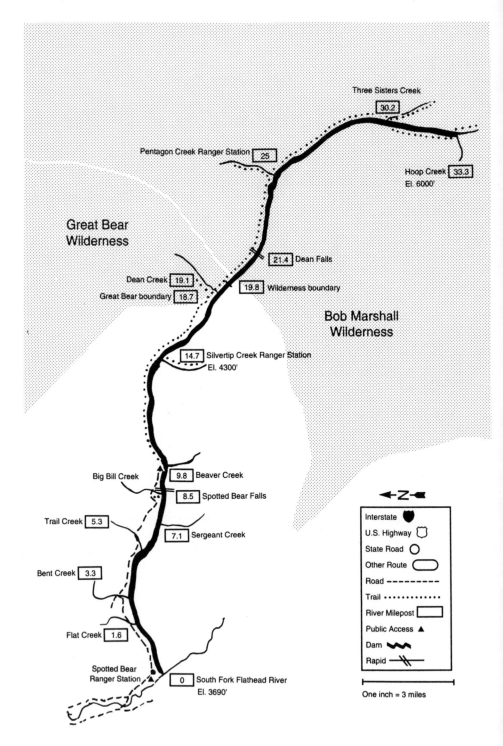

Great Bear
Wilderness

Three Sisters Creek

30.2

Pentagon Creek Ranger Station 25

Hoop Creek 33.3
El. 6000'

21.4 Dean Falls

Dean Creek 19.1

19.8 Wilderness boundary

Great Bear boundary 18.7

Bob Marshall
Wilderness

14.7 Silvertip Creek Ranger Station
El. 4300'

Big Bill Creek

9.8 Beaver Creek

8.5 Spotted Bear Falls

Trail Creek 5.3

7.1 Sergeant Creek

Bent Creek 3.3

Flat Creek 1.6

Spotted Bear
Ranger Station

0 South Fork Flathead River
El. 3690'

←Z←

Interstate
U.S. Highway
State Road
Other Route
Road ---------
Trail ••••••••••••
River Milepost
Public Access ▲
Dam
Rapid

One inch = 3 miles

Spotted Bear

STILLWATER (Flathead)

ORIGIN: Russky Creek northeast of Stryker, MT El.5800'

END: Flows into Flathead River at Kalispell, MT El. 2930'

LENGTH: 79.3 total miles (73.5 river miles + 3 lakes 5.8 miles)
(45 air miles)

FLOATABLE: 57.2 river miles   Mile "63" to End "0"
Duck Lake 2.0 miles
Upper Stillwater Lake 2.3
Lower Stillwater Lake 1.5
All floatable   5.8 miles

SECTIONS: Upper (16.3 mi.) Origin "79.3" to "63"
Middle (21.0 mi.) Hwy "63" to Star Meadow Br. "42"
Lower (42.0 mi.) Star Meadow Br. "42" to End - "0"

DAMS: None

WATERFALLS: None

WHITEWATER: 1.5 miles Mile "55.3" to "53.8" (5.3 mi. float to exit)
Class III in a narrow canyon

DANGERS: Whitewater portion, numerous logjams, fences

DEWATERED: Can be low in fall

PORTAGES: Whitewater portion (RIGHT). Numerous logjams

SPEC. AGENCIES: None

REGS - PERMITS: None

ACCESS-SHUTTLE: Not too difficult. Access can be round-about. Study a
good map. No formal access sites, but many bridges.

SERVICES: Limited in Stryker, MT. All services in Whitefish or
Kalispell, MT.

CAMPING: No formal campgrounds or access sites, but plenty of
places to choose from in the upper & middle sections.
Lower section mostly private property.

GAMEFISH: Cutthroat, brookies, pike

VESSEL:	Canoe, small boat (lots of slow water and logjams)
	Whitewater - Whitewater canoe, small raft, kayak
SKILL LEVEL:	Beginner.
	Whitewater portion - Experienced
FLOAT TIMES:	Slow
FLOW INFO:	(406) 449-5263 USGS - Helena

HYDROGRAPH

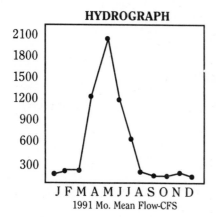

2100
1800
1500
1200
900
600
300

J F M A M J J A S O N D
1991 Mo. Mean Flow-CFS

Gage Sta: Milepost "19.3"
Drain Area: 524 sq. mi. (at this locale)
Ave. Flow: (38 years) 343 cfs
Ext. Max: 4,330 cfs - 20.9' ga. ht. 5/26/48
Ext. Min: 32 cfs 9/9/88
Gradient: 2870' in 79.3 mi. = 36.2' pma
Float Grad: 420' in 63.0 mi. =   6.7' pma
Clarity: Clear to murky
Temp: Jan. 32° F.
        Apr. 45° F.
        Jul. 75° F.
        Oct. 48° F.

DRAINAGE:	(West) Flathead, Clark Fork, Pend Oreille, Columbia, Pacific Ocean
MAPS:	BLM - #9 "Whitefish" (upper) - #10 "Kalispell" (lower)
	USFS - Flathead NF (North) entire river - Kootenai NF (upper only)
	USGS - "Kalispell"
	CO. - Lincoln, Flathead

STILLWATER (Flathead)

The origin of the river is at Russky Creek, northeast of Stryker, Montana and flows into the Flathead nearly eighty miles distant, at Kalispell. After spring run-off the river runs deep and quite clear, interrupted frequently by logjams. The river is certainly befitting its name, and does freeze over during winter.

The stream begins small and tumbles out of the mountains, congested with downfall and boulders. After passing under Highway 93 "68.4" near Stryker, the stream attains a more normal gradient. Logjams infest the river down to milepost "63". At this point, Highway 93 comes close to the river, three miles above Duck Lake. Floating can begin here.

The best choice of vessel is a canoe. Many locals prefer a small boat with motor to go from lake to lake. A beginner can handle the river during normal conditions, except for a 1.5 mile stretch below Upper Stillwater Lake outlet "55.3". At this point the channel has a steep gradient through a curvy and narrow gorge. During high water this boulder portion is solid class III whitewater. This whitewater should only be approached by an experienced paddler in a kayak or whitewater canoe. The next access below is at a forest service road bridge "50". This bridge is at a sawmill near Olney and the Stillwater State Forest Headquarters. West of this bridge is an old forest service road going up to the lake outlet and a neat informal campsite.

Cutthroat, brookies and pike are present in the river. Lower Stillwater Lake can be excellent for pike, especially through the ice. Many old campsites and bridges occur. Explore a little and "pick and choose".

Below Lower Stillwater Lake "48.2", three major logjams require portage. Logan Creek at river milepost "44" adds volume to the river. The Star Meadow Road bridge "42" is just below.

Below Star Meadow Road the river has four major logjams and three fences. Also, a few partial logjams exist. Bridges are frequent and their locations can be found on the river milepost.

The Whitefish River joins at the Highway 2 bridge "3.1" in Kalispell. The "Old Steel Bridge Road" bridge "2.5" is just below, and offers the last exit off the Stillwater River. Floating beyond involves the remaining 2.5 miles of the Stillwater and 3.5 miles of the Flathead River down to Foys Bend Access.

LOGAN CREEK

A newly discovered kayakers run on Logan Creek is gaining popularity. Logan Creek is a tributary of the Stillwater River at milepost "44". A three mile run begins at the second bridge above Tally Lake, and ends at the lake. Boating above this bridge is not possible as an 8' waterfall interrupts. The overall gradient of this run is 125 fpm, with places up to 175 fpm. The stream is narrow and has a gorge appearance, with boulders and some downfall. During April and May it is really "cookin" and is an adventurous class IV-V. This portion requires expert paddling skills.

A class III run can be found at the bridge below the lake. An experienced pilot can handle this portion. A campsite at Sanko Creek and a campground at Tally Lake offer a weekend stay.

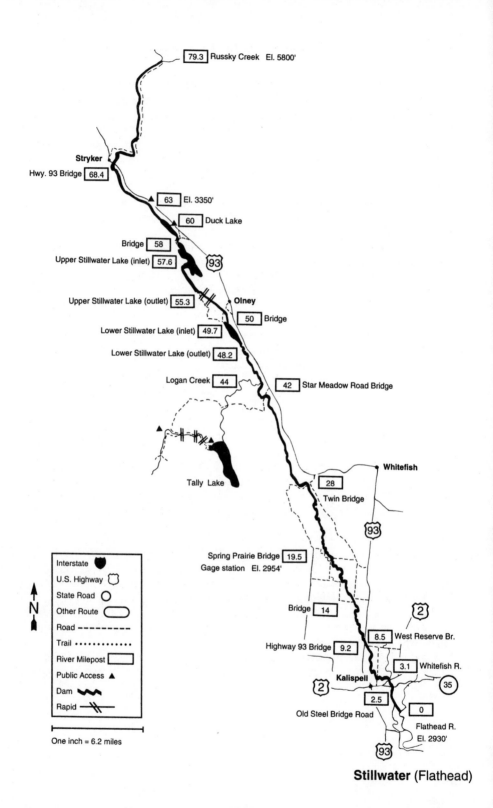

79.3 Russky Creek El. 5800'

Stryker
Hwy. 93 Bridge 68.4

63 El. 3350'

60 Duck Lake

Bridge 58

Upper Stillwater Lake (inlet) 57.6

Upper Stillwater Lake (outlet) 55.3

Olney

50 Bridge

Lower Stillwater Lake (inlet) 49.7

Lower Stillwater Lake (outlet) 48.2

Logan Creek 44

42 Star Meadow Road Bridge

Whitefish

Tally Lake

28

Twin Bridge

Spring Prairie Bridge 19.5
Gage station El. 2954'

Bridge 14

8.5 West Reserve Br.

Highway 93 Bridge 9.2

3.1 Whitefish R.

Kalispell

35

2.5

0

Old Steel Bridge Road

Flathead R.
El. 2930'

Interstate
U.S. Highway
State Road
Other Route
Road ‐ ‐ ‐ ‐ ‐ ‐ ‐ ‐
Trail • • • • • • • • • •
River Milepost
Public Access ▲
Dam
Rapid

N

One inch = 6.2 miles

Stillwater (Flathead)

STILLWATER (Yellowstone)

ORIGIN:	At Goose Creek in Beartooth Mountains southwest of Absarokee, MT El. 7100'
END:	Flows into Yellowstone River just above Columbus. El. 3500'
LENGTH:	67.7 miles (50 air miles)
FLOATABLE:	47 miles (Whitewater beginning at wilderness boundary El. 5600' to end)
SECTIONS:	Upper (26.7 mi.) Origin "67.7" to Old Nye Access "41" Middle (17.0 mi.) Old Nye "41" to Cliff Swallow "24" Lower (24.0 mi.) Cliff Swallow "24" to End - "0"
DAMS:	Johnson Creek Diversion Dam - Mile "14"
WATERFALLS:	None - Some severe whitewater drops
WHITEWATER:	15 miles Milepost "47" to "45" Class V to VI Milepost "45" to "41" Class IV to V Milepost "33" to "24" Class III
DANGERS:	Diversion dam. Severe whitewater, whitewater drop at Mile "5.3", low bridge (mile "39")
DEWATERED:	Can get low, but usually floatable.
PORTAGES:	Johnson Creek Dam or use RIGHT channel to avoid
SPEC. AGENCIES:	Beartooth Wilderness (extreme upper)
REGS - PERMITS:	10 hp maximum on all streams in Park County
ACCESS-SHUTTLE:	Numerous access sites and roads parallel river.
SERVICES:	All services in Absarokee or Columbus. Limited at Nye, MT. Commercial raft trips available (lower section).
CAMPING:	Numerous campgrounds and access sites.
GAMEFISH:	Upper - Rainbow, cutthroat, brook trout Middle - Brown, rainbow, brook trout Lower - Brook, rainbow, brown, whitefish
VESSEL:	Raft, whitewater canoe. Extreme upper whitewater - Kayak only Lower whitewater - Raft, kayak, whitewater canoe

SKILL LEVEL:	Upper 2 miles Whitewater - Expert only
	Next 4 miles Whitewater - Highly skilled
	Lower Whitewater - Experienced
	At least Intermediate skills for balance of river.
FLOAT TIMES:	Fast flow entire river.
FLOW INFO:	(406) 449-5263 USGS - Helena

HYDROGRAPH

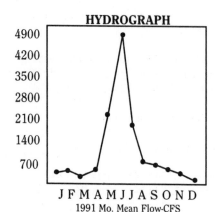

J F M A M J J A S O N D
1991 Mo. Mean Flow-CFS

Gage Sta: Mile "9.4"
Drain Area: 975 sq. mi. (at this gage)
Ave. Flow: (56 years) 950 cfs
Ext. Max: 12,000 cfs - 7.17' ga. ht. 6/15/67
Ext. Min: 58 cfs 4/2/36
Gradient: 3600' in 67.7 mi. = 53.1' pma
Float Grad: 2100' in 47.0 mi. = 44.7' pma
Clarity: Clear
Temp: Jan. 32⁰ F.
       Apr. 40⁰ F.
       Jul. 55⁰ F.
       Oct. 40⁰ F.

DRAINAGE:	(East) Yellowstone, Missouri, Mississippi, Gulf of Mexico
MAPS:	BLM - #35 "Beartooth"
	USFS - Custer NF (Beartooth) entire river
	Gallatin NF (upper)
	USGS - "Billings"
	CO. - Park, Stillwater.

STILLWATER (Yellowstone)

The Stillwater is a gross misnomer. It is anything but still! Etymologists seem to agree it has Native American origin. It seems Weeluna (Little Moon), a beautiful Indian maiden, married Nemidji. She was washed away in the flooding river, and Nemidji drowned also. As the water receded, the backwater remaining was called "Hallowed Place" or Stillwater.

The origin of the river is in the Absaroka-Beartooth Wilderness, declared in 1978. A trailhead and campground at Woodbine offers trails into the backcountry.

Big whitewater approaching Class VI, begins a mile inside the wilderness boundary, and extends 2 miles out to the trailhead. Below the trailhead is a four mile Class V stretch, down to the Old Nye Access and picnic area "41". At the peak of runoff these rapids are unfloatable! At other times it requires an expert in a kayak, properly equipped. Big drops are prevalent.

Floating for the less reckless begins at Old Nye. At this point the river still has good velocity, but is less of a "bull". If flow is high, a low bridge on private property "39" may cause a clearance problem. Nye Bridge Access "36.5" is also a camping possibility. It is at this site that I saw a Northern Swift Fox on one float trip. The river remains normal to Moraine Access "33". Below Moraine, the river gets moderately "bouncy". Castle Rock Access "32" would also be a nice campsite. "Moraine" and "Castle Rock" rapids are named for their proximity.

Beehive Access "31" marks the beginning of the annual kayak race down to Cliff Swallow Campground "24". This stretch of whitewater requires an experienced skill level. A good raft or a skilled pilot in a whitewater canoe would also work. This stretch is nearly continuous II-III. Low bridges are hazards. Above the Cliff Swallow bridge is "Rosco" or "Midnight" rapids.

Below Cliff Swallow, the lower section of the river could be handled by a paddler with strong intermediate skills. Spring Creek Bridge "20.5" and Johnson Creek Bridge "14" offer access. Just below Johnson Bridge is a small diversion dam in the left channel. Use the right channel above, to avoid. A bridge "11.6" just below the Rosebud River confluence, or White Bird Access "5.4" offer ingress or egress. Immediately below White Bird is a Class III drop. Swinging Bridge Access is just below. Firemans Point Access "1.5" is the last opportunity to exit on the Stillwater. Floaters could continue into the Yellowstone River and float downstream a couple miles to the Columbus bridge access.

The upper section of the river contains rainbow, cutthroat and brook trout. The middle section is predominately browns, and brookies are the most common in the lower section. There is a definite hatch on this river beginning with the caddis in May. The salmonfly and stoneflies follow into the summer. Spinfishing can be nearly as productive as flies.

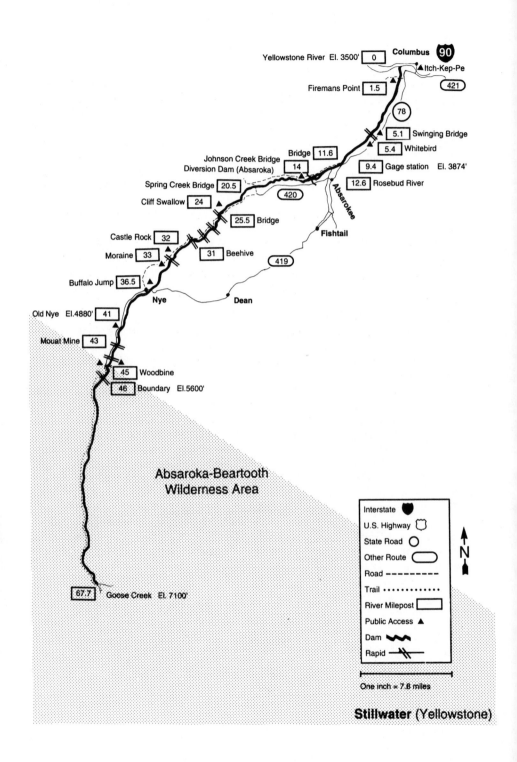

Yellowstone River El. 3500' [0] **Columbus** 90
Itch-Kep-Pe
Firemans Point [1.5]
421
78
[5.1] Swinging Bridge
[5.4] Whitebird
Bridge [11.6]
Johnson Creek Bridge [9.4] Gage station El. 3874'
Diversion Dam (Absaroka) [14]
[12.6] Rosebud River
Spring Creek Bridge [20.5]
Absarokee
Cliff Swallow [24]
420
[25.5] Bridge
Castle Rock [32] **Fishtail**
Moraine [33] [31] Beehive
419
Buffalo Jump [36.5]
Nye **Dean**
Old Nye El.4880' [41]
Mouat Mine [43]
[45] Woodbine
[46] Boundary El.5600'

Absaroka-Beartooth
Wilderness Area

Interstate	
U.S. Highway	
State Road	
Other Route	
Road	- - - - - - - -
Trail	• • • • • • • • • • •
River Milepost	
Public Access	▲
Dam	～～
Rapid	╫

N

One inch ≈ 7.6 miles

Stillwater (Yellowstone)

[67.7] Goose Creek El. 7100'

250

SUN

ORIGIN:	Gibson Dam - northwest of Augusta. El. 4400'
END:	Flows into Missouri River at Broadwater Bay in Great Falls. El. 3300'
LENGTH:	100.8 miles (70 air miles)
FLOATABLE:	100.8 miles (Class I designation = 100.8 miles)
SECTIONS:	Upper (29.5 mi.) Gibson Dam "100.8" to Hwy 287 "71.3" Middle (33.9 mi.) Hwy 287 "71.3" to Fort Shaw "37.4" Lower (37.4 mi.) Fort Shaw "37.4" to End - "0"
DAMS:	Gibson (Forms reservoir and controls flow) Sun River Div. Dam (large) (Pishkun Canal) 6 diversion dams (major)
WATERFALLS:	None
WHITEWATER:	11.5 mi. Gibson Dam to downstream 2.5 mi. (Class V) Pishkun Div. Dam to downstream 9 mi. (Class III)
DANGERS:	6 diversion dams, whitewater, remote area (upper)
DEWATERED:	Can get low, depending on dam releases and irrig. use.
PORTAGES:	Sun River Dam (Major portage RIGHT) "97.3" Floweree (RIGHT) "74.1" Crown Butte (LEFT) "58.1" Fort Shaw (LEFT) "53" Diversion dam (RIGHT) "47" Rocky Reef (RIGHT) "40" Sun River Valley (portage) "34.2"
SPEC. AGENCIES:	None
REGS - PERMITS:	None
ACCESS-SHUTTLE:	Upper - Access infrequent - shuttle round-about Middle & Lower - Hwy and intersecting road bridges.
SERVICES:	All services in Augusta and Great Falls, MT. Limited in Simms, Fort Shaw, Sun River and Vaughn, MT
CAMPING:	Upper - Good campsites by Gibson Reservoir area. Below float spots only. Middle & Lower - Camping at access sites only

GAMEFISH:	Upper - Rainbow, brown, brook, cutthroat, whitefish Middle & Lower - Some trout, pike, burbot
VESSEL:	Extreme upper Whitewater - Kayak Mi. "97.3" to "71.3" - Raft, whitewater canoe, kayak Middle - Raft, whitewater canoe, canoe Lower - Canoe, small boat
SKILL LEVEL:	Extreme upper Whitewater (2.5 miles) Highly skilled 26 mile remote section - Experienced Middle - Intermediate Lower - Beginner
FLOAT TIMES:	Moderate flows. Lower 17.1 miles slow. 26 mile remote section 1 extremely long day (2 days better)
FLOW INFO:	(406) 449-5263 USGS - Helena 2.0' minimum at Hwy 287 gage sta.

HYDROGRAPH

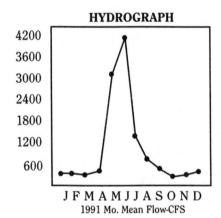

JFMAMJJASOND
1991 Mo. Mean Flow-CFS

Gage Sta: Milepost "13.6"
Drain Area: 1,854 sq. mi. (at this gage)
Ave. Flow: (57 years) 707 cfs
Ext. Max: 53,500 cfs - 23.4' ga. ht. 6/9/64
Ext. Min: 20 cfs 4/24/44
Gradient: 1100' in 100.8 miles = 10.9' pma
Float Grad: Same
Clarity: Cloudy to murky
Temp: Jan. 32° F.
          Apr. 50° F.
          Jul. 70° F.
          Oct. 50° F.

DRAINAGE:	(East) Missouri, Mississippi, Gulf of Mexico
MAPS:	BLM - #29 "Choteau" (upper) - #39 "Great Falls N." (lower) - #40 "Great Falls S." (extreme lower) USFS - Lewis & Clark NF (RMD) (Gibson to Augusta) USGS - "Choteau" (upper) - "Great Falls" (lower) Sp. - "Bob Marshall, Great Bear, Scapegoat Wilderness" (upper) USFS CO. - Lewis & Clark, Cascade

SUN

The main stem of the Sun used to begin at the confluence of the North and South Forks 5.6 miles above Gibson Dam. Since the dam was built as an irrigation project in 1913, and the reservoir formed; the Sun River now begins at the dam outlet.

The Blackfeet Indians called the river "Medicine", because of the healing properties in the minerals along the upper river. Since the river flows from the setting sun and into the rising sun, it is presumed this is why the river has its present name.

A trailhead near Gibson Dam, affords access by hiking or horse, up the two forks and into the Sun River Game Preserve and the Bob Marshall Wilderness. Boating on Gibson Reservoir and rock climbing below the dam, are each possible.

Below Gibson Dam "100.8" is some big whitewater, composed mainly of two big drops. These drops are 8' high and only 15' wide, due to canyon walls. Strong water hydraulics lie below. Lives have been lost in these drops and only the expert in kayak or good raft should risk it. This 2.5 mile whitewater section is followed by a mile of calm water just above the Sun River Diversion Dam forming Pishkun Canal.

An access exists just below the Sun River Dam "97.3". This is the beginning of the most popular floating portion of the Sun. A 26 mile, remote and inaccessible wonderland lies below. The first nine miles is moderate, nearly continuous whitewater. Whitewater canoes or a good raft are the most popular. A canyon with a solid bedrock floor and intermittent slabs, exposed from thrust faulting and boulder gardens cause the whitewater. It takes an experienced paddler. Get an early start and don't loiter long, if you plan on completing this trip in one day. An overnight trip is perfect, allowing you to fish and relax.

Fishing is wonderful for rainbow and browns. Whitefish and a few cutts and brookies also call this "home". There are distinct hatches on the river. Muddlers, caddis, salmon or mayflies along with the common dry flies would be possibilities depending on time of year, weather and water conditions. Small Mepps (brass) or the old red/white Dardevle are good. On one trip, I believe we caught fish on everything we had along.

After leaving the canyon area, limestone formations and shale with very little vegetation, is the backdrop for the long riffles and deep green pools. The Floweree Diversion Dam at milepost "74.1" requires a portage RIGHT. You are now entering the prairie hills and ranchland, which are still nearly void of vegetation. The Highway 287 Bridge Access "71.3" offers easy exit or entry.

Below this bridge are three 4' drops between mileposts "67" and "65". The Crown Butte Diversion Dam "58.1"requires a portage LEFT, and at mile "53" is the dangerous 9' Fort Shaw Dam (portage LEFT), built in 1908. With no further interruptions the Lory Bridge "49.4" follows. Below Lory Bridge is a 8' diversion dam which demands a portage RIGHT at mile "47.4". From Simms Bridge "45" to the Fort Shaw Bridge Access "37.4" there is the Rocky Reef diversion at Mile "40" (portage RIGHT). The Sun River Valley Diversion Dam occurs nearly four miles above the Highway 200 bridge at Sun River "30.4". An access under this bridge is usable. A county road bridge southeast of Vaughn "17.1" marks the end of obvious current, and murky water begins. Above this bridge, intermediate skills are necessary. Below this bridge a beginner can handle the rest of the river in any moderately sized vessel. I have even seen small motors being used. Bait fishing obviously, would be the most successful. Pike and ling and a few browns are the most common catch. Only a couple exit opportunities occur before Broadwater Bay Access, at the 10th Avenue South Bridge in Great Falls.

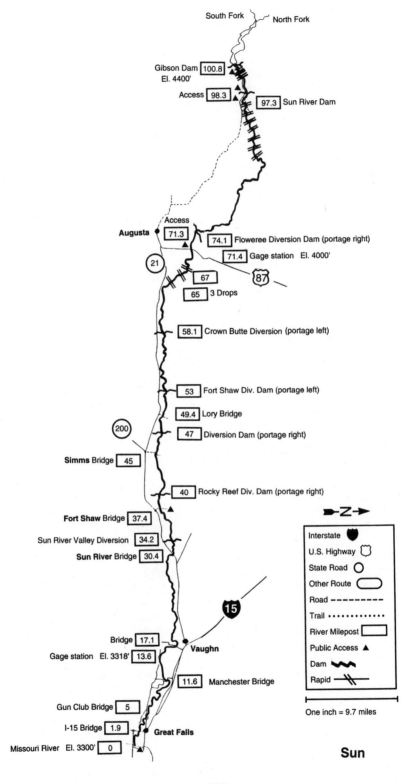

South Fork   North Fork

Gibson Dam 100.8
El. 4400'

Access 98.3

97.3 Sun River Dam

Access
Augusta   71.3

74.1 Floweree Diversion Dam (portage right)

71.4 Gage station El. 4000'

21

87

67

65 3 Drops

58.1 Crown Butte Diversion (portage left)

53 Fort Shaw Div. Dam (portage left)

49.4 Lory Bridge

200

47 Diversion Dam (portage right)

Simms Bridge 45

40 Rocky Reef Div. Dam (portage right)

Fort Shaw Bridge 37.4

Sun River Valley Diversion 34.2

Sun River Bridge 30.4

15

Bridge 17.1

Gage station El. 3318' 13.6

Vaughn

11.6 Manchester Bridge

Gun Club Bridge 5

I-15 Bridge 1.9   Great Falls

Missouri River El. 3300' 0

N

Interstate
U.S. Highway
State Road
Other Route
Road -----
Trail ••••••
River Milepost
Public Access ▲
Dam
Rapid

One inch = 9.7 miles

Sun

254

SWAN

ORIGIN:	Gray Wolf Lake above Lindberg Lake. El. 6646'
END:	Flows into Flathead Lake at Bigfork, MT. El. 2893'
LENGTH:	93 total mi. (78.1 river mi. + 3 lakes & 1 res. = 14.9 mi.) (54 air miles)
FLOATABLE:	66.1 river mi. (Lindberg Lake Rd. El. 4015' to End Lindberg & Cygnet L. 5.5 miles Swan Lake 8.2 Bigfork Dam Reservoir 1.2 All floatable 14.9 miles
SECTIONS:	Upper (43.0 mi.) Origin "93" to Piper Creek "50" Middle (48.2 mi.) Piper Cr. Br. "50" to Bigfork Dam "1.8" Lower (1.8 mi.) Bigfork Dam "1.8" to Flathead Lake "0"
DAMS:	Bigfork Dam (Forms small res. & controls flow below)
WATERFALLS:	None
WHITEWATER:	1.0 mile Bigfork Dam "1.8" to Flathead Lake Bay Bridge ".8" Class V, continuous whitewater called "Wild Mile"
DANGERS:	Dam and whitewater below, numerous logjams.
DEWATERED:	Can be low in fall.
PORTAGES:	Bigfork Dam (portage RIGHT)
SPEC. AGENCIES:	None
REGS - PERMITS:	None
ACCESS-SHUTTLE:	Highway 83 with many intersecting road bridges. A few formal access sites.
SERVICES:	Limited in Condon, MT. All in Bigfork, MT
CAMPING:	A few formal campgrounds and access sites.
GAMEFISH:	Rainbow, cutthroat, bulls, brook trout Also pike in lower river.
VESSEL:	1.0 mile Whitewater section - Kayak or good raft. Rest of river - Canoe, medium raft, small boat.

SKILL LEVEL:	Whitewater section - Highly skilled
	Rest of river - Beginner to Inter. (depending on flow)
FLOAT TIMES:	Mod. fast except last 8 mi. above Bigfork Dam - slow. Below Bigfork Dam - Screamin'
FLOW INFO:	(406) 449-5263 USGS - Helena

HYDROGRAPH

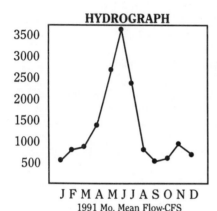

J F M A M J J A S O N D
1991 Mo. Mean Flow-CFS

Gage Sta: Immediately down from Swan Lake
Drain Area: 671 sq. mi. (at this gage)
Ave. Flow: (69 years) 1,167 cfs
Ext. Max: 8,890 cfs - 7.34' ga. ht. 6/20/74
Ext. Min: 193 cfs - .04' ga. ht. 1/29/30
Gradient: 3753' in 93.0 miles = 40.4' pma
Float Grad: 1122' in 75.5 miles = 14.9' pma
Clarity: Clear

DRAINAGE:	(West) Flathead, Clark Fork, Pend Oreille, Columbia, Pacific Ocean
MAPS:	BLM - #20 "Seeley Lake" (upper) - #19 "Swan River" (lower) - #18 "Hungry Horse" (extreme lower). USFS - Flathead NF (South) entire river - Flathead NF (North) lower only USGS - "Choteau" (most of river) - "Cut Bank" & "Kalispell" (lower) CO. - Missoula, Lake, Flathead

256

SWAN

The etymology of the Swan is cloudy. Some say it was named for great numbers of Trumpeter Swan that formerly gathered in the area. Others, say it may have been named after Emmett Swan, an early resident of the area.

The origin of the river is at Gray Wolf Lake "93", above Lindberg Lake. Lindberg Lake offers all of the boating activities. A public campground is located between Lindberg Lake and the small Cygnet Lake. The river below Cygnet Lake has a steep gradient, many boulders, and downfall. Lindberg Lake Road Bridge "75.5", marks the beginning of difficult floating on the Swan.

This 25 mile stretch requires a patient and healthy person. Many exhausting, wall to wall logjams require portage. In high water these logjams can appear quickly around a curve and getting stopped to portage can be difficult. I can personally attest to this, as on an early spring float, I got caught in a sudden snowstorm. Being tired from portages, I hit a logjam, which twisted and bent in half the canoe I was in and sucked it under. Grabbing a log I pulled myself out and to avoid the brushy banks I had to walk the river out two miles to my vehicle. Talk about a hypothermia candidate!

Floating gets better below Piper Creek bridge "50". Bridges remain your only opportunity to access. Fatty Creek bridge "43" and Point Pleasant Campground "37" occur before Porcupine Bridge Access "28.6". An intermediate paddler in a canoe, medium sized raft, or small boat can handle all of the river, excepting the whitewater section, if flow is normal.

Piper Creek to Porcupine Bridge is the most popular float fishing portion on the Swan. Rainbow, cutthroat, brookies and bulls make possible a mixed creel. Pike and bass are found in Swan Lake and below. Below Porcupine Bridge the river slows to a crawl before entering Swan Lake. Swan Lake is a popular summer resort lake offering all of the popular boating activities.

Below the Swan Lake outlet "15.3", the river has good velocity and some boulders for five miles. Slow water then exists for eight miles to the Bigfork Dam.

Below Bigfork Dam "1.8", and depending on dam discharge, is a dangerous Class IV-V whitewater run. This 1 mile run, with a gradient of 95' is called the "Wild Mile", and ends at the Bigfork Bridge on Flathead Lake. A May kayak race has great participation and is well attended by spectators. This whitewater festival is a fun filled weekend affair, with slalom and down river events. This lower section of whitewater can only be run by the highly skilled, in a kayak or good raft.

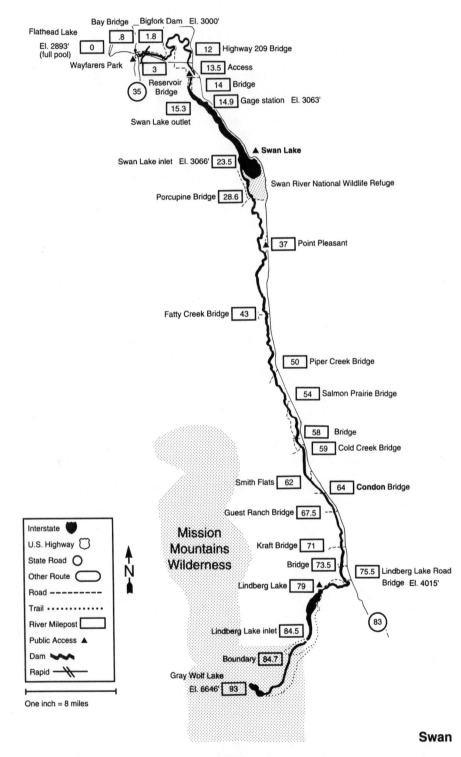

Flathead Lake
El. 2893'
(full pool) | 0

Bay Bridge | .8
Bigfork Dam   El. 3000' | 1.8
12 | Highway 209 Bridge

Wayfarers Park
3

Reservoir
Bridge
35

13.5 | Access
14 | Bridge
14.9 | Gage station   El. 3063'

15.3
Swan Lake outlet

▲ Swan Lake

Swan Lake inlet   El. 3066' | 23.5

Swan River National Wildlife Refuge

Porcupine Bridge | 28.6

▲ 37 | Point Pleasant

Fatty Creek Bridge | 43

50 | Piper Creek Bridge

54 | Salmon Prairie Bridge

58 | Bridge
59 | Cold Creek Bridge

Smith Flats | 62
64 | **Condon** Bridge

Guest Ranch Bridge | 67.5

Kraft Bridge | 71
Bridge | 73.5
75.5 | Lindberg Lake Road
Bridge   El. 4015'

Lindberg Lake | 79 ▲
83

Lindberg Lake inlet | 84.5

Boundary | 84.7

Gray Wolf Lake
El. 6646' | 93

Legend

Interstate
U.S. Highway
State Road
Other Route
Road - - - - - - - -
Trail • • • • • • • • •
River Milepost [ ]
Public Access ▲
Dam
Rapid

One inch = 8 miles

Mission
Mountains
Wilderness

Swan

SWIFTCURRENT

ORIGIN:	Swiftcurrent Mtn. in Glacier National Park. El. 5600'
END:	Flows into Lower St. Mary Lake, near Babb, MT El. 4471'
LENGTH:	21 total miles (13 river mi. + 5 lakes & reservoir 8 mi.) (15 air miles)

FLOATABLE: 7 river miles (Mile "7" to "0")

Bullhead Lake	.5 miles
Red Rock Lake	.5
Fishercap Lake	.5
*Swiftcurrent Lake	1.0
*Sherburne Reservoir	5.5
Floatable *	8.0 miles

SECTIONS:	Upper (6.5 mi.) Origin "21" to Swiftcurrent Falls Middle (7.5 mi.) Swiftcurrent Falls "14.5" to "7" Lower (7.0 mi.) Sherburne Dam "7" to "0"
DAMS:	Sherburne Dam (Forms reservoir & controls flow)
WATERFALLS:	Red Rock Falls Mile "18" Swiftcurrent Lake Falls Mile "14.5"
WHITEWATER:	3 miles Mile "4" to Bridge "1" Dangerous Class III when dam discharge high.
DANGERS:	Swift, moderate whitewater in a narrow, channeled streambed with debris, for 3 miles.
DEWATERED:	Usually extremely dewatered late in fall.
PORTAGES:	None
SPEC. AGENCIES:	Glacier National Park (upper) - Blackfeet Indian Reservation (lower)
REGS - PERMITS:	If camping overnight in the back-country, a permit is required. No firearms in Glacier National Park. If you leave the river on reservation you need a recreation or fish permit.
ACCESS-SHUTTLE:	Easy. Highway parallels river. Informal access points.
SERVICES:	All services in summer at Many Glacier. Limited in Babb, MT. Boat trips on Swiftcurrent Lake, and guided hikes and horseback trips.

CAMPING:	Formal campground at Many Glacier. No formal camp-grounds or access sites on reservation.
GAMEFISH:	Cutthroat, rainbow, whitefish, pike
VESSEL:	Canoe, medium raft, small boat Whitewater - Whitewater canoe, medium raft, kayak
SKILL LEVEL:	Intermediate Whitewater portion - Experienced
FLOAT TIMES:	Quite fast.
FLOW INFO:	(406) 449-5263 USGS - Helena

HYDROGRAPH

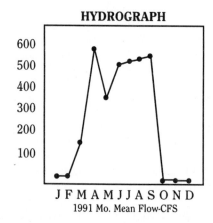

600
500
400
300
200
100

J F M A M J J A S O N D
1991 Mo. Mean Flow-CFS

Gage Sta: Below Sherburne Dam
Drain Area: 65 sq. mi. (at this gage)
Ave. Flow: (7 years) 199 cfs
Ext. Max: 2,420 cfs - 7.63' ga. ht. 6/25/69
Ext. Min: No flow at times (dam gates shut)
Gradient: 1129' in 21 miles = 53.8' pma
Float Grad: 279' in 7 miles = 39.9' pma
Clarity: Cloudy
Temp: Jan. 32⁰ F.
        Apr. 34⁰ F.
        Jul. 66⁰ F.
        Oct. 36⁰ F.

DRAINAGE:	(North) St. Mary, Oldman, South Sask., Saskatchewan, Nelson, Hudson Bay
MAPS:	BLM - #17 "St. Mary" USGS - "Cut Bank" Sp. - "Glacier National Park" USGS CO. - Glacier

SWIFTCURRENT

Swiftcurrent is Blackfoot for "swift flowing stream". The origin of the river is near Swiftcurrent Mountain in magnificent Glacier National Park. The river leaves the park and enters the Blackfeet Indian Reservation at Sherburne Reservoir, and flows into Lower St. Mary Lake.

A trailhead at Many Glacier, leads upstream along the river to Swiftcurrent Pass and beyond. A horse concession offers guided trail rides, and ranger guided hiking tours are offered. This small stream tumbles down through Bullhead, Redrock and Fishercap Lakes before reaching Swiftcurrent Lake. Waterfalls can be viewed above Redrock Lake and at the outlet of Swiftcurrent Lake.

The rugged towering peaks with glaciers offer a panorama for hikers and photographers. A park resort complex, including a campground can be found at Many Glacier. Canoeing is permitted on the lake and boat tours are offered.

The Sherburne Reservoir and dam are eight miles below the resort. Floating can begin at an access below the dam at river milepost "7". A short and moderate rapids exists 1/2 mile below the dam. Although the river has a steep gradient, an intermediate skill level in a medium raft, canoe or small boat can handle the river for three miles below the dam, to milepost "4". The highway comes close to the river and ingress or egress is possible.

Below milepost "4" the next three miles can be dangerous class III whitewater when flow is up. The gradient is steep, through a narrow and channeled streambed where downfall protrudes out from the banks. This whitewater run ends at a reservation road bridge south of Babb at river milepost "1". The river then flows into Lower St. Mary Lake. This lower three miles of potential whitewater should only be approached by an experienced pilot, in a whitewater canoe, medium raft or kayak.

Although not a popular fishing stream, cutthroat, rainbow, whitefish and pike can be found. A fishing license is not needed in the park, however bank fishing below the dam requires a tribal permit. Extreme low to high water releases from Sherburne Dam, for irrigation purposes, detract from fishery and floating values.

Swiftcurrent River

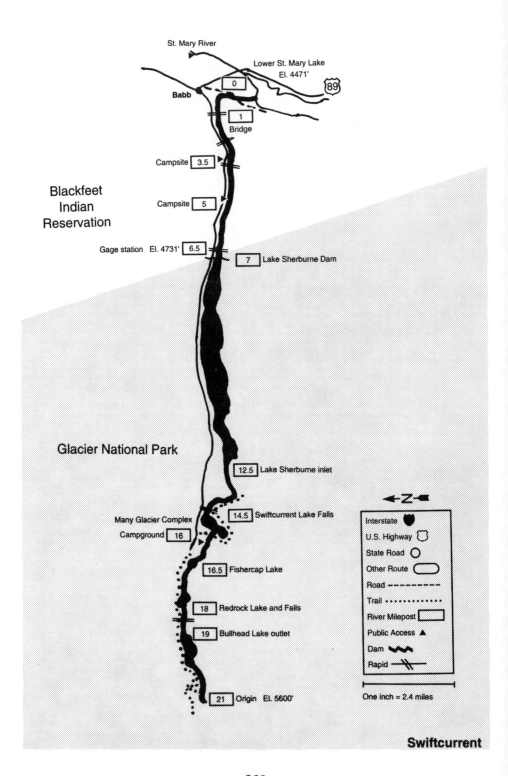

St. Mary River

Lower St. Mary Lake
El. 4471'

89

Babb

0

1
Bridge

Campsite 3.5

Campsite 5

**Blackfeet
Indian
Reservation**

Gage station   El. 4731'   6.5

7   Lake Sherburne Dam

Glacier National Park

12.5   Lake Sherburne inlet

14.5   Swiftcurrent Lake Falls

Many Glacier Complex
Campground   16

16.5   Fishercap Lake

18   Redrock Lake and Falls

19   Bullhead Lake outlet

21   Origin   El. 5600'

N

Interstate
U.S. Highway
State Road
Other Route
Road ----------
Trail ••••••••••••
River Milepost
Public Access ▲
Dam
Rapid

One inch = 2.4 miles

Swiftcurrent

TETON

ORIGIN:	Confluence of North & South Forks, northwest of Choteau, MT El. 4900'
END:	Flows into Marias River at Loma, MT El. 2570'
LENGTH:	195.8 miles (100 air miles)
FLOATABLE:	195.8 miles
SECTIONS:	Upper (30.2 mi.) Origin "195.8" to Highway 89 Bridge "165.6" Middle (64.9 mi.) Highway 89 Access "165.6" to Kerr Bridge "100.7" Lower (100.7 mi.) Kerr Bridge "100.7" to End - "0"
DAMS:	Bynum (Concrete-entire river) portage Mile "188" Farmers (Rock-partial) possible portage Mile "186.6" Eldorado (Rock-partial) possible portage Mile "182" Eureka (Rock-partial) possible portage Mile "179" Old Diversion Dam-possible portage Mile "51"
WATERFALLS:	None
WHITEWATER:	None
DANGERS:	Irrigation diversions, fences
DEWATERED:	Often
PORTAGES:	5 diversion dams (above)
SPEC. AGENCIES:	None
REGS - PERMITS:	None
ACCESS-SHUTTLE:	Access points often longer distances, but quite easy with a good map.
SERVICES:	All in Choteau or Fort Benton, MT. Limited in Loma.
CAMPING:	Few formal campgrounds or access sites.
GAMEFISH:	Upper - Rainbow, brown, brook trout Middle - Brown, whitefish, rainbow, brook Lower - Sauger, walleye, burbot, catfish, pike
VESSEL:	Canoe, small boat, medium raft

SKILL LEVEL:	Upper - Intermediate Middle & Lower - Beginner
FLOAT TIMES:	Upper - Moderately fast. Middle - Slow & curvy Lower - Moderate
FLOW INFO:	(406) 449-5263 USGS - Helena

HYDROGRAPH

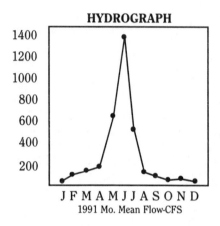

JFMAMJJASOND
1991 Mo. Mean Flow-CFS

Gage Sta: Kerr Bridge
Drain Area: 1308 sq. mi. (at this gage)
Ave. Flow: (37 years) 148 cfs
Ext. Max: 71,300 cfs - 20.48' ga. ht. 6/9/64
Ext. Min: No flow at times.
Gradient: 2330' in 195.8 miles = 11.9' pma
Float Grad: Same
Clarity: Cloudy to turbid
Temp: Aug 7   78⁰ F.
          Sep 5   63⁰ F.

DRAINAGE:	(East) Marias, Missouri, Mississippi, Gulf of Mexico
MAPS:	BLM - #29 "Choteau" (upper) - #39 "Great Falls North" - #14 "Highwood" (lower) USFS - Lewis & Clark NF (R M Div.) upper only USGS - "Choteau" (upper) - "Great Falls" (lower) Sp. - "Bob Marshall, Great Bear, Scapegoat Wilderness" (extreme upper) USFS CO. - Teton, Chouteau

TETON

The Teton has been called the "Rose" River, obviously for the wild roses frequenting the area. The Indians called it "Titan", which means "land without trees". The French called it Teton (breasts), for the image the mountains created. A tribe of the Sioux nation, living along the Missouri, was called Tetons. And so hangs the cloud of namesake.

The main stem of the Teton begins at the confluence of the North and South Forks "195.8", west of Choteau, MT. The headwaters area above, offers diversified recreation opportunities. A trailhead leads into the vast backcountry, while a ski resort and snowmobile trails offer winter fun. Indian Head Rock a natural landmark, guards the canyon.

Floating can begin at the North & South Fork confluence, or you may begin higher on either fork. The upper section, beginning at the edge of the Rockies is magnificent. The river begins flowing through a streambed of large gravel. This section has a rather steep gradient in places. The river is interrupted by four diversion dams in only a nine mile span. Campgrounds are found in the headwaters area and at Eureka Reservoir, just off the river. These are the only formal campgrounds along the course of the river. County road bridges occur sporadically, often distant, causing all day floats.

Below Choteau, the river flows through hilly farm and ranch land. The streambed, due to natural siltation is muddy or sandy, creating turbidity. The river picks up velocity as it approaches the Marias. The banks are not as undercut and support more vegetation. As a result the stream begins to clear.

The upper river requires at least intermediate skills. The middle and lower sections can be handled by a beginner. A canoe, small boat or raft are the best vessels. The middle section, with a lot of slow water, might test the patience of a raft oarsman. A few fences and irrigation jettys disrupt floating. An old diversion, partially washed out occurs midway between Kerr Bridge and the end of the river. A fine place to exit at the mouth to the Marias, is at the Highway 87 bridge in Loma.

Teton River

265

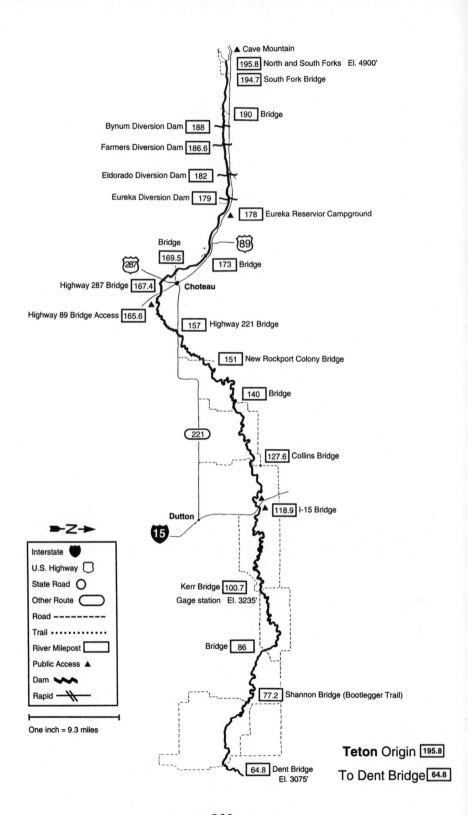

▲ Cave Mountain

195.8 North and South Forks   El. 4900'

194.7 South Fork Bridge

190 Bridge

Bynum Diversion Dam 188

Farmers Diversion Dam 186.6

Eldorado Diversion Dam 182

Eureka Diversion Dam 179

▲ 178 Eureka Reservior Campground

Bridge
169.5

89

287

173 Bridge

Highway 287 Bridge 167.4

Choteau

Highway 89 Bridge Access 165.6 ▲

157 Highway 221 Bridge

151 New Rockport Colony Bridge

140 Bridge

221

127.6 Collins Bridge

Dutton

15

▲ 118.9 I-15 Bridge

Kerr Bridge 100.7
Gage station   El. 3235'

Bridge 86

77.2 Shannon Bridge (Bootlegger Trail)

Teton Origin 195.8

64.8 Dent Bridge
El. 3075'

To Dent Bridge 64.8

Legend

Interstate 🛡
U.S. Highway ⬡
State Road ◯
Other Route ⬭
Road -----------
Trail ••••••••••
River Milepost ☐
Public Access ▲
Dam 〰〰
Rapid —⫽—

One inch = 9.3 miles

➤-Z-➤

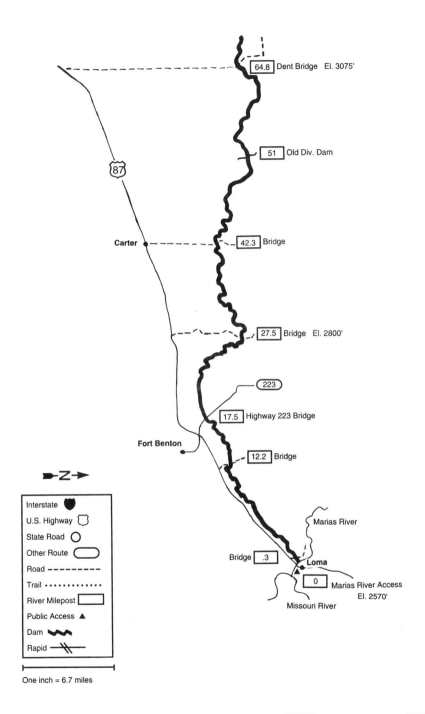

64.8 Dent Bridge   El. 3075'

51 Old Div. Dam

42.3 Bridge

27.5 Bridge   El. 2800'

223

17.5 Highway 223 Bridge

12.2 Bridge

Marias River

Bridge .3

Loma

0 Marias River Access
El. 2570'

Missouri River

87

Carter

Fort Benton

➡-Z-➡

Interstate	(shield)
U.S. Highway	(shield)
State Road	◯
Other Route	⬭
Road	- - - - - -
Trail	• • • • • • • •
River Milepost	☐
Public Access	▲
Dam	〰
Rapid	⧸⧸

One inch = 6.7 miles

Teton Dent Bridge 64.8 to Marias River 0

267

THOMPSON

ORIGIN: Upper Thompson Lake outlet, southwest of Kalispell. El. 3300'

END: Flows into Clark Fork River east of Thompson Falls. El. 2400'

LENGTH: 55.5 total miles (51.3 river miles & Middle & Lower Thompson Lakes 4.2 miles) (33 air miles)

FLOATABLE: 50.1 miles (Logging Road Bridge "50.1" to End "0") 3 lakes are floatable.

SECTIONS: Upper (5.4 mi.) Origin "55.5" to Logging Road Bridge "50.1"
Middle (32.2 mi.) Logging Road "50.1" to Little Thompson River & Bridge "17.9"
Lower (17.9 mi.) Little Thompson R. "17.9" to "0"

DAMS: None

WATERFALLS: None

WHITEWATER: 4 miles Copperking Campground "4" to End "0" (When water high) Class II - III
Also, a stretch below milepost "16" - when water high (Class II)

DANGERS: Fences (middle), logjams. Curvy and narrow - can be a problem when current strong.

DEWATERED: Can be low in fall.

PORTAGES: A low bridge, some fences, logjams in middle section.

SPEC. AGENCIES: None

REGS - PERMITS: None

ACCESS-SHUTTLE: Thompson River Road along with a logging road parallel the river, and cross it a number of times.

SERVICES: All in Thompson Falls, MT only, and gas, food, cabins at Thompson Lake.

CAMPING: 3 formal campgrounds and numerous informal places.

GAMEFISH:	Upper - Brook, rainbow, largemouth bass
	Lower - Brook, cutthroat, rainbow, whitefish, bulls
VESSEL:	Canoe, medium raft (some slow water in places)
	4 miles Whitewater - Whitewater canoe, kayak, raft
	(when water high)
SKILL LEVEL:	Beginner, if flows are normal.
	Milepost "16" to end "0" - Intermediate
FLOAT TIMES:	Moderate flow. These mileposts are very slow:
	"50.1" to "42.5"
	"40.0" to "36.6"
	"24.6" to "23.0"
FLOW INFO:	(406) 449-5263 USGS - Helena

HYDROGRAPH

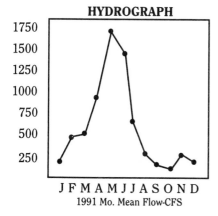

1991 Mo. Mean Flow-CFS

Gage Sta: 1 mile upstream from mouth
Drain Area: 642 sq. mi.
Ave. Flow: (35 years) 456 cfs
Ext. Max: 6,080 cfs - 8.53' ga. ht. 06/09/64
Ext. Min: 60 cfs - 1.96' ga. ht. 11/20/77
Gradient: 900' in 55.5 mi. = 16.2' pma
Float Grad: 870' in 50.1 mi. = 17.4' pma
Clarity: Clear
Temp: Jan. 34^0 F.
     Apr. 45^0 F.
     Jul. 63^0 F.
     Oct. 45^0 F.

DRAINAGE:	(West) Clark Fork, Pend Oreille, Columbia, Pacific
MAPS:	BLM - #10 "Kalispell" (extreme upper) - #11 "Polson"
	(upper) - #6 "Thompson Falls" (lower).
	USFS - Lolo NF (entire river) best map - Kootenai NF
	(extreme upper only)
	USGS - "Kalispell" (extreme upper only) - "Wallace"
	(most of river)
	CO. - Lincoln, Flathead, Sanders

THOMPSON

The Thompson River was named after David Thompson, an early explorer. The river properly begins at the outlet of Upper Thompson Lake, and extends for nearly 56 miles to the Clark Fork River, east of Thompson Falls, MT.

The upper section consists of three nearly continuous lakes, and a mile of marsh below. All of these lakes furnish numerous boating activities. Rainbow, brookies and largemouth bass are present.

Floating can begin as high as the logging road bridge "50.1" at Lang Creek. Marshland grasses along the rivers undercut banks and muddy to sandy streambed, is the scene as you begin floating. The slow moving stream passes through private land with ranching activity of pasture and hay land. You soon enter the Lolo National Forest, at the Thompson River Road bridge "42.5" near Murr Creek. Two low, private equipment bridges, require an easy portage in this stretch above Murr Creek.

1.5 miles below Murr Creek bridge is a small informal campsite. These informal campsites are frequent and unmarked along the rest of the river, now on public land. This Thompson River Road and the private logging road may be used by the public, but watch for logging trucks that have the right-of-way. These two roads cross and recross the river many times, offering bridge access. They connect Hwy 2 and Hwy 200.

Slow moving water, again occurs between the bridge at Schroeder Creek "40", and the Bend Bridge "36.6". Below Bend the river current increases, down to the bridge near Chippy Creek "24.6". A medium-sized raft would work nicely as well as a canoe. Below Chippy Creek is 1.6 miles of "dead" water. On one trip I paddled by a young bull moose standing in the river, not a paddle length away. Just below, I spotted a moose calf in the willows, and shortly here comes "mama". She chased me until I reached current again and was able to outdistance her.

Below the bridge at Bear Creek "23" the river's slow sections end. Below the Little Thompson River confluence is a bridge "16". Some bouncy water occurs below this bridge when the water is high. A steeper gradient and some boulders make the remaining river difficult for a beginner.

Clark Memorial Campground "5.5" and the Copper King Campground "4" occur before the whitewater section. This whitewater is during high water only, and offers a 4 mile Class II - III run. A 4' drop in a narrow corridor, exists at milepost "2.5". A few deep, green pools break up the boulder caused waves. A kayaker or a whitewater canoer would enjoy this portion. A medium-sized raft also works nicely. Spotting Bighorn Sheep is probable on the mountain sides. A jeep trail under the Highway 200 bridge at the mouth of the river offers exit.

Brookies, rainbow, cutthroat and a few bulls are present in the river. And let us not forget the ubiquitous whitefish. A distinguishable hatch occurs: salmonfly in the spring, followed by the caddis and mayfly. Spinning with brass colored lures is equally productive.

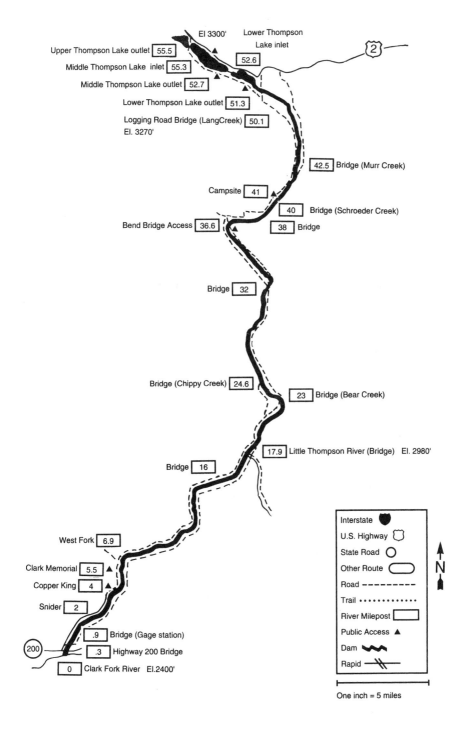

El 3300'

Lower Thompson
Lake inlet

Upper Thompson Lake outlet 55.5

Middle Thompson Lake inlet 55.3

52.6

Middle Thompson Lake outlet 52.7

Lower Thompson Lake outlet 51.3

Logging Road Bridge (LangCreek) 50.1
El. 3270'

42.5 Bridge (Murr Creek)

Campsite 41

40 Bridge (Schroeder Creek)

Bend Bridge Access 36.6   38 Bridge

Bridge 32

Bridge (Chippy Creek) 24.6

23 Bridge (Bear Creek)

17.9 Little Thompson River (Bridge)   El. 2980'

Bridge 16

West Fork 6.9

Clark Memorial 5.5

Copper King 4

Snider 2

.9 Bridge (Gage station)

200

.3 Highway 200 Bridge

0 Clark Fork River   El.2400'

Interstate
U.S. Highway
State Road
Other Route
Road --------
Trail •••••••••••
River Milepost
Public Access ▲
Dam
Rapid

N

One inch = 5 miles

Thompson

LITTLE THOMPSON

ORIGIN:	Alder Creek near Thompson Peak, northwest of Hot Springs, MT El. 4500'
END:	Flows into Thompson River northwest of Plains, MT El. 2980'
LENGTH:	17 miles (12 air miles)
FLOATABLE:	2 miles (Middle section - Mile "3" to "1")
SECTIONS:	Upper (12.7 mi.) Origin "17" to Mudd Creek Br. "4.3" Middle (3.3 mi.) Mudd Creek "4.3" to Canyon "1" Lower (1.0 mi.) Canyon "1" to End "0"
DAMS:	None
WATERFALLS:	None
WHITEWATER:	None floatable
DANGERS:	Logjams, fences, remote area, 1 mile canyon
DEWATERED:	Usually low in fall.
PORTAGES:	Logjams
SPEC. AGENCIES:	None
REGS - PERMITS:	None
ACCESS-SHUTTLE:	Easy, road along river for middle & lower sections.
SERVICES:	None
CAMPING:	A few informal campsites.
GAMEFISH:	Rainbow, brook, cutthroat, bulls, whitefish
VESSEL:	Small raft
SKILL LEVEL:	Intermediate
WATER:	Moderate flow, clear, 129 square miles (drainage) Jan. 32⁰ F. Apr. 42⁰ F. Jul. 65⁰ F. Oct. 45⁰ F.
GRADIENT:	1520' in 17 miles = 89.4' pma. Floatable 2 miles moderate gradient.

DRAINAGE: (West) Thompson, Clark Fork, Pend Oreille, Columbia.

MAPS: BLM - #11 "Polson"
USFS - Lolo NF
USGS - "Wallace"
CO. - Sanders

Gray Squirrel

LITTLE THOMPSON

The origin of the river is at Alder Creek near Thompson Peak, northwest of Hot Springs, Montana. Seventeen miles later it flows into the Thompson River.

The upper section is difficult to find. A road north of Plains leads to its origin. This road follows the river for four miles down to a bridge "13.3" at McGinnis Creek. The river then departs from all roads and is accessible only by hiking to a ford across the stream, near Indian Gulch. This is a five-mile hike. Below Indian Gulch, the river leaves its narrow canyon of boulders and downfall, and flows through a very thick willow habitat. These willows are difficult to traverse. The first sign of civilization is at a bridge at Mudd Creek "4.3".

The river continues to be a jungle of downfall, down to a campsite at river milepost "3". A very short two-mile float could begin at this campsite. Although the river remains small, less downfall and fewer boulders make a small raft float possible. Intermediate skills are necessary. Low water makes floating impossible in the fall. Floating must end at a large meadow, as a steep gorge exists the last mile to the Thompson River. This narrow gorge has a steep gradient with numerous boulder drops and is unfloatable and dangerous.

Fishing can be quite good as rainbow, brookies, cutts, bulls and whitefish offer a mixed creel.

Little Thompson River

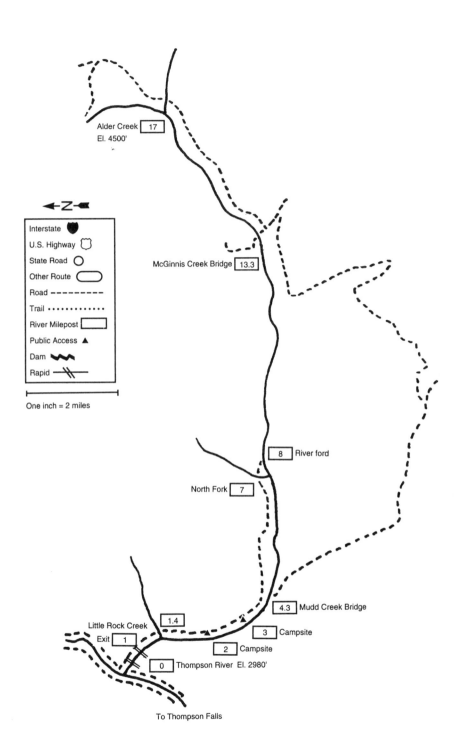

Alder Creek [17]
El. 4500'

McGinnis Creek Bridge [13.3]

Interstate 🛡
U.S. Highway ⬭
State Road ◯
Other Route ⬭
Road - - - - - -
Trail •••••••
River Milepost ▭
Public Access ▲
Dam 〰
Rapid ╱╱

One inch = 2 miles

[8] River ford

North Fork [7]

[4.3] Mudd Creek Bridge

Little Rock Creek [1.4]
Exit [1]   [3] Campsite

[2] Campsite

[0] Thompson River El. 2980'

To Thompson Falls

Little Thompson

TOBACCO

ORIGIN:	Confluence of Fortine & Grave Creeks, southeast of Eureka, MT El.2780'
END:	Flows into Koocanusa Reservoir west of Eureka, MT El. Full pool 2459' - Low pool 2287'
LENGTH:	15.2 miles (12 air miles)
FLOATABLE:	15.2 miles
SECTIONS:	Upper (6.7 mi.) Origin "15.2" to Eureka Bridge "8.5" Middle (5.3 mi.) Eureka Bridge "8.5" to Reservoir inlet (Full pool) "3.2" Lower (3.2 mi.) Reservoir Full-pool "3.2" to Reservoir Low-pool "0"
DAMS:	None
WATERFALLS:	None
WHITEWATER:	None
DANGERS:	Logs, low bridge Mile "6"
DEWATERED:	Can be low in fall
PORTAGES:	Low bridge
SPEC. AGENCIES:	None
REGS - PERMITS:	None
ACCESS-SHUTTLE:	Round-about but quite easy. Highways 93 & 37. Good access at Eureka city park. Formal access site near reservoir below Highway 37 bridge.
SERVICES:	All in Eureka, MT
CAMPING:	Good informal campsites near reservoir at access site.
GAMEFISH:	Cutthroat, bulls

VESSEL:	Canoe, medium raft, small boat
SKILL LEVEL:	Beginner, if flows are normal
FLOAT TIMES:	Moderate flow
FLOW INFO:	(406) 449-5263 USGS - Helena

HYDROGRAPH

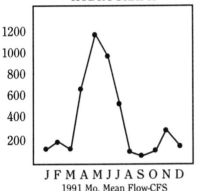

1200
1000
800
600
400
200

J F M A M J J A S O N D
1991 Mo. Mean Flow-CFS

Gage Sta: NW of Eureka, MT
Drain Area: 440 sq. mi.
Ave. Flow: (33 years) 269 cfs
Ext. Max. 3180 cfs - 7.16' ga. ht. 5/13/91
Ext. Min: 20 cfs 1/11/63
Gradient: 405' in 15.2 mi. = 26.6' pma
Float Grad: Same
Clarity: Clear to cloudy
Temp: Jan. 32^0 F.
          Apr. 43^0 F.
          Jul. 66^0 F.
          Oct. 43^0 F.

| DRAINAGE: | (West) Kootenai, Columbia, Pacific Ocean |
| MAPS: | BLM - #9 "Whitefish" (upper) - #4 "Yaak" (lower)
USFS - Kootenai NF entire river (best map)
USGS - "Kalispell"
CO. - Lincoln |

TOBACCO

The namesake of Tobacco is derived from the Kootenai Indians who grew tobacco in the valley. The mainstem of the river begins at the confluence of Fortine and Grave Creeks, southeast of Eureka.

A bridge, just off Highway 93, occurs at this confluence. Floating can begin at this bridge "15.2". The river meanders along rocky bluffs with mountain and valley foliage. The gravel streambed gradually becomes sandy with undercut banks as you approach the reservoir. The Eureka City Park offers the first access at river milepost "8.5". Each year fun seekers enjoy the annual float race to Koocanusa.

Cutthroat and bulls frequent the river. A beginner can handle the river if flow is normal. A medium sized raft, canoe or small boat would work fine. The river can be low in the fall.

Below Eureka, midway to the Highway 37 bridge, is a low bridge that requires portage. The river is slow and affords ample time to stop. Between the Highway 37 bridge "4.5" and the reservoir are numerous campsites. The reservoir inlet at full pool, is at river milepost "3.2". When the reservoir is low, the river continues further towards the original streambed of the Kootenai River. The reservoir offers all boating activities and fishing can be quite good.

Tobacco River

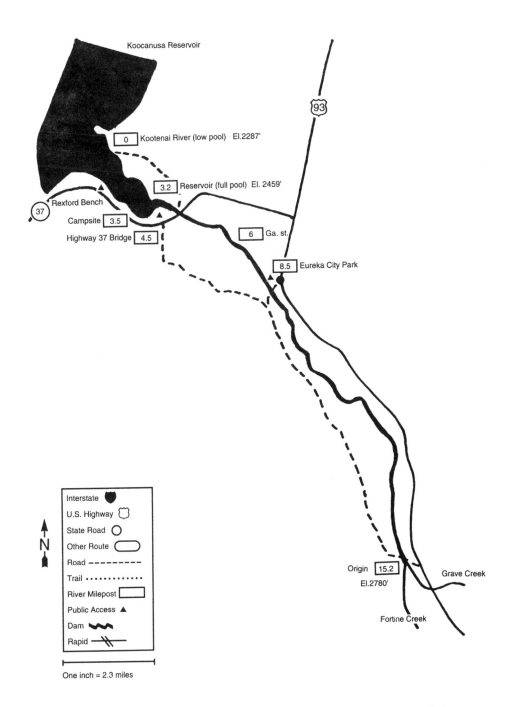

Koocanusa Reservoir

0 Kootenai River (low pool) El.2287'

3.2 Reservoir (full pool) El. 2459'

37 Rexford Bench

Campsite 3.5

Highway 37 Bridge 4.5

6 Ga. st.

8.5 Eureka City Park

93

Interstate
U.S. Highway
State Road
Other Route
Road - - - - - - -
Trail ••••••••••
River Milepost
Public Access ▲
Dam
Rapid

N

Origin 15.2
El.2780'

Grave Creek

Fortine Creek

One inch = 2.3 miles

Tobacco

TONGUE

ORIGIN: In Bighorn Mountains near Dayton, WY. Enters Montana near Decker, MT El. 3450'

END: Flows into Yellowstone River at Miles City, MT. El. 2350'

LENGTH: 206.7 total mi. in MT. (198.8 river mi. + Tongue Reservoir 7.9 mi.) (110 air mi.)

FLOATABLE: 198.8 river mi. and 7.9 reservoir miles
Class I portion is 189.1 mi. (Tongue Res. Dam to end)

SECTIONS: Upper (17.6 + 2.8 WY) WY border 206.7 to Dam "189.1"
Middle (168.7 mi.) T.R. Dam "189.1" to T-Y (12 mi.) Dam "20.4"
Lower (20.4 mi.) T-Y Dam "20.4" to End - Yellowstone River "0"

DAMS: Tongue River (Forms reservoir & controls flow)
Sitting Man (Mobeley) diversion dam
S-H diversion dam
T-Y (12 mi.) diversion dam
Numerous low float over or easy portage irrigation jettys (above Birney)

WATERFALLS: None

WHITEWATER: None

DANGERS: Tongue River Dam, 3 major diversion dams, numerous low irrigation jettys, fences, logjams, rattlesnakes.

DEWATERED: Can be dewatered below diversion dams during irrigation or in fall, depending on dam releases.

PORTAGES: Tongue River (LEFT), Sitting Man (LEFT), S-H (LEFT). T-Y (RIGHT) - a few low jettys, a few fences and logjams.

SPEC. AGENCIES: Northern Cheyenne Indian Reservation borders on west for part of the river.

REGS - PERMITS: None

ACCESS-SHUTTLE: Roads parallel and intersect river. Very few formal access sites.

SERVICES:	Limited in Ashland, MT. All services in Miles City, MT.
CAMPING:	Very few campgrounds and very few access sites.
GAMEFISH:	Upper below dam - Rainbow, brown, catfish. Middle below Birney - Small & largemouth bass, pike, walleye, sauger, catfish
VESSEL:	Any moderate-sized craft, unless flows are low.
SKILL LEVEL:	Beginner - if flows are normal and caution for dangers.
FLOAT TIMES:	Flows are moderate to slow, under normal conditions.
FLOW INFO:	(406) 449-5263 USGS - Helena

HYDROGRAPH

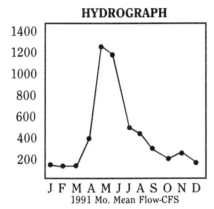

1991 Mo. Mean Flow-CFS

Gage Sta: Just below Tongue River Dam
Drain Area: 1,770 sq. mi. (at this location)
Ave. Flow: (52 years) 445 cfs
Ext. Max: 10,800 cfs - 20' ga. ht. 5/20/78
Ext. Min: 0 cfs 11/13/69
Gradient: 1100' in 206.7 mi. = 5.3' pma
Float Grad: Same
Clarity: Cloudy to murky
Temp: Jan. 34^0 F.
Apr. 46^0 F.
Jul. 71^0 F.
Oct. 54^0 F.
Total Drain Area: Approximately 5500 sq. mi.

DRAINAGE:	(East) Yellowstone, Missouri, Mississippi, Gulf of Mexico
MAPS:	BLM - #38 "Tongue" (upper) - #28 "Rosebud" (short section between) - #29 "Custer" (lower) USFS - Custer NF (Ashland Division) Birney to Brandenberg only USGS - "Hardin" (upper) - "Forsyth" (short section between) - "Miles City" (lower) CO. - Bighorn, Rosebud, Custer

TONGUE

There is some confusion over the etymology of the Tongue River. One theory, is that the Indians called it "crooked as the tongue of the white man". Also, they called it the "Talking River".

The Tongue begins in Wyoming and flows into Montana at milepost "209.5". It re-enters Wyoming at "205.7" and again enters Montana at "202.9". This upper section in ranching and "hay" country is floatable to the Decker county road bridge "197.3" or on into the reservoir. Any moderately sized vessel will work when the wind isn't blowing! Although I have only seen one, it is my understanding that rattlesnakes are abundant in this area.

Below the Tongue River Dam "189.1" and its numerous campsites, begins the most popular floating section. Locals call it the "canyon area". Below the dam, the terrain has the appearance of a badlands and is magnificent, especially in autumn. If flow is normal, a beginner in a canoe, medium raft, or small boat can handle the entire Tongue. Whitetail, mulies, turkey, waterfowl, pheasants and birds of prey are all common sights. The numerous turtles have an acute preservation system, for they slide off their sundecks into their watery escape routes well ahead of you.

Formal campgrounds or access sites are non-existent, forcing you to make bridges suffice. A few washed out diversion jettys will appear above Birney. These can be bypassed or floated over. Locals speak of an excellent smallmouth bass fishery in this area. Rainbow and browns use the "above Birney zipcode", and largemouth bass, pike, walleye, sauger and catfish are common below. On a recent canoe trip down the entire Tongue, I spotted a huge fish, struggling upstream in the murky water. Since paddlefish cannot get above the three diversion dams below, I have since deduced that it must have been a huge pike.

The south boundary of the Northern Cheyenne Indian Reservation, is at Cook Creek "149.8". Cook Creek being between Birney and Birney Village, and the reservation is on the left bank only. A community park at the Ashland Bridge "113" offers a potential campsite. A beautiful spot at the St. Labre School Park "111" might be a better choice if you will simply gain administrative approval.

The Sitting Man (Mobeley) Diversion Dam "104.8" is visible from Highway 332. This dangerous rock structure mandates a portage LEFT. The north boundary of the Indian reservation is at milepost "101". The next access, without any interruptions between, is at the Highway 332 bridge "83". The S-H diversion dam "70.5" requires a portage LEFT. Below this dam is the S-H road bridge "59". If you desired, and used a good map, you could find your way to the S-H dam by crossing to the west side and going south on an old road.

Below S-H bridge is the old Garland bridge "53". The next 33 miles have no public access, except the river coming close to the road in a couple places. Below the T-Y (12 mi.) Diversion Dam "20.4" is a fine access and campsite. This dam offers only a "lousy" portage RIGHT. At the time of this writing, only a canoe will squeeze through the narrow trail and unnecessary fences.

The river below T-Y Dam is often dewatered due to huge withdrawals, and access in this last section is nearly non-existent. The river flows under the I-90 Bridge and along the south edge of Miles City. An access point occurs on the dike road (right bank) right at the mouth to the Yellowstone River.

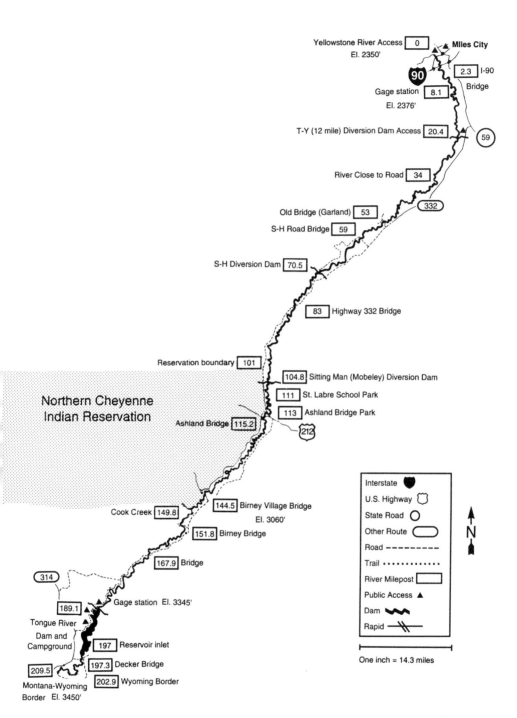

Yellowstone River Access [0] ▲ Miles City
El. 2350'

90

2.3 I-90
Bridge

Gage station [8.1]
El. 2376'

T-Y (12 mile) Diversion Dam Access [20.4] ▲

59

River Close to Road [34]

332

Old Bridge (Garland) [53]
S-H Road Bridge [59]

S-H Diversion Dam [70.5]

[83] Highway 332 Bridge

Reservation boundary [101]
[104.8] Sitting Man (Mobeley) Diversion Dam

Northern Cheyenne
Indian Reservation

[111] St. Labre School Park
[113] Ashland Bridge Park

Ashland Bridge [115.2]

212

Cook Creek [149.8] [144.5] Birney Village Bridge
El. 3060'

[151.8] Birney Bridge

[167.9] Bridge

314

[189.1] ▲
▲ Gage station El. 3345'
Tongue River ▲
Dam and
Campground [197] Reservoir inlet

[209.5] [197.3] Decker Bridge
Montana-Wyoming [202.9] Wyoming Border
Border El. 3450'

Interstate 🛡
U.S. Highway ⬡
State Road ◯
Other Route ⬭
Road - - - - - - -
Trail • • • • • • • •
River Milepost ☐
Public Access ▲
Dam 〰
Rapid ⧸⧸

N

One inch = 14.3 miles

Tongue

TWO MEDICINE

ORIGIN:	In Glacier National Park at Upper Two Medicine Lake. El. 5400'
END:	Joins Cut Bank Creek to form Marias River south of Cut Bank MT. El. 3300'
LENGTH:	92.1 total mi. (86.4 river mi. + 3 Lakes 5.7 mi.) Two Medicine 2.3 mi. Pray .2 Lower Two Medicine 3.2 All floatable 5.7 mi. (57 air mi.)
FLOATABLE:	77.1 river mi. (portions not floatable!) "83.1" to end
SECTIONS:	Upper (17.3 mi.) Origin "92.1" to East Glacier "74.8" Middle (34.8 mi.) Gallup private property "74.8" to Gustafson Ranch "40" Lower (40 mi.) Gustafson priv. prop. "40" to End "0"
DAMS:	Lower Two Medicine (Forms reservoir & controls river flow) Mi. "81.3" Diversion Dam "53.2" Dangerous
WATERFALLS:	Upper Two Medicine Falls "92.1" Running Eagle "Trick" "86.5" Two Medicine "77.7" (Dangerous - no portage possible)
WHITEWATER:	29.3 miles Mileposts "74.8" to "64" Class III waves (no takeout to "60") Mileposts "21" to "2.5" 3 Class IV and many III - no access to "0" Unfloatable canyon with falls that cannot be portaged 2 moderate rapids Class II at mi. "33" and "31"
DANGERS:	Diversion dam, remote area in lower section, Do not float beyond Highway Bridge at milepost "79". Dangerous falls in canyon that cannot be portaged. Whitewater
DEWATERED:	Often
PORTAGES:	Two Medicine Falls cannot be portaged Mi. "77.7" Diversion Dam Mi. "53.2" portage RIGHT
SPEC. AGENCIES:	Glacier National Park, Blackfeet Indian Reservation

REGS - PERMITS:	Overnight camp permit in back country of Glacier National Park. No firearms in Glacier National Park. Fishing or Recreation use permit on reservation if you leave the river.
ACCESS-SHUTTLE:	Difficult. Long floats between access points. Private property most of the river. Use good map.
SERVICES:	Two Medicine Lake, East Glacier
CAMPING:	Campground only at Two Medicine Lake. Very few access sites, and mostly private property.
GAMEFISH:	Rainbow, brook, cutthroat
VESSEL:	Canoe, medium raft, small boat Whitewater portions - Whitewater canoe, good raft, kayak
SKILL LEVEL:	Intermediate - except whitewater portions which would require portage or a skill level of Experienced.
FLOAT TIMES:	Moderately fast if flows are normal.
FLOW INFO:	(406) 449-5263 USGS - Helena

Wilderness Campsite

Two Medicine River

HYDROGRAPH

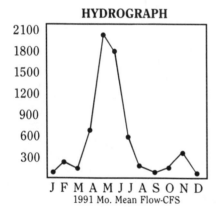

2100
1800
1500
1200
900
600
300

J F M A M J J A S O N D
1991 Mo. Mean Flow-CFS

Gage Sta: Hwy 1 Br. - 10 mi. S. of Browning
Drain Area: 250 sq. mi. (at this location)
Ave. Flow: (14 years) 338 cfs
Ext. Max: 11,700 cfs - 7.78' ga. ht. 5/19/91
Ext. Min: 10 cfs 1/6/82
Gradient: 2100' in 92.1 mi. = 22.8' pma
Float Grad: 1400' in 77.1 mi. = 18.2' pma
Clarity: Cloudy
Temp: Jan. 32⁰ F.
        Apr. 43⁰ F.
        Jul. 71⁰ F.
        Oct. 43⁰ F.

DRAINAGE: (East) Marias, Missouri, Mississippi, Gulf of Mexico

MAPS: BLM - #17 "St. Mary" (extreme upper) - #18 "Hungry Horse Reservoir" (upper) - #28 "Valier" (lower) - #27 "Cut Bank" (short section).
USFS - Lewis & Clark NF (R. Mtn. Div.) (short upper)
USGS - "Cut Bank"
Sp. - "Glacier National Park" (upper) USGS
CO. - Glacier, Pondera

286

TWO MEDICINE

Two versions of the etymology of this river exist. The Blackfeet name is "Natoki-Okasi". One explanation is, that they felt the high mountains had spiritual powers and that two streams flowing out of the mountains, brought this power with them. Another theory is, that two medicine lodges for the sun dance were set up on opposite sides of the stream.

The "Two Med" is a wonderful river. It has everything! The river's origin is at Upper Two Medicine Lake and Falls, in the beautiful high country of Glacier National Park. The small river drops quickly in the first two miles to Two Medicine Lake. It's a wonderful canoe trip up the lake or you can take the old tour boat during tourist season. A hiking trail leads past Twin Falls (on a feeder stream) to the upper lake. This is an especially beautiful sight in autumn.

Below Two Medicine and Pray Lakes is Trick Falls (Running Eagle), before flowing into Lower Two Medicine Lake. This lake is the boundary between Glacier National Park and the Blackfeet Indian Reservation. The river flows through the reservation for its duration. Boating is possible on Lower Two Medicine, but a 10 hp maximum is enforced on Two Medicine.

Below Lower Two Medicine Lake Dam, floating can begin. This float must only be 2.3 miles to the Highway 49 bridge. A mile below this bridge is Two Medicine Falls. There is no warning of this beautiful but dangerous 20' waterfall and it is impossible to portage. While exploring this canyon in a tiny raft, I had to scale a cliff with the raft rope tied to my waist and the raft dangling. I luckily made it around the falls. The river below the falls remains bouncy through a canyon strewn with boulders and containing some ledges.

There is no public access in the East Glacier area. I have used on occasion the Gallup private property, with permission. It is a four wheel drive jaunt to the river. Locals float below East Glacier annually in rafts after the high water recedes. On one occasion, a friend and I floated in a 12' aluminum boat. The river was wild and dirty with runoff, and contrary to the advise of locals, floated it anyway. We wrecked twice and ended up on opposite sides of the river. We gathered up what we had left and finished the trip (no way out). The beautiful day ended in a snowstorm. Talk about hypothermia candidates! I didn't' realize it until recently, that we made that trip two days after the record high flow. This section between East Glacier and the Heart Butte Road is 15 miles, with the upper 11 miles being whitewater during high water. The scenery in this area is great and after the high water recedes an experienced floater in a raft or whitewater canoe would enjoy the trip.

Below the Heart Butte bridge, the river flows gently through a wide valley with cottonwood bottoms and rolling prairie hills. A dangerous diversion dam, which requires a portage RIGHT, is midway to the Highway 89 bridge "47.1". Below the 89 bridge, two moderate rapids occur at mileposts "33" and "31". Formal campgrounds or access sites are non-existent, so infrequent bridges must suffice. Landowners seem very congenial if you seek permission.

Six miles below the Carroll Road "27" is the beginning of the whitewater. In the next seven miles down to the Highway 44 bridge, are nine Class II-III rapids. A Class IV is just upstream and visible from the Highway 44 bridge "14".

Below the 44 bridge the river is lined with unique limestone formations and the area is nearly void of vegetation. Five miles below the bridge a Class IV and III rapids occur. Below Birch Creek "4.5" a Class IV and two Class III rapids exist. Below these rapids the river is mild-mannered.

2 1/2 miles below the last rapid the river joins Cut Bank Creek, and together they form the Marias River. A bridge access on a county road south of Cut Bank, MT is at this point.

A strong intermediate in a canoe, medium raft, or small boat can handle the river, when the flow is normal, by portaging the whitewater. Although not a popular fishing stream, rainbow, brookies and cutthroat are present. Spinning, especially in the deeper pools can be as productive as a fly.

Wilderness Float Trek

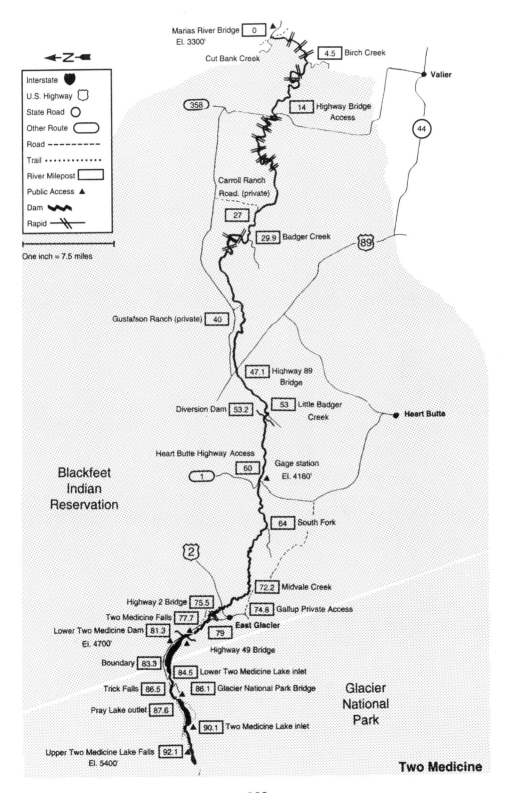

One inch = 7.5 miles

Marias River Bridge [0] ▲
El. 3300'

Cut Bank Creek

[4.5] Birch Creek

Valier

(358)

[14] Highway Bridge
Access

(44)

Carroll Ranch
Road. (private)

[27]

[29.9] Badger Creek

(89)

Gustafson Ranch (private) [40]

[47.1] Highway 89
Bridge

Diversion Dam [53.2]

[53] Little Badger
Creek

Heart Butte

Heart Butte Highway Access

(1) [60]

Gage station
▲ El. 4180'

Blackfeet
Indian
Reservation

[64] South Fork

(2)

[72.2] Midvale Creek

Highway 2 Bridge [75.5]

[74.8] Gallup Private Access

Two Medicine Falls [77.7]

East Glacier

Lower Two Medicine Dam [81.3]
El. 4700'

[79]
Highway 49 Bridge

Boundary [83.3]

[84.5] Lower Two Medicine Lake inlet

Trick Falls [86.5]

[86.1] Glacier National Park Bridge

Glacier
National
Park

Pray Lake outlet [87.6]

▲ [90.1] Two Medicine Lake inlet

Upper Two Medicine Lake Falls [92.1] ▲
El. 5400'

Two Medicine

Legend

Interstate 🛡
U.S. Highway ⬭
State Road ◯
Other Route ⬭
Road - - - - - -
Trail • • • • • • •
River Milepost ▭
Public Access ▲
Dam 〰
Rapid ╫

←Z←

VERMILION

ORIGIN:	Freezout Creek near Vermilion Peak, north of Thompson Falls, MT. El. 5800'
END:	Flows into Clark Fork drainage at Noxon Reservoir near Trout Creek, MT. El. 2332'
LENGTH:	19.7 miles (11 air mi.)
FLOATABLE:	4.8 mi. (Mi. "4.8" to end "0")
SECTIONS:	Upper (8.3 mi.) Origin "19.7" to Vermilion Falls "11.4" Middle (6.6 mi.) Vermilion Falls "11.4" to Close to road "4.8" Lower (4.8 mi.) Road "4.8" to End - Clark Fork R. "0"
DAMS:	None
WATERFALLS:	Vermilion Falls (Mi. "11.4")
WHITEWATER:	None floatable
DANGERS:	Narrow, curvy, brush, 300 yard gorge with 10' and 5' drops and waves at end (1 1/2 mi. below Lyons Creek)
DEWATERED:	Can be low in fall.
PORTAGES:	None in floatable section.
SPEC. AGENCIES:	None
REGS - PERMITS:	None
ACCESS-SHUTTLE:	Road parallels river on west side, close to river. No formal access sites.
SERVICES:	Limited in Trout Creek, MT
CAMPING:	Formal campsite in upper section.
GAMEFISH:	Cutthroat, brook, bulls, whitefish (upper best)
VESSEL:	Small raft, canoe
SKILL LEVEL:	Intermediate (if flows are normal)

| **FLOAT TIMES:** | Moderately fast flow. |

| **FLOW INFO:** | 847-2462 Kootenai NF (Cabinet Dist. at Trout Cr.) |

HYDROGRAPH

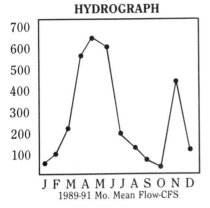

J F M A M J J A S O N D
1989-91 Mo. Mean Flow-CFS

Gage Sta: at mouth of river
Ave. Flow: (3 years) 305 cfs
Gradient: 3468' in 19.7 mi. = 176' pma
Float Grad: 518' in 4.8 mi. = 108' pma
Clarity: Cloudy

| **DRAINAGE:** | (West) Clark Fork, Pend Oreille, Columbia, Pacific |

MAPS:	BLM - #6 "Thompson Falls"
	USFS - Kootenai NF (entire river) - Lolo NF (upper
	USGS - "Wallace"
	CO. - Sanders

Becoming more common

291

VERMILION

The namesake of the Vermilion is derived from the Kootenai Indians, who found ochre paint in the area, circa 1865. The origin of the river is at Freezout Creek near Vermilion Peak, north of Thompson Falls, Montana.

This small stream tumbles down from the open high valley, through a gravel and sand streambed with an occasional boulder. The banks are lined with brush. Beaver dams and some downfall can be found in the upper area. The river soon enters a narrow valley and is surrounded by timber.

A forest service road parallels the river and crosses three times. A campsite can be found at Willow Creek. Just below Willow Creek is Vermilion Falls "11.4". A short but steep trail leads down to a precarious point to view the falls. The river remains inaccessible down to Lyons Gulch "6.5". Below Lyons Gulch the river is dimensionally floatable, except that a gorge lies just below. This gorge at river milepost "5" contains a ten foot and five foot drops. These drops are in a tight turn and are followed by 300 yards of rapids. Portaging this gorge is extremely difficult.

Floating can begin just below this gorge, at milepost "4.8". The rest of the river can be floated by a strong intermediate in a small raft, if flow is normal. The river has some sharp turns, boulders, and downfall in its steep gradient. An experienced paddler in a whitewater canoe or kayak would enjoy this during high water. Floating can continue into the Clark Fork drainage at Noxon Reservoir, near Trout Creek, Montana.

Cutthroat, brookies, bulls and whitefish can be found. The portion above Vermilion Falls is the best. Fly fishing is preferred, although spinning in the beaver dams or occasional deeper pools could be productive.

Vermilion River

292

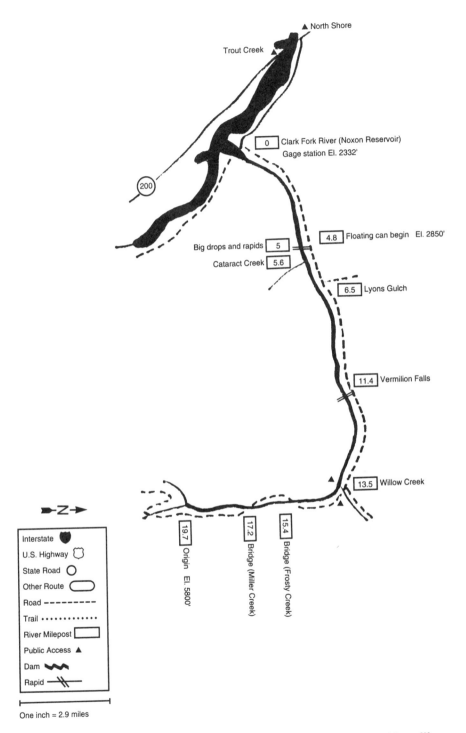

▲ North Shore

Trout Creek ▲

200

| 0 | Clark Fork River (Noxon Reservoir)
Gage station El. 2332'

| 4.8 | Floating can begin   El. 2850'

Big drops and rapids | 5 |

Cataract Creek | 5.6 |

| 6.5 | Lyons Gulch

| 11.4 | Vermilion Falls

▲ | 13.5 | Willow Creek

| 19.7 | Origin   El. 5800'

| 17.2 | Bridge (Miller Creek)

| 15.4 | Bridge (Frosty Creek)

Interstate 🛡
U.S. Highway ⬡
State Road ◯
Other Route ⬭
Road - - - - - - -
Trail • • • • • • • • •
River Milepost ▢
Public Access ▲
Dam 〰〰
Rapid ⫽

One inch = 2.9 miles

Vermilion

293

WATERTON

ORIGIN:	At Nahsukin Lake in Glacier National Park. El. 5410'
END:	Flows into Waterton Lake and on into Canada El. 4196'
LENGTH:	20 total mi. in MT (17 river mi. + 3 mi. of Waterton Lake) (12 air mi.)
FLOATABLE:	0.8 mi. (Footbridge below Rainbow Falls to Waterton Lake) Waterton Lake is floatable.
DAMS:	None
WATERFALLS:	Rainbow Falls (1 mi. above Goat Haunt on Waterton Lake)
WHITEWATER:	None floatable
DANGERS:	Primitive park.
DEWATERED:	Can be low in fall
PORTAGES:	None in the .8 floatable portion.
SPEC. AGENCIES:	Glacier National Park
REGS - PERMITS:	Back-country permit if camping overnight. No fire-arms. U.S. Immigration & Customs service at Goat Haunt for overnight campers.
ACCESS-SHUTTLE:	Hiking or horse trail along west side of Waterton Lake, or you can take the boat down the lake, get off, and return in a few days, to Waterton Village, Alberta.
SERVICES:	None
CAMPING:	Back-country campsites. No facilities except those at the campsite at Goat Haunt.
GAMEFISH:	Cutthroat, rainbow, brook, whitefish
VESSEL:	Small raft.
SKILL LEVEL:	Beginner.
FLOAT TIMES:	Moderate flow in the .8 floatable portion.

FLOW INFO: Call Glacier National Park at Many Glacier. They can radio Goat Haunt Ranger Station.

HYDROGRAPH

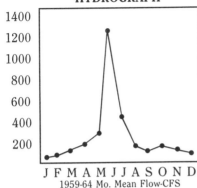

J F M A M J J A S O N D
1959-64 Mo. Mean Flow-CFS

Gage Sta: International Border (Disc. 1978)
Drain Area: 238 sq. mi.
Ave. Flow: (5 years) 220 cfs
Ext. Max: 7280 cfs 6/08/64
Ext. Min: 20 cfs 1/21/62
Gradient: 1214' in 20 mi. = 60.7' pma
Float Grad: 20' in .8 mi. = 25.0' pma
Clarity: Clear

DRAINAGE: (North) Belly, Oldman, South Saskatchewan, Saskatchewan, Nelson, Hudson Bay

MAPS: BLM - #7 "St. Mary"
USGS - "Cut Bank"
Sp.   - "Glacier National Park" USGS
CO.   - Glacier

Gros Ventre Falls (Mokowanis River)

WATERTON

The Waterton area was named after English naturalist, Charles Waterton. The origin of the river is at Nahsukin Lake in beautiful Glacier National Park. The river then flows into Waterton Lake and on for about eighty five miles in Canada, to the Belly River and eventually to Hudson Bay.

The Nahsukin Lake area is inaccessible even by trail. After nine miles the river tumbles down a boulder and downfall infested streambed, to a patrol cabin at the Waterton and Stoney Indian Trail junction.

Hiking or horse trails lead through remote park backcountry in all four directions. Up the Belly and Mokowanis River valleys and over Stoney Indian Pass from the east, or the Highline or Fifty Mountain trails from the south. Trails also lead from the Kintla Lake area over Browns Pass. A few years ago, a friend and I made an extensive horsepack trip through the entire area. We explored, floated and fished the Waterton, Belly and the unfloatable Mokowanis Rivers. Since then I have returned backpacking a small raft. Access can also be gained on the Canadian side from Waterton Townsite to Goat Haunt. Goat Haunt is a "hub" on the Montana end of Waterton Lake. An elaborate park headquarters, campsites and customs and immigration all can be found. A trail on the west side of the lake or a tour boat offers access. Should you desire, you can get off the boat and report through immigration with a park ranger. You may recreate in the area for up to one week, and take the boat back.

Below the patrol cabin at Stoney Indian Junction the river flows into Kootenai Lakes. Camping is permitted, fishing is great and moose can be seen feeding in the lakes. Rainbow Falls occur three miles below Kootenai Lakes. Just below the falls is the Browns Pass Trail footbridge. A short float of .8 mile is possible from this point to Waterton Lake. The International border is three miles down the lake from Goat Haunt.

A beginner can make this float in a small raft. Fishing is quite good, especially in Kootenai Lakes, for cutthroat, rainbow, brookies and whitefish.

The campsites at Goat Haunt are quite elaborate. Three sided structures with a roof, firewood and toilets are a luxury to the weary hiker. All boating activities are offered on Waterton Lake.

Waterton River

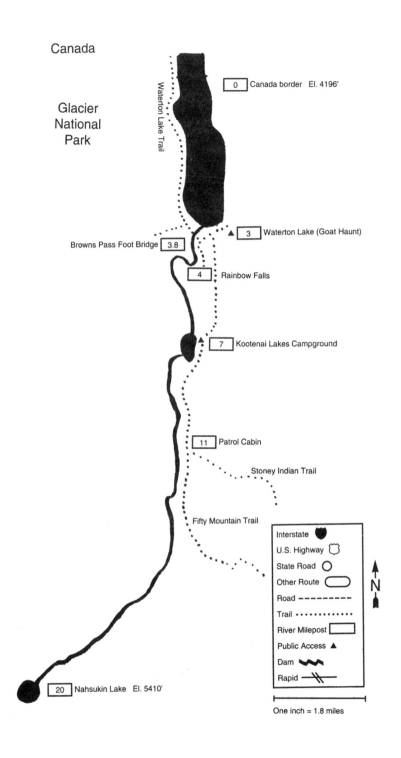

Canada

Glacier
National
Park

Waterton Lake Trail

0 | Canada border   El. 4196'

▲ | 3 | Waterton Lake (Goat Haunt)

Browns Pass Foot Bridge | 3.8

4 | Rainbow Falls

▲ | 7 | Kootenai Lakes Campground

11 | Patrol Cabin

Stoney Indian Trail

Fifty Mountain Trail

Interstate	⬟
U.S. Highway	⬡
State Road	◯
Other Route	⬭
Road	– – – – –
Trail	· · · · · · ·
River Milepost	▭
Public Access	▲
Dam	〰
Rapid	⫻

N

20 | Nahsukin Lake   El. 5410'

One inch = 1.8 miles

Waterton

WHITE

ORIGIN:	Rooney Creek near Silvertip Mountain in Bob Marshall Wilderness. El. 6300'
END:	Flows into South Fork (Flathead) River. El. 4400'
LENGTH:	20 miles (11 air mi.)
FLOATABLE:	6 miles (Ford at South Fork "6" to End - South Fork Flathead River "0"
SECTIONS:	Upper (11.2 mi.) Origin "20" to Needle Falls "8.8" Middle (2.8 mi.) Needle Falls "8.8" to Ford below South Fork "6" Lower (6.0 mi.) Ford "6" to End "0"
DAMS:	None
WATERFALLS:	Needle Falls (Mi. "8.8")
WHITEWATER:	None floatable
DANGERS:	Wilderness area
DEWATERED:	Can be low in fall.
PORTAGES:	None
SPEC. AGENCIES:	Bob Marshall Wilderness
REGS - PERMITS:	No motors in wilderness
ACCESS-SHUTTLE:	Hiking or horse trail up north side of the river, to the river ford, just below the South Fork confluence.
SERVICES:	None. Pack trips and float trips offered by guest ranches at Spotted Bear.
CAMPING:	You may camp nearly anywhere of your choice.
GAMEFISH:	Above Needle Falls - Cutthroat Below Needle Falls - Cutthroat, Dolly Varden
VESSEL:	Small raft
SKILL LEVEL:	Intermediate
FLOAT GRAD:	380' in 6 mi. = 63.3' pma (overall river 95' pma)

WATER:	Fast flowing, cloudy and cold.
DRAINAGE:	(West) South Fork Flathead, Flathead, Clark Fork, Pend Oreille, Columbia, Pacific Ocean
MAPS:	BLM - #19 "Swan River" USFS - Flathead NF (South) entire river - Lewis & Clark NF (R Mtn.) entire river USGS - "Choteau" Sp. - "Bob Marshall - Great Bear - Scapegoat Wilderness" entire river USFS CO. - Flathead, Powell

Hittin' the back country

WHITE

The White River lies entirely within the Bob Marshall Wilderness Area. It is accessible only by hiking and horse trails, over Spotted Bear Pass or up the South Fork of the Flathead. This White River area is one of the prettier places in the wilderness. The namesake of the river is not clear. Some say the name comes from the whiteish appearance of the water. Others say it was named after the author, S.E. White.

The rivers origin is at Rooney Creek near Silvertip Mountain, and twenty miles later flows into the South Fork of the Flathead below Big Prairie. A forest service trail follows the river.

The beautiful Needle Falls is at river milepost "8.8". Below the falls the South Fork of the White adds volume to the river. The trail fords the river just below the South Fork and floating can begin at this point. The river has a steep gradient in its streambed of small rounded boulders, for the six mile float.

The Big Prairie Trail ford is at milepost ".7". Floating could continue to the mouth of the river, or on down the beautiful South Fork of the Flathead.

The river requires strong intermediate skills in a small raft. Cutthroat are common above Needle Falls. Below the falls, cuts and bulls are present.

Trail Ford - White River

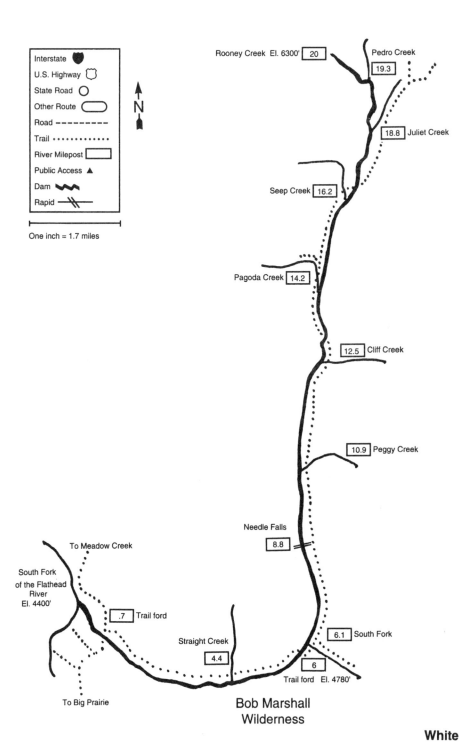

One inch = 1.7 miles

Interstate
U.S. Highway
State Road
Other Route
Road ---------
Trail ············
River Milepost
Public Access ▲
Dam
Rapid

N

Rooney Creek El. 6300' 20
Pedro Creek
19.3
18.8 Juliet Creek
Seep Creek 16.2
Pagoda Creek 14.2
12.5 Cliff Creek
10.9 Peggy Creek
Needle Falls
8.8
To Meadow Creek
South Fork
of the Flathead
River
El. 4400'
.7 Trail ford
Straight Creek
4.4
6.1 South Fork
6
Trail ford El. 4780'
To Big Prairie
Bob Marshall
Wilderness

White

WHITEFISH

ORIGIN:	Whitefish Lake. El. 2995'
END:	Flows into Stillwater River at Kalispell, MT. El. 2950'
LENGTH:	25.5 mi. (16 air mi.)
FLOATABLE:	25.5 mi.
SECTIONS:	Upper (6.3 mi.) Origin "25.5" to Hwy. 40 Bridge "19.2" Middle (9.4 mi.) Hwy 40 Br. "19.2" to Airport Br. "9.8" Lower (9.8 mi.) Airport Bridge "9.8" to End "0"
DAMS:	None
WATERFALLS:	None
WHITEWATER:	None
DANGERS:	Low irrigation jettys, fences, logs
DEWATERED:	Can be low in fall.
PORTAGES:	Usually none
SPEC. AGENCIES:	None
REGS - PERMITS:	None
ACCESS-SHUTTLE:	Highway 2 and Whitefish Stage Road parallel river, with intersecting roads and bridges. No formal access sites.
SERVICES:	All services in Whitefish or Kalispell, MT.
CAMPING:	No formal campgrounds or access sites. Mostly private property.
GAMEFISH:	Cutthroat, pike, whitefish
VESSEL:	Canoe, small boat, medium raft
SKILL LEVEL:	Beginner.
FLOAT TIMES:	Slow flow.

HYDROGRAPH

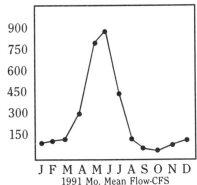

900
750
600
450
300
150

J F M A M J J A S O N D
1991 Mo. Mean Flow-CFS

Gage Sta: 8 mi. north of Kalispell, MT
Drain Area: 170 sq. mi. (at this locale)
Ave. Flow: (39 years) 192 cfs
Ext. Max: 1580 cfs - 4.91' ga. ht. 06/24/74
Ext. Min: 4 cfs - .83' ga. ht. 10/18/34
Gradient: 45' in 25.5 mi. = 1.8' pma
Float Grad: Same
Clarity: Cloudy
Temp: Jan. 32⁰ F.
       Apr. 45⁰ F.
       Jul. 71⁰ F.
       Oct. 50⁰ F.

DRAINAGE: (West) Stillwater, Flathead, Clark Fork, Pend Oreille, Columbia, Pacific Ocean

MAPS: BLM - #10 "Kalispell"
              USFS - Flathead NF (North) entire river (best map)
              USGS - "Kalispell"
              CO.   - Flathead

Whitetail Ptarmigan - Ready for winter

WHITEFISH

The namesake of the Whitefish area is derived from great catches of whitefish long ago. The Whitefish River begins at the outlet of Whitefish Lake and flows 25.5 miles into the Stillwater River, near the Highway 2 bridge in Kalispell.

The river is noted for its annual lake to lake canoe race. The race begins at Whitefish Lake, and courses its way through the Whitefish River, into the Stillwater and later the Flathead River. Upon entering Flathead Lake a 2 1/2 mile paddle across the lake is required to finish at Bigfork. This race is 52.7 miles long. Some years it is shortened to 26.1 miles and ends .6 mile below Whitefish River, at bridge.

The Whitefish area and its proximity to Glacier National Park offers superb recreational opportunities. The Big Mountain Ski Resort, overlooking Whitefish Lake and the Flathead Valley offers world class skiing. The area offers all boating activities, groomed cross-country and snowmobile trails, hiking trails, and golf courses.

The river meanders slowly through the agricultural valley with intermittent timber groves. The sandy streambed with undercut banks is lined with meadow and marsh grass and the ubiquitous willow. The deep, slow moving water is not highly regarded for fishing, although cutthroat, pike and whitefish are residents.

A beginner can handle the river and a canoe is the best choice of vessel. Although no formal campgrounds are found on the river, numerous camping facilities are nearby. Bridges must suffice for ingress or egress. Bridges occur frequently with no more than five river miles between.

Whitefish River

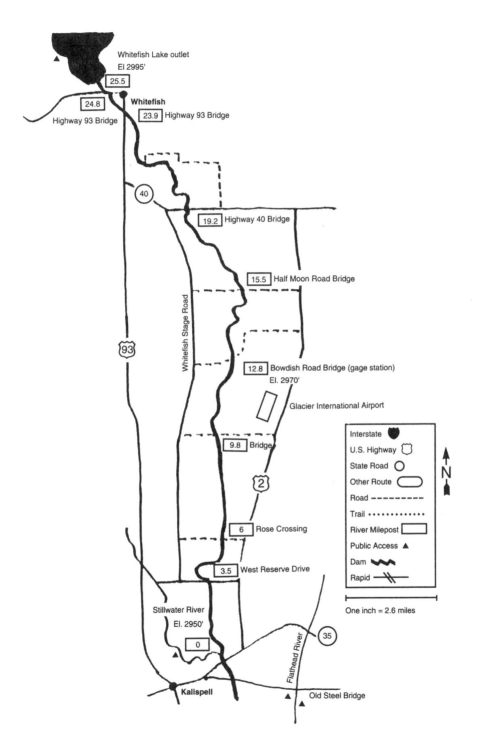

Whitefish Lake outlet
El 2995'
25.5

24.8
Highway 93 Bridge

Whitefish

23.9 Highway 93 Bridge

40

19.2 Highway 40 Bridge

15.5 Half Moon Road Bridge

Whitefish Stage Road

93

12.8 Bowdish Road Bridge (gage station)
El. 2970'

Glacier International Airport

9.8 Bridge

2

6 Rose Crossing

3.5 West Reserve Drive

Stillwater River

El. 2950'

0

Kalispell

Flathead River

35

Old Steel Bridge

Interstate	
U.S. Highway	
State Road	
Other Route	
Road	– – – – –
Trail	• • • • • • • •
River Milepost	
Public Access	▲
Dam	
Rapid	

N

One inch = 2.6 miles

Whitefish

WISE

ORIGIN:	Confluence of Mono and Jacobson Creeks, southwest of Wise River, MT. El. 6800'
END:	Flows into Bighole River near Wise River, MT. El. 5810'
LENGTH:	27.9 miles (16 air miles)
FLOATABLE:	27.9 mi.
SECTIONS:	Upper (7.5 mi.) Origin "27.9" to Elk Cr. Br. "20.4" Middle (12.4 mi.) Elk Cr. "20.4" to Butler Cr. Br. "8" Lower (8 mi.) Butler Cr. Br. "8" to Bighole R. "0"
DAMS:	None
WATERFALLS:	None
WHITEWATER:	Can be whitewater in high water. "14.7" to end "0"
DANGERS:	High water, boulders, steep gradient, narrow, curvy, beaver dams, 3 irrigation jettys
DEWATERED:	Often too low to float in fall
PORTAGES:	Numerous beaver dams upper & middle sections. 3 irrigation jettys at Mi. "6" - "4.5" - "3"
SPEC. AGENCIES:	None
REGS - PERMITS:	10 hp maximum on all streams in Beaverhead County
ACCESS-SHUTTLE:	Easy. Road parallels river with intersecting bridges. Numerous campgrounds and access sites.
SERVICES:	Limited in Wise River, MT (gas, food)
CAMPING:	Numerous campgrounds
GAMEFISH:	Brook, rainbow, whitefish, burbot
VESSEL:	Canoe, small raft.
SKILL LEVEL:	Intermediate (if flows are normal)

FLOAT TIMES: Upper & upper middle sections - slow (beaver dams)
Lower portion - quite fast.

FLOW INFO: 832-3178 Wise River Ranger Dist. of Beaverhead NF

HYDROGRAPH

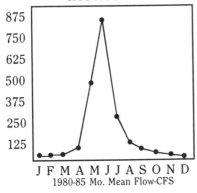

875
750
625
500
375
250
125

J F M A M J J A S O N D
1980-85 Mo. Mean Flow-CFS

Gage Sta: near Wise River, MT
Drain Area: 214 sq. mi.
Ave. Flow: (13 years) 189 cfs
Ext. Max: 2450 cfs 06/16/74
Ext. Min: 14 cfs 12/24/83
Gradient: 990' in 27.9 mi. = 35.5' pma
Float Grad: Same
Clarity: Clear

DRAINAGE: (East) Bighole, Jefferson, Missouri, Mississippi,

MAPS: BLM - #31 "Bighole" (upper) - #32 "Dillon" (lower)
USFS - Beaverhead NF (Interagency) entire river
USGS - "Dillon"
CO.   - Beaverhead

Wise River Corps of Engineers

WISE

The namesake of the river is a little cloudy. Some sources feel "Wise" is derived from the Wiser family, who drove herds of horses from Texas to this area. One son is buried here. Others feel the name is a spinoff from the Bighole ("Wisdom") River.

The mainstem of the river begins at the confluence of Mono and Jacobson Creeks, south of Wise River, Montana. More campgrounds occur along this river per mile, than any other river in Montana. A good road parallels and crosses the river up to its origin and beyond. Trailheads, a ski resort, rock climbing, snowmobiling and cross country skiing are all activities in the smorgasbord of fun.

The beautiful upper river, surrounded by mountains, is full of beaver dams. The clear water, in a sandy streambed that channels frequently, is surrounded by meadow grasses and some willows. The banks are undercut in places, creating outstanding fish habitat. Brookies, rainbow, whitefish and ling inhabit the river.

The upper river requires intermediate skills in a canoe. The lower river has a different complexion. It tumbles with a steep gradient through boulders and sharp curves. High water requires an experienced paddler in a whitewater canoe, kayak or medium raft. Three diversion jettys in the lower section add to the excitement. The river is often too low to float in the fall.

The last place to exit on the river is at the Highway 43 bridge ".7" in Wise River, Montana. One could float on and into the Bighole River, and exit at Jerry Creek Access, three miles downstream.

Wise River

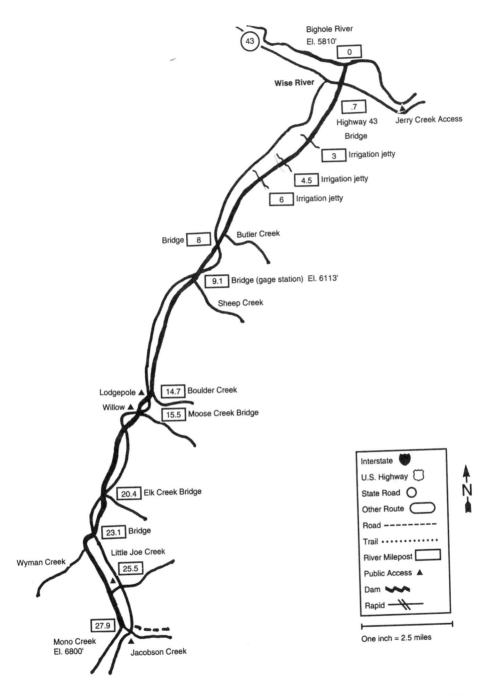

Bighole River
El. 5810'

43

0

Wise River

.7

Highway 43
Bridge

Jerry Creek Access

3 Irrigation jetty

4.5 Irrigation jetty

6 Irrigation jetty

Bridge 8

Butler Creek

9.1 Bridge (gage station) El. 6113'

Sheep Creek

Lodgepole ▲

14.7 Boulder Creek

Willow ▲

15.5 Moose Creek Bridge

20.4 Elk Creek Bridge

23.1 Bridge

Little Joe Creek

Wyman Creek

25.5

27.9

Mono Creek
El. 6800'

Jacobson Creek

Interstate
U.S. Highway
State Road
Other Route
Road --------
Trail ••••••••••••
River Milepost
Public Access ▲
Dam
Rapid

N

One inch = 2.5 miles

Wise

YAAK

ORIGIN:	Near Yahk Mountain in the vicinity of Moyie, BC. Enters MT north of Libby, MT. El. 4300'
END:	Flows into Kootenai River near Troy, MT. El. 1830'
LENGTH:	53.6 miles in MT (36 air mi.)
FLOATABLE:	52 miles (1.6 mi. below Canada border to end) Class I portion is 9.2 mi. (Yaak Falls to Kootenai River)
SECTIONS:	Upper (19.3 mi.) Origin - Border "53.6" to Yaak Village Access "34.3" Middle (25.1 mi.) Yaak "34.3" to Yaak Falls "9.2" Lower (9.2 mi.) Yaak Falls "9.2" to Kootenai R. "0"
DAMS:	None
WATERFALLS:	Yaak Falls
WHITEWATER:	13 mi. 17 mi. Bridge "13" to Kootenai River "0" (portage Yaak Falls) Class III above falls - Class IV-V below falls.
DANGERS:	Yaak Falls, whitewater above and below Yaak Falls, remote area last 9 mi.
DEWATERED:	Can be low in fall.
PORTAGES:	Yaak Falls (major portage RIGHT to Campground below (steep put in)
SPEC. AGENCIES:	None
REGS - PERMITS:	None
ACCESS-SHUTTLE:	Road parallels river all except the last 9 mi. (remote). Intersecting roads and a few access points.
SERVICES:	Limited in Yaak Village. Gas, grocery, food. Guest ranch located below Yaak Village.
CAMPING:	5 campgrounds.
GAMEFISH:	Rainbow, brook, cutthroat, whitefish

VESSEL:	Upper - Canoe, medium raft, small boat Whitewater (lower 13 mi.) Medium raft, kayak whitewater canoe
SKILL LEVEL:	Upper & Middle to Milepost "13" - Beginner (normal conditions) Whitewater - Mi. "13" to Mi. "9.2" - Intermediate to Experienced. Whitewater - Mi. "9.2" to End "0" - Highly skilled.
FLOAT TIMES:	Upper - Moderate to slow flow Middle - Moderate flow Last 13 mi. - Fast (8.0' = 7200 cfs - 7.3' = 5200 cfs)
FLOW INFO:	(406) 449-5263 USGS - Helena

HYDROGRAPH

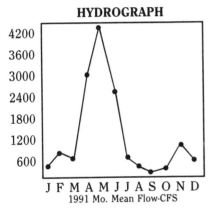

1991 Mo. Mean Flow-CFS

Gage Sta: Hwy 2 Br. northwest of Troy, MT
Drain Area: 766 sq. mi.
Ave. Flow: (35 years) 885 cfs
Ext. Max: 12,100 cfs - 9.7' ga. ht. 5/21/56
Ext. Min: 50 cfs 12/9/72
Gradient: 2470' in 53.6 mi. = 46' pma
Float Grad: Same
Clarity: Clear to cloudy
Temp: Jan. 32^0 F.
       Apr. 41^0 F.
       Jul. 75^0 F.
       Oct. 43^0 F.

DRAINAGE:	(West) Kootenai, Columbia, Pacific Ocean
MAPS:	BLM - #4 "Yaak" USFS - Kootenai NF (Best map) USGS - "Kalispell" CO. - Lincoln

YAAK

The namesake of this area has a Native American origin. The Yaak River flowing into the curved Kootenai River, has the resemblance of an arrow on a strung bow. The Indians called it "Yakt" or "Yhak". The river flows for approximately 25 miles in British Columbia before crossing the international boundary at milepost "53.6".

Highway 508, beginning at Highway 2 and the mouth of the river northwest of Troy, parallels the river upstream to the village of Yaak. A paved road connecting Yaak Village to the Koocanusa Reservoir continues access to the river further upstream.

Floating can begin 1 1/2 miles below the Canadian border. A boulder garden exists from this point and continues along under the bridge and to the East Fork. Below the East Fork the river curves often with an occasional partial logjam, down to Ford Bridge "43.4". An experienced paddler in a canoe can handle this portion.

Below Ford, a beginner in any moderately sized vessel, can handle the river all the way down to the 17 Mile Road Bridge "13". Intermittent "dead" water and the possibility of headwinds makes rafting difficult. A fine access in Yaak Village "34.3" offers ingress or egress. This unique backcountry village consists of a convenience store and gas pump, "Dirty Shame" Saloon, and a few wonderful year-round inhabitants.

Wildlife abounds in the area. In one day I paddled by a bull moose standing in the river, a mountain lion on the river bank, and a huge black bear. The black bear followed me for 1/4 mile trying to figure out what I was. Below Yaak Village are four campgrounds. Rainbow, brookies, cutts and whitefish are also residents. Below Yaak Falls bull trout are also common. Fishing is excellent for the fly or spin fisherperson.

17 Mi. Road Bridge "13" is the beginning of the whitewater. Moderate Class III rapids occur above Yaak Falls "9.2". This stretch is best run by an experienced paddler in a whitewater canoe, medium raft, or kayak. Yaak Falls commands a major portage RIGHT for those daring few that wish to continue on. Below the falls is nine miles of big whitewater. Two Class IV-V drops, followed by huge waves and long Class II-III rapids, through a narrow gorge, offer quite a challenge. Portaging the rapids would be difficult. I floated this a number of years ago with no advance information available and found myself in a "pucker" state! I use a little two man raft that I have modified for all of these "unknown" runs, enabling me to roll out quickly or portage up cliffs if I have to. This is probably the best run in Montana at 6' - 8' gage height.

A campground just below Yaak Falls offers a steep entrance to the river. A kayak or medium sized raft piloted by a highly skilled individual is my recommendation. A companion would be advisable through this remote and inaccessible canyon, surrounded by a pristine forest of hemlock, fir and ponderosa pine. A beautiful campground at the Highway 2 Bridge and the confluence to the Kootenai River offers a rest stop.

Trailheads leading into the backcountry and skiing at Turner Mountain offer diverse season recreational opportunities.

Canada

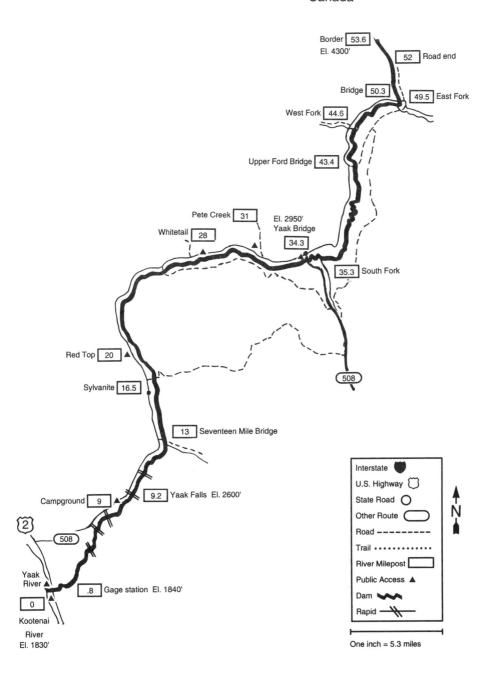

Border 53.6
El. 4300'

52 Road end

Bridge 50.3

49.5 East Fork

West Fork 44.6

Upper Ford Bridge 43.4

Pete Creek 31

El. 2950'
Yaak Bridge

Whitetail 28

34.3

35.3 South Fork

Red Top 20

508

Sylvanite 16.5

13 Seventeen Mile Bridge

Campground 9

9.2 Yaak Falls El. 2600'

2

508

Yaak
River

.8 Gage station El. 1840'

0

Kootenai
River
El. 1830'

Interstate
U.S. Highway
State Road
Other Route
Road - - - - - - - -
Trail • • • • • • • • • • •
River Milepost
Public Access ▲
Dam
Rapid

N

One inch = 5.3 miles

Yaak

YELLOWSTONE

ORIGIN:	In Wyoming. Flows into Montana near Gardiner, MT. El. 5600'
END:	Flows into North Dakota and the Missouri River near Fairview, MT. El. 1800'
LENGTH:	553.7 miles (379 air mi.)
FLOATABLE:	543.1 miles (Yellowstone National Park boundary to North Dakota border) Class I portion is 543.1 mi. "Navigable river" below Billings
SECTIONS:	Upper (112.7 mi.) Origin - WY border "553.7" to Big Timber "441" Middle (104.2 mi.) Big Timber "441" to Huntley Diversion Dam "336.8" Lower (336.8 mi.) Huntley Diversion Dam "336.8" to End - North Dakota border "0"
DAMS:	6 Diversion Dams (major) Huntley, Waco, Custer, Meyers, Forsyth, and Intake.
WATERFALLS:	None
WHITEWATER:	12.9 mi. Yellowstone National Park boundary "543.1" to Corwin Sp. Bridge "534.7" = 8.4 mi. Class III Joe Brown "530" to Carbella "525.5" (Yankee Jim Canyon) Class III. 4.5 mi. - 3 rapids
DANGERS:	Diversion dams, Buffalo Rapids, whitewater
DEWATERED:	No
PORTAGES:	6 diversion dams: Huntley (LEFT) - Waco (LEFT) - Custer (LEFT) - Meyers (bypass or portage LEFT) - Forsyth (RIGHT) - Intake (RIGHT) - Buffalo Rapids (bypass or portage LEFT - part of irrig. project)
SPEC. AGENCIES:	Yellowstone National Park
REGS - PERMITS:	Floating streams not allowed in Yellowstone National Park. 10 hp maximum on all streams in Park County (upper). Below Springdale Bridge no restrictions.

ACCESS-SHUTTLE:	Highways parallel and roads intersect. Upper - access sites are frequent. Middle & Lower - less frequent.
SERVICES:	All services in many towns entire river. Commercial raft trips available, on upper and middle sections.
CAMPING:	Upper - numerous campgrounds. Middle & Lower - less frequent, but adequate access sites.
GAMEFISH:	Upper (Blue Ribbon) - Brown, rainbow, cutthroat, whitefish. Middle - Brown, rainbow, whitefish, burbot (big), catfish. Lower - Walleye, sauger, catfish, shovelnose sturgeon, paddlefish.
VESSEL:	Upper whitewater - Medium to large raft, whitewater canoe, kayak. Rest of river - any moderate-sized vessel. Caution - portages of diversion dams.
SKILL LEVEL:	Upper Whitewater - Intermediate to Experienced Rest of river - Beginner (Caution diversion dams and short whitewater rapids)
FLOAT TIMES:	Upper & Middle - Flows moderately fast. Lower - Flows slower.
FLOW INFO:	(406) 449-5263 USGS - Helena

HYDROGRAPH

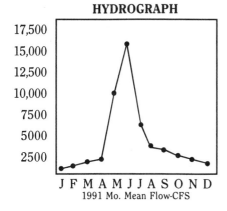

17,500
15,000
12,500
10,000
7500
5000
2500

J F M A M J J A S O N D
1991 Mo. Mean Flow-CFS

Gage Sta: Hwy 540 Br. S. of Livingston
Drain Area: 3,551 sq. mi. (at this location)
Ave. Flow: (66 years) 3,717 cfs
Ext. Max: 36,300 cfs - 9.21' ga. ht. 6/17/74
Ext. Min: 540 cfs 2/5/89
Gradient: 3800' in 553.7 mi. = 7' pma
Float Grad: Same
Clarity: Clear to murky
Temp: Jan. 34^0 F.
        Apr. 50^0 F.
        Jul. 69^0 F.
        Oct. 48^0 F.
Total Drain Area: Approx. 68,000 sq. mi. (MT)

DRAINAGE: (East) Missouri, Mississippi, Gulf of Mexico

MAPS: BLM - #34 "Park" - #35 "Beartooth" - #36 "Pryor" #27 "Sumatra" - #28 "Rosebud" - #29 "Custer" - #30 "Fallon" - #20 "Savage".
USFS - Gallatin NF (Yellowstone National Park to Reed Point) - Custer NF (Beartooth) Gray Bear to Billings.
USGS - "Bozeman" - "Billings" - "Forsyth" - "Miles City" - "Glendive".
Sp.   - "Upper Yellowstone River Guide" (Gardiner to Gray Bear Access) DFWP
"Float Guide to the Yellowstone" (Billings to Missouri River) DFWP
CO.   - Park, Sweetgrass, Stillwater, Yellowstone, Treasure, Rosebud, Custer, Prairie, Dawson, Richland, Carbon, Wibaux

Missouri - Yellowstone Big Game

YELLOWSTONE

From a sparkling mountain stream in Yellowstone National Park to a prairie waterway, the Yellowstone is the longest free-flowing river in the "lower 48". The Indians called it the Elk River, and the French explorers called it "Roche Jaune" (yellow rock); thereby the etymology of this fascinating stream.

The 678.2 mile river flows from its headwaters south of Yellowstone Park in Wyoming for 109.5 miles; through Montana, and 15 miles in North Dakota before reaching the Missouri. The river enters Montana and then re-enters Montana before reaching the Yellowstone National Park boundy "543.1". Floating streams is not allowed in Yellowstone National Park and since there is no access, floating may begin at Gardiner, Montana at the confluence of the Gardiner River.

Moderate whitewater occurs down to Corwin Springs and again from Joe Brown, through the Yankee Jim Canyon to Carbella "525.5". This Class III portion can be handled by experienced paddlers in rafts, kayaks, or whitewater canoes. "Revenge", "Big Rock" and "Boxcar" are three major rapids in the Yankee Jim Canyon. Guided raft trips are available through the whitewater, and guided fishing floats are offered below.

Carbella begins the "blue ribbon" stretch and a very scenic Paradise Valley float. A practiced beginner can handle most of the remaining Yellowstone if flow is normal, in any moderately sized vessel. Browns, rainbow and cutts are prized in this upper section. Very frequent access sites and campgrounds occur in this upper section.

The 9th St. Bridge in Livingston demands some attention, as a steeper gradient leads to the debris collecting pillars. Just below this bridge is a short Class II rapids. Springdale Bridge "459.6" marks the point where motor restrictions have been removed (10 hp maximum above). The annual "fun run" from Livingston to Billings attracts all ages in many configurations called "vessels".

Below Livingston the river channels more often so be alert for waves as these channels rejoin. Floating pressure decreases as you go downstream and so does the availability of access sites and campgrounds. The 160.4 mile "transition" section lies between Big Timber and the Bighorn River. In this section the river gradually changes from a clear mountain stream to a warmer prairie river. Near Park City some short moderate rapids should cause little concern for the alert pilot.

Below Billings Highway 87 bridge "345.6" is the dangerous Huntley Diversion Dam "336.8" which requires a portage LEFT. Since the Yellowstone is considered a "navigable river" below Billings I do not understand how six big, wall-to-wall diversion dams could be "navigable". On a recent, extended trip from Yellowstone National Park all the way into North Dakota, portaging these diversion dams is not my fondest memory of the trip. We must try and remember however, that water is prized on the dry plains.

Pompeys Pillar "313.5" is a historical landmark, followed by the Waco Diversion Dam "301", which requires a portage LEFT. The Custer Diversion Dam "278.4" and its counterpart "rock dam" in the other channel (right), each require portage. The Meyers Diversion Dam "264" can often be bypassed on the left, or portaged if desired. The Forsyth Diversion Dam "222.5" requires a portage RIGHT. The Buffalo Rapids "138.5" can be portaged LEFT if desired.

Agate hounding in the riverbed or the surrounding tributaries is popular. Looking for fossils in the Billings and Glendive areas or a visit to Makoshika State Park near Glendive can be interesting.

Intake Diversion Dam "56.1" requires a portage RIGHT. Early June the paddlefish congregate below the dam, blocking their upstream spawning run. As the fish gather, so do the fish poles. Paddlefish do not take bait or lures, as ingested plankton is their diet. Snagging one of these tasty monsters usually means a 30 minute - 1/4 mi. tussle. Catfish, shovelnose sturgeon, walleye and sauger offer a mixed creel in this warm water fishery.

Below Intake Dam "56.1" are the Elk Island and Seven Sisters Recreation Areas at mileposts "36" and "24". Sydney Highway 23 Bridge Access "14.5" is the last Montana exit. Floating across the North Dakota border "0", access can next be found east of Fairview, Montana at the North Dakota Highway 200 bridge, 3 miles downstream. Continuing on 12 more miles to the Missouri you may utilize the super facilities at Fort Buford, North Dakota. A boat ramp and campground awaits.

Yellowstone River

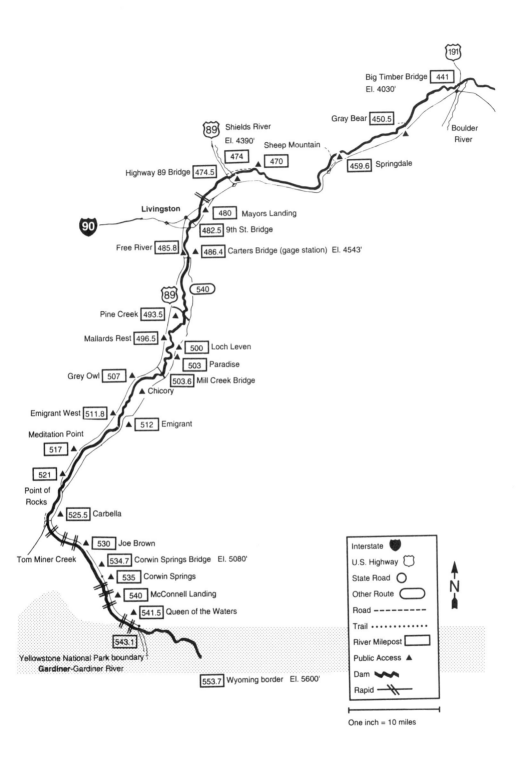

191

Big Timber Bridge 441
El. 4030'

Gray Bear 450.5

Boulder
River

89 Shields River
El. 4390'

Sheep Mountain

474

470

459.6 Springdale

Highway 89 Bridge 474.5

Livingston

90

480 Mayors Landing

482.5 9th St. Bridge

Free River 485.8

486.4 Carters Bridge (gage station) El. 4543'

89 540

Pine Creek 493.5

Mallards Rest 496.5

500 Loch Leven

503 Paradise

Grey Owl 507

503.6 Mill Creek Bridge

▲ Chicory

Emigrant West 511.8

512 Emigrant

Meditation Point

517

521

Point of
Rocks

525.5 Carbella

530 Joe Brown

Tom Miner Creek

534.7 Corwin Springs Bridge   El. 5080'

535 Corwin Springs

540 McConnell Landing

541.5 Queen of the Waters

543.1

Yellowstone National Park boundary
Gardiner-Gardiner River

553.7 Wyoming border   El. 5600'

Interstate	
U.S. Highway	
State Road	
Other Route	
Road	--------
Trail	••••••••
River Milepost	
Public Access	▲
Dam	〰〰
Rapid	

N

One inch = 10 miles

Yellowstone   Origin 553.7 to Big Timber 441

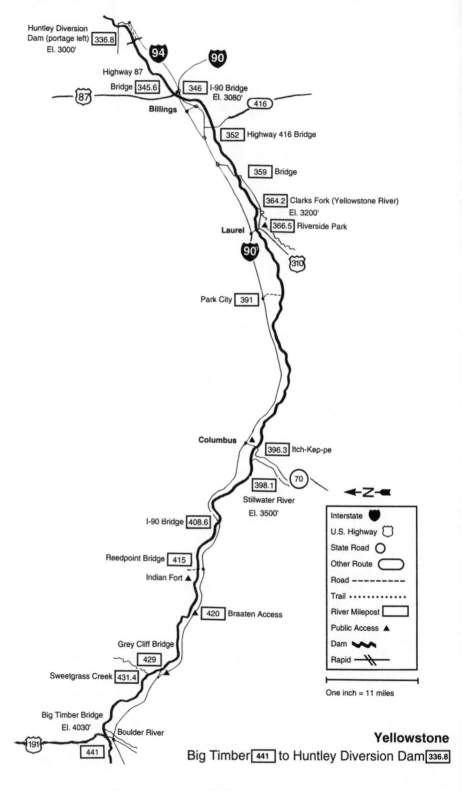

Huntley Diversion
Dam (portage left) 336.8
El. 3000'

Highway 87
Bridge 345.6

87

346 I-90 Bridge
El. 3080'

Billings

416

352 Highway 416 Bridge

359 Bridge

364.2 Clarks Fork (Yellowstone River)
El. 3200'

Laurel

▲ 366.5 Riverside Park

90

310

Park City 391

Columbus ▲

396.3 Itch-Kep-pe

398.1

70

Stillwater River
El. 3500'

I-90 Bridge 408.6

Reedpoint Bridge 415

Indian Fort ▲

▲ 420 Braaten Access

Grey Cliff Bridge
429

Sweetgrass Creek 431.4 ▲

Big Timber Bridge
El. 4030'

Boulder River

191

441

←N←

Interstate	⬟
U.S. Highway	◯
State Road	◯
Other Route	⬭
Road	- - - - - - -
Trail	· · · · · · ·
River Milepost	▭
Public Access	▲
Dam	〰
Rapid	╱╱

One inch = 11 miles

Yellowstone
Big Timber 441 to Huntley Diversion Dam 336.8

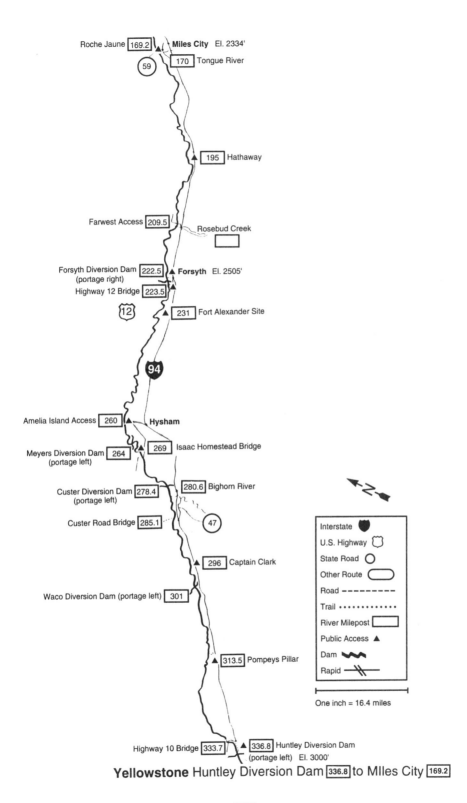

Roche Jaune 169.2 **Miles City** El. 2334'
59
170 Tongue River

▲ 195 Hathaway

Farwest Access 209.5
Rosebud Creek

Forsyth Diversion Dam 222.5 ▲ **Forsyth** El. 2505'
(portage right)
Highway 12 Bridge 223.5

12
▲ 231 Fort Alexander Site

94

Amelia Island Access 260 ▲ **Hysham**
269 Isaac Homestead Bridge
Meyers Diversion Dam 264
(portage left)

Custer Diversion Dam 278.4 280.6 Bighorn River
(portage left)
Custer Road Bridge 285.1
47

▲ 296 Captain Clark

Waco Diversion Dam (portage left) 301

Legend:
Interstate
U.S. Highway
State Road
Other Route
Road ----------
Trail ············
River Milepost
Public Access ▲
Dam
Rapid

One inch = 16.4 miles

▲ 313.5 Pompeys Pillar

Highway 10 Bridge 333.7 ▲ 336.8 Huntley Diversion Dam
(portage left) El. 3000'

Yellowstone Huntley Diversion Dam 336.8 to MIles City 169.2

321

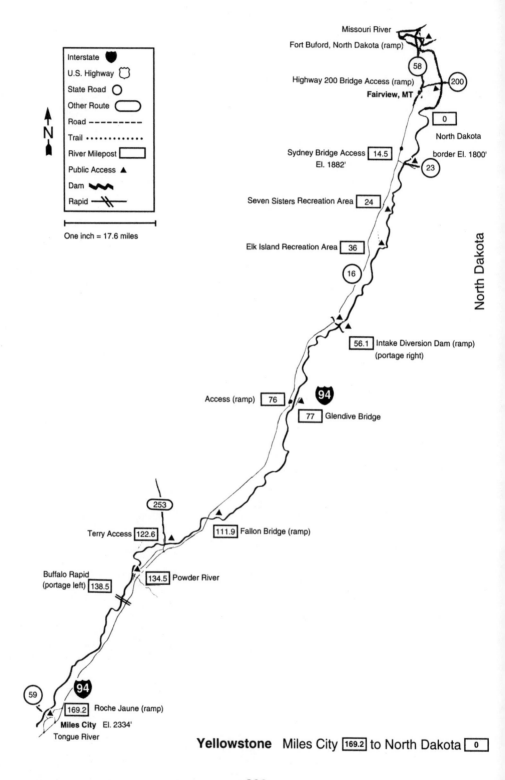

Missouri River

Fort Buford, North Dakota (ramp)

58

Highway 200 Bridge Access (ramp) | 200

Fairview, MT

0

North Dakota

Sydney Bridge Access | 14.5 | border El. 1800'
El. 1882'

23

Seven Sisters Recreation Area | 24

Elk Island Recreation Area | 36

16

56.1 | Intake Diversion Dam (ramp)
(portage right)

Access (ramp) | 76 | **94**

77 | Glendive Bridge

North Dakota

253

Terry Access | 122.6 | 111.9 | Fallon Bridge (ramp)

Buffalo Rapid
(portage left) | 138.5 | 134.5 | Powder River

59 | **94**

169.2 | Roche Jaune (ramp)

Miles City El. 2334'
Tongue River

Yellowstone Miles City 169.2 to North Dakota 0

Legend

Interstate
U.S. Highway
State Road
Other Route
Road ----------
Trail ....
River Milepost
Public Access ▲
Dam
Rapid

N

One inch = 17.6 miles

ARROW

Called "Slaughter River" by Lewis and Clark on 5/29/1805, due to 120' high buffalo jump at mouth. The river begins at Birch Creek, northwest of Geyser, Montana at an elevation of 4200'. It empties into the Missouri west of Judith Landing (Highway 236) at an elevation of 2450'. The river is 100 miles long, covering 45 air miles. The stream usually has water only during spring runoff and flows muddy through remote areas, with fences and debris. There are no camp or access sites. The upper portion has brook trout, while the lower has some warm water species. BLM maps #14 "Highwood" (upper) and #15 "Judith" (lower) cover the river.

LITTLE BOULDER (Jefferson)

The river origin is at Little Boulder Park, southwest of Boulder, Montana at elevation 7250'. It flows for 15 miles (10 air) into the Boulder River with a gradient of 164 fpm. The stream channel is narrow, curvy and brushy. Brookies and rainbow inhabit the upper portion, and browns the lower. Elder Gulch Campground can be found half way up the forest service road paralleling the river. The Little Boulder is within the Deer Lodge NF or use BLM map #22 "Avon". It is a pretty stream with clear water and a few beaver dams.

SOUTH BOULDER (Jefferson)

The river flows for 17 miles from Curly Creek, near Hollowtop Mountain, south of Whitehall, elevation 7600'. The river has a 200 fpm gradient, flowing through the boulder streambed, infested with downfall. The stream is narrow, brushy and remote. Rainbow and brookies are found up high and browns lower. A forest service road parallels the river up to a trailhead and numerous informal campsites. The mouth of the river is near the Lewis and Clark Caverns on the Jefferson River. Use Deer Lodge or Beaverhead NF map. BLM maps #32 "Dillon" (upper) and #33 "Madison" (lower).

BROADWATER

This alpine river flows for only 6.7 miles. It begins at the confluence of Star and Zimmer Creeks near Cooke City, Montana. After an 800' tumble it flows into the Clarks Fork of the Yellowstone, elevation 7900'. A hiking trail leads into Broadwater and Curl Lakes that are part of the system. The upper two miles are grassy meadow and the river offers fair fishing for brookies. The area is beautiful. Gallatin or Custer-Beartooth NF maps and #35 "Beartooth" BLM show area.

ELK

The Elk River begins at Rossiter Creek near Monument Hill, west of Hebgen Lake at an elevation of 8800'. It then flows into the West Fork of the Madison River 13.7 miles later with a drop of 2400'. The West Fork Road leads up to a trailhead at the mouth of the Elk. A campsite can be found there and a jeep trail goes upstream another mile. The rest of the stream is by trail only and later cross country. Rainbow, cutts and browns call this home. The streambed is boulders and very narrow and brushy. The stream is clear and mouths in a large alpine meadow. The lower 1/2 mile could be canoed or use a small raft or inner tube. The river is in the Beaverhead National Forest.

LITTLE ELK

The Little Elk flows for 2.6 miles into the Elk River. A trail goes up a short distance, and the rest is cross country climbing. The stream has a 538.5 fpm gradient. The stream is clear and cold, with boulders and brushy banks and is six feet wide. Rainbow and cutts can be found. The origin is at Blue Lake.

GARDINER

This river was named after Johnston Gardiner, a trapper and mountain man in the area in the 1830's. The stream flows for 17.6 miles in Wyoming (Yellowstone National Park) before entering Montana, near Gardiner. All 2.9 miles of flow in Montana occurs within Yellowstone Park, and no floating is allowed on streams in the park. The river has a gradient of 138 fpm as it tumbles into the Yellowstone River right at the park boundary. The river is warm having a 50° F. average in January. The river does have brookies and browns. The BLM #34 "Park" or Gallatin NF maps show the lower portion, or use the Yellowstone National Park map.

LOST

The river originates near Onefour, Alberta and flows into Montana west of Wild Horse Port of Entry. It flows four miles in Montana and enters the Milk River northwest of Havre. The gradient is 100' beginning with an elevation of 2700' at the border. The country is very remote and one must cross miles of private fenced property, with no roads to find the river. The river only has water during run-off or after heavy rains, and therefore is extremely muddy. A few catfish, walleye and sauger can be found in the backwater mouth. BLM map #4 "Fresno" or USGS "Shelby" map show the area.

MOKOWANIS

The river begins above Atsina Lake in Glacier National Park, near Stoney Indian Pass (Elevation 6700'). It flows into the Belly River just above the ranger station at 4600' elevation. The total length is 12 miles including Atsina, Glenns and Cosley Lakes. This valley is spectacularly beautiful with towering peaks and has five waterfalls in the river system. Atsina, three unnamed and Gros Ventre Falls are gorgeous. This small boulder strewn and brushy stream is accessible by trail only. Rainbow and grayling can be found in the stream and lakes. A float tube or small raft could be packed into Glenns or Cosley Lakes. Use Glacier National Park (USGS) map. Mokowanis is a Blackfeet name for the Belly Indians who lived in the area. The name refers to the digestive system of the buffalo.

LITTLE POWDER

The river originates near Weston, Wyoming and flows into Montana south of Biddle (Elevation 3500'). It flows into the Powder River just northeast of Broadus, after dropping 495' in 66.4 miles. There are numerous small irrigation dams and fences in this small stream. The river is dewatered after spring run-off and allows only "tubing" in the slow water for short stretches. Highway 59 parallels the river and the east side Powderville Road goes up to the mouth of the river and an access site. Catfish can be found in the lower portion only. BLM #39 "Powder" or USGS "Ekalaka" maps show the area.

ROE

"The Worlds Shortest River", proclaimed recently by the Guinness Book of Records! The river has an average length of 201', originating at Giant Springs and flowing into the Missouri River. Floating is not allowed in this Giant Springs State Park. The name of the river comes from fish eggs at the on-sight fish hatchery. The springs puts out an average flow of 220 cfs and the water is clear and cool. The state park offers picnicing and camping and tours of the fish hatchery. Take the Giant Springs Road in north Great Falls along the Missouri River dams and falls.

SACAJAWEA

Also called Crooked Creek. The name Sacajawea comes from the Lewis and Clark Expedition, honoring their Indian maiden guide. The origin of the stream is north of Roy, Montana and flows 100 miles to the Fort Peck Reservoir in the Musselshell River drainage. The river is murky, warm and often has no flow. Access to the stream is difficult as roads are few and can be impassable if wet. At the mouth is the Crooked Creek Campground with boatramp, which is now part of the C.M. Russell Wildlife Refuge. Short portions of this stream are canoeable when water is high, if you can find access. The streambed is silt and has a 10.5 fpm gradient. BLM maps #68 "Winnett" (upper) and #77 "Sand Springs" (lower) show the area.

WIGWAM

Algonquin name for tipi (siouan). The origin of the stream is at Therriault Lakes, northeast of Eureka at an elevation of 5450'. It flows over Therriault Falls in its eight mile journey to the Canada border. This small stream has a gravel and boulder streambed infested with logjams. The lakes are boatable and a trailhead leads into the backcountry. The panorama of the towering peaks is magnificent. The stream has a 93.8 fpm gradient of clear cold water, inhabited by cutthroat trout. BLM map #9 "Whitefish", Kootenai NF or USGS "Kalispell" show the area. The river flows into the Elk River in Canada and eventually into the Kootenai River.

MAP INFORMATION

Montana Highway maps are available free from nearly any place of business.

BLM - Good maps. Show private and public land. Some are topo. Available at all Bureau of Land Manage ment offices. $4.00 all maps.

USFS - Good maps. Forest service also has smaller ranger district maps. Not topo. Available at all National Forest Service offices. $2.00 or Ranger District maps usually free.

USGS - Good for topography. Difficult to read and many are outdated. Available at Montana Tech. or Denver U.S. Geological Service office only. $2.50 for most maps.

COUNTIES - County court houses have maps of county with possiblility of detailed or "blown up" sectionals. Usually inexpensive.

DFWP - Some maps distributed by Regional Offices. Usually free.

SPECIAL MAPS:

"Glacier National Park" (USGS). Excellent map shows trails and topography.
Available at NFS-offices. $7.95

"Bob Marshall, Great Bear and Scapegoat Wilderness Complex" (USFS)
Excellent map shows trails and topography. Available at some NFS offices. $2.00

"Three Forks of the Flathead River". A great second map. Waterproof.
Available at some NFS offices. $4.95

"Upper Missouri National Wild & Scenic" 2 water resistant maps. Excellent as
a second map. Covers Fort Benton to James Kipp State Park.
Available at Lewistown BLM office. $4.00 each.

* For addresses or phone numbers see Fed. and State offices
* Many of these maps are available at bookstores, sporting goods stores or other retail outlets.
* For guides and outfitters see Montana Recreation Guide (Dept. of Commerce)

RIVER ETIQUETTE and SAFETY

Leader - Understand abilities and limitations of yourself and those in the party. Know rules for the river and the activities. Inform party members. Advise someone of your float plans! Permits? Licenses? Weather forecasts? Life jackets (under 12 - wear). First aid and life saving skills. Be familiar with "Z" drag and removing pinned vessel.
Stream Access and Trespass Law. Respect for landowners.

"Pack it in - Pack it out." Pick up after less concerned people and leave the river better than it was. "Leave only footprints - take only memories". Pack out or burn fish entrals.
Please report: Fishermans log, misconduct, rare wildlife sightings, fires, river dangers
Extreme temperature changes - From need of suntan lotion to hypothermia. Dress in layers.
Plan trips carefully - Study maps, talk to locals, (river could change daily) dewatered, rapids, dams?
Do not impose pets. Keep all noises minimal. Do not discharge firearms and similar devices or harass livestock. No profanity, disorderly conduct or drunkeness. Do not drive off roads.

Leave cultural materials for others to enjoy. Do not destroy, deface or damage.
No Glass - Do not dig trenches or leave evidence of campsite - use toilets or bury 100' from water
Use dead and downed firewood only. Use existing fire ring if possible. Reclaim when finished. Beware of
    winds! Use fire pan to prevent earth scars. Observe fire danger ratings.
Stop and study rapids. Proceed or portage?
Courtesy to bank and wader fishermen. (Go behind if possible and retreive lines)
Boil water to prevent Giardiasis or use water purify tablets.
Wood ticks, poisonous plants and rattlesnakes necessitate precautions.
Equipment:

Waterproof containers	Baler
Spare paddle (secured to vessel)	Compass
Basic repair material - tools	Knife (Axe - shovel)
Biodegradable soap & toilet paper	Waterproof matches
Drinking water	Rescue equipment
First Aid & Snake bite	Rope & pulleys
Insect repellant - sun screen	Hat & gloves
Camping gear (if applicable)	Rain gear
Maps - camera - binocs	Dry clothes
Whistle - flares - mirror	Duct tape
Food - beverage	Eyeglass neck straps

Vessel: Good condition and test before trip. Multiple airchambers or install floatation devices. Pad sharp
    projections. Rescue lines on vessel. Check trailer, car top rack and vehicle, for safety. Secure oars
    to vessel. Do not overload vessel.

If upset occurs:
    1. Hold onto craft on upstream side.
    2. Leave boat if log jams, brush or rapids below.
    3. Get into "sitting position" with feet downstream. Look downstream and attempt to get to shore as
soon as current allows.
    4. Rescue boat and equipment only after all people are safe.

American Whitewater Association Safety Code:
    1. Be a competent swimmer
    2. Wear a life jacket
    3. Keep craft under control (reach shore before danger)
    4. Be aware of hazards and avoid them.
    5. Boating alone is not recommended (3 recommended minimum)
    6. Know your boating ability
    7. Good physical condition
    8. Be practiced in escape, rescue and first aid.
    9. Master eskimo roll
    10. Wear crash helmet in difficult water
    11. Be suitably equipped. Shoes to swim or walk in. Knife and waterproof matches. Tie eyeglasses on.
        Avoid bulky clothing.

Grizzly encounter: (Do not recreate alone, make noise as you progress)
    1) Remain calm, talk softly, walk slowly backward, look for climbable tree, do not run (you cannot outrun
        a bear and running may induce attack).
    2) If bear charges:
        A) Drop coat or pack to distract.
        B) Climb a tree
        C) Play dead, assume fetus position protecting head and stomach.

Mountain lion encounter:
    Make noise and create aggressive behavior.

SHUTTLING: Using 2 vehicles or employing a commercial shuttle service found at a very few rivers are
popular ways. Have a friend drive and meet you. They can sun, read or fish while waiting. Take a mountain
bike or a small trail motorcycle along and leave it off downstream locked to a tree, if you're alone or in one
vehicle. Hitch-hiking is also a possibility, if roads are well traveled. Carry a paddle or fish pole to identify
yourself. Lock vehicle.

BASIC BOATING FIRST AID

Preventive maintenance of course, is best; however, undesirable situations may occur. Party members should be in good physical condition, wear proper layered clothing, including hats and good traction river shoes that can be hiked in. Persons with allergies or other unique problems should state that fact to the group and take precautions. Eyeglasses should be tied on.

Listed are the most common problems involving boating and some basic first aid to make a victim more comfortable or sustain life until medical help can be reached:

CPR (Cardio-pulmonary resuscitation)
  Lay victim on back, elevate legs, neck and head arched back.
  Place heel of hand on the lower part of the breastbone and the other hand on top of the first hand.
    5 chest compressions (1 each second)
    1 full lung inflation (mouth-to-mouth)
    Repeat!

Mouth-to-mouth (Check mouth and throat for obstructions!)
  Lay on back, tilt head back, pinch nostrils. Open your mouth wide, take a deep breath and seal your mouth tightly around victims mouth and blow.
  Approximately 1 breath each 5 seconds.

Problems:
HYPOTHERMIA
  Get out of water quickly.
  Get dry clothes on or rainsuit or wetsuit.
  Move around to improve circulation or get into sleeping bag if severe.
  Build fire if necessary.

  If in lake:
    Get out of water - stay with boat and get as far out of water as possible.
    Curl up to retain body heat.
    If several people are in the water, huddle close in a circle.
      Place children in middle of circle.

  If a victim has no pulse or respiration, make sure airway is open and begin CPR. Do not rub skin or give anything to drink (including hot drinks or alcohol).

SHOCK - CONCUSSION - UNCONSCIOUS
  Lay victim down (elevate feet if no upper injuries exist)
  On warm days covering is not necessary.
  Treat for injury.
  Offer water if he does not vomit.
  Use tactful encouragement.
  Wake up occassionally to check.

HYPERVENTILATION
  Breathe into a bag or hat

BLEEDING
  Elevate wounded area. Direct pressure over wound with clean cloth if possible. Until direct pressure can be applied at wound, use pressure against bone in the upper arm area between armpit and elbow; or below groin in front.
  Bandage snugly, and add more bandages on top as necessary.
  For nosebleed - lay down, tip head back, and pinch nostrils.

SPRAINS - DISLOCATIONS - BREAKS
  Immobilize with inflatable splints or improvise with sticks and wrapping duct tape.

SNAKEBITE (Poison attacks the circulatory system)
  Immobilize bite area in lower-than-the-heart position.
  Apply lightly constricting band just above bite.
  Sterilize sharp knife and make short incision through skin only, at fang marks.
  Apply suction with suction cup provided in snakebite kit or use your mouth. Continue sucking
    for at least 30 minutes. If swelling moves above constricting band, apply another above and
    leave first band in place.
  Cleanse wound and watch for shock.
  If victim must walk, move very slowly.
  A new theory of 12 volt shock at the bite appears to work.
  Use car battery or carry a "stun gun"

SUNBURN (Very intense on water-use sunglasses and hat)
  Cover with long pants and long sleeved shirt. Protect exposed areas with zinc oxide or creams.
  If burned use burn spray.

BLISTERS (Use gloves if hands are tender)
  Break blisters only if necessary. Use pin and press out water or blood. Cleanse area and apply
  antibiotic.

POISON PLANTS
  Wash affected area in soapsuds. Apply cream or lotion.

SUGGESTED FIRST AID SUPPLIES (Waterproof bag)

First Aid Manual	Band Aids
Aspirin	Sterile gauze squares
Diarrhea tablets	Gauze rolls
Sunburn (lotion and burn)	Q-tips
Insect repellant	Elastic bandages
Poison plant cream	Adhesive tape
Antihistimine	Safety pins
Antiseptic	Sharp knife
Antibiotic	Tweezers
Oil of cloves (toothache)	Thermometer
Eyewash	Magnify glass
Salt tablets	Inflatable splints
Dextrose tablets	Waterproof matches
Antacid tablets	Chapstick
Vitamins	Water purification tablets (or boil)
Earache drops	Bar soap
Snakebite kit	Duct tape
Prescription drugs for special people	

Hypothermia Chart

Water Temp. (^{0}F)	Exhaustion or Unconsciousness	Expected time of survival
32.5^0	Under 15 minutes	Under 15-45 minutes
32.5-40	15-30 minutes	30-90 minutes
40-50	30-60 minutes	1-3 hrs.
50-60	1-2 hrs.	1-6 hrs.
60-70	2-7 hrs.	2-40 hr.
70-80	3-12 hr.	3-Indefinite
over 80^0	Indefinite	Indefinite

If combined air and water temperature do not exceed 100^0 hypothermia can be a greater problem.

Ave. Temp. - Great Falls, MT
(Western MT is slightly warmer in winter & cooler in summer)

Mo.	Ave. High	Ave. Low
Jan.	32	14
Feb.	35	15
Mar.	43	22
Apr.	56	33
May	66	42
Jun.	73	49
Jul.	84	55
Aug.	81	53
Sept.	69	44
Oct.	59	37
Nov.	45	26
Dec.	35	18

Annual Precipitation:

Northwest - MT 24" - 48"
West - MT 12" - 24"
East - MT 0" - 12"

CONVERSION TABLE

Length
1 in. = 2.54 cent.
1 ft. = .3048 meter
1 yard (3 ft.) = .9144 meter
1 mile = 5280' or 1760 yds.
1 mi. = 1.61 kilometers
6 ft. = 1 fathom
1.1508 mi. = 1 nautical mi.

Volume
1 sq. mi. = 640 acres
1 cu. ft. = 144 cu. in.

Liquid
1 oz. = .02958 liter
1.0567 qt. = 1 liter
1 gal. = 3.7853 liters
British Imp. gal. = 4.546 liters or 1.2 gal.

Speed
1 m.p.h. (statute) = 1.61 kilometers per hour (55
  m.p.h. = 88.55 kph)
1.15 m.p.h. = 1 knot (nautical) per hour

Fahrenheit degrees		Celsius degrees
-60^0	=	-51^0
-50^0	=	-46^0
-40^0	=	-40^0
-30^0	=	-35^0
-20^0	=	-29^0
-10^0	=	-23^0
0^0	=	-18^0
10^0	=	-12^0
20^0	=	-6^0
32^0	=	0^0
40^0	=	4^0
50^0	=	10^0
60^0	=	15^0
70^0	=	21^0
80^0	=	27^0
90^0	=	32^0
100^0	=	38^0
110^0	=	43^0
120^0	=	49^0

RIVER DIFFICULTY
"International Grading Scale"

Whitewater Rating:

I PRACTICED BEGINNER	Easy - Sand banks, bends without difficulty, occasional small rapids with waves regular and low. Correct course easy to find; but care needed with minor obstacles like pebble banks, fallen trees, etc., especially on narrow rivers. River speed less than hard back paddling speed.
II INTERMEDIATE	Medium - Fairly frequent but unobstructed rapids, usually with regular waves, easy eddies, and easy bends. Course generally easy to recognize. River speeds occasionally exceeding hard back-paddling speed.
III EXPERIENCED	Difficult - Maneuvering in rapids necessary. Small falls, large regular waves covering boat, numerous rapids. Main current may swing under bushes, branches or overhangs. Course not always easily recognizable. Current speed usually less than fast forward paddling speed.
IV HIGHLY SKILLED (Several years exp. with group)	Very difficult - Long, rocky rapids with difficult and completely irregular broken water which must be run head on. Very fast eddies, abrupt bends and vigorous cross currents. Difficult landings increase hazard. Frequent inspections necessary. Extensive experience necessary.
V TEAM OF EXPERTS	Exceedingly difficult - Either very long or mean waves usually wild turbulance capable of picking up a boat and boater and throwing them several feet. Extreme congestion in cross current. Scouting difficult from shore and some danger to life in the event of mishap.
VI TEAM OF EXPERTS (Taking precaution)	Limit of navigability - All previously mentioned difficulties increased to the limit. Only negotiable at favorable water levels. Cannot be attempted without risk of life.

BOATING LAW

Montana boating law: (Only in part)

All recreation vessels must have a life preserver aboard for each person (Coast Guard approved Type I - II - III - IV). All under the age of 12 must have it on. If vessel is over 16' in length, 1 throwable seat cushion with handle or ring buoy must be aboard. Vessels need a hand lantern showing a white light if underway between sunset and sunrise. Must be temporarily exhibited to prevent collision. No discharge of any kind of garbage or waste.

Motors are uncommon on rivers and laws are complicated concerning the following items:

Ventilation systems
Fire extinguishers
Lights
Sound producing devices
Registration and decals
Noise limitation
Navigation rules
Liability
Use of alcohol & drugs

Refer to "Montana Boating Laws and Rules" - "U.S. Coast Guard Requirements" publications for complete laws. Available Fish, Wildlife and Parks offices or many sporting goods stores.

Montana motor restrictions: (Only in part)

Closed to any motor-propelled watercraft:
Bighole River (entire)
Bighorn River (Afterbay Dam to Bighorn Access)
Flathead (Middle Fork) - (Origin to Essex)
Flathead (North Fork) - (Canada border to Big Creek)
Flathead (South Fork) - (Origin to Spotted Bear River confluence)
Missouri (From 10th Ave. S. Bridge to Black Eagle)
Smith (entire river)
All section of rivers in "wilderness" designated areas.

Closed to over 10 hp:
All rivers and streams in the following counties:

Beaverhead
Broadwater (Exception - Missouri R. downriver from Gallatin Co. line)
Gallatin (Exception - downriver from Headwaters State Park)
Jefferson
Madison
Park (Exception - downriver from Springdale Bridge on Yellowstone)
Silverbow
Also:
Flathead (Middle Fork) - Essex to S.F. confluence
Flathead (North Fork) - Big Creek to Blankenship Bridge
Flathead (South Fork) - Spotted Bear R. to H.H. Reservoir
Flathead (Main stem) - Blankenship Br. to S.F. confluence

Limited to "no wake" speed (no whitewater in waves)

Missoula Co. - Clearwater River from outlet of Seeley Lake to the first bridge downstream from Camp Paxson swim dock.

"Wild" and "Scenic Missouri"   Refer to Special Agencies - "Wild - Scenic Rivers Act"
in appendix or Missouri mileage maps for exact designation.

Other floating variances:

Yellowstone National Park - no floating streams allowed.
Red Rock Lakes Wildlife Refuge - numerous rest. (See Red Rock River)
Flathead Indian Reservation - No motors on Lower Flathead R. 3/15 to 6/30
15 hp maximum other times of year.
Rock Creek - No fishing while floating 7/1 - 11/30.
Madison River - No fishing while floating at certain times and places.
Gallatin - No fishing while floating above Gallatin Forks.
Missouri and Smith - Permits required, in certain sections. See individual river information.

Fishing Licenses: Required of persons 15 years or older. Special license situation for those under 15 or over 62 and for paddlefish. Non-residents can obtain 2 day or season licenses. Available from FWP offices or many retail outlets. Annual licenses good from March 1 through February. Lakes are open year around. Rivers and streams in the Western and Central Fishing Districts open the third Saturday in May and close November 30. Eastern District streams are open year around. The regulations are very complex. Catch and release, no float fishing, and catch and release for some species only, in certain stretches of river. Check current local restrictions. Some Indian reservations require fishing or recreational permits. National Parks do not require a fishing license.

MONTANA STREAM ACCESS LAW
H.B. # 265 - 1985

Class 1 - Those streams which are capable of recreational use and have been declared navigable or which are capable of specific kinds of commercial activity, including commercial outfitting with multi-person watercraft.

Class 2 - All rivers and streams of recreational use that are not Class 1 waters.

Stream Access Law: The law says that, in general, all surface water capable of recreational use may be so used by the public without regard to ownership of the land underlying the waters. It also states that recreationists can use rivers and streams up to the ordinary high-water mark. The law does not address recreational use of lakes; only rivers and streams.

Surface water: a natural river or stream, its beds and banks up to the ordinary high-water mark.

Recreational use: fishing, hunting, swimming, floating in small craft or other floatation devices, boating in motorized craft (except where prohibited by law), boating in craft propelled by oars or paddles, other water-related pleasure activities, and related unavoidable or incidental uses. Certain restrictions are listed.

Ordinary high-water mark: the line that water impresses on land covering it for sufficient time to cause different characteristics below the line, such as deprivation of the soil of substantially all its terrestrial vegetation and destruction of its value for agricultural vegetation. Flood plains next to streams are considered to be above the ordinary high-water mark, and are not open for recreation without permission.

Portage: The law states that recreationists using a stream may go above the ordinary high-water mark to portage around barriers, but must do so in the least intrusive manner possible, avoiding damage to the landowners property and violation of his rights. Barrier is defined as an artificial obstruction in or over the water which totally or effectively obstructs the recreational use of the surface water. The law does not address portage around natural barriers, and does not make such a portage either legal or illegal.

Landowner Liability: The legislature has limited the situations in which a landowner or his agent or tenant may be liable for injuries to people using a stream flowing through his property. They are liable only for acts or omissions that constitute "willful or wanton misconduct".

Landowners: The Department of Fish, Wildlife and Parks will provide assistance to any landowner in designing and locating fences that do not interfere with recreational use of streams. Contact Department Portage Coordinator at 444-2449.

Restrictions: Landowner permission is required for the following recreational uses between ordinary high-water marks:
* operating all-terrain vehicles or other motorized vehicles not intended for use on the water.
* making recreational use of stock ponds or private impoundments fed by intermittent streams. Although this restriction deals specifically with only those stock ponds or impoundments fed by intermittent streams, the Department recommends, as a matter of courtesy, that recreationists obtain permission before using any private ponds.
* making recreational use of water diverted away from a stream, such as an irrigation canal or ditch.
* big game hunting
* overnight camping, unless the camping is necessary for the enjoyment of the water resource and it is done out of sight of, or more than 500 yards from, any occupied dwelling.
* the placement or creation of any permanent duck blind boat moorage or any other permanent object.
  the placement or creation of any seasonal objects such as a duck blind or boat moorage, within sight of, or within 500 yards of an occupied dwelling (whichever is less).
* using a streambed as a right-of-way when no water is flowing.
* any other pleasure activity not primarily water related.

TRESPASS LEGISLATION (HB 911 - 1985): This legislation states that a member of the public has the privilege to enter or remain on private land by the explicit permission of the landowner or his agent or by the failure of the landowner to post notice denying entry onto the land. The landowner may revoke permission by personal communication.

The law states that notice denying entry must consist of written notice or of notice by painting a post, structure or natural object with at least 50 sq. in. of fluorescent orange paint. In the case of a metal fencepost, the entire post must be painted. This notice must be placed at each outer gate and all normal points of access to the property and wherever a stream crosses an outer boundary line.

National parks, Indian reservations and wildlife refuges may have specific rules. Also big game hunting and trapping may have variances.

ASK FIRST - AND RESPECT THE RIGHTS AND REQUESTS OF LANDOWNERS WHENEVER YOU RECREATE ON PRIVATE LANDS.

SPECIAL AGENCIES

WILD-SCENIC-Rivers Act (Public Law 90-542 10/2/68)

The National Wild and Scenic Rivers Act declared that "certain selected rivers of the nation which, with their immediate environments, possess outstandingly remarkable scenic, recreational, geologic, fish and wildlife, historic, cultural or other similar values, shall be preserved in free-flowing condition, and that they and their immediate environments shall be protected for the benefit and enjoyment of present and future generations"....

1) WILD - Those rivers or sections of rivers that are free of impoundments and generally inaccessible except by trail, with watersheds or shorelines essentially primitive and waters unpolluted. These represent vestiges of primitive America.

2) SCENIC - Those rivers or sections of rivers that are free of impoundments, with shorelines or watersheds still largely primitive and shorelines largely undeveloped, but accessible in places by roads.

3) RECREATIONAL - Those rivers or sections of rivers that are readily accessible by road or railroad, that may have some development along their shorelines, and that may have undergone some impoundment or diversion in the past.

In Montana, the Missouri River had sections designated in 1976, and the Flathead River had designations in 1980.

WILD:

MF Flathead Headwaters to Bear Creek confluence.
SF Flathead Headwaters to Spotted Bear River confluence.
Missouri   .5 miles below Pilot Rock to Deadman Rapid.
Missouri   Holmes Rapid to .5 miles above Little Dog Rapid.
Missouri   End of SCENIC portion to lower end of Cow Island.

SCENIC:

NF Flathead Canada Border to Camas Bridge
Missouri   Little Dog Rapid to downstream 5 miles
Missouri   Cow Island to James Kipp State Park.

RECREATIONAL:

NF Flathead Camas Bridge to Middle Fork confluence.
MF Flathead Bear Creek to South Fork confluence.
SF Flathead Spotted Bear R. to Hungry Horse Reservoir
Missouri   Fort Benton to .5 miles below Pilot Rock
Missouri   Deadman Rapid to Holmes Rapid

Each river has its own specific rules. On the Flathead sections, WILD or SCENIC means NO MOTORS. RECREATION means up to 10 hp motors. On the Missouri those sections of WILD or SCENIC means WAKELESS SPEED. Detailed information on the Flathead is available from the Flathead Forest Service - Kalispell. Information on the Missouri is available from BLM - Lewistown.

WILDERNESS ACT:

This act insures that the area will remain untrammeled by man, retaining it primeval character and influence, and provide outstanding opportunities for solitude or primitive and unconfined recreation.

Montana Wilderness Areas: National Forest: (Dept. of Agric.)

Absaroka-Beartooth   Custer-Gallatin
Anaconda-Pintler   Beaverhead-Bitterroot-Deer Lodge
Bob Marshall   Flathead-Lewis & Clark (R. Mtn. Div.)
Cabinet Mountains   Kootenai
Gates of the Mountains   Helena
Great Bear   Flathead
Lee Metcalf   Gallatin-Beaverhead
Mission Mountains   Flathead
Rattlesnake   Lolo
Scapegoat   Helena-Lewis & Clark (R. Mtn. Div.)
Selway-Bitterroot   Bitterroot-Lolo
Welcome Creek   Lolo

Numerous restrictions apply, but basically no motorized equipment of any kind allowed. Detailed information available from Forest Service.

WILDLIFE REFUGES:

Benton Lake - North of Great Falls. 12,383 acres
Bowdoin - East of Malta. 15,500 acres
Charles M. Russell and UL Bend - Missouri River near James Kipp State Park. (1976)
         1,100,000 land acres and 245,000 acres Fort Peck Reservoir
Hailstone - 35 miles west of Billings. 1,913 acres and 767 acres of private land. (1942)
Halfbreed - 5 miles south of Hailstone. (1942)
Lake Mason - Northwest of Roundup. (1941) 18,600 acres.
Lee Metcalf - Bitterroot Valley
Medicine Lake - Northeast Montana.
National Bison Range, Ninepipe Reservoir and Pablo - Near Charlo
Red Rock Lakes - On Red Rock River in Centennial Valley. 40,000 acres.
War Horse - Near Winnett. (1958)

Numerous special restrictions apply. Most forms of recreation are permitted. Contact Department of Interior Refuge Office for detailed information.

Bowdoin Wildlife Refuge
    Box J
    Malta, MT 59538
    645-2863

CM Russell Wildlife Refuge
    Box 110
    Lewistown, MT 59457
    538-8706

Lee Metcalf Wildlife Refuge
    Box 257
    Stevensville, MT 59870
    777-5552

Medicine Lake Wildlife Refuge
    HC 53, Box 2
    Medicine Lake, MT 59247
    789-2305

National Bison Range
    Moiese, MT 59824
    644-2211

Red Rock Lakes Wildlife Refuge
    Monida Star Rt. - Box 15
    Lima, MT 59739
    276-3347

INDIAN RESERVATIONS:

Blackfeet	Blackfeet	Browning, MT	338-7179
Crow	Crow	Crow Agency, MT	638-2601
Flathead	Salish-Kootenai	Pablo, MT	675-2700
Fort Belknap	Assiniboine-Gros Ventres	Fort Belknap, MT	353-2205
Fort Peck	Assiniboine-Sioux	Poplar, MT	768-5155
Northern Cheyenne	Northern Cheyenne	Lame Deer, MT	477-6284
Rocky Boy	Chippewa-Cree	Rocky Boy, MT	395-4282

Many restrictions apply. Some activities are available for non-members, others are not. Some reservations have special recreation, hunting, or fishing permits available for non-members to buy. Contact the specific reservation for current details.

Blackfeet Fish, Wildlife & Parks Department
    Browning, MT 59417
    338-7179

Flathead Indian Reservation
    Tribal Fish & Game, Conservation and Recreation Department
    Box 278
    Pablo, MT 59855
    675-2700
    675-4700   Weekends or evenings

Fort Belknap Recreation Department
    Fort Belknap, MT
    353-2205

NATIONAL PARKS:

Glacier and Yellowstone National Parks are under the control of the U.S. Department of Interior. Many special restrictions apply. Contact the respective park (address and phone numbers under Fed. Offices) for detailed current information.

OTHER SPECIAL AGENCIES:

Many areas have special designation with certain rules applicable. Study the maps and talk to local people about special areas!

> Game Ranges
> Primitive Areas
> Preserves
> Natural Landmark areas
> State - Local parks
> Government and Private joint venture areas
> Historical - Geology - Archaeology sites
> Some lakes and reservoirs

National Monuments, Historical & Recreation Sites:
> Bighole National Battlefield - West of Wisdom, MT
> Bighorn Canyon - Wyoming border
> Custer Battlefield - Southeast of Hardin, MT
> Fort Union Trading Post - North Dakota border - Missouri River
> Grant Kohrs Ranch - Historical site - Deer Lodge, MT

Montana State Parks:
> Bannack - Gold mining town - West of Dillon, MT
> Giant Springs - Missouri River springs - Great Falls, MT
> Lewis & Clark Caverns - Limestone caves - East of Whitehall, MT
> Lone Pine - Overlook - West of Kalispell, MT
> Lost Creek - Scenic - North of Anaconda, MT
> Makoshika - Badlands scenery - Glendive, MT
> Medicine Rocks - Sandstone scenery - North of Ekalaka, MT
> Missouri Headwaters - Three rivers join - North of Three Forks, MT
> Ulm Pishkun - Buffalo jump - West of Great Falls, MT
> West Shore - Flathead Lake
> Wild Horse Island - Flathead Lake

Montana State Monuments:
> Beaverhead Rock - Historic landmark - Northeast of Dillon, MT
> Chief Joseph Battleground - South of Chinook, MT
> Chief Plenty Coups - Pryor, MT
> Citadel Rock - Missouri river landmark - East of Fort Benton, MT
> Council Grove - Missoula, MT - Clark Fork River
> Fort Owen - Stevensville, MT
> Greycliff Prairie Dog Town - East of Big Timber, MT
> Madison Buffalo Jump - Southeast of Three Forks, MT
> Natural Bridge - Boulder River landmark - South of Big Timber, MT
> Purgatory Hill - Paleontology site - South of Fort Peck
> Pictograph Cave - Archeology site - Southeast of Billings, MT
> Rosebud Battlefield - South of Busby, MT
> Sluice Boxes - Mining landmark - Southeast of Great Falls, MT

BLACKFOOT RIVER RECREATION CORRIDOR
SPECIAL PUBLIC USE REGULATIONS

By order of the Department of Fish, Wildlife & Parks the attached rules and regulations shall govern the recreational use in the designated Blackfoot River Recreation Corridor for the purpose of gaining recreational privileges on private land.

The designated area for the recreational corridor shall begin at Johnsrud Park, then upstream along the Blackfoot River to the Missoula-Powell County line. The corridor shall also include that portion of the Clearwater River from its confluence with the Blackfoot River upstream to Highway 200

Public access is limited to only the designated areas and a corridor on both sides of the river fifty (50) feet from the normal high water mark.

WHERAS, the public enjoyment of the recreational facilities of these lands necessitates rules, regulations and enforcement of certain protection of property requirements for persons using these facilities for recreational purposes, now, therefore, pursuant to the provisions of 23-1-106 and 87-1-201 M.C.A.:

It is ordered that it shall be unlawful for any person while recreating in the corridor to:

1. Discharge any firearm, fireworks, air or gas weapon, or arrow from a bow, on or over either land or water, except when and where specifically allowed.

2. Permit a pet animal to run at large in a designated public camping area. Persons in possession of pet animals must restrain them and keep them under control on a leash in a manner which does not cause or permit a nuisance or any annoyance or danger to others. The leash may not exceed fifteen (15) feet in length and must be in hand or anchored at all times. Pet animals may not be kept in or permitted to enter areas or portions of areas posted to exclude them. Persons in possession of pet animals who cause or permit said animals to create a nuisance or an annoyance to others or who do not restrain pet animals properly may be expelled from the area in addition to being subject to any other penalty provided. Animals owned or possessed by persons who are not staying in the area will be captured and will not be returned to the owner or possessor until the costs of capture and holding the animal are reimbursed to the Department.

3. Drive vehicle off authorized roads, except onto parking areas provided.

4. Park any vehicle, trailer, camper or other vehicle except in designated parking areas, nor shall any person pitch a tent or build a fire or otherwise set up camp other than in a designated camping area.

5. Maintain occupancy of camping facilities or space in any one designated recreation area for a period longer than seven (7) days during any thirty (30) day period. Such thirty (30) day periods shall run consecutively during the year commencing with the first day each person camps in a designated recreation area each year. No person may leave a set up camp, trailer, camper or other vehicle unattended for more than forty-eight (48) hours unless the area is otherwise posted.

6. Build fires on private land except in designated campsites.

7. Leave a camping area without completely extinguishing all fires started or maintained by such person.

8. Destroy, deface, injure, remove or otherwise damage any natural or improved property (including but not limited to, machinery, buildings, equipment, fences, gates, signs, sprinkler systems and irrigation pumps), or willfully or negligently cut, destroy, or mutilate any tree, including dead trees, shrubs, plants or other geological, historical or archaeological features.

9. Disturb or remove the top soil cover or permit the disturbance or removal of top soil cover, including, but not limited to, digging for worms, burying of garbage and allowing pets to dig holes.

10. Enter upon any portion of the area that is posted as restricted to public passage. Public access along the river corridor is limited to fifty (50) feet from the high water mark except in areas so designated. Adoption of these regulations shall constitute notice to the public that entry upon any property not subject to public access as herein provided shall be deemed a trespass without the necessity of providing any further written or verbal notice.

11. Disturb, harass or otherwise interfere with livestock.

12. Post commercial, political or other unauthorized signs.

13. Use these lands for any commercial purpose without permit.

14. Disorderly conduct such as drunkenness, use of vile or profane language, fighting, indecent exposure, or operation of a motor vehicle in a manner as to create a nuisance or annoyance or danger to others or loud or noisy behavior is prohibited; and in addition to any other penalty provided, the participant may be expelled from the area.

15. No group of more than thirty (30) persons may use a Department administered recreation area except with the prior permission of the director or his agent. Groups may be assessed user fees as determined by the Commission and may be required to surrender a deposit to defray additional or unusual Department expenses caused by their use of recreation areas.

16. The dumping of trash, garbage or litter.

The Montana Department of Fish, Wildlife & Parks, after consultation with and subject to the advance approval of affected landowners, shall have the power to alter present regulations or institute any new regulations deemed necessary for optimum management of the Blackfoot River Recreation Corridor. However, these changes can only be accomplished through the existing Administrative Rules of Montana.

VESSEL

There is no such thing as a perfect all-around vessel. Each design has a special application.

RAFTS:

2 man	3'9" x 6'	(1 person)
4 man	4.5' x 9'	(2 people)
6 man	5.5' x 12'	(3 people)
7 man	6.5' x 12'	(4 people)
10 man	8.0' x 16'	(6 people)
14 man	8.0' x 20'	(8 person pontoon)

Rafts can be lashed together to make floating "islands"

Advantages: Rafts are very forgiving. Good whitewater or comfort vessels. Carry large loads. One person can row or paddle as a group. Rowing frames add oar power and a place for cargo. Can be easily repaired in an hour with small repair kit and portable pump. Some have motor transoms or mounting brackets. Can be horse, back or airplane packed.

Disadvantages: Need inflation, not good in slow water or wind. Big rafts can be difficult to portage or go through shallow boulder gardens.

CANOE (Open):

Advantages: Enchanting, quiet, navigate narrow streams or boulder gardens. Faster than a raft. New FRP (fiberglass reinforced plastic) material is light, has no rivets to leak, and is nearly indestructable. Easy to portage.

Disadvantages: Paddling proficiency necessary. 3 adults normal maximum. Long on curvy streams with brush. Can take in water in waves or whitewater. Learn paddling skills in slow water.

CANOE (Whitewater):

Advantages: More maneuverable in whitewater. Air bags displace water internally, and add floatation. Can be eskimo-rolled like a kayak with proficiency.

Disadvantages: Not as tracking in slow water or lakes. Kneeling on long trips. Lacking cargo space of an open canoe. Usually 1 or 2 paddlers.

CANOE (Square stern): Good all-around vessel. Can be paddled, rowed or use motor. Not as maneuverable as a canoe or as stable as a boat, but adequate.

KAYAK: Great personal adventure! The ultimate whitewater vessel. Very fast and maneuverable. Requires great skill. Strokes, eskimo-roll and wet exits must be learned in still water. Gradually graduating into current and bigger whitewater. Very little room for camp gear for "tripping". Not good in slow water (unless you have 1 or 2 person sea-going kayak, thus losing whitewater capability). Can be pinned in vessel under "strainers".

INFLATABLES: Fun. Can be packed into remote places. Puncture quite easily. Require some paddling skills.

BOAT: More stable and shorter than a canoe. Haul more cargo. Not as maneuverable as a canoe, but can be rowed quite well by going bow facing upstream. A small boat is quite portable and can handle a motor. A 7.5 hp motor will allow some upstream travel in mild current.

DORY: The banana shaped river boat. The high sides allow a fisher to stand up. Very stable and fair whitewater capability. Can be used with or without a motor. Difficult to portage. The ultimate fishing vessel as it requires little draft.

FLOAT TUBE: Great fun and fishing slow water. Dangerous with waders in fast water.

JET BOATS (Tunnel-prop): Great to go upstream. Require little draft. Portaging impossible, but good for big rivers, fishing or for scenic trips for the disabled. Motors are frowned upon by the true floater, so respect must be illustrated. Common for search and rescue.

FEDERAL OFFICES

Bureau of Land Management (MT office)
222 N. 32nd St.
Box 36800
Billings, MT 59107
(406) 255-2938

BLM - District office
P.O. box 1160 - Airport Road
Lewistown, MT 59457
538-7461

BLM - District office
P.O. Box 940
Miles City, MT 59301
232-4331

BLM - District office
Box 3388 - Indust. Park
Butte, MT 59702
494-5059

BLM - Resource Area Offices:
Billings (406)	657-6262
Dillon	683-2337
Glasgow	228-4316
Great Falls	727-0503
Havre	265-5891
Malta	654-1240
Miles City	232-7000
Missoula	329-3914

U.S. Geological Survey - Map Sales
P.O. Box 25286
Denver, CO 80225
(303) 236-7477

U.S. Geological Survey
Fed. Office Bldg.-Room 428-Drawer 10076
301 South Park Ave.
Helena, MT 59626
449-5263

Bureau of Reclamation - Montana
P.O. Box 30137
Billings, MT 59107
657-6202

Clark Canyon	683-6472
Fresno	265-2927
Hungry Horse	387-5241
Tiber	456-3226

U.S. Corp. of Eng. - Missouri R. Div.
Box 103 - Downtown Station
Omaha, Neb. 68101-0103

U.S. Corp. of Eng. - N. Pacific Div.
Box 2870
Portland, OR 97208-2870

U.S. Army Corps of Engineers
P.O. Box 208
Fort Peck, MT 59223
526-3411

Agric. Stab. & Con. Service
35 West Reserve Dr.
Kalispell, MT 59901
752-4896

U.S. Fish & Wildlife Service
P.O. Box 25486
Federal Center
Denver, CO 80225
(303) 236-8148

U.S. Customs Service
Glacier International Airport
Kalispell, MT 59901
(406) 257-7034

U.S. Geological Survey
1013 Hwy. 2 East
Kalispell, MT 59901
755-6686

Soil Conservation Office
(406) 587-4843

Int. Dept. - Bonneville Power
Kerr Dam
Polson, MT 59860
883-5872

Nat. Park Service (Rocky Mtn. Div.)
12795 W. Alameda Parkway
Denver, CO 80225-0281
(303) 969-2504

Glacier Nat. Park (U.S. Dept. Int.)
West Glacier, MT 59936
(406) 888-5441

Yellowstone National Park
Park Headquarters
Yellowstone Nat. Park, WY 82190
(307) 344-7381

Water & Power Resource Service
Dept. of the Interior
Box 11568
Salt Lake City, UT 84111

Water & Power Resource Service
Dept. of the Interior
Box 2553
Billings, MT 59103

Office of Equal Opportunity
U.S. Department Interior
Washington, D.C. 20240

NATIONAL FOREST SERVICE (U.S. Dept. Agric.)

Northern Region Headquarters
P.O. Box 7669
Missoula, MT 59807
(406) 329-3511

Beaverhead National Forest
610 North Montana
Box 1258 Dillon, MT 59725
683-3900

Ranger District:	
Madison-Ennis, MT 59729	682-4253
Sheridan-Sheridan, MT 59749	842-5432
Wisdom-Wisdom, MT 59761	689-3243
Wise River-W.R., MT 59762	832-3178

Bitterroot National Forest
316 N. Third St.
Hamilton, MT 59840
363-3131

Ranger District:	
Darby-Darby, MT 59829	682-3913
Stevensville-St., MT 59870	777-5461
Sula-Sula, MT 59871	832-3201
West Fork-Darby, MT 59762	821-3269

Custer National Forest
2602 First Ave. N.
Box 2556
Billings, MT 59103
657-6361

Ranger District:	
Ashland-Billings 59103	784-2344
Beartooth-Billings 59103	446-2103
Sioux-Billings 59103	657-6361

Deer Lodge National Forest
Federal Building
Box 400
Butte, MT 59703
496-3400

Ranger District:	
Butte-Butte, MT 59701	494-2147
Deer Lodge-D.L., MT 59722	846-1770
Jefferson-Whitehall, 59759	287-3223
Philipsbrug-P-burg 59858	859-3211

Flathead National Forest
P.O. Box 147
1935 3rd Ave. E.
Kalispell, MT 59901
755-5401
758-5368 (Rec. Recording)

Ranger District:
Glacier View-CF 59912   892-4372
Hungry Horse-HH 59919   387-5243
Spotted Bear-HH 59919   752-7345
Swan Lake-BF 59911   837-5081
Tally Lake-WF 59937   862-2508

Gallatin National Forest
Federal Building
Box 130
Bozeman, MT 59715
587-6701

Ranger District:
Big Timber-B.T., MT 59011   932-5155
Bozeman-Boze., MT 59715   587-6920
Gardiner-Gard., MT 59030   848-7375
Hebgen L.-W. Yellow, MT 59758 646-7369
Livingston-Living., MT 59047   222-1892

Helena National Forest
Fed. Bldg. Room 334-Drawer 10014
301 South Park
Helena, MT 59626
449-5201

Ranger District:
Helena-Helena 59601   449-5490
Lincoln-Lincoln 59639   362-4265
Townsend-Townsend 59644   266-3425

Kootenai National Forest
506 Hwy # 2 W.
Libby, MT 59923
293-8861

Ranger District:
Cabinet-Trout Cr., 59874   847-2462
Fisher River-LIbby 59923   293-7773
Fortine-Fortine 59918   882-4451
Libby-Libby 59923   293-7741
Rexford-Eureka 59917   295-4693
Yaak-Troy 59935   295-4717

Lolo National Forest
Fort Missoula - Bldg. 24
Missoula, MT 59801
329-3750

Ranger District:
Ninemile-Huson 59846   626-5201
Plains-Plains 59859   826-3821
Seeley Lake-SL 59868   677-2233
Superior-Sup. 59872   822-4233
Thompson Falls-59873   827-3589

MONTANA - FISH, WILDLIFE and PARKS

MT. Dept. of FWP - State Headquarters
1420 East 6th Ave.
Helena, MT 59620
(406) 444-2535

MT Dept. FWP - Region 1
490 N. Meridian Rd.
Kalispell, MT 59901
752-5501

MT Dept. FWP - Region 2
3201 Spurgin Rd.
Missoula, MT 59801
542-5500

MT Dept. FWP - Region 3
1400 S. 19th
Bozeman, MT 59715
994-4042

MT Dept. FWP - Region 4
4600 Giant Springs Rd.
Great Falls, MT 59406
454-3441

MT Dept. FWP - Region 5
2300 Lake Elmo Drive
Billings, MT 59105
252-4654

MT Dept. FWP - Region 6
Route 1 - 4210
Glasgow, MT 59230
228-9347

MT Dept. FWP - Region 7
RR1 - box 2004
Miles City, MT 59301
232-4365

MT Dept. FWP - Region 8
1404 - 8th Ave.
Helena, MT 59620
444-4720

MONTANA - STATE LANDS

Montana Dept. of State Lands
1625 11th Ave.
Helena, MT 59620
(406) 444-2074

Area Offices:

Central Land Office
8001 N. Mont. Ave.
Helena, MT 59601
444-3633
Eastern Land Office
Box 1794
321 Main St.
Miles City, MT 59301
232-2034
NE Land Office
Box 12021
USDA Bldg. - 613 NE Main
Lewistown, MT 59457
538-5989
Southern Land Office
528 S. Moore Lane
Billings, MT 59101
259-3264
SW Land Office
1401 27th Ave.
Missoula, MT 59801
542-4200

Unit Offices:

Anaconda (406)	563-6078
Bozeman	586-5243
Clearwater	793-5757
Conrad	278-7869
Dillon	683-6305
Glasgow	228-2430
Hamilton	363-1585
Helena	444-3633
Libby	293-2711
Lincoln	362-4999
Missoula	542-4201
Plains	826-3791
Stillwater	881-2371
Swan River	654-2301

Forestry Div. Headquarters
705 Spurgin Road
Missoula, MT 59801
542-4300

Montana State Div. of Forestry
2350 Hwy # 93 N.
Kalispell, MT 59901
756-6575

Dept. Natural Resources & Conser.
32 S. Ewing
Helena, MT 59620
444-6601

Field Offices:

Billings	657-2105
Bozeman	586-3136
Glasgow	228-2561
Havre	265-5516
Kalispell	752-2288
Lewistown	538-7459
Miles City	232-6359
Missoula	721-4284

MONTANA COUNTIES (56)
c/o Court House

Beaverhead Co.	Dillon, MT	59725
Bighorn	Hardin	59034
Blaine	Chinook	59523
Broadwater	Townsend	59644
Carbon	Red Lodge	59068
Carter	Ekalaka	59324
Cascade	Great Falls	59401
Chouteau	Fort Benton	59442
Custer	Miles City	59301
Daniels	Scobey	59263
Dawson	Glendive	59330
Deer Lodge	Anaconda	59711
Fallon	Baker	59313
Fergus	Lewistown	59457
Flathead	Kalispell	59901
Gallatin	Bozeman	59715
Garfield	Jordan	59337
Glacier	Cut Bank	59427
Golden Valley	Ryegate	59047
Granite	Phillipsburg	59858
Hill	Havre	59501
Jefferson	Boulder	59632
Judith Basin	Stanford	59479
Lake	Polson	59860
Lewis & Clark	Helena	59601
Liberty	Chester	59522
Lincoln	Libby	59923
McCone	Circle	59215
Madison	Virginia City	59755
Meagher	While Sulphur Springs	59645
Mineral	Superior	59872
Missoula	Missoula	59801
Musselshell	Roundup	59072
Park	Livingston	59047
Petroleum	Winnett	59087
Phillips	Malta	59538
Pondera	Conrad	59425
Powder River	Broadus	59317
Powell	Deer Lodge	59722
Prairie	Terry	59349
Ravalli	Hamilton	59840
Richland	Sidney	59270
Roosevelt	Wolf Point	59201
Rosebud	Forsyth	59327
Sanders	Thompson Falls	59873
Sheridan	Plentywood	59254
Silverbow	Butte	59701
Stillwater	Columbus	59019
Sweetgrass	Big Timber	59011
Teton	Choteau	59422
Toole	Shelby	59474
Treasure	Hysham	59038
Valley	Glasgow	59230
Wheatland	Harlowton	59036
Wibaux	Wibaux	59353
Yellowstone	Billings	59100

MONTANA

Montana Chamber of Commerce
  Box 1730
  Helena, MT 59624
  (406) 442-2405

Montana Travel Promotion
  1424 9th Ave.
  Helena, MT 59620
  444-2654
  800-541-1447

Montana Magazine
  Box 5630
  Helena, MT 59601

Montana Historical Society
  225 N. Roberts
  Helena, MT 59620
  449-3770

Glacier Natural Hist. Assoc.
  Box 428
  West Glacier, MT 59936
  888-5441

Yellowstone Hist. Assoc.
  Box 117
  Yellowstone N.P., WY 82180
  307-344-2349

Montana Outfitters & Guides Assoc.
  Box 9070
  Helena, MT 59604
  449-3578

Montana Board of Outfitters
  Dept. of Commerce
  111 N. Jackson
  Helena, MT 59620
  444-3738

Fishing Outfitters-Assoc. of Montana
  Box 67
  Gallatin Gateway, MT 59730
  763-4761

Montana Campground Assoc.
  Box 215
  West Glacier, MT 59936

Montana Power Co.   800-247-9131

Travel Montana
  Room 259
  Deer Lodge, MT 59722
  800-541-1447

Bureau of Mines & Geology
  Montana Tech. - Main Hall
  Butte, MT 59701
  494-4167

Dept. of Geology
  Univ. of Montana
  Missoula, MT 59801

Dept. of Earth Sciences
  Montana State Univ.
  Bozeman, MT 59717

Montana Dept. of Transportation
  2701 Prospect Ave.
  Helena, MT 59620
  444-6200
  444-6339 (Recording)

Montana Highway Patrol
  303 N. Roberts
  Helena, MT 59620
  444-7000

Area Road Reports:	800-332-6171
Billings	252-2806
Bozeman	586-1313
Butte	494-3666
Glasgow	245-6193
Glendive	365-2314
Great Falls	453-1605
Havre	265-1416
Helena	444-6354
Kalispell	755-4949
Lewistown	538-7445
Miles City	232-2099
Missoula	728-8553
Wolf Point	653-1692

National Weather Service 449-5204

Disaster & Emergency 911

OUT-OF-STATE INFORMATION

Division of Economic & Comm. Affairs
State Capitol Bldgs. - 108
Boise, Idaho 83720
(208) 334-2470
800-635-7820

Idaho Dept. of Fish & Game
600 S. Walnut - Box 25
Boise, Idaho 83707

North Dakota Tourism Promotion
Liberty Mem. Bldg. - Capitol
Bismarck, N. Dak. 58505
(701) 224-2525
800-437-2077

North Dakota Game & Fish Dept.
100 N. Bismarck Expressway
Bismarck, N. Dak. 58501-5095
(701) 221-6300

South Dakota Div. of Tourism
Box 6000
Pierre, S. Dak. 57501
(605) 773-3301
800-843-1930

South Dakota Game, Fish & Parks Dept.
445 E. Capitol
Pierre, S. Dak. 57501

Wyoming Game & Fish Dept.
5400 Bishop Blvd.
Cheyenne, WY 82009

Alberta Energy-Forestry-Lands & Wildlife
Info. Centre
9920-108 St.
Edmonton, Alberta Canada T5K2M4

Ministry of Tourism
Parliament Bldgs.
Victoria, B.C. Canada V8V 1X4

Tourism Saskatchewan
Trade & Convention Centre
1919 Sask. Drive
Regina, Sask. Canada S4P 3V7

DISABLED

Dream
1st & Main Bldg. - Box 1058
Kalispell, MT 59903
752-6565

Eagle Mount
6901 Goldenstein Lane
Bozeman, MT 59715
586-1781

Accent on Living
Box 700
Bloomington, IL 61702

American Canoe Association
7432 Albon Station Blvd.
Suite B-226
Springfield, Virginia 22150
703-451-0141

Camp ASCCA - Easter Seals
Box 21
Jackson Gap, AL 36861
205-825-9226

Chairshooters - Dr. Hugo Keim
Silver Dollar Ranch #38
17000 Patterson Road
Odessa, FL 33556
813-920-2737

Disabled Boaters and Campers News
Box 173
Lyons, IL 60534

Disabled Outdoors Magazine
2052 W. 23rd St.
Chicago, IL 60608
708-358-4160

Paralized Veterans of America
801 18th St. N.W.
Washington, D.C. 20006
202-USA-1300

Special K Ranch
Box 372
Billings, MT 59103
406-255-7476

Mt. Independent Living Project
38 S. Last Chance Gulch
Helena, MT 59601
442-5755

Summit Independent Living Center
1280 S. 3rd West
Missoula, MT 59801
728-1630

Fishing Has No Boundaries
Box 375
Hagward, Wis. 54843
715-634-3185

Ntl. Assoc. Handicapped Sportsmen
R.R. 6 - Box 25
Centralia, IL 62801
618-532-4565

National Wheelchair Shooting Fed.
3595 E. Fountain Blvd.
Suite L-1
Colorado Springs, CO 80910
719-574-1150

Outdoor Buddies
Box 37283
Denver, CO 80237
303-771-8216

Outdoors Forever
Box 4832
East Lansing, Mich 48823
517-337-0018

Palaestra
Box 508
Macomb, IL 61455
309-833-1902

Shake-A-Leg
Box 1002
Newport, RI 02840
401-849-8898

Wilderness Inquiry
1313 Fifth St. S.E.
Box 84
Minneapolis, MN 55414
800-728-0719

MONTANA and its HISTORY

Montana (Mountainous in Spanish)
      "Treasure State" - "Big Sky Country" - "Land of Shining Mountains"
      Capitol: Helena (since 1875) - Virginia City (1865-1875) - Bannack (1864-65)
      Area: 147,138 sq. mi. (1,746 sq. mi. of inland water) - 550 mi. long - 275 mi. wide - 4th largest state.
      Elevation: Highest - Granite Peak (Park Co.) 12,799'
                     Lowest - Kootenai River (at Idaho border) 1800'
      Population: 799,065 (1990 census) - 5.4 people per sq. mi. ave. - 12,375 person growth in 10 years.

Flower:	Bitterroot (Lewisia rediviva)
Bird:	Western Meadowlark (Sturnella neglecta)
Tree:	Ponderosa Pine (Pinus ponderosa)
Gemstone:	Agate and Sapphire
Grass:	Bluebunch Wheatgrass (Agropyron spicatum)
Fish:	Blackspotted Cutthroat Trout (Salmo clarkii)
Animal:	Grizzly Bear (Ursus Arctos horribilis)
Fossil:	Duck-billed Dinosaur (Maiasaura peeblesorum)
Motto:	ORO Y PLATA (1893) Spanish for Gold and Silver
Song:	"Montana" (by Cohan & Howard)

1803 - Eastern Montana became U.S. Territory through Louisiana Purchase.
1805 - Lewis & Clark Expedition began.
1807 - Trapping gained popularity
1846 - NW Montana became part of US - Oregon Treaty with England.
1860 - Cattle ranching began
1862 - Gold rush began
1864 - Congress established Montana Territory
1872 - Yellowstone National Park
1876 - General Custer defeat
1880 - Utah and Northern Railroads entered Montana
1883 - Northern Pacific crossed Montana
1889 - Montana statehood - 11/8/1889 - 41st state - First governor J.K. Toole
1910 - Congress established Glacier National Park
1937 - Fort Peck Dam completed

DAMS & RESERVOIRS

MONTANA POWER CO.

Hebgen (1915)	Madison River
Madison (1906)	Madison River
Hauser (1911)	Missouri River
Holter (1918)	Missouri River
Black Eagle (1891)	Missouri River
Rainbow (1910)	Missouri River
Cochrane (1958)	Missouri River
Ryan (1915)	Missouri River
Morony (1930)	Missouri River
Mystic (1925)	West Rosebud (Stillwater)
Flint Cr. (1897)	Georgetown Lake
Milltown (1906)	Clark Fork River
Thompson Falls (1915)	Clark Fork River
Kerr (1938)	Flathead River
Bigfork	Swan River

WASHINGTON POWER CO.

Cabinet Gorge   Clark Fork River
Noxon   Clark Fork River

BUREAU OF RECLAMATION - CORPS OF ENGINEERS

Anita Reservoir (irrig.)
Barretts (1963) (irrig.) Beaverhead River
Bitterroot River Projects (irrig.)
Clark Canyon (1964) (irrig.) Beaverhead River
Clarks Fork (Yellowstone) Projects (irrig.)
Como (1910) (irrig.)
Divide (water supply) (1898) Bighole River
Fort Peck (1937) (elect.) Missouri River (Corps of Engineers)
Frenchman (irrig.) Frenchman River
Frenchtown (1937) (irrig.) Clark Fork River
Fresno (1939) (irrig.) Milk River
Hubbart (irrig.) Little Bitterroot River
Huntley (irrig.) Yellowstone River
Libby (elect.) (1972) Kootenai River (Cors of Engineers)
Lima (irrig.) Red Rock River
Milk River Projects (irrig.)
Musselshell River Projects (irrig.)
Red Rocks Lake (irrig. - refuge) Red Rock River
Ruby (irrig.) Ruby River
Sun River Projects (1927) (irrig.)
Teton River Projects (irrig.)
Tiber (Elwell) (1956) (irrig.) Marias River
Tongue (irrig.) Tongue River
Toston (1954) (irrig.) Missouri River
Troy (water supply) Lake Creek
Two Medicine (irrig.) Two Medicine River
Yellowstone River Projects (1909) (irrig.)

Bureau of Rec. (Reservoirs supervised by):

    MT Department of Fish, Wildlife & Parks:

        Canyon Ferry (1954) (elect.) Missouri River
        Greenfields (Freezeout) (irrig. - refuge)
        Helena Valley (irrig.)
        Intake (irrig.) (1947) Yellowstone River
        Nelson Reservoir (1915) (irrig.)
        Pishkun (irrig.)
        Sleeping Buffalo (irrig.)
        Willow Creek (irrig.)

    National Forest Service:

        Gibson (1913) (irrig.) Sun River
        Hungry Horse (1953) (elect.) South Fork Flathead River

    National Park Service:

        Sherburne (irrig.) (1921) Swiftcurrent River
        Yellowtail (Bighorn) (1966) (elect.) Bighorn River

CAMPGROUNDS - ACCESS SITES

Map Coordinates	Site Name	Directions	Camping	Day use only	Trailers	Toilets	Water	Boat Launch	Fishing	Swimming	Trails	Stay Limit	Fee	Season	Handicapped
H7	Absaroka FAS	1 1/2 miles W of Absarokee on Secondary and Country Rds.	•		•	•		A	•						
E7	Ackley Lake FAS	17 miles W of Lewistown, milepost 58 at Hobson, then 5 miles S on Secondary 400, then 2 miles SW on Cty. Rd.	•		•	•	•	C	•	•		14	•		
G2	Alta FS	4 miles S of Darby on U.S. 93, then 22 miles S on Cty. Rd. 473, then 6 miles S on Cty. Rd. 96	15		•	•	•					10	•	6/1-9/15	
F10	Amelia Island FAS	1 mile N of Hysham's Main Street on County Road						C	•						
F8	Anita Reservoir USBR	4 miles S of I-94 Pompeys Pillar exit	•					A	•			14			
G9	Arapooish FAS	1/2 mile N of Hardin on Mt. 47, then 1 mile E on County Road.		•				C	•	•					
C4	Arod Lake FAS	1 mi. E of Choteau on Secondary 221, then 6 mi. N on Secondary 220, then 5 mi. E on County Rd, then 6 1/2 miles N on County Rd,	•		•	•		B	•			14			
B2	Ashley Lake SRA	16 miles W of Kalispell on U.S. 2, milepost 15, then 13 miles N on County Rd. (Trailers not recommended)	12		•	•	•	C	•	•		7	•	5/15-9/15	
E6	Aspen FS	5 miles N of Neihart on Mt. 89	6		•	H	•			•		14	•	6/1-10/15	
E4	Aspen Grove FS	7 miles E of Lincoln on Mt. 200	25		•	•	•			•		14	•	6/1-9/30	
G5	Axtell Bridge FAS	10 miles S of Belgrade on U.S 191, milepost 77, then 1 mile W on Axtell Road.	•		•	•		A	•			14			
B1	Bad Medicine FS	3 mi. SE of Troy on U.S. 2, then 19 mi. S on Mt. 56, then 1 mi. W on For. Rd. 398, then 1 mi. N on For. Rd. 7170	11		•	•	•	•		•		15	•	5/20-9/30	
I5	Bakers Hole FS	3 miles N of West Yellowstone on U.S. 191	72		•	H	•			•		15	•	6/1-9/15	
H3	Bannack SP	5 miles S of Dillon on I-15, then 21 miles W on Secondary 278, then 4 miles S on County Road.	•		•	•			•			14			
H7	Basin FS	1 mile S of Red Lodge on U.S. 212, then 7 miles W on For. 71.	28		•	•	•			•		10	•	6/15-9/15	•
F4	Basin Canyon FS	4 miles NW of Basin on For. Rd. 172	12		•	•						14		6/1-9/15	
G8	Battle Ridge FS	21 miles NE of Bozeman on Mt. 293	13		•	•	•					14		6/10-9/30	
D4	Bean Lake FAS	15 miles S of Augusta, on Secondary 434	•		•	•		c	•			14			
C10	Bear Creek CE	11 miles SE of Fort Peck on 24 - 7 miles W.	•		•	•				•		14			
F2	Bear Creek Pass FS	7 miles N of Darby on U.S. 93, then 18 miles W on For. Rd. 429.	5		•	•						10		7/15-9/15	
B7	Bear Paw Lake FAS	17 miles S of Havre on Secondary 234.	•		•	•		A	•			7			
E5	Beartooth SRA	2 miles W of Wolf Creek on Recreation Road, across bridge, then 3 miles E and 5 miles S on the Cty. Rd.	•		•	•	•	C	•	•		14	•		
I5	Beaver Creek FS	8 miles N of West Yellowstone on U.S. 191, then 17 miles W on U.S. 287	63		•	•	•					15	•	6/1-9/15	
F4	Beaver Dam FS	7 miles W of Butte - 18 miles S and 6 miles west.	•		•	•	•			•		14		5/15-11/15	
H7	Beaver Lodge FAS	7 miles N of Red Lodge on U.S. 212, then 1/4 mile E on county road, then 1 1/4 miles N on county road	•		•					•					
E3	Beavertail Hill SRA	26 miles SE of Missoula on I-90 to milepost 130 Beavertail Hill Exit, then 1/4 mile S on county Road.	25		•	F	•	A	•			14	•	4/15-9/15	
F2	Bell Crossing FAS	2 miles N of Victor in U.S. 93, then 1/2 mile E on Secondary 370.		•				A	•						
D4	Benchmark FS	30 miles W of Augusta on Benchmark Rd. 235.	32		•	•	•			•		14	•	6/1-11/15	
C2	Big Arm SRA	12 miles N of Polson on U.S. 93, milepost 74 (ramp suitable for sailboats).	35		8		•	C	•	•		7	•	5/19-9/15	
A2	Big Creek FS	21 miles N of Columbia Falls	20		•	•	•	A	•			14	•	6/1-9/30	•
G3	Big Hole Battlefield NB	12 miles W. of Wisdom on Mt. 43.		•		•	•			•					
H9	Big Horn FAS	29 mile S of Hardin on Secondary 313.	•		8	8		C	•						
F3	Big Horn FS	15 miles W of Phillipsburg on Mt. 348, or 5 miles SE of Clinton on I-90 , then 8 miles S on For. Rd. 102	6									14		5/20-9/30	
G9	**Bighorn Canyon:**														
	Afterbay NPS	1 mile NE of Yellowtail Dam	48		•	H	•	C	•		N	14			
	Barrys NPS	27 miles N of Lovell, Wyoming.	9		•	H		C	•		•	14			
D3	Big Larch FS	2 miles NW of Seeley Lake on Mt. 83	50		•	•	•	•	•	•	•	14	•	5/15-10/15	•
E3	Big Nelson FS	7 miles E of Ovando on Mt. 200, then 12 miles NE on For. Rd. 500	11		•	•				•		14	•	6/15-9/15	
E2	Big Pine FAS	18 miles S of Superior on I-90 to Fish Creek Exit, then 5 miles NW on County Road.	10		•	•				•		7			
G7	Big Rock FAS	1/2 mile E of Big Timber on U.S. 10, then 4 miles S on county road on E side of Boulder River	•		•	•		A	•						
A2	Big Therriault FS	3 mi. NW of Fortine on U.S. 93, then 3 mi. NE on Cty. Rd. 14, then 11 mi. NE on For. Rd. 114, then 9 mi. W on For. Rd. 319	11		•	•			•	•	•	14		6/15-10/1	
C2	Bigfork FAS	Montana 35 at Bigfork, milepost 31 under bridge on south side.		•		•	•	C	•						
H9	Bighorn Canyon NRA	Entrances at Ft. Smith and from Lovell, Wy via Wy 37.													
	Afterbay NPS	1 1/2 miles S of Fort Smith	48		•	•	•	•	•		N	14		all year	
F8	Billings Mem FS	4 miles S of Darby 13 miles SW Rt. 473 and 1 mile NW	11		•	•				•		10		6/1-9/15	
F3	Bitterroot Flat FS	5 miles SE of Clinton on I-90, then 23 miles S on For. Rd. 102	16		•	•	•			•		14		5/26-9/10	
B2	Bitterroot Lake SRA	20 miles W of Kalispell on U.S. 2, milepost 101, then 5 miles N.	20			H	•	C	•	•		14	•	5/15-9/15	
B9	Bjomberg Bridge FAS	8 miles W of Hinsdale on Mt. 2, then 4 miles N on County Road to Milk River, then across bridge.	8					A	•						
B7	Black Bear FS	3 miles S of Hamilton on U.S. 93, then 13 miles E on Mt. 38	10		•	•	•					10		6/1-9/15	
E5	Black Sandy SRA	7 miles N of Helena on I-15, then 4 miles E on Secondary 453, then 3 miles N.	•			H	•	C	•	•		•	•	5/15-9/15	
H6	Blackmore FS	8 miles S of Bozeman on Cty. Rd. 243, then 9 miles SE on For. Rd. 62.	11		•	•	•			•		14	•	6/15-9/15	

350

CAMPGROUNDS - ACCESS SITES

Map Coordinates	Site Name	Directions	Camping	Day use only	Trailers	Toilets	Water	Boat Launch	Fishing	Swimming	Trails	Stay Limit	Fee	Season	Handicapped
G5	Black's Ford FAS	23 miles W of Bozeman on Mt. 84.	•			•		A	•			14			
B2	Blanchard Lake FAS	2 miles S of Whitefish on U.S. 93, milepost 125, then 3 miles W on County Road.	•	•				C	•						
H8	Bluewater FAS	30 miles S of Laurel on U.S. 310 to milepost 32 at Fromberg, then 9 miles SE on County Road.				•			•						
C10	Bonetrail CE	60 miles SW of Fort Peck.	•		•	•		B	•	•		14			
G2	Boulder Creek FS	4 miles S of Darby on U.S. 93, then 13 miles SW on Cty. Rd. 473, then 1 mile NW on For. Rd. 5631.	12	•	•							10		6/1-9/15	
G6	Boulder Forks FAS	17 miles S of Big Timber on Secondary 298.	•			•		A							
G5	Bozeman Pond FAS	U.S. 191, W edge of Bozeman, milepost 87.		•		•			•	•					
H4	Branham Lakes FS	14 miles E of Sheridan on Mill Cr. Rd.	6	•		•			•	•		•	14		7/1-9/15	
G7	Bratten FAS	16 miles E of Big Timber on Secondary 298.	•		•	H		C	•						
H8	Bridger Bend FAS	30 miles S of Laurel on U.S. 310 to Bridger, then 13 miles S on Mt. 72.	•					A	•						
G8	Broadview Pond FAS	25 miles N of Billings on Mt. 3 at Broadview.	•					C	•						
G4	Browne's Lake FAS	8 miles S of Melrose on I-15, Glen Exit, then 7 miles W on County Road.	•		•	•		D	•			14			
E3	Browns Lake FAS	10 miles SE of Ovando on County Road.	•		•	•		C	•			14			
H7	Buffalo Jump FAS	21 miles SW of Absaroke on secondary 419.	•		•	•		A	•						
G8	Buffalo Mirage FAS	7 miles E of Laurel on I-90 at Park City Exit, then 6 miles SE on County Road.	•		•	•		B	•						
C7	Buffalo Wallow Res. BLM	U.S. 191 N of Lewistown to Junction with Montana 19, then 7 mi. N on U.S. 191, then 14 mi. E on Wilder Trail.	•		•	•			•					5/1-10/30	
B1	Bull River FS	6 miles NW of Noxon on Mt. 200.	18	•		•	•			•				5/1-10/30	•
H7	Bull Springs FAS	7 miles N of Red Lodge on U.S. 212 at milepost 77, then E on county Road 1/4 mile.	•			•			•						
H5	Burnt Tree Hole	1 mile W of Ennis on Montana 287, then 2 miles S on County Road.	•		•	•		C	•			14			
C4	Bynum Reservoir FAS	14 miles N of Choteau on U.S. 89 to Bynum, then 4 miles W on couty Road, then 1 mile S.	•		•	•		B	•			14			
D1	Cabin City FS	3 miles SE of Deborgia on I-90, then 2 miles NE on For. Rd. 977, then .2 mile N on For. Rd. 352.	24	•	•	•	•			•		•	14	•	5/28-9/11	
I5	Cabin Creek FS	8 miles N of West Yellowstone on U.S. 191, then 15 miles W on U.S. 287	15	•	•	•	•			•		•	14	•	6/1-9/15	
F3	Cable Mountain FS	12 miles S of Phillipsburg on U.S. 10A, then 3 miles N on For. Rd. 676, then 1 mile S on For. Rd.8617.	11	•	•	•	•			•			14		6/15-9/30	
G5	Cameron Bridge FAS	2 miles S of Belgrade on Mt. 85, at milepost 5, then 2 miles W on West Cameron Bridge Road.	•		•	•		A	•			14			
E5	Camp Baker FAS	13 miles NW of White Sullphur Spring on Secondary 360 at milepost 126, then 10 miles N on Couty Road.	•		•	•		A	•			14			
C8	Camp Creek BLM	1 mile NE of Zortman on Cty. Rd.	9	•	•	•				•			14			
G9	Captain Clark FAS	8 miles W of Custer on the Frontage Road. (no facilities)	•					A	•						
G5	Carbella BLM	20 miles N of Gardiner.	10	•					B	•			14			
G4	Cardwell FAS	1 mile S of Cardwell on Secondary 359.	5	•	•				B	•			14			
H6	Carter's Bridge FAS	3 miles S of Livingston on U.S. 89, then 1 mile E on Secondary 540.	•		•			B	•			14			
D2	Cascade FS	3 miles SE of Paradise on Mt. 200, then 6 miles SW on For. Rd. 3836.	12		H	•			•	•	•	14	•	5/15-10/31	
H7	Cascade FS	2 miles S of Red Lodge on U.S. 212, then 10 miles W on For. Rd. 71.	30	•	•	•			•			10	•	6/15-9/15	
D5	Cascade Bridge SRA	Highway 330.													
H7	Castle Rock FAS	23 miles W of Absarokee on Secondary 420.	•		•	•		A	•						
E5	Causeway FAS	7 miles N of Helena on I-15 at milepost 200, then 5 miles E on Secondary 453.	•		H			A	•						
C4	Cave Mountain FS	6 miles W of Choteau on U.S. 89, then 25 miles W on For. Rd. 144.	14	•	•	•			•		•	14	•	6/1-11/15	
E5	Cemetery Island SRA	Canyon Ferry (Boat access only.)	•		•			•							
E5	Chalet SRA	9 miles E of Helena on U.S. 287, then 8 miles NE on Sec. 284 to Yacht Basin, then 1/2 miles S on gravel road (Group use area)	•		H				•	•				All Year	
E2	Charles Waters FS	2 miles NW of Stevensville on Cty. Rd 269, then 4 miles N on U.S. 93, then 2 miles W on Cty. Rd. 22, then 1 mile W on For. Rd. 1316.	18	•	H	•			•	•		14	•	5/1-9/30	
H6	Chicory FAS	18 miles S of Livingston on Secondary 540, then 1 mile W on County Road.	•					A	•						
B7	Chief Joseph SM	16 miles S of Chinook on Secondary 240.	•		•										
H7	Chief Joseph FS	5 miles E of Cooke City on U.S. 212	6	•	•	•			•		•	15	•	7/1-9/10	
E2	Chief Looking Glass FAS	14 miles S of Missoula on U.S. 93 to milepost 77, then 2 miles E on Couty Road.	25	•	•	•		A	•			7			
H8	Chief Plenty Coups SM	1 mile W of Pryor on County Road.		•		H			•		N				
E5	Chinaman's SRA	Canyon Fery 9 miles E of Helena on U.S. 287 at milepost 55, then 10 miles NE on Sedonary 284.	•		•	•		C	•	•		•		5/15-9/15	
G6	Chippy Park FS	25 miles S of Big Timber on then, 10 miles S on 212.	7	•	H	•			•	•		15			
G5	Chisolm FS	8 miles S of Bozeman.	9	•	H	•			•	•		15	•	6/1-9/15	
C6	Citadel Rock SM	On Wild and Scenic Missouri River NE of Geraidine. (No vehicle access.)	•					•							
H3	**Clark Canyon:**														
	Barretts USBR	5 miles S of Dillon on I-15	•		•	H	•	B	•			14			•
	Beaverhead USBR	At Reservoir	•		•	H	•	C	•			14			•

CAMPGROUNDS - ACCESS SITES

Map Coordinates	Site Name	Directions	Camping	Day use only	Trailers	Toilets	Water	Boat Launch	Fishing	Swimming	Trails	Stay Limit	Fee	Season	Handicapped
	Cameahwait USBR	At Reservoir	•			•	H	•		•		14			
	Fish Access USBR	AT Reservoir	•			•	H	•	C	•		14			•
	hap Hawkins USBR	At Reservoir	•			•	H	•		•		14			
	Horse Prairie USBR	At Reservoir	•			•	H	•	C	•		14			•
	Lewis & Clark USBR	At Reservoir	•			•	H	•		•		14			
	Lone Tree USBR	At Reservoir	•			•	H	•	B	•		14			•
	West Cameahwait USBR	At Reservoir	•			•	H	•		•		14			
C1	Clark Memorial FS	5 miles E of Thompson Falls on Mt. 200, then 5 miles NE on For. Rd. 56.	5		•					•		14		6/1-9/30	
E3	Clearwater Crossing FAS	31 miles E. of Bonner on Montana 200 at milepost 31.	•		•	•				•		7			
I5	Cliff Point FS	12 miles N of West Yellowstone on U.s. 191, then 27 miles W on Mt. 449, then 4 miles S on Mt. 287, then 7 miles W on For. Rd. 5721.	6		•	•	•			•		•	14		6/15-9/15	
H7	Cliff Swallow FAS	10 miles W of Absarokee on Secondary 420.	•		•	•		A	•						
C8	Coal Banks Landing SRA	20 miles N of Fort Benton on U.S. 87 to milepost 67, then 8 miles S on county road.	•		•	•	•	C	•			14			
G5	Cobblestone FAS	3 miles W of Logan on U.S. 10, then 7 miles S on Madison River Road.	6		•			A	•			14			
B9	Cole Ponds FAS	7 miles N of Saco on Secondary 243, to end of pavement, then 6 miles W on County Road.	•	•				A	•						
H7	Colter FS	3 Miles E of Cooke City on U.S. 212.	23		•	•	•			•		•	15	•	7/1-9/10	
F5	Confederate SRA	Canyon Ferry, 2 miles E of Townsend on U.S. 12 at milepost 2, then 18 miles N on Secondary 284.	•		•	•		A	•						
H7	Cooney SRA	22 miles SW of Laurel at Boyd, milepost 90, then 5 miles W on county road.	•		•	H	•	C	•	•			•		
E4	Copper Creek FS	7 miles E of Lincoln in Mt. 200, then 9 miles NW on For. Rd. 330	20		•	•	•			•			14	•	6/15-9/30	
F3	Copper Creek FS	6 miles S of Phillipsburg on U.S. 10A, then 9 miles SW on Mt. 38, then 10 miles S on For. Rd. 80.	7		•	•	•			•			14		6/15-9/30	
C1	Copper King FS	5 miles E of Thompson Falls on Mt. 200, then 4 miles NE on For. Rd. 56	5		•	•				•					6/1-9/30	
H6	Corwin Springs FAS	48 miles S of Livingston on U.S. 89, milepost 7.	•					A	•			14			
F5	Cottonwood SRA	Canyon Ferry 1 1/2 miles N of Townsend on U.S. 287 at milepost 75		•		•	•		•						
E5	Coulter FS	15 miles N of Helena on I-15, then 3 miles E on Cty. Rd. 17, then 4 miles NE on Lake (boat access only)	7			•			•		•	15		6/1-9/15	
E2	Council Grove SM	I-90 W of Missoula to Reserve St. Exit, 2 miles S on Reserve St., then 10 miles W on Mullan Road.	•			H	•		•						
E3	County Line FAS	35 miles E of Bonner on Montana 200 to milepost 35.	•		•	•		A	•			7			
E5	Court Sheriff SRA	Canyon Ferry 9 miles E of Helena on U.S. 287 at milepost 55, then 9 miles NE on Secondary 284.	•		•	•	•	B	•	•			•	5/15-9/15	
H11	Cow Creek FS	8 miles N of Otter on For. Rd. 51, then 5 miles W on For. Rd. 95.	8		•	•	•			•			14			
C8	Cow Island SRA	Wild and Scenic Missouri kRiver SW of Landusky. (No vehicle access)	•			•				•			14			
E4	Craig SRA	I-15 at Craig Exit, then 1/2 mile E at bridge.	•		•	•	•	C	•			14			
G2	Crazy Creek FS	5 miles NW of Sula on U.S. 93, then 1 mile SW on For. Rd. 370.	14		•	•	•					•	14		6/1-11/30	
E5	Crittendon SRA	Canyon Ferry 9 miles E of Helena on U.S. 287 at milepost 55, then NE on Secondary 284 to Yacht Basin, then 4 miles S on Gravel road.				•				•	•	•				
G4	Cromwell Dixon FS	17 miles SW of Helena on U.S. 12	14		•	•	•						15	•	6/1-9/15	
C9	Crooked Cr.	48 miles NE of Winnett - F.P. Res.	•			•				•			14			
E7	Crystal Lake FS	9 miles W of Lewistown, on U.S. 87, then 16 miles S on Cty. Rd. then 9 miles S on For. Rd. 275.	28		•	H	•			•		•	14	•	6/15-9/15	
E5	Cemetery Island SRA	Canyon Ferry (Boat access only.)	•			•				•			14			
H9	Custer Battlefield NM	2 miles S of Crow Agency on I-90, then 1 mile E on US. 212.		•		•	•			•		•	14			
H4	Dailey Lake FAS	1 mile E of Emigrant, then 4 miles S on Secondary 240, then 6 miles SE on County Road.	•		•	•	•	C	•			14			
F3	Dalles FS	5 miles SE of Clinton on I-90, then 15 miles S on For. Rd. 102	10		•	•	•			•		•	14		5/25-9/10	
F7	Deadman's Basin SRA	20 miles E of Harlowton on U.S. 12 to milepost 120, then 1 mile N on County Road.	•		•	•	•			•		•	14		5/25-9/10	
F11	Dean S. BLM	8 miles E of Miles City on U.S. 12, then 2 miles S on Cty. Rd.	•		•		•			•					5/1-10/1	
D5	Dearborn SRA	14 miles S of Cascade on I-15 at Canyon Exit 244, then 6 miles S on Recreation Road.	•		•	•				•			14			
F5	Deepdale FAS	4 miles S of Townsend on U.S. 287 to milepost 82, then 1 mile W.	•		•	•		C	•						
E4	Departure Point BLM	Holter Lake.	10		•	•		A	•			14	•		
B3	Devil Creek FS	45 miles SE of West Glacier on U.S. 2.	12		•	•	•					•	14		6/1-9/15	
C9	Devils Cr. CE	45 miles NW of Jordan.	•			•		C	•			14			
F3	Dickie Br. BLM	10 miles W of Divide on Mt 43	5		•	•				•			14			
H3	Dinner Station FS	12 miles N of Dillon on I-15, then 12 miles NW on Birch Cr. Rd.	13		•	H	•			•		•	15	•	5/15-9/15	
G4	Divide Bridge	1 mile W of Divide on Montana 43.	•		•	H		C	•			14			•
B2	Doris Point FS	8 miles SE of Hungry Horse on Rd. 895.	18		•	•				•	•		14	•	6/15-9/30	
B1	Dorr Skeels FS	3 miles SE of Troy on U.S. 2, then 14 miles S on Mt. 56.	6		•	•				•	•	•	14	•	5/20-9/15	•
C10	Downstream CE	Fort Peck Dam	57		•	H	•	C	•			14	•	5/15-10/15	

352

CAMPGROUNDS - ACCESS SITES

Map Coordinates	Site Name	Directions	Camping	Day use only	Trailers	Toilets	Water	Boat Launch	Fishing	Swimming	Trails	Stay Limit	Fee	Season	Handicapped
D6	Drag Reservoir BLM	U.S. 191 N of Lewistown to Junction with Montana 19, then 35 miles E on Balentine Rd.	•		•	•			•					5/1-10/1	
G5	Drouillard FAS	2 miles W of Three Forks on U.S. 10.	6		•	•		C	•			14			
E6	Dry Wolf FS	18 miles SW of Stanford on Cty. Rd, then 6 miles SW on For. Rd. 251.	33		•	•	•				•	14	•	5/20-10/15	
C10	Duck Cr. CE	4 miles S of Fort Peck	•			•		C				14			
C6	Eagle Creek BLM	South of Big Sandy (no vehicle access).	•			•			•						
F3	East Bank BLM	17 miles W of Divide on Mt. 43	1		•	H		C	•	•		14			
H4	East Cr. FS	8 miles SW of Lima then 1 mile S then 1 miles SE.	4		•	•	•					14		5/15-10/1	
F3	East Fork FS	8 miles S of Philipsburg on U.S. 10A, then 1 mile SE on For. Rd. 1090.	10		•				•			14		6/1-9/30	
H7	East Rosebud Lake FS	7 miles SW of Roscoe on Cty. Rd. 177, then 6 miles SW on For. Rd. 177.	12		•	•	•		•	•	•	10		6/15-9/15	
D5	Eden Bridge FAS	10 Miles S of Ulm on Secondary 330.		•		•		B	•						
H5	Eight Mile Ford FAS	1 mile W of Ennis on Mt. 287, then 4 milew S on County Road.	•		•	•		C	•						
G12	Ekalaka Park FS	3 miles SE of Ekalaka on Mt. 323, then 1 mile W on Cty. Rd., then 5 miles on Couty Road.	9		•	•	•		•			14		5/1-11/30	
B3	Elk Island FS	13 miles SE of Martin City on For. Rd. 38 (boat access only)	7			•			•	•		14		6/1-9/15	
D12	Elk Island SRA	29 miles S of Sidney on Montana 16, milepost 30 then 1 mile E on county Road.	•					B	•			14			
C2	Elmo SRA	2 miles N of Elmo on U.S. 93, milepost 78.	35		•	•	•	C	•	•		7	•	5/15-9/15	
H7	Emerald Lake FS	7 miles W of Fishtail on Mt. 425, then 12 miles S on For. Rd. 72.	31		•	•	•		•			10	•	6/15-9/15	
B3	Emery Bay FS	7 miles SE of Martin City on For. RD. 38.	8		•	•	•		•	•	•	14		6/1-9/15	
H6	Emigrant FAS	22 miles S of Livingston on U.S. 89 to milepost 31, then E across bridge.	•		•	•		C	•			14			
H6	Emigrant FAS	22 miles S of Livingston on U.S. 89 at milepost 31.	•					A	•			14			
H5	Ennis FAS	U.S. 287 at Ennis, milepost 48.	•		•	•	•	C	•			14	$3	5/15-9/15	
E2	Erskine FAS	15 miles W of Missoula on I-90 to Frenchtown Exit, milepost 89, then through Frenchtown, then mi. W on Mulan Rd.		•					•						
C4	Eureka Reservoir FAS	4 miles N of Choteau on U.S. 89 at milepost 345, then 4 miles NW on County Road.		•	•	•		C	•			14			
G5	Fairweather FAS	1 mile W of Logan on U.S. 10, then 3 1/2 miles N on Logan Trident Road, then 10 miles NE on Clarkston Road.		•		•		C	•			14			
G8	Fairy Lake FS	22 miles NE of Bozeman on Mt. 86, then 6 miles W on For. Rd.	8			•			•			14		7/1-9/15	
E12	Fallon Bridge FAS	9 miles NEL of Terry on I-94 on Fallon Exit, then 1 mile N on County Road.	•			•		B	•			14			
H6	Falls Creek FS	25 miles SW of Big Timber on Mt. 298, then 4 miles S on Cty. Rd. 212	11		•	•	•		•			14	•	6/15-10/15	
F10	Far West SRA	1mile N of Rosebud on Secondary 446, then 1/2 mile W on county Road.	•		•	•		C	•	•		14			
C2	Finley Point SRA	11 miles N of Polson on Montana 35, then 4 miles W.	18		•	•	•	C	•	•		7	•	5/15-9-15	
G7	Fireman's Point FAS	2 miles SW of Columbus on Montana 78 at milepost 44, then 1/2 mile W on County Road.	•					A	•						
E5	Fish Hawk SRA	Canyon Ferry 9 miles E of Helena on U.S. 287 at milepost 55, then 8 miles NE on Seconday 284. (tent camping only)	•			•			•				•	5/19-9/15	
G3	Fishtrap Creek FAS	23 miles N of Wisdom on Montana 43.	•		•	•		C	•			14			
C1	Fishtrap Lake FS	5 miles E of Thompson Falls on Mt. 200, then 13 miles NE on For. Rd. 56, then 15 miles NW on For. Rd. 518, then 2 miles W. on For. Rd. 7493.	11		•	•	•		•	•	•	14		6/1-9/30	
A4	Fitzpatrick Lake FAS	10 miles W of Sunburst on Secondary 214, then 2 miles S and 3 miles W on county Road.	•			•			•			14			
C1	Flat Iron Ridge FAS	5 miles NW of Thompson Falls on Montana 200, milepost 49.	•					A	•						
C10	Flat Lake CE	6 miles E of Fort Peck.	•		•	•		C	•			14			
E3	Flint Cr. FS	6 miles S of Philipsburg then 1 miles SE.	10		•	H			•			14		5/1-10/31	
E2	Florence Bridge FAS	17 miles S of Missoula on U.S. 93 to Secondary 203, then 1 mile E.		•		•		A	•						
E2	Forest Grove FAS	13 miles E of Superior on I-90 at Tarkio Exit, then 5 miles W on Frontage Road.	10		•	•		C	•			7			
E2	Forks FAS	18 miles S of Superior on I-90 to Fish Creek Exit, then 7 miles SW on County Road.	•		•	•			•			7			
F2	Fort Owen SM	U.S. 93 S of Missoula to Stevensville Junction, then1 mile E on Secondary 269.		•		•	•								
C10	Fort Peck Dredge Cuts FAS	3 miles N of Fort Peck on Mt. 117, then 1/2 mile W on gravel road.	•		•	•		C	•						
D5	Fort Shaw FAS	1/2 mile N of Fort Shaw on County Road.		•		•		A	•						
B12	Ft. Union Trading Post NHS	13 miles SE of Bainville on Cty. Rd. or 15 N of Fairview on Cty. Rd.		•	•	•					N				
C9	Fourchette Creek CE	60 miles S of Malta.	•		•	•		C	•			14			
G5	Four Corners FAS	I-90 at Manhattan, milepost 288, then 3 miles E on Secondary 346.	•			•		A	•			14			
D6	Fred Ellis FAS	S of Hobson on Secondary 239 to Utica, then 13 miles S of Judith River Road.	•						•			14			
G6	Free River FAS	2 1/2 miles S of Livingston on U.S. 89.	•					A	•			14			
E2	Frenchtown Pond SRA	15 miles W of Missoula on I-90, milepost 89, Frenchtown Exit, then 1 mile W on Frontage Road.		•		F		A	•	•					
A6	**Fresno Res:**														
	Fresno Beach USBR	At Reservoir	•			H		C	•	•		14			
	Kiehns USBR	At Reservoir	•	•		·			•	•		14			

353

CAMPGROUNDS - ACCESS SITES

Map Coordinates	Site Name	Directions	Camping	Day use only	Trailers	Toilets	Water	Boat Launch	Fishing	Swimming	Trails	Stay Limit	Fee	Season	Handicapped
	Kremlin USBR	At Reservoir	•					H	•	•		14			
	River Run USBR	At Reservoir	•					H	•			14			
G5	Gallatin Forks FAS	I-90 at Manhattan milepost 288, then 2 miles N on Nixon Gulch Road.	•					C	•						
D5	Giant Springs/Heritage SP	U.S. 87 N through Great Falls, milepost 1.7, then 3 miles E on River Drive.		•		•	•				•				
B3	**Glacier NP:**	Entrances from U.S. 2 at West Glacier and from U.S. 89 near East Glacier Park, St. May and Babb													
	Apgar NPS	1 mile NW of West Entrance on Going-to-theSun Road	196		•	F	•	•	•			7	•	5/15-10/18	
	Avalanche Creek NPS	5 miles NE of Lake McDonald on Going-to-the-Sun Road	87h		•	F	•					7	•	6/29-9/6	
	Bowman NPS		6		•	•						7		6/4-9/30	
	Bowman Lake NPS	8 miles NE of Polebridge	48		•	F	•	•	•	•		7	•	5/22-9/30	
	Cut Bank NPS	15 miles S of St. Mary on U.S. 89, then 5 miles W on primitive road	19		•	•						7	•	6/1-9/15	
	Fish Creek NPS	5 miles N of West Glacier on North Fork Road	180		•	F	•					7	•	6/15-8/25	
	Kintla Lake NPS	15 miles N of Polebridge on North Fork Road	19		•	•	•	•	•			7	•	5/4-9/30	
	Logging Creek NPS	7 miles SE of Polebridge on North Fork Road	8		•	•	•					7	•	5/4-9/30	
	Many Glacier NPS	10 miles SW of Babb	117h		•	F	•	•				7	•	6/1-9/6	
	Quartz Creek NPS		7		•	•	•					7	•	6/4-9/30	
	Rising Sun NPS	5 miles SW of St. Mary on Going-to-the-Sun Road	83		•	F	•	•				7	•	6/1-9/6	
	River NPS		7		•	•	•					7			
	Sprague Creek NPS	8 miles NE of West Glacier on Going-to-the-Sun Road	25			F	•		•			7	•	6/15-9/6	
	St. Mary Lake NPS	In St. Mary	156		•	F	•	•				7	•	6/13-9/30	
	Two Medicine NPS	3 miles N of East Glacier Park on MT 49, then 2 miles W	99		•	F	•	•	•			7	•	6/1-9/6	
B10	Glasgow Base Pond FAS	1 1/2 miles E of Glasgow, then 19 miles N on Mt. 247 to milepost 20, then 3/4 mile W on dirt road.	•			•		A	•						
H4	Glen FAS	19 miles N of Dillon on I-15 to milepost 85, Glen Exit, then 6 miles S on Frontage Road.	•		•	•		A	•			14			
A2	Glen Lake FAS	6 miles S of Eureka on U.S. 93, then 6 miles E on County Road.	5			•	•	C	•	•					
E2	Gold Creek FS	1 mile S of Stevensville route 269 - 11 miles SE - 4 miles S	5			•			•		•	14		6/1-9/15	
D1	Gold Rush FS	9 miles S of Thompson Falls on For. Rd. 352	7		•	•								6/1-10/30	
F4	Grant-Hohrs Ranch NHS	N edge of Deer Lodge on U.S. 10		•		•	•								
H3	Grasshopper FS	4 miles S of Dillon on I-15, then 27 miles NW on Mt. 278, then 13 miles N on Wise River Road	28		•	•			•		•	15		6/15-9/15	
F6	Grasshopper Creek FS	7 miles NE of White Sulphur Springs on U.S. 12, then 4 miles S on For. Rd. 211	12		•	•			•		•	14		6/1-10/15	
A2	Grave Creek FS	3 miles NW of Fortine on U.S. 93, then 2 miles NE on Cty. Rd. 114, then 1 mile E on For. Rd. 7019	8			•			•			14		all year	
H5	Greek Creek FS	9 miles N of Big Sky Junction on U.S. 191	14		•	•			•		•	14		6/15-9/15	
17	Greenough Lake FS	12 miles SW of Red Lodge on U.S. 212, then 1 mile SW on For. Rd. 421	17		•	H	•				•	10		6/15-9/15	•
G6	Grey Bear FAS	5 miles W of Big Timber on I-90 at DeHart Exit, then 1/2 mile E on Frontage Road, then 1 mile NW on County Road.	•		•	•		C	•						
G5	Grey Cliff FAS	23 miles W of Bozeman on Mt. 84, then 6 miles N on Madison River Road.	30		•	•	•	A	•			14			
H6	Grey Owl FAS	3 miles n of Emigrant on U.S. 89	•		•	•		C	•			14			
G7	Greycliff Prairie Dog Town SM	9 miles E of Big Timber on I-90 at Greycliff Exit, milepost 390.		•											
E3	Grizzly FS	5 miles SE of Clinton on I-90 to Rock Cr. Exit, then 13 miles S on For. Rd. 102	9		•	•			•		•	14		5/25-9/10	
G6	Half Moon FS	12 miles N of Big Timber on U.S. 191, then 8 miles W on Cty. Rd. 197, then 2 miles W on For. Rd. 197	9		•	•	•		•			14		6/15-10/15	
B3	Handkerchief FS	35 miles SE of Hungry Horse on For. Rd. 895, then 2 miles NW on For. Rd. 897	9		•	•			•			14		6/1-9/15	
G2	Hannon Memorial FAS	20 miles S of Hamilton on U.S. 93 to milepost 27.	•		•				•			7			
D5	Hardy Bridge SRA	4 miles S of Cascade on I-15 at Hardy Exit 247, then 4 miles S on Recreation Road.	•			•			•			14			
E3	Harper Lake FAS	14 miles S of Seeley Lake on Secondary 209 to milepost 1.	•		•	•		C	•			7			
G5	Harrison Lake FAS	5 miles E of Harrison on County Road.	•		•	•		C	•			14			
E3	Harry Morgan FAS	4 miles S of Ovando on County Road.	•		•			A	•			7			
F3	Harry's Flat FS	5 miles SE of Clinton on I-90, then 18 miles S on For. Rd. 102	14		•	•	•		•					5/20-9/30	
E6	Hay Canyon FS	12 miles W of Hobson on Mt. 239, then 12 miles SW on Cty. Rd., then 5 miles SW on For. Rd. 487	9		•	•			•					5/20-9/30	
E5	Helena Valley Reservoir FAS	8 miles NE of Helena on Secondary 280.		•		•		A	•						
D10	Hell Creek SRA	Montana 200 at Jordan, milepost 213, then 24 miles N on County road.	•		•	•		C	•	•		14	•		
F5	Helligate SRA	Canyon Ferry 9 miles E of Helena on U.S. 287 at milepost 55, then 18 miles NE on Secondary 284.		•		H	•	C	•	•			•	5/15-9/15	
H6	Hell Canyon FS	25 miles S of Big Timber on Mt. 298, then 14 miles S on Mt. 298.	11		•	•			•			14		6/15-10/1	
H6	Hicks Parks FS	25 miles S of Big Timber on Mt. 298, then 14 miles S on Cty. Rd. 212.	27		•	•	•		•			14		6/15-10/1	
H4	High Road FAS	1 mile S of Twin Bridges on Mt. 41, then 3 miles W on County Road.	•			•		C	•			14			
15	Hilltop FS	12 miles N of West Yellowstone on U.S. 191, then 31 miles W on U.s. 287, then 7 miles w on For. Rd. 572	18		•	•	•					14		6/15-9/15	

CAMPGROUNDS - ACCESS SITES

Map Coordinates	Site Name	Directions	Camping	Day use only	Trailers	Toilets	Water	Boat Launch	Fishing	Swimming	Trails	Stay Limit	Fee	Season	Handicapped
B9	Hinsdale (East Area) FAS	2 miles N of Hinsdale on Secondary 537.	•					A	•			14			
B9	Hinsdale (West Area) FAS	3 miles N of Hinsdale on Secondary 537, then 1 1/2 miles W on dirt road.	•					A	•			14			
C6	Hole in the Wall SRA	Wild and Scenic Missouri River NE of Geraldine. (No vehicle access)	•			•			•			14			
D3	Holland Lake FS	9 miles SE of Condon on Mt. 83, then 3 miles E on For. Rd. 44	41	•	•	•	•	•	•	•	•	14	•	5/28-9/17	
E4	Holter Lake BLM	2 miles N of Wolf Creek on Recreation Road, across bridge, then 3 miles E on Cty. Rd.	28	•	•	•		C	•	•		14	•		•
C4	Home Gulch FS	20 miles NW of Augusta on Sun R. Canyon Cty. Rd., then 21 miles W on For. Rd. 108	15	•	•	•			•			14	•	5/25-11/15	
H8	Homestead Isle FAS	Yellowstone River S of Park City. (No vehicle access)							•						
H6	Hood FS	8 miles S of Bozeman on MT 345, then 10 miles SE on Hyalite Canyon Rd. (For. Rd. 62)	16	•	•	•	•		•			14	•	6/15-9/15	•
H7	Horsethief Station FAS	7 miles N of Red Lodge on U.S. 212, then 1/4 mile E on County Road, then 3 miles N on County Road.	•	•	•				•						
B1	Howard Lake FS	12 miles S of Libby on U.S. 2, then 12 miles S on For. Fd. 231	7	•	•	•	•		•			14		6/1-9/15	
E9	Howay Island BLM	26 miles W of Forsyth - 3 miles N - 8 miles W	•	•	•			C	•		•	14		5/1-10/31	
F3	Humbug Spires BLM	3 miles NE Moose Cr. Rd.	•	•	•				•		•	14			
F8	Huntley Div. Dam USBR	1 mile W of Huntley	•					B	•			14			
G3	Indian Creek FS	4 miles S of Darby on U.S. 93, then 14 miles SW on Cty. Rd. 473, then 37 miles W on For. Rd. 468, then 5 miles N on For. Rd. 6223	8	•	•							10		6/15-11/30	
G7	Indian Fort FAS	1 mile N of Reedpoint on County Road.	•	•	•	•		C	•						
E6	Indian Hill FS	12 miles W of Hobson on Mt. 239, then 12 miles SW on Cty. Rd., then 3 miles SW on For. Rd. 487	7	•	•	•			•		•	14		5/20-10/15	
F5	Indian Road SRA	1 mile N of Townsend on U.S. 287, milepost 75.	•	•	•	•		C	•		•				
G2	Indian Trees FS	6 miles S of Sula on U.S. 93, then 1 mile SW on For. Rd. 729	18	•	•	•			•			14	•	6/15-9/30	
D12	Intake FAS	16 miles N of Glendive on Montana 16, then S on County Road.	•	•	•	•		C	•			14	•		
F9	Isaac Homestead SWMA	5 miles E of Hysham on County Roads.	•	•	•	•		A	•			14			
G7	Itch-Kep-Pe FAS	1/4 miles S of Columbus on Mt. 78 at Yellowstone River Bridge.	•	•	•	•		C	•			14			
H5	Jack Creek FS	4 miles SE of Ennis on U.S. 287, then 12 miles E on Jack Creek Rd.	6	•	•	•			•			14		6/15-9/15	
C8	James Kipp SRA	28 miles N of Lewistown on U.S. 191, at Fred Robinson Bridge.	•	•	•	•		C	•			14	•		•
G2	Jennings Camp FS	3 miles W of Sula on U.S. 93, then 10 miles NE on Cty. Rd. 472	5	•	•	•						14		6/15-11/30	
H7	Jimmy Joe FS	7 miles SW of Roscoe on Cty. Rd. 177, then 3 miles SW on For. Rd. 177	10	•	•				•			10		6/15-9/15	
E5	Jo Bonner SRA	Canyon Ferry. 9 miles E of Helena on U.S. 287 at milepost 55, then 12 miles NE on Secondary 284.	•	•	•									5/15-9/15	
E3	Johnsrud FAS	11 miles E of Bonner on Montana 200. Then 1 mile NE on Blackfoot River Road.	•	•	•	•		A	•			7			
C7	Judith Landing SRA	U.S. 87 at Big Sandy, milepost 79, then 44 miles S on Secondary 236. Site closed 10-15 through 5-15	•	•	•	•		C	•			14			
E6	Jumping Creek FS	22 miles NE of White Sulphur Springs on U.S. 89	15	•	•	•			•		•	14	•	6/1-10/15	
E4	Juniper Bay SRA	3 miles N of Wolf Creek on Recreation Road, then 6 miles S on County Road.	•	•	•	•			•			14	•		
F4	Kading FS	22 miles SW of Helena on U.S. 12, then 12 miles S on Cty. Rd. 227	16	•	•	•			•		•	15		6/1-9/15	
E2	Kelly Island FAS	I-90 at Missoula, Reserve St. Exit to Spurgin Road, then 2 miles W.	•					C	•						
B2	Kila FAS	7 miles W of Kalispell on U.S. 2, milepost 112, then one mile S on County Road.	•	•	•			•	•			14		5/20-9/30	
A1	Kilbrennen Lake FS	3 miles NW of Troy on U.S. 2, then 9 miles NE on For. Rd. 2394	5	•	•	•			•	•		14			
E6	Kings Hill FS	9 miles S of Neihart on U.S. 89	21	•	H	•			•		•	14	•	7/1-9/15	
B2	Kiwanis Lane FAS	U.S. 2 at Kalispell, milepost 123, then S on Shady Lane, then E on Conrad Drive.	•		•	•		C	•						
F4	Kohrs Bend FAS	6 miles N of Deer Lodge on I-90 to milepost 178 at Beck Hill Exit, then 1 mile W on Frontage Road.	•												
B2	Kokanee Bend FAS	14 miles N of Kalispell on U.S. 2, milepost 136, then 3 miles W on County Road.	•		•										
C12	Kuester Reservoir FAS	5 miles NE of Richey on Montana 200.	•					A	•						
F4	Lady Smith FS	4 miles W of Basin on Mt. 91, then 3 miles W on For. Rd. 82	5	•	•							14		5/15-9/15	
D3	Lake Alva FS	13 miles NW of Seeley Lake on Mt. 83	41	•	H	•			•			14	•	6/15-9/15	
F2	Lake Como FS	5 miles N of Darby on U.S. 93, then 1 mile SW on Cty. 321, then 4 miles W on For. Rd. 550	10	•	H	•	•	•	•	•	•	10	•	6/1-9/15	
G8	Lake Elmo SRA	3 miles NE of Billings on U.S. 87 to Pemberton Lane, then 1/2 mile W.	•	•				C	•	•		•			
B5	Lake Elwell (Tiber Reservoir)		•												
	Island Area USBR	At Reservoir	•		H	•		C	•			14			•
	North Bootlegger USBR	AT Reservoir	•		H	•		A	•			14			
	Sanford Park USBR	At Reservoir	•		H	•		B	•			14			•
	South Bootlegger USBR	At Reservoir	•		H	•		C	•			14			•
	VFW Campground USBR	At Reservoir	•		H	•		C	•			14			•
	Willow Cr. USBR	At Reservoir	•		H	•		C	•			14			•
G8	Lake Josephine SRA	1 mile S of Billings on Secondary 416 at the Blue Creek Bridge. (maintained by city)	•	•					•	•					
C2	Lake Mary Ronan FWP	7 miles NW of Dayton.	27	•	•		•	C	•						

355

CAMPGROUNDS - ACCESS SITES

Map Coordinates	Site Name	Directions	Camping	Day use only	Trailers	Toilets	Water	Boat Launch	Fishing	Swimming	Trails	Stay Limit	Fee	Season	Handicapped
B3	Lakeview FS	24 miles SE of Hungry Horse on For. Rd. 895.	5	•	•				•			14		6/1-9/15	
C2	Lambeth Memorial SRA	U.S. 93 at Dayton milepost 83, then 7 miles NW	20	•	•	•	•	C	•			7	•	5/15-9/15	
H6	Langhor FS	8 miles S of Bozeman on Mt. 345, then 5 miles SE on Hyalite Canyon Rd. (For. Rd. 62)	11	•	•	•			•			14	•	6/15-9/15	•
G12	Lantis Spring FS	3 miles W of Camp Crook, SD, on State Highway 20, then 11 miles NW on For. Rd. 117.	5	•	•	•						14		5/1-11/15	
E2	Lee Creek FS	24 miles W of Lolo on U.S. 12.	22	•	•	•			•	•	•	14	•	5/20-9/30	
E5	Lewis & Clark SRA	Canyon Ferry 9 miles E of Helena on U.S. 287, then 8 miles NE on SEc. 284 to Yacht Basin, then 2 mi. S on gravel rd.	•		•	•	•		•	•						
G5	Lewis & Clark Caverns SP	19 miles W of Three Forks on U.S. 10, milepost 271.	•		•	F	A					N 14	•	6/15-9/15	
E2	Lewis & Clark FS	16 miles W of Lolo on U.S. 12	17	•	•	•			•			14		5/25-9/10	
B3	Lid Creek FS	15 miles SE of Hungry Horse on For. RD. 895.	22	•	•			•	•	•		14		6/1-9/15	
I7	Limber Pine FS	12 miles SW of Red Lodge on U.S. 212, then 1 mile SW on For. Rd. 421.	11	•	•	•			•		•	10	•	6/15-9/15	
F3	Little Joe FS	20 miles SW of Wise River.	4		•	•					•	15		5/25-9/15	
A2	Little Therriault FS	3 miles NW of Fortine on U.S. 93, then 3 miles NE on Cty. Rd. 114 then 11 miles NE on For. Rd. 114, then 10 miles on For. Rd. 319.	6	•	•				•		•	14		6/15-11/15	•
H6	Loch Leven FAS	9 miles S of Livingston on U.S. 89 to milepost 44, then 2 mile E. then 4 miles S on Secondary 540.	•	•	•	•	•	C	•			14			
F3	Lodgepole FS	11 miles S of Philipsburg on U.S. 10A	31	•	•	•	•		•	•	•	14		6/15-9/30	
G3	Lodgepole FS	13 miles SW of Wise River on Wise River - Polaris Rd.	6	•	•	•					•	15		6/15-10/15	
B1	Logan SRA	37 miles W of Kalispell on U.S. 2, milepost 77. (Dump station for park patrons only).	30	•	•	•		C	•	•		7	•	5/15-9/15	
D4	Logging Creek FS	3 miles N of Monarch on Mt. 89, then 6 miles W on Cty. Rd. 427, then 6 miles SW on For. Rd. 253	26	•	H	•			•		•	14		6/15-10/15	
D4	Log Gulch BLM	Holter Lake	80	•	•	•		C	•			14			
C6	Loma Access Site BLM	1 mile E of Loma on Cty. Rd.	•		•			C	•						
B2	Lone Pine SP	4 miles SW of Kalispell on Foys Lake Road, then 1 mile N on Lone Pine Estates Rd.	•		•	•									
H5	Lonesomehurst FS	8 miles W of West Yellowstone - 3 miles N	26	•	H	•		C	•	•	•	15		5/22-9/15	
E5	Loreiel SRA	Canyon Ferry. 9 miles E of Helena on U.S. 287 at milepost 55, then 8 miles NE on Secondary 284 to Yacht Basin, then 1 1/2 miles S on gravel road.	•		•				•	•					
F4	Lost Creek SP	1 1/2 miles E of Anaconda on U.S. 10A, milepost 5, then 2 miles N on Secondary 273, then 6 miles W.	40	•	H	•			•		•	N 14			
B3	Lost Johnny Point FS	9 miles SE of Hungry Horse on For. Rd. 895	21	•	•			•	•	•		14	•	6/1-9/15	
F4	Lowland FS	9 miles NE of Butte on I-15, then 7 miles W on For. Rd. 442	7	•	•	•						14		5/15-11/1	
I7	M-K FS	12 miles SW of Red Lodge on U.S. 212, then 4 miles SW on For. Rd. 421	10	•	•				•		•	10		6/15-9/15	
G12	Macnab Pond FS	7 miles SE of Ekalaka on Mt. 323, then 1 mile E on Cty. Rd.	5	•	•	•			•			14		5/1-11/30	
G5	Madison Buffalo Jump SM	23 miles W of Bozeman on I-90 at Logan Exit, then 7 miles S on Buffalo Jump Road.	•		•	•						14			
I5	Madison River FS	24 miles S of Cameron U.S. 287, then 1 mile SW on Cty. Rd. 8381, then 1 mile S on For. Rd. 8381	10	•	•	•			•			14		6/15-9/15	
E5	Mahogany Cove SRA	Canyon Ferry. (Boat access only.)	•		•				•					5/15-9/15	
G4	Maldenrock FAS	I-15 at Melrose, milepost 93, then 6 miles W & N on County Road	•		•	•	•	A	•			14			
D12	Makoshika SP	2 miles SE of Glendive on Snyder Avenue.	•		•	•	•					N 14			
H6	Mallard's Rest FAS	13 miles S of Livingston on U.S. 89 to milepost 42.	•		•	•	•	C	•			14			
F9	Manuel Lisa FAS	6 miles E of Custer on Frontage Road.	•		•			A	•						
E6	Many Pines FS	4 miles S of Neihart on Mt. 89	23	•	•	•			•		•	14	•	6/1-10/15	
G3	Martin Creek FS	3 miles W of Sula on U.S. 93, then 15 miles NE on Cty. Rd. 472	7	•	•	•						14		6/15-11/30	
F6	Martinsdale Reservoir FAS	1 mile E of Martinsdale on County Road.	•		•			C	•			14			
G2	May Creek FS	17 miles W of Wisdom on Mt. 43	21	•	•	•			"		•	15	•	7/4-9/15	
B1	McGillivray FS	13 miles NE of Libby on Mt 37, then 10 miles N on For. Rd. 228	58	•	•	•	•	•	•	•	•	14	•	5/20-10/15	
B1	McGregor Lake FS	32 miles W of Kalispell on U.s. 2	15	•	•	•		C	•	•	•	14	•	5/10-9/15	
C10	McGuire Creek CE	44 miles SE of Fort Peck	•		•	•		A	•			14			
H5	Meadow Lake FAS	6 miles N of Ennis on U.S. 287 to milepost 55, then 2 miles E on County Road.	•		•	•		B	•			14			
F12	Medicine Rocks SP	25 miles S of Baker on Montana 7, milepost 10, then 1 mile W on County Road.	•		•	•	•					14			
E5	Meriwether FS	18 miles NE of Helena on I-15 (boat access only)			•	•			•	•	•			6/15-9/15	
H4	Mill Creek FS	7 miles E of Sheridan on Mill Cr. Rd.	13	•	•	•						14		6/1-10/31	
H3	Miner Lake FS	19 miles SW of Wisdom at Jackson on Mt. 278, then 7 miles W on Cty. Rd. 182, then 3 miles W on For. Rd. 182	25		•	•	•		•		•	15		7/4-9/15	
G5	Missouri Headwaters SP	3 miles E of Three Forks on U.S. 10, then 3 miles N on Secondary 286.	•		•	F		C	•			14		5/15-9/15	
H3	Mono Creek FS	23 miles SW of Wise River on Wise River - Polaris Rd.	5	•	•	•					•	15		6/15-9/30	
C8	Montana Gulch BLM	1/2 mile NW of Landusky on Cty. Rd.	5		•							14			
E3	Monture FAS	39 miles E of Bonner on Montana 200, milepost 39.	•		•	•			•			7			
E3	Monture FS	9 miles N of Ovando on For. Rd. 89	5		•				•		•	14		6/15-9/30	

CAMPGROUNDS - ACCESS SITES

Map Coordinates	Site Name	Directions	Camping	Day use only	Trailers	Toilets	Water	Boat Launch	Fishing	Swimming	Trails	Stay Limit	Fee	Season	Handicapped
E6	Moose FS	18 miles N of White Sulphur Springs on U.S. 89, then 6 miles W on For. Rd. 119, then 3 miles N on For. Rd. 204	9	·	·	·			·			14		6/1-10/15	
F4	Moose Creek FS	9 miles SW of Helena on U.S. 12, then 4 miles SW on Rimini Rd.	11	·	·	·	·					15		6/1-9/15	
H5	Moose Flat FS	5 miles N of Big Sky on U.S. 191	22	·	·		·		·			14	·	8/15-9/15	
H7	Moraine FAS	24 miles W of Absarokee on Secondary 420.		·		H	·		·						
F4	Mormon Gulch FS	4 miles W of Basin on Mt. 91, then 1 mile W on For. Rd. 82	16	·	·							14		5/15-9/15	
D5	Morony Dam FAS	Below Great Falls - below dam	·												
B3	Murray Bay FS	22 miles SE of Martin City on For. Rd. 38	46	·	·	·	·	·	·	·		14		6/1-9/15	
A2	N. Dickey Lake FS	5 miles NW of Stryker on U.S. 93	16	·	·	·	·	·	·	·		14	·	5/15-11/15	·
H6	Natural Bridge SM	27 miles S of Big Timber on Montana 298.		·		·			·						
C10	Nelson Creek CE	49 miles SE of Fort Peck - 7 miles W		·	·	·							14			
B9	Nelson Reservoir SRA	17 miles E of Malta on U.S. 2, milepost 488, then 2 miles N on County Road.		·	·	·	·	C	·				7			
D4	Nilan Reservoir FAS	10 miles W of Augusta on County Road.		·		·	·	B	·				14			
E3	Ninemile Prairie FAS	25 miles E Bonner on Montana 200 to milepost 26, then 4 miles W on County Road.		·		·	·	A	·				7			
D2	Ninepipe Reservoir FAS	6 miles S of Ronan at Allentown. (Boats not allowed)		·		·					·					
C1	North Shore FS	2 miles NW of Trout Creek on Mt. 200	19	·	·	·	·	·	·	·		14	·	5/1-10/30	
H6	Norton FS	5 miles SE of Clinton on I-90 to Rock Cr. Exit, then 11 miles S on For. Rd. 102	10	·	·	·			·		·	14		5/20-9/30	
G7	Nye FAS	SW of Absarokee	·						·						
G7	Old Nye FAS	SW of Absarokee		·					·						
B2	Old Steel Bridge FAS	U.S. 2 at Kalispell, milepost 123, then S on Shady Lane; then E on Conrad Drive.	6	·	·		B	·							
E5	Orchard SRA	Canyon Ferry. 9 miles E of Helena on U.S. 287 at milepost 55, then 8 miles NE on Secondary 284 to Yacht Basin, then 3 miles S on gravel road.		·		·				·	·				
F4	Orofino FS	13 miles SE of Deer Lodge on For. Rd. 82	10	·	·							14		6/15-9/1	
E5	Overlook SRA	Canyon Ferry. 9 miles E of Helena on U.S. 287 at milepost 55, then NE on Secondary 284 to Yacht Basin, then 1 mile S.		·		·				·			·	5/15-9/15	
G2	Painted Rocks SRA	20 miles S of Hamilton on U.S. 93, then 23 miles SW on Secondary 473.	32	·	·	·		C	·			14			
H7	Palisades FS	2 miles S of Red Lodge on For. Rd. 71, then 2 miles W on Cty. Rd. 3010, then 1 mile NW on For. Rd. 3010	7	·	·				·			10		6/15-9/15	
H6	Paradise FAS	9 miles S of Livingston on U.S. 89 to milepost 44, then 2 miles E, then 4 1/2 miles S on Secondary 540.		·		·		A	·				14			
F4	Park Lake FS	1 mile N of Clancy on Cty. Rd. 426, then 6 miles W on For. Rd. 4000, then 2 miles SW on For. Rd. 426, then 5 miles W on For. Rd. 4009	22	·	·	·	·		·			15		6/11-9/15	
F4	Park Lakes FAS	1 mile N of Clancy on Cty. Rd. 426, then 6 miles W on For. Rd. 4000, then 2 miles SW on For. Rd. 426, then 5 miles W on For. Rd. 4009.		·		·		A	·				14			
17	Parkside FS	12 miles SW of Red Lodge on U.S. 212, then 1 mile SW on For. Rd. 421	25	·	H	·			·		·	10	·	6/15-9/15	·
A1	Peck Gulch FS	17 miles SW of Rexford on Mt. 37	5	·	H	·	·	·	·	·	·	14	·	5/15-10/15	·
G7	Pelican FAS	1 mile NE of Greycliff on County Road.		·		·		C	·						
A1	Pete Creek FS	10 miles NW of Troy on U.S. 2, then 20 miles NE on Mt. 508	10	·	·				·			14	·	all year	
H5	Petrified Forest FS	16 miles NW of Gardiner on U.S. 89, then 12 miles SW on Cty. Rd. 63, then 4 miles SW on For. Rd. 63	12	·	·				·		·	15		5/15-11/30	
E2	Petty Creek FAS	27 miles W of Missoula on I-90 to Petty Creek Exit, then 1 mile S on County Road.		·		·		C	·				7			
F3	Philipsburg Bay FS	9 miles S of Philipsburg on U.S. 10A, then 2 miles SW on For. Rd. 406, then 1 mile SE on For. Rd. 9460	69	·	·	·	·	·	·			14		6/15-9/30	
G8	Pictograph Cave SM	8 miles E of Billings on I-90 to Lockwood Exit, milepost 452, then 6 miles S on County Road.		·		·					N				
G4	Pigeon Creek FS	16 miles W of Whitehall on Mt. 10, then 5 miles S on For. Rd. 668	6	·	·				·		·	14		5/15-9/15	
E5	Pikes Gulch FS	11 miles E of Helena on U.S. 12, then 9 miles N on Mt. 284, then 14 miles N on For. Rd. 138	5	·	·							15		6/1-9/30	
H6	Pine Creek FAS	3 miles S of Livingston on U.S. 89, then 7 miles S on Secondary 340 to Pine Creek, then 1 mile W on County Road.		·		·		C	·				14			
H6	Pine Creek FS	10 miles S of Livingston on U.S. 89, then 2 miles W on Cty. Rd. 540, then 3 miles W on For. Rd. 202	24	·	·		B		·			14	·	6/1-9/30	·
H7	Pine Grove FS	7 miles W of Fishtail on Mt. 425 then 8 miles SW on For. Rd.72	46	·	·				·		·	10	·	6/15-9/15	
C10	Pines CE	33 miles SW of Fort Peck		·		·	·	C	·				14			
F3	Piney FS	9 miles S of Philipsburg on U.S. 10A, then 3 miles SW on For. Rd. 406, then 1 mile SE on For. Rd. 505	36	·	·	·	·	·	·	·		14	·	6/15-9/30	
13	Pipe Organ FAS	8 miles S of Dillon on I-15 at Barretts Exit, then 7 miles S on Frontage Road.		·		·		A	·				14			
F11	Pirogue Island SRA	1 mile N of Miles City on Montana 22, then 2 miles E on Kinsey Road then 2 miles S on gravel road.		·		·			·				14			
C4	Pishkun Reservoir FAS	1/2 mile S of Choteau on U.S. 287, then 19 miles SW on County Road.		·		·		C	·				14			
D3	Placid Lake SRA	3 miles S of Seeley Lake on Montana 83, then 3 miles W on County Road.	42	·	FH	·		C	·	·	·	14	·	4/15-9/15	
B1	Pleasant Valley FS	31 miles SE of Libby on U.S. 2	18	·	·		B		·		·	14	·	5/25-9/15	
H4	Poindexter Slough FAS	2 miles S of Dillon on Montana 41.		·		·			·				14			

CAMPGROUNDS - ACCESS SITES

Map Coordinates	Site Name	Directions	Camping	Day use only	Trailers	Toilets	Water	Boat Launch	Fishing	Swimming	Trails	Stay Limit	Fee	Season	Handicapped
H6	Point of Rocks FAS	30 miles S of Livingston on U.S. 89 at milepost 21.	•						•			14			
C2	Point Pleasant FAS	S of Swan Lake	•						•						
F2	Poker Joe FAS	19 miles S of Missoula on U.S. 93 to milepost 72, then E 1/2 mile on County Road.		•					•						
E5	Ponderosa SRA	Canyon Ferry. 9 miles E of Helena on U.S. 287 at milepost 55, then 9 miles NE on Secondary 284.	•		•	•	•		•	•			•		5/15-9/15	
F4	Porcupine FS	13 miles SW of Helena on U.S. 12.	18		•	•	•		•			15	•	6/1-9/15	
H5	Potosi FS	3 miles SE of Pony on Cty. Rd. 1601, then 5 miles SW on For. Rd. 1601	15		•	•	•		•			14		6/15-9/15	
B2	Pressentine Bar FAS	7 miles NE of Kalispell on U.S. 2, then N on LaSalle to Birch Grove Road.	•					B	•						
D5	Prewett Creek SRA	4 miles S of Cascade on I-15 at Hardy Creek Exit 247, then 3 miles S on Recreation Road.	•			•	•	C	•			14			
E4	Prickly Pear SRA	26 miles N of Helena on I-15 at Spring Creek Exit 219, then 3 miles N on Recreation Road.	•			•	•		•			14			
E2	Quartz Flat FS	15 miles SE of Superior on I-90 at Tarkio Exit	52		•	•	•				•	14	•	5/28-9/25	•
F3	Race Track FS	3 miles E of Anaconda on U.S. 10A, then 7 miles N on Mt. 48, then 4 miles N on Cty. Rd., then 3 miles NW on For. Rd. 169	8		•	•			•			14		6/15-11/15	
I5	Rainbow Point FS	5 miles N of West Yellowstone on U.S. 191, then 5 miles W on For. Rd. 610	86		•	•	•	•	•	•	•	15	•	6/1-9/15	
I7	Ratine FS	5 miles SW of Red Lodge on U.S. 212, then 3 miles SW on For. Rd. 379	8		•	•	•		•			10	•	6/15-9/15	
I5	Raynolds Pass FAS	31 miles NW of West Yellowstone on U.S. 287 to milepost 8, then 1/2 mile S to bridge.	•					A	•			14			
H5	Red Cliff FS	6 miles S of Big Sky Junction on U.S. 191	67		•	•	•		•			14	•	6/15-9/15	•
H5	Red Mountain BLM	9 miles NE of Norris on MT 84	22		•	•	•		•			14	•		
G11	Red Shale FS	6 miles SE of Ashland on U.S. 212	17		•	•	•					14	•	5/1-11/15	
H3	Reservoir Lake FS	19 miles S of Dillon on U.S. 91, then 17 miles W on Mt. 324, then 15 miles NW on Bloody dick Rd.	22		•	•	•	•	•	•		15		6/15-9/15	
A1	Rexford Bench FS	1 mile N of Rexford on For. Rd. 7940	52		•	•	•	•	•	•	•	14	•	5/1-10/30	•
E6	Richardson Creek FS	7 miles E of White Sulphur Springs - 5 miles S	4								•	14		6/1-10/15	
E3	River Bend FAS	35 miles E of Missoula on Montana 200 to milepost 26 then 6 miles W on County Road.	•		•		A		•			7			
E3	River Junction FAS	39 miles E of Bonner on Montana 200, milepost 39, then 9 miles S on County Road.	•		•		A		•			7			
D3	River Point FS	1 mile SW of Seeley Lake on Mt. 83, then 2 miles NW on Cty. Rd. 77	26		•	•	•		•			14	•	6/24-9/7	
E5	Riverside SRA	9 miles E of Helena on U.S. 287, then 9 miles NE on Secondary 284 1 mile NW on Cty. Rd.	•		•	•		C	•				•	5/15-9/15	
F11	Roche Jaune FAS	Truscott Street & N Sixth in Miles City.		•				C	•						
C8	Rock Creek FWP	Below Fred Robinson Br.	•		•	•			•	•				5/1-10/1	
C10	Rock Creek SRA	43 miles S of Glasgow on Montana 24, then 7 miles W on County Road.	•		•	•		C	•	•		7			
A1	Rocky Gorge FS	30 miles SW of Eureka on Mt. 37	120		•	•		C	•	•	•	14	•	5/1-9/15	•
G2	Rombo FS	4 miles S of Darby on U.S. 93, then 18 miles SW on Cty. Rd. 473	16		•	•	•					10	•	6/1-9/15	•
B7	Rookery SRA	N on 7th Avenue in Havre across Milk River Bridge to River Road, then 4 1/2 miles W		•				A	•						
F10	Rosebud (East Unit) SRA	I-94 at Forsyth, East Exit, then n Yellowstone River.	•		•	•	•	B	•			14	•		
F10	Rosebud (West Unit) SRA	W of Forsyth on U.S. 12 at south end of Yellowstone River Bridge, milepost 270.	•		•	•	•	C	•			14			
H10	Rosebud Battlefield SM	15 miles N of Decker on Secondary 314, then 3 miles W on County Road.	•		•	•						14			
H7	Rosebud Isle FAS	3 miles S of Absarokee on Montana 78, then 3 miles SW on Secondary 419.	•		•				•						
E3	Roundup FAS	25 miles E of Bonner on Montana 200 to milepost 25 then W on Ninemile Prairie Road.	•		•			A	•						
G4	Ruby Res. BLM	Ruby Res. - S of Alder	10		•			C	•		8	14			
E12	Rush Hall FAS	26 miles S of Wibaux on Montana 7 at milepost 52, then 3 miles W on County Road.	•			•		A	•			14			
D3	Russell Gates FWP	35 miles E of Bonner on Mt. 200	12		•	•	•	A	•			7	•		
A2	S. Dickey Lake FS	5 miles NW of Stryker on U.S. 93, then 1 mile SW on Cty. Rd. 3785, then 2 miles SE on For. Rd. 3788	20		•	•	•	•	•	•		14	•	5/15-11/15	
H8	Sage Creek FS	3 miles S of Bridger on U.S. 310, then 22 miles SE on Cty. Rd., then 1 mile E on For. Rd. 50	12		•	•			•			10		6/15-9/15	
D3	Salmon Lake SRA	5 miles S of Seeley Lake on Montana 83.	20	•	FH	•		C	•	•			•	4/15-9/15	
G5	Sappington Bridge FAS	11 miles W of Three Forks on U.S. 10, then 1 mile S on U.s. 287 to bridge.	•		•			C	•			14			
B1	Savage Lake FS	10 miles E of Troy on U.S. 2, milepost 17, then 2 miles S on Secondary 202.	•					C	•						
F2	Schumaker FS	7 miles W of Darby on U.S. 93, then 2 miles W on Cty. Rd., then 16 miles W on For. Rd. 429, then 2 miles N on For. Rd. 5605	5		•	•						10		7/15-9/15	
D3	Seeley Lake FS	1 mile S of Seeley Lake on Mt. 83, then 3 miles NW on Cty. Rd. 77	29	*	FH	•	•	•	•	•		14	•	6/10-9/15	•
F6	Selkirk FAS	19 miles W of Harlowton on U.S. 12 at milepost 80.	•		•	•	•	A	•						
C8	Sentinel Reservoir BLM	Junction of U.S. 191 and Montana 66 S of Landusky, then 7 miles E on U.S. 191, then 6 miles E on BLM Dry Creek Rd., then 3 miles S on BLM Rd.	•		•	•								5/1-10/1	
C12	Seven Sisters FAS	10 miles S of Sidney on Montana 16, milepost 41, then 1 mile E on County Road.		•					•	•					
G3	Seymour FS	11 miles W of Wise River on Mt.43, then 4 miles N on Mt. 274, then 8 miles NW on For. Rd. 934	17		•	•	•				•	15		6/15-9/30	
E5	Shannon SRA	Canyon Ferry. 9 miles E of Helena on U.S. 287 at milepost 55, then 8 miles NE on Secondary 284.	•		•	•		•	•			•			

CAMPGROUNDS - ACCESS SITES

Map Coordinates	Site Name	Directions	Camping	Day use only	Trailers	Toilets	Water	Boat Launch	Fishing	Swimming	Trails	Stay Limit	Fee	Season	Handicapped
G5	Sheds Bridge FAS	7 miles W of Bozeman on Montana 84.	•					A	•			14			
G6	Sheep Mountain FAS	4 miles E of Livingston on I-90 to milepost 340, then 2 miles N on U.S. 89, then 4 miles E on County Road.	•			•		A	•			14			
17	Sheridan FS	5 miles SW of Red Lodge on U.S. 212, then 2 miles SW on For. Rd. 379	8		•	•	•		•			10	•	6/15-9/15	
F5	Silos SRA	Canyon Ferry. 7 miles N of Townsend on U.S. 287, milepost 70, then 1 mile E on County Road.	•		•	H	•	C	•	•			•		
C8	Siparyann USFW	Below Fred Robinson Bridge.	•		•					•					
D5	Skidway FS	23 miles E of Townsend on U.S. 12, then 2 miles S on For. Rd. 4042	11		•	•	•				•	15		6/15-9/30	
B2	Skyles Lake FS	3 1/2 miles W of Whitefish on U.S. 93, milepost 131.	•					A	•						
G2	Slate Creek FS	4 miles S of Darby on U.S. 93, then 22 miles Cty. Rd. 473, then 2 miles S on Cty. Rd. 96	13		•	H			•			10		5/1-9/15	•
C7	Slaughter River SRA	Wild and Scenic Missouri River S of big Sandy. (No vehicle access)	•			•			•			14			
D1	Sloway FS	7 miles SE of St. Regis on I-90.	21		•	•	•		•			14	•	5/28-9/11	
D6	Sluice Boxes SM	15 miles S of Belt on U.S. 89 at milepost 190, then 2 miles W on County Road.	•						•		B	14			
E5	Smith River FAS	13 miles NW of White Sulphur Springs on Secondary 30, then 6 miles N on County Road.	•			•			•			14			
H6	Snow Bank FS	20 miles S of Livingston on U.S. 89, then 15 miles SE on Cty. Rd. 466	11		•	•	•		•			14	•	6/1-9/30	
H7	Soda Butte FS	1 mile E of Cooke City on U.S. 212	21		•	•	•					15	•	7/1-9/10	
A1	Sophie Lake FAS	4 miles NW of Eureka on Montana 37, milepost 65, then 4 miles N on County Road.	•		•	•		C	•	•					
D4	South Fork FS	31 miles W of Augusta on Benchmark Rd. 235	7		•	•	•		•		•	14	•	6/1-9/15	
15	South Madison BLM	15 miles S of Cameron on U.S. 287, then 1 mile W	11		•	•	•		•						•
F12	South Sandstone SRA	13 miles W of Baker on U.S. 12 to Plevna, then 7 miles S on County Road.	•			•	•	C	•	•		14		6/15-10/15	
H5	Spanish Creek FS	8 miles S of Gallatin Gateway on U.S. 191, then 5 miles W on Cty. Rd. 982, then 4 miles S on For. Rd. 982	6		•	•	•		•			14		5/20-9/30	
B1	Spar Lake FS	3 miles SE of Troy on U.S. 2, then 16 miles S on For. Rd. 384	8		•	•	•	•	•	•		14		6/15-9/30	
F3	Spillway FS	6 miles S of Philipsburg on U.S. 10A, then 6 miles SW on Mt. 38, then 5 miles SE on For. Rd. 5141	13		•	•	•		•	•		14		6/15-9/15	
H5	Spire Rock FS	11 miles S of Gallatin Gateway on U.S. 191, then 3 miles E on For. Rd. 1321	17		•	•	•		•			14		6/15-9/15	
E4	Spite Hill SRA	41 miles N of Helena on I-15 at Craig Exit 234, then 5 miles N on Recreation Road.	•			•	•	A	•			14			
B2	Sportsman's Bridge FAS	6 miles S of Kalispell on U.S. 93, milepost 104, then 6 miles E on Montana 82.	•			•		C	•						
C3	Spotted Bear FS	55 miles SE of Martin City on For. Rd. 38	13		•	•	•		•			14			
E7	Spring Creek FAS	2 miles N of Lewistown on U.S. 191, then 4 miles W on Secondary 505.	•						•			14			
F6	Spring Creek FS	33 miles W of Harlowton on U.S. 12, then 4 miles N on For. Rd. 274	10		•	•	•		•			14	•	5/1-11/30	
G2	Spring Gulch FS	5 miles NW of Sula on U.S. 93	10		•	•	•		•			14	•	5/1-11/30	
F3	Spring Hill FS	11 miles NW of Anaconda on U.S. 10A	16		•	•	•					14	•	6/15-9/1	
F4	Spring Meadow Lake SRA	U.S. 12 on W edge of Helena.		•						•					
G6	Springdale Bridge FAS	21 miles E of Livingston on I-90 to Springdale Exit, then 1 mile N on County Road.	•			•		C	•			14			
F3	Squaw Rock FS	14 miles W of Philipsburg on Cty. Rd. 348, then 5 miles W on Cty. Rd. 102, then 1 mile SW on For. Rd. 9346	10		•	•	•		•			14		6/1-10/15	
C7	Stafford Access BLM	16 miles NE of Winifred on Montana 236.		•		•		B	•						
G3	Steel Creek FS	1 mile N of Wisdom on Mt. 43, then 5 miles E on Steel Cr. Rd.	9		•	•	•		•		•	15		7/4-9/15	
D5	Stickney Creek SRA	41 miles N of Helena on I-15 at Craig Exit 234, then 4 1/2 miles N on Recreation Road.		•		•		C	•			14			
B3	Summit FS	13 miles SW of East Glacier on U.S. 2	17		•	H	•				•	14	•	6/1-9.7	
H5	Swan Creek FS	8 miles N of Big Sky Junction on U.S. 191, then 1 mile S on For. Rd. 481	13		•	•	•		•			14		6/15-9/15	
C3	Swan Lake FS	1 mile NW of Swan Lake on Mt. 83	42		•	•	•	•	•	•		14		5/28-9/1	
H7	Swinging Bridge FAS	6 miles SW of Columbus on Mt. 78, then 1 mile W on gravel road.		•		•		A	•						
B2	Tally Lake FS	6 miles W of Whitefish on U.S. 93, then 15 miles W on For. Rd. 113	36		•	•	•	•	•	•	•	14	•	6/1-9/7	
B2	Teakettle FAS	Montana 40 at Columbia Falls, milepost 7.		•		•		C	•						
A2	Tetrault FAS	4.5 miles NW of Eureka on Montana 37, milepost 55, then 3 miles N on County Road.	8		•	•	•	C	•						
D6	Thain Creek FS	6 miles E of Great Falls on U.S. 89, then 13 miles E on Mt. 228, then 16 miles E on Cty. Rd. 121, then 2 miles E on For. Rd. 8840	22			•	•		•		•	14		5/20-10/15	
E3	Thibodeau FAS	11 miles E of Bonner on Montana 200 then 6 miles NE along Blackfoot River Road.	•		•	•		A	•			7			
C1	Thompson Falls SRA	1 mile NW of Thompson Falls on Montana 200, milepost 50	20		•	•	•	C	•			14	•	5/15-9/15	
B1	Timberlane FS	1 mile NE of Libby on Mt. 37, then 8 miles N on For. Rd. 63	11		•	•	•		•			14	•	5/15-9/15	
F5	Tizer Lake FAS	18 miles S of Helena on I-15 at Jefferson City Exit, then 3 miles SE on gravel road, then 8 miles E on pack trail.	•						•			14			
F4	Toll Mountain FS	13 miles W of Whitehall - 2 miles N	14		•	•			•		•	14		5/15-9/15	
G5	Tom Miner FS	16 miles NW of Gardiner	12		•	•	•					15		5/15-11/30	
H10	Tongue River Canyon FAS	6 miles N of Decker on Secondary 314, then 5 miles E on County Road.	•			•		A	•	•		14			
H10	Tongue River Reservoir SRA	6 miles N of Decker on Secondary 314, then 1 mile E on County Road.	•			•		A	•	•		14			

CAMPGROUNDS - ACCESS SITES

Map Coordinates	Site Name	Directions	Camping	Day use only	Trailers	Toilets	Water	Boat Launch	Fishing	Swimming	Trails	Stay Limit	Fee	Season	Handicapped
F5	Toston FAS	U.S. 287 at Toston.	•					C	•			14			
D2	Trout Creek FS	7 miles SE of Superior on For. Rd. 250	10		•	•	•		•			14		6/11-9/11	
B10	Trout Pond FWP	3 miles N of Fort Peck	10		•	•		C	•			14			•
A2	Tuchuck FS	53 miles N of Martin City - 10 miles W	7		•	•			•			14		6/15-9/30	
E3	Turah FAS	6 miles E of Missoula on I-90 to milepost 113, then 2 miles SE on County Road.		•				A	•						
F11	Twelve Mile Dam FAS	11 miles S of Miles city on Montana 59, then 1 mile S on Tongue River Road (Secondary 332).			•	•		C	•						
H3	Twin Lakes FS	17 miles S of Wisdom on Mt. 278, then 8 miles W on Cty. Rd. 1290, then 5 miles S on For. Rd. 945, then 6 miles SW on For. Rd. 183	22		•	•	•	•	•		•	15		7/4-9/15	
G9	Two Leggins FAS	8 miles S of Hardin on Secondary 313 at Two Leggins Bridge.			•			C	•						
D5	Ulm Bridge FWP	Hwy. 330			•			C							
D5	Ulm Pishkun SM	10 miles S of Great Falls on I-15 at Ulm Exit, milepost 274, then 4 miles NW on County Road. Site closed 11-1 through 3-31.		•		•									
E3	Upsata Lake FAS	34 miles W of Lincoln on Montana 200 to milepost 38, then 4 miles N on County Road.		•		•		C	•			7			
H5	Valley Garden FAS	U.S. 287 1/4 mile S of Ennis to milepost 48, then 2 miles N on County Road.		•		•		C	•			14			
H5	Varney Bridge FAS	1 mile W of Ennis on U.S. 287, then 10 miles S on County Road.		•		•		C	•			14			
E5	Vigilante FS	11 miles E of Helena on U.S. 12, then 9 miles N on Mt. 284, then 7 miles N on For. Rd. 280	21		•		H		•		•	15		6/1-9/15	
15	Wade Lake FS	12 miles N of West Yellowstone on U.S. 191, then 27 miles W on Mt. 449, then 4 miles N on Mt. 287, then 7 miles W on For. Rd. 5721	13		•	•	•	•	•			14		6/15-9/15	
C2	Walstad Memorial SRA	10 miles N of Polson on U.S. 93, milepost 72.		•		•		C	•						
F3	Warm Springs FS	11 miles NW of Augusta on U.S. 10A and 2 miles N on For. Rd. 170	6		•	•	•		•			14	•	6/15-9/1	
G2	Warm Springs FS	5 miles NW of Sula on U.S. 93, then 1 mile SW on Cty. Rd. 100	15		•	•	•					14	•	5/20-9/30	
H7	Water Birch FAS	9 miles N of Red Lodge on U.S. 212 to milepost 79.		•		•			•						
B2	Wayfarers SRA	1/2 mile W of Bigfork on Montana 35. (Dump station for park patrons only).	20		•	•		C	•	•		7	•	5/15-9/15	
H6	West Boulder FS	20 miles SW of Big Timber on Mt. 298, then 7 miles W on Cty. Rd. 35, then 5 miles SW on For. Rd. 35	10		•	•	•		•			14	•	6/15-10/15	
C10	West End CE	2 miles SW of Fort Peck	12	•		H	•	C	•	•	•	14	•	5/15-10/15	•
15	West Fork FS	24 miles S of Cameron on U.S. 287, then 1 mile W on For. Rd. 8381	5		•	•	•		•			14		6/15-9/15	
C4	West Fork FS	6 miles N of Choteau on U.S. 89, then 33 miles NW on Cty. Rd. 144. (wilderness access)	5			•	•		•		B	14		6/1-11/5	
15	West Madison BLM	7 miles S of Cameron on U.S. 287, cross McAttee Bridge, then 3 miles S on BLM Rd.	28		•	•	•	•	•			14	•		
C2	West Shore SP	20 miles S of Kalispell on U.S. 93, milepost 93	30		•	•	•	C	•	•		7	•	5/15-9/15	
H7	White Bird FAS	8 miles S of Columbus on Montana 78.			•	•		A	•						
F5	White Earth SRA	Canyon Ferry. 5 miles E of Winston on County Road.		•		H	•	C	•					5/15-9/15	
C4	Whitehorse FS	4 miles W of Basin - 7 miles W on Forest Rd. 82	4		•	•	•		•		•	14		6/1-9/15	
E5	White Sandy SRA	7 miles N of Helena on I-15, then 4 miles E on Secondary 453, then 3 miles N.		•		•	•	A	•	•	•				
B2	Whitefish Lake SRA	1/2 mile W of Whitefish on U.S. 93, milepost 129, then one mile N.	25		•	•	•	C	•	•		7	•	5/15-9/15	
B2	Whitefish Satellite FAS	1 mile W of Whitefish on U.S. 93 to milepost 129, then 1 mile N. (Recommended boat access only.)			•			A	•						
A1	Whitetail FS	10 miles NW of Troy on U.S. 2, then 16 miles Ne on Mt. 508	12		•	•			•			14		6/15-9/30	
A11	Whitetail Reservoir FAS	14 miles N of Flaxville on Mt. 511.			•	•		B	•			7			
F2	Whittecar Rifle Range SRA	1 mile W of Hamilton on Main Street, then 1/2 mile N on Gerer Road, then E and N 1 1/4 miles on Ricketts Road, then 2 miles W on Blodgett View Road.		•		•							•		
C2	Wild Horse Island SP	Access from Big Arm SRA via boat to Little Sheeko Bay (NW side of island).		•					•						
G5	Williams Bridge FAS	I-90 W of Three Forks, Exit 274, then 6 miles SW on U.S. 10, then 2 miles S on Williams Bridge Road.		•		•		A	•			14			
G3	Willow FS	14 miles SW of Wise River on Wise River - Polaris Rd.	6		•	•	•		•		•	15		6/15-9/30	
C1	Willow Creek FS	19 miles E of Trout Cr.	4		•	•			•		•	14		6/1-9/30	
D6	Willow Creek Reservoir FAS	5 miles NW of Augusta on Gibson Reservoir Road.		•		•		C	•			14			
E4	Wolf Creek Bridge SRA	35 miles North of Helena on I-15 at Wolf Creek Exit 226, then 2 miles N on Recreation Road.		•		•		C	•			14			
D4	Wood Lake FS	24 miles W of Augusta on Benchmark Rd. 235	7		•	•	•		•	•	•	14	•	6/1-11/15	
H7	Woodbine FS	8 miles S of Nye on Mt. 419	46		•	•	•		•		•	10	•	6/15-9/15	
C7	Woodhawk Bottom BLM	38 miles N of Lewiston - 12 miles E - 16 miles NE	5		•	•		A	•			14		5/30-10/31	
C2	Woods Bay SRA	14 miles S of Bigfork on Montana 35, milepost 27, then one mile W.		•		•	•	C	•	•					
A1	Yaak FS	8 miles NW of Troy on U.S. 2	43		•	•	B		•			14	•	5/20-9/30	
A1	Yaak Falls FS	10 miles NW of Troy on U.S. 2, then 6 miles NE on Mt. 508	7		•	•			•		•	14		5/20-9/30	
C2	Yellow Bay SRA	15 miles N of Polson on Montana 35, milepost 17.	25		•	•	•	C	•	•		7	•	5/15-9/15	
H6	Yellowstone NP	Entrances in Montana and Wyoming. See insert		•		•	•	•	•	•	•		•		

CAMPGROUNDS - ACCESS SITES

Map Coordinates	Site Name	Directions	Camping	Day use only	Trailers	Toilets	Water	Boat Launch	Fishing	Swimming	Trails	Stay Limit	Fee	Season	Handicapped
	Bridge Bay NPS	3 miles S of Lake Village	438		•	•	•	•	•			•	14	•	5/1-10/1	
	Canyon NPS	1/4 mile E of Canyon Junction	280h		•	•	•		•			•	14	•	6/1-9/15	
	Fishing Bridge NPS	1 mile E of Fishing Bridge Junction	308h		•	•	•	•	•			•	14	•	5/25-9/30	
	Grant Village NPS	2 miles S of West Thumb Junction	438		•	•	•	•	•			•	14	•	6/15-10/1	
	Indian Creek NPS	7 1/2 miles S of Mammoth Junction	78		•	•	•		•			•	14	•	6/15-9/15	
	Lewis Lake NPS	10 miles S of West Thumb	1(		•	•	•		•			•	14	•	6/15-10/15	
	Madison NPS	1/4 mile W of Madison Junction	292		•	•	•		•			•	14	•	5/1-10/31	
	Mammoth NPS	1/2 mile N of Mammoth Junction	87		•	•	•		•			•	14	•	all year	
	Norris NPS	1 mile N of Norris Junction	116		•	•	•		•			•	14	•	6/7-9/15	
	Old Faithful NPS	At Old Faithful		•		•	•					•			all year	
	Pebble Creek NPS	7 miles S of Northeast entrance	36		•	•			•			•	14	•	5/15-10/31	
	Slough Creek NPS	10 miles NE of Tower Junction	30		•	•			•			•	14	•	5/21-10/31	
	Tower Falls NPS	3 miles SE of Tower Junction	32		•	•	•		•			•	14	•	6/1-9/15	

LEGEND

Recreation Map Coordinates -

Name - Official site name.

Type -   FS -   Forest Service Campground
         BLM -   Bureau of Land Management Campground
         NP -   National Park
         NRA -   National Recreation Area
         NHS -   National Historic Site
         NB -   National Battlefield
         NPS -   National Park Service Campground
         SP -   State Park
         SM -   State Monument
         SRA -   State Recreation Area
         FAS -   State Fishing Access Site

Fee -   There is a Camping Fee.

Camping -   Camping is allowed at this site. Number indicates number of camping spaces available
            H - Hard sided units only; no tents.

Day Use
only -   Day use only.

Trailers -   Trailer units allowed.

Toilets -   Toilets on the site.
            H - Handicapped Latrine
            F - Flush Toilet
            FH - Flush toilets, handicapped accessible

Water -   Drinking water on the site.

Boat -   Type of boat ramp on site

Launch -   A - Carry-in launch
           B - 4-Wheel drive with trailer
           C - 2-Wheel drive with trailer

Fishing -   A visitor can fish on the site.

Swimming -   There is a designated swimming area

Trails -   There are trails on site.
           B - Backpacking Trails
           N - Nature/Interpretive

Stay
Limit -   The maximum length of stay in days

Season -   The season in which camping fees are collected.

Fishing

	Coldwater Species												Warmwater Species										Facilities					
RIVERS AND STREAMS	Brook Trout	Mountain Whitefish	Lake Whitefish	Golden Trout	Cutthroat Trout	Brown Trout	Rainbow Trout	Kokanee Salmon	Bull Trout	Lake Trout	Arctic Grayling	Burbot	Largemouth Bass	Smallmouth Bass	Walleye	Sauger	Northern Pike	Shovelnose Sturgeon	Channel Catfish	Yellow Perch	Crappie	Paddlefish	Vehicle Access	Campgrounds	Toilets	Docks	Boat Ramps	Motor Restrictions
Bear Creek					•																		•					
Belly River							•				•																	
Bitterroot River	•	•			•	•	•																•	•	•		•	
Blackfoot River	•	•			•	•	•		•														•	•	•		•	
Bull River	•	•			•	•																	•	•				
Clark Fork River		•			•	•	•		•				•				•						•	•	•		•	
Clearwater River	•	•			•		•		•														•	•	•	•	•	
East Fork Bitterroot River		•			•		•		•														•					
Fish Creek	•	•			•	•	•		•														•	•	•			
Fisher River	•	•			•		•																•					
Flathead River		•	•		•				•	•			•				•						•	•	•		•	
Jocko River	•	•			•	•	•		•														•	•	•			
Kootenai River		•					•	•	•														•	•	•		•	
Lake Creek	•	•			•		•																					
Little Bitterroot River	•	•			•		•										•						•	•				
Logan Creek	•	•			•				•														•					
Lolo Creek	•	•			•	•	•		•														•	•				
Middle Fork Flathead River		•			•				•														•	•	•		•	•
Mokowanis River							•				•																	
Ninemile Creek	•	•			•	•	•																•					
North Fork Blackfoot River	•	•			•		•		•														•	•	•			•
North Fork Flathead River		•			•				•														•	•	•		•	
Rattlesnake Creek		•			•				•																			
St. Mary River		•			•		•		•														•	•	•	•	•	
St. Regis River	•				•																		•	•	•			
Skalkaho Creek		•			•																							
South Fork Flathead River		•			•				•														•	•	•		•	
Spotted Bear River		•			•				•														•	•	•			
Swan River	•	•			•		•		•														•	•	•			
Thompson River	•	•			•	•	•		•														•	•	•			
Tobacco River							•	•	•														•					
South Fork Two Medicine River					•																							
Two Medicine River	•				•		•																•	•	•	•	•	•
Vermilion River	•	•			•				•														•	•	•			
Waterton River	•	•			•																		•	•	•	•	•	
West Fork Bitterroot River		•			•	•	•																•	•	•			
White River		•							•																			
Whitefish River			•		•														•				•					
Wigwam River					•																							
Yaak River	•	•			•																		•	•	•		•	
LAKES AND RESERVOIRS																												
Ashley Lake					•		•													•			•	•	•	•	•	
Bitterroot Alpine Lakes					•																							
Blanchard Lake													•							•			•					
Bob Marshall Wilderness Lakes		•			•		•																					•
Church Slough													•				•			•							•	
Clark Fork alpine lakes	•				•	•																						
Echo Lake													•				•			•			•	•	•	•	•	
Flathead Lake			•		•			•	•														•	•	•	•	•	
Foy Lake							•																•			•	•	
Glen Lake		•					•	•															•	•	•		•	
Handkerchief Lake					•						•												•	•	•			
Harper's Lake							•																•	•	•		•	
Hubbart Reservoir	•						•	•															•					
Hungry Horse Reservoir		•			•				•														•	•	•		•	
Lake Alva		•			•			•	•				•										•	•	•		•	
Lake Inez		•			•			•	•				•										•	•	•		•	
Lake Koocanusa		•			•		•	•				•								•			•	•	•	•	•	
Lake Mary Ronan					•		•	•					•							•			•	•	•	•	•	
Little Bitterroot Lake							•	•															•	•	•		•	
Lower Stillwater Lake																	•			•			•					
McGregor Lake		•			•				•											•			•	•	•	•	•	
Mission Mtn. Wilderness Lakes	•			•	•																							•
Noxon Rapids Reservoir		•	•		•	•	•		•				•	•			•			•			•	•	•	•	•	
Placid Lake		•			•	•	•	•	•				•							•			•	•	•	•	•	
Rainy Lake		•			•		•																	•	•			
Salmon Lake		•			•	•	•	•	•				•							•			•	•	•	•	•	
Seeley Lake		•			•		•	•	•				•							•			•	•	•	•	•	
Smith Lake																				•			•			•	•	
Swan Lake		•			•		•	•	•											•			•	•	•	•	•	
Thompson Lakes					•	•	•		•				•	•						•			•	•	•	•	•	
Upper Stillwater Lake					•															•			•				•	
Whitefish Lake			•		•			•	•											•			•	•	•	•	•	

RIVERS AND STREAMS	Brook Trout	Mountain Whitefish	Lake Whitefish	Golden Trout	Cutthroat Trout	Brown Trout	Rainbow Trout	Kokanee Salmon	Bull Trout	Lake Trout	Arctic Grayling	Burbot	Largemouth Bass	Smallmouth Bass	Walleye	Sauger	Northern Pike	Shovelnose Sturgeon	Channel Catfish	Yellow Perch	Crappie	Paddlefish	Vehicle Access	Campgrounds	Toilets	Docks	Boat Ramps	Motor Restrictions
Coldwater Species →													**Warmwater Species** →										**Facilities** →					
Beaver Creek						•	•																•	•	•			
Beaverhead River		•				•	•																•	•	•		•	
Big Hole River	•	•				•	•																•	•	•		•	
Big Sheep Creek		•				•	•																•	•	•			
Blackfoot River		•			•	•	•		•														•	•	•		•	
Blacktail Deer Creek	•	•			•	•	•																					
Boulder River	•					•	•																					
Clark Fork River	•	•			•	•	•		•														•	•	•		•	
Cottonwood Creek	•	•			•	•	•																					
Crow Creek	•						•																					
Dearborn River		•			•	•	•																•					
Elk River					•	•	•																•					
Jefferson River		•				•	•																•	•	•		•	
Little Blackfoot River		•			•	•	•																					
Little Boulder River	•					•	•																•	•				
Little Elk River					•	•	•																					
Little Prickly Pear Creek	•	•				•	•																•	•	•			
Madison River		•				•	•																•	•	•		•	•
Missouri River		•				•	•																•	•	•		•	•
North Fork Sun River	•				•		•																					•
Odell Creek						•	•																					
Poindexter Slough		•				•	•																					
Prickly Pear Creek	•					•	•																					
Red Rock River		•				•	•																					
Rock Creek	•	•			•	•	•		•														•	•	•			
Ruby River		•			•	•	•																•	•	•			
Silverbow Creek	•					•	•																•	•				
South Boulder River	•					•	•																					
South Fork Sun River	•				•		•																					•
Sun River		•				•	•																•	•	•			
West Fork Madison River						•	•																•	•	•			
Wise River	•	•			•	•	•				•												•	•	•			
LAKES AND RESERVOIRS																												
Bean Lake							•																•	•	•		•	
Branham Lakes	•																						•					
Browns Lake							•																•	•	•		•	
Canyon Ferry Lake						•	•								•					•			•	•	•	•	•	•
Clark Canyon Reservoir		•				•	•								•								•	•	•		•	
Cliff Lake					•		•																•	•	•			
Coopers Lake					•																		•	•	•			
East Pioneer alpine lakes	•			•	•		•				•													•				
Elk Lake					•					•	•												•	•	•		•	
Elkhorn Mountains alpine lakes	•				•	•																						
Ennis Lake						•	•								•								•	•	•		•	
Georgetown Lake	•					•	•																•	•	•		•	
Gibson Reservoir							•																•	•	•			
Harrison Lake						•	•																•	•	•			
Hauser Lake						•	•													•			•	•	•	•	•	
Helena Valley Regulating Res.							•																•	•	•		•	•
Hidden Lake							•																					
Holter Lake						•	•	•											•				•	•	•	•	•	•
Madison alpine lakes					•		•																					
Nilan Reservoir							•																•	•	•		•	
Park Lake					•						•												•	•	•			•
Ruby River Reservoir		•				•	•																•	•	•		•	•
Twin Lakes	•									•	•												•	•	•		•	•
Upsata Lake							•						•							•						•		
Wade Lake					•		•																•	•	•		•	
West Big Hole alpine lakes	•			•	•		•		•	•	•												•	•	•		•	
Willow Creek Reservoir							•																•	•	•		•	
Wood Lake							•																•	•	•		•	

363

RIVERS AND STREAMS	Coldwater Species												Warmwater Species										Facilities					
	Brook Trout	Mountain Whitefish	Lake Whitefish	Golden Trout	Cutthroat Trout	Brown Trout	Rainbow Trout	Kokanee Salmon	Bull Trout	Lake Trout	Arctic Grayling	Burbot	Largemouth Bass	Smallmouth Bass	Walleye	Sauger	Northern Pike	Shovelnose Sturgeon	Channel Catfish	Yellow Perch	Crappie	Paddlefish	Vehicle Access	Campgrounds	Toilets	Docks	Boat Ramps	Motor Restrictions
Arrow Creek	•																						•					
Beaver Creek	•				•	•	•																•	•	•			
Belt Creek	•	•				•	•																•	•	•			
Big Spring Creek		•				•	•																•		•			
Cut Bank Creek	•				•		•					•											•					
Hound Creek		•				•	•																					
Judith River	•	•				•	•																•	•	•			
Lost River															•	•				•								
Marias River		•				•	•					•	•	•	•	•	•	•	•				•	•	•		•	
Milk River			•				•					•	•	•	•	•	•			•			•	•	•			
Missouri River		•				•	•					•	•	•	•	•	•	•	•			•	•	•	•	•	•	•
MusselshellRiver	•	•				•	•																•	•	•			
Red River																				•			•					
Roe River																							•	•	•			
Sacajawea River																							•					
Sheep Creek	•	•				•	•																•	•	•			
Smith River	•	•				•	•					•											•	•	•		•	•
Teton River	•	•			•	•	•																•	•	•			
Warm Springs Creek							•							•									•					
LAKES AND RESERVOIRS																												
Ackley Lake							•																•	•	•		•	
Bailey Reservoir													•				•			•			•	•	•		•	•
Bair Reservoir							•																•	•	•		•	
Bearpaw Lake					•		•																•	•	•		•	
Beaver Creek Reservoir							•								•		•			•			•	•	•		•	•
Bynum Reservoir							•								•					•			•	•	•			
Crystal Lake							•																•	•	•		•	
Deadman's Basin Reservoir						•	•	•															•	•	•		•	
Eureka Reservoir							•																•	•	•		•	
Faber Reservoir							•																•	•	•			•
Fresno Reservoir			•												•		•			•			•	•	•	•	•	•
Grasshopper Reservoir							•																•	•	•			
Lake Frances												•			•		•			•			•	•	•		•	
Lake Sutherlin												•											•	•	•		•	
Martinsdale Reservoir						•	•																•	•	•		•	
Newlan Creek Reservoir					•		•																•	•	•		•	
Petrolia Reservoir															•		•			•			•	•	•		•	
Pishkun Reservoir							•										•			•			•	•	•		•	
Reser Reservoir							•						•							•	•		•					
Split Rock Lake																	•			•			•					
Tiber Reservoir							•					•			•		•			•			•	•	•		•	

364

Region Map 1

Coldwater Species | **Warmwater Species** | **Facilities**

RIVERS AND STREAMS

	Brook Trout	Mountain Whitefish	Lake Whitefish	Golden Trout	Cutthroat Trout	Brown Trout	Rainbow Trout	Kokanee Salmon	Bull Trout	Lake Trout	Arctic Grayling	Burbot	Largemouth Bass	Smallmouth Bass	Walleye	Sauger	Northern Pike	Shovelnose Sturgeon	Channel Catfish	Yellow Perch	Crappie	Paddlefish	Vehicle Access	Campgrounds	Toilets	Docks	Boat Ramps	Motor Restrictions
Boulder River	•	•			•	•	•																•	•	•			
Broadwater River	•																											
East Gallatin River	•	•				•	•																•					
Gallatin River	•	•				•	•																•					
Gardiner River	•					•																	•	•	•			
Grayling Creek					•		•																•					
Hyalite Creek	•				•		•																•	•	•			
Rock Creek	•					•	•																•					
Rosebud River						•	•																					
Shields River		•			•	•	•																•					
Sixmile Creek					•	•																						
South Fork Madison River						•	•																•	•				
Squaw Creek	•					•	•																•	•	•			
Stillwater River	•	•				•	•																•	•	•			
Taylor Fork					•	•	•																•	•				
West Fork Gallatin River						•	•																•					
Yellowstone River		•			•	•	•					•											•	•	•	•	•	•

LAKES AND RESERVOIRS

	Brook Trout	Mountain Whitefish	Lake Whitefish	Golden Trout	Cutthroat Trout	Brown Trout	Rainbow Trout	Kokanee Salmon	Bull Trout	Lake Trout	Arctic Grayling	Burbot	Largemouth Bass	Smallmouth Bass	Walleye	Sauger	Northern Pike	Shovelnose Sturgeon	Channel Catfish	Yellow Perch	Crappie	Paddlefish	Vehicle Access	Campgrounds	Toilets	Docks	Boat Ramps	Motor Restrictions
Beartooth Plateau alpine lakes	•			•	•	•	•				•																	
Cooney Reservoir						•	•								•						•		•	•	•	•	•	•
Crazy Mountains alpine lakes	•			•	•		•																					
Dailey Lake							•								•					•			•	•	•		•	
Emerald Lake	•	•			•	•	•																•	•	•			
Gallatin Mountains alpine lakes				•	•		•				•																	
Greenough Lake							•																•	•	•			
Hebgen Lake						•	•																•	•	•	•	•	
Hyalite Reservoir					•																		•	•	•	•	•	•
Mystic Lake	•				•																							
Quake Lake						•	•																•	•	•	•	•	
Three Forks Ponds							•						•										•					
West Rosebud Lake	•	•			•	•	•																•	•	•			
Wild Bill Lake							•																•	•				

Region Map 2

Coldwater Species | **Warmwater Species** | **Facilities**

RIVERS AND STREAMS

	Brook Trout	Mountain Whitefish	Lake Whitefish	Golden Trout	Cutthroat Trout	Brown Trout	Rainbow Trout	Kokanee Salmon	Bull Trout	Lake Trout	Arctic Grayling	Burbot	Largemouth Bass	Smallmouth Bass	Walleye	Sauger	Northern Pike	Shovelnose Sturgeon	Channel Catfish	Yellow Perch	Crappie	Paddlefish	Vehicle Access	Campgrounds	Toilets	Docks	Boat Ramps	Motor Restrictions
Bighorn River	•				•	•	•					•	•						•				•	•	•	•		•
Little Bighorn River						•						•							•				•	•	•			•
Clarks Fork	•	•			•	•	•					•							•				•	•	•			•
Frenchman River															•	•	•		•				•					
Little Missouri																												
Milk River													•	•	•	•	•		•	•	•		•	•	•	•	•	•
Missouri River						•		•							•	•	•	•	•			•	•	•	•			
Musselshell River		•				•											•		•				•					
Poplar River												•	•		•	•	•		•				•					
Powder River																•			•				•					
Little Powder River																•			•				•	•				
Redwater River												•					•		•				•					
Tongue River												•	•	•	•	•	•		•				•					
Yellowstone River					•	•						•	•	•	•	•	•	•	•			•	•	•	•	•	•	•

LAKES AND RESERVOIRS

	Brook Trout	Mountain Whitefish	Lake Whitefish	Golden Trout	Cutthroat Trout	Brown Trout	Rainbow Trout	Kokanee Salmon	Bull Trout	Lake Trout	Arctic Grayling	Burbot	Largemouth Bass	Smallmouth Bass	Walleye	Sauger	Northern Pike	Shovelnose Sturgeon	Channel Catfish	Yellow Perch	Crappie	Paddlefish	Vehicle Access	Campgrounds	Toilets	Docks	Boat Ramps	Motor Restrictions
Bighorn Lake						•	•					•	•		•	•			•	•	•		•	•	•	•	•	
Box Elder Reservoir							•													•			•	•	•		•	•
Broadview Pond													•								•		•			•		
Castle Rock Lake													•		•		•			•	•		•		•	•	•	
Dredge Cut trout pond													•			•				•			•	•	•	•	•	•
Flat Lake							•																•					•
Fort Peck Dredge Cuts								•					•	•	•	•	•		•	•		•	•	•	•			
Fort Peck Lake								•					•	•	•	•	•	•	•	•			•	•	•	•		
Glasgow AFB Pond							•													•			•					
Homestead Reservoir													•	•									•					
Kuester Reservoir																	•						•		•		•	•
Lake Elmo													•						•	•	•		•		•		•	•
Lake Josephine																							•					
Laurel Pond							•																•	•	•			•
Medicine Lake															•		•			•	•		•	•	•		•	
Nelson Reservoir													•		•		•		•	•			•	•	•	•	•	
South Sandstone Reservoir													•	•	•		•			•	•		•	•	•	•	•	
Tongue River Reservoir													•	•	•	•	•		•	•	•		•	•	•	•	•	
Whitetail Reservoir																	•						•	•	•		•	•
Yellowtail Afterbay					•	•																	•	•	•	•	•	

MONTANA'S RECORD-SETTING FISH (1991)

SPECIES	WEIGHT	ANGLER	YEAR	LOCATION
Arctic grayling	2 lbs. 10.5 ozs.	Steve Houser	1986	Hyalite Reservoir
Bigmouth buffalo	35 lbs. 8 ozs.	John P. Cotton	1991	Missouri River
Black bullhead	1 lb. 11 ozs.	Mike Mitchell	1977	Horse Creek
Black crappie	3 lbs. 2 ozs.	Al Elser	1973	Tongue River Reservoir
Blue sucker	11.46 lbs.	Doug Askin	1989	Yellowstone River
Bluegill	2.64 lbs.	Brent Fladmo	1983	Peterson's Stock Dam
Brook trout	9 lbs. 1 oz.	John R. Cook	1940	Lower Two Medicine L.
Brown trout	29 lbs. 0 ozs.	E.H. "Peck" Bacon	1966	Wade Lake
Bull trout	25 lbs. 10 ozs.	James Hyer	1916	unknown
Burbot (ling)	17.08 lbs.	Jeff E. Iwen	1989	Missouri River
Carp	38 lbs. 8 ozs.	Don Bagley	1986	Eyraud Lakes
Channel catfish	25.89 lbs.	Gordon Wentworth	1984	Fort Peck Reservoir
		Tom Hilderman (tie)	1988	
Chinook (king salmon)	31 lbs. 2 ozs.	Carl L. Niles	1991	For Peck Reservoir
Cisco	1.46 lbs.	Jim Liebelt	1990	Dredge Cut Trout Pond
Coho salmon	4 lbs. 14 ozs.	Irven Stohl	1973	Fort Peck Reservoir
Cutthroat trout	16 lbs. 0 ozs.	William D. Sands	1955	Red Eagle Lake
Freshwater drum	20 lbs. 7 ozs.	Richard C. Lee	1987	Fort Peck Reservoir
Golden trout	4 lbs. 8 ozs.	Tom McGillvray	1989	Lightning Lake
Goldeye	2 lbs. 14.5 ozs.	Vance "Bubba" Kielb	1989	Irrigation canal (west of Malta)
Green sunfish	0.56 lbs.	Roger Fliger	1991	Castle Rock Reservoir
Kokanee (salmon)	5 lbs. 15 ozs.	Forrest Johnson	1976	Pishkun Reservoir
Lake trout	42 lbs. 0 ozs.	Dave Larson	1979	Flathead Lake
Lake whitefish	10 lbs. 0 ozs.	Ruby Mutch	1986	Lower St. Mary Lake
Largemouth bass	8 lbs. 2.5 ozs.	Juanita A. Fanning	1984	Milnor Lake
Longnose sucker	3.27 lbs.	Ray Quigley	1988	Marias River
Mountain whitefish	5 lbs. 1.5 ozs.	Mervin "Frog" Fenimore	1987	Kootenai River
Northern pike	37 lbs. 8 ozs.	Lance Moyler	1972	Tongue River Reservoir
Northern squawfish	7 lbs. 14 ozs.	Darrel Torgrimson	1991	Noxon Rapids Reservoir
Paddlefish	142 lbs. 8 ozs.	Larry Branstetter	1973	Missouri River
Pallid sturgeon	60 lbs. 0 ozs.	Gene Sattler	1979	Yellowstone River
Peamouth	0.64 lbs.	Gordon Stewart	1991	Ashley Creek
Pumpkinseed	0.95 lbs.	Tim Colver	1985	Milnor Lake
Pygmy whitefish	0.16 lbs.	Orlin Iverson	1982	Ashley Lake
Rainbow trout	29.02 lbs.	Stanley Ross	1991	Kootenai River
Rainbow-cutthroat hybrid	30 lbs. 4 ozs.	Pat Kelly	1982	Ashley Lake
River carpsucker	3.50 lbs.	James Jessen	1991	Yellowstone River
Rock bass	0.57 lbs.	Don Holzheimer	1989	Tongue River Reservoir
Sauger	7.57 lbs.	James Jessen	1990	Yellowstone River
Shorthead redhorse sucker	4.68 lbs.	Ray Quigley	1985	Marias River near Loma
Shortnose gar	3 lbs. 1 oz.	John Johnson	1977	Fort Peck dredge cuts
Shovelnose sturgeon	13.72 lbs.	Sidney L. Storm	1986	Missouri River
Smallmouth bass	6.09 lbs.	Terry L. Druyvestein	1990	Fort Peck Reservoir
Smallmouth buffalo	10 lbs. 4 ozs.	Ron Skirvin	1989	Fort Peck dredge cuts
Stonecat	0.42 lbs.	Robert M. Garwood	1985	Milk River at Havre
Tiger muskellunge	11.59 lbs.	Jay Watson	1991	Lebo Lake
Utah chub	1.47 lbs.	Jan R. Mack	1991	Canyon Ferry Reservoir
Walleye	14 lbs. 14 ozs.	Duane A. Leidholt	1989	Yellowstone River
White bass	1 lb. 2 ozs.	Ludwig Dubbe	1986	Fort Peck dredge cuts
White crappie	2 lbs. 6 ozs.	Greg Johnson	1990	Tongue River Reservoir
Whitesturgeon	96 lbs. 0 ozs.	Herb Stout	1968	Kootenai River
White sucker	5 lbs. 5 1/3 ozs.	Fred Perry	1983	Nelson Reservoir
Yellow bullhead	0.72 lbs.	Wade Fredenberg	1987	Yellowstone River
Yellow perch	2.37 lbs.	Vernon Schmid	1988	Ashley Lake

CONSERVATION GROUPS

American Rivers Conservation Council
   317 Penn. Ave. SE
   Washington, DC 20003

American Wilderness Alliance
   324 Fuller
   Helena, MT 59601

Defenders of Wildlife
   304 E. Franklin
   Missoula, MT 59801
   549-0761

Montana Envir. Info. Center
   Box 1184
   Helena, MT 59601
   443-2520

Montana Wilderness Assoc.
   Box 635
   Helena, MT 59624
   443-7350

Montana Wildlife Fed.
   Box 6537
   Bozeman, MT 59715
   587-1713

The Wilderness Society
   1400 I St. NW - 10th Floor
   Washington, DC 20005
   (202) 842-3400

Trout Unlimited
   Montana State Council
   19 Park Dr.
   Bozeman, MT 59715

National Wildlife Fed.
   240 N. Higgins
   Missoula, MT 59802
   721-6705

American River Touring Assoc.
   1016 Jackson St.
   Oakland, CA 94607

American Forestry Assoc.
   919 17th St. NW
   Washington, DC 20016

Env. Defense Fund
   2728 Durant
   Berkeley, CA 94704

Friends of the Earth
   230 Park Ave.
   New York, NY 10017

Sierra Club
   730 Polk St.
   San Francisco, CA 94109
   (415) 776-2211

Back Country Horsemen
   Box 1192
   Columbia Falls, MT 59912

Pheasants Forever
   Box 75473
   St. Paul, Minn. 55175

Ducks Unlimited
   1 Waterfowl Way
   Long Grove, IL 60047

Rocky Mountain Elk Foundation
   2291 W. Broadway
   Box 8249
   Missoula, MT 59807-8249

National Rifle Assoc.
   1600 Rhode Is. Ave. NW
   Washington, DC 20036-3268

Sport Fishing Institute
   1010 Mass. Ave. NW - Suite 320
   Washington, DC 20001
   (202) 898-0770

BASS Sportsman Society
   Box 17116
   Montgomery, AL 36141

National Audubon Society
   950 Third Ave.
   New York, NY 10022

American League of Anglers
   810 18th St. NW
   Washington, DC 20036

SOME RELATED BOOKS & VIDEOS

"River Rescue" Bechdel & Ray
"ACA Canoeing and Kayaking" Gullion
"The Big Drops" Nash
"Guide to WW in Calif." Holbeck & Stanley
"Idaho - The WW State" Amaral
"Sea Kayaking" Dowd
"First Descents" O'Connor & Lazenby
"The Squirt Book" Snyder
"Calif. WW" Cassady & Calhoun
"Whitewater Kayaking" Rowe
"The Inflatable Kayak" Allen
"Basic Essentials of Rafting" Ellison
"Guide to the WW Rivers of Wash." Bennett
"The Canoe Handbook" Ray
"Wildwater" Flores
"Whitewater Rafting" McGinnis
"Kayak" Nealy
"Wildwater Touring" Arighi
"Kayaking" Evans & Anderson
"Intro. to WW and Kayaking" Hartline
"River Running" Huser
"Wild Rivers of North Amer." Jenkinson
"All Purpose Guide to Paddling" Norman
"Exploration of the Colo. River" Powell
"Canoeing and Kayaking" Ruck
"A WW Handbook for Canoe & Kayak" Urban
"Boatbuilders Manual" Walbridge
"Roads & Trails - Glac. NP" Ruhle
"Hells Canyon - The Deepest Gorge on Earth" Ashworth
"Hells Canyon" Bailey
"Canyonlands River Guide" Belknap
"Down the Worlds Most Dangerous River" Eddy
"Dinosaur River Guide" Evans
"Delightful Journey - Green & Colo." Goldwater
"Guidebook to the Colo. R." Hamblin
"Rivers of the West" Hogan
"Middle Fork Salmon River" NW Cartographics
"Rogue River Canyon" NW Cartographics
"Running the Rivers of NA" Wood
"WW Tales of Terror" Nealy
"Carolina Whitewater" Benner
"Wildwater West Virginia" Davidson
"Paddlers Guide to Arkansas & Missouri" Kennon
"Canoe & Kayak Guide to Florida" Carter
"Rivers of Costa Rica" Mayfield
"Guide to Wisconsin, Mich. & Minn." Palzer
"Georgia Canoeing" Sehlinger
"Canoe & Kayak Guide to Kentucky" Sehlinger
"Canoe & Kayak Guide to Tennessee" Sehlinger
"Canoe & Kayak Guide to Ohio" Combs
"Harsh Weather Camping" Curtis
"Modern Outdoor Survival" Schuh
"Yukon Solo" Dohnal
"Appalachian Whitewater" Menasha
"Boundary Waters Canoe Area" Beymer
"Canoeing Wild Rivers" Jacobson
"Class V Briefing" McGinnis
"Coastal Kayaker" Washburne

"Colorado River - Grand Canyon" Stevens
"Complete Whitewater Source Book" Penny
"Desolation River Guide" Belknap - Evans
"Family Canoe Trip" Shepardson
"Floaters Guide to Colo." Wheat
"Gila Descending" Salmon
"The Guide's Guide" McGinnis
"Handbook of the Deschutes" Quinns - King
"Handbook to the Illinois River" Quinns - King
"Hells Canyon of the Snake" Quinn
"Idaho River Tours" Garren
"New England Whitewater Guide" Gabler
"Oregon River Tours" Garren
"Ozark Whitewater" Kennon
"Paddling Hawaii" Sutherland
"River of No Return" Carrey & Conley
"Rivers of the Southwest" Anderson - Hopkins
"Snake River Guide" Huser - Belknap
"Floating Montana" Thompson
"Washington Whitewater" North
"Idaho Whitewater Guide" Moore & McLaren

VIDEOS:

"Costa Rica - Whitewater Paradise"
"Kayak Handling"
"River Rescue"
"Solo Playboating"
"Open Canoe Roll"
"Solo Canoe Instruction"
"Calif. Whitewater"
"Canon - The Grand Canyon"
"Southeast Whitewater"
"Southwest Whitewater"
"West Virginia Whitewater"
"Wilderness Rivers"
"Canoe Basics"
"Grand Canyon Experience"
"Guide to Canoeing"
"Middle Fork - Salmon River"
"NF Payette - SF Salmon"
"Selway and Lochsa"
"Wild & Scenic Rogue River"
"Northwest Whitewater"
"Kayakers Edge"
"Kayak Roll"

RIVER TALK

ABOVE	Upriver.
ALLUVIUM	Material deposited by streams (gravel, sand, clay)
BACK ROLLER	A reversal.
BAR	A shallow accumulation of alluvium.
BEAM	The width of a boat at its widest point.
BELAY	Wrap a rope around tree to slow slippage.
BELOW	Downriver.
BLIND	Can not see.
BOAT	Any vessel or craft.
BOIL	A water current upheaving into a convex mound.
BOULDER GARDEN	Dense boulders that necessitate intricate maneuvering.
BOW (Stern)	Front of boat. Stern is rear of boat.
BROACH	Broadside to the current or an obstacle.
CANOE-BOAT	Decked canoe.
CARTWHEELING (pivot)	Spinning a boat to avoid collision.
CFS	Volume of flow in cubic feet per second.
CHANNEL	Main boatable route.
CHUTE	Channel between obstructions.
CONFLUENCE	Point where two streams meet.
CURLER	A reversal. Wave that falls back upstream.
DOUBLE OAR TURN	Technique of pulling on one oar while pushing the other.
DOWNRIVER	A race for speed with no mandatory maneuvers.
DRAWSTROKE	A paddler pulls his boat toward a "planted paddle". Pry away.
DROP (Pitch)	A sudden descent in a stream. 6' or more is a waterfall.
EDDY	Whirlpool or current heads upstream.
EDDY CUSHION (Pillow)	Slack water on upstream face of rocks.
EDDY FENCE	Current line between river flow and an eddy.
ENDER	Standing the kayak on end while surfing. Also back-ender or pirouette (ender with twist).
ESKIMO ROLL	A maneuver where a kayaker or canoer rights his over turned craft, by using underwater paddle strokes.
FEATHERED	Paddle blades set at angle to each other.
FERRYING	Moving across a river.
FLOOD PLAIN	Ground covered when river overflows at flood stage.
FOOT PEGS	Two pegs kayaker uses to brace his feet.
FREEBOARD	Distance from water level to lowest point of hull.
FRP	Fiberglass reinforced plastic.
GAUGE HEIGHT	A calibrated rod showing river level. CFS can be determined.
GRADIENT	Streambed descent expressed in feet per mile.
HAIR	Fast, turbulent water covered with white foam.
HAYSTACK	A succession of standing waves.
HIGH BRACE (Low)	A stabilizing or uprighting paddle stroke.
HIGH SIDE	Everyone moving to downstream side of vessel to avoid wrapping or flipping.
HIP SNAP	Hip snap used in eskimo roll to right vessel.
HOLE (Souse-suck)	A reversal where the current is falling back in on itself.
KAYAK	A 1 or 2 cockpit, whitewater or sea vessel. Very streamlined and maneuverable. Cockpit is covered with sprayskirt.
KEEPER	A reversal capable of trapping a vessel for long periods.
LEFT (Right)	Direction going downriver.
LEDGE (Shoal)	Streambed stratum causing drops.
LINING	Working a boat down through a rapid with ropes, from shore.
PAINTER	A line attached to bow or stern of vessel.
PANCAKE	Boat flipped over.
POGIES	Cold water mitts attached to paddle shaft.
POOL	Deep calm water above or below a rapid.

PORT (Starboard)	Left side of vessel. Starboard is right.
PORTAGE	Carrying a vessel around obstacles or to another waterway.
PORTEGEE	Moving a vessel by pushing on the oars.
POUROVER (Sleeper)	Water passing over a submerged rock or ledge.
RAPID	A fast bouncy stretch of river. Usually whitewater with obstacles. Classified I-VI by difficulty.
REVERSAL	Currents meeting and revolving back on itself. Specific reversals have names. Very dangerous.
RIFFLE (Sandpaper)	A shallow rapid with small waves. No whitewater.
ROOSTERTAIL	A fountain caused by water striking an obstacle and spewing it up.
ROWING FRAME	A rigid frame for rowing with long oars and serves as a gear rack.
SCOUTING	Looking ahead for obstacles by bank or boat.
SECTION	Stretch of river between two points.
SHUTTLE	Going to and from put-in and take-out, for vehicles.
SKI JUMP	Use lip of a drop as a launching pad and paddle-shoot over what lies below.
SKULLING	Figure eight stroke used to pull boat to that side.
SLALOM	A race downstream with mandatory maneuvers.
SLUICE	A narrow channel in a rapid with no eddies.
SNEAK	River rat language for taking the easy way through a rapid or portaging.
SPONSON	Added pontoons for greater stability.
SQUIRT BOAT	A small decked boat that can ender in eddylines or flatwater.
STAIRCASE	Stream pouring over a series of drops.
STOPPER	A reversal that can stop a boat momentarily.
STRAINER	Brush, debris or anything that current passes through but pins boats and occupants.
SURFING	Riding a wave on its upstream lip or in the hole.
SWEEP	Forward arcing stroke that induces turning to opposite side.
THOLE PIN	Fulcrum pin for oars on rowing frame.
THROAT	Point on a paddle where the blade meets the shaft.
THWARTS	Place for paddlers to brace their knees for power strokes.
THROW BAG	Safety rope coiled in bag for easy throwing.
TONGUE	V-shaped smooth water leading into a rapid.
TRIM	The angle that a boat rides in relation to the water.
TUBER	Float tube users or kids on inner-tubes
TWOSOME	Two vessels lashed together.
VOLUME	Enclosed capacity in a vessel.
WASHED OUT	High water where most obstacles are submerged and the rapid become technically easier.
WAVES	Formed when water flows over an obstacle. Vee, brain, breaking, curler, diagonal, explosion, offset, reaction, standing or tail waves are expressions to describe different wave hydraulics.
WET EXIT	A paddler leaving his craft, while underwater.
WINDOW-SHADED	A paddler flips on upstream side of a big hole while side surfing.
WRAPPING	A broached craft is bent sideways around an obstacle by the force of the current.
WETSUIT (Dry)	Used in extremely cold conditions, to keep warm.